THE FLETCHER JONES FOUNDATION

HUMANITIES IMPRINT

The Fletcher Jones Foundation has endowed this imprint to foster innovative and enduring scholarship in the humanities.

The publisher and the University of California Press
Foundation gratefully acknowledge the generous support
of the Fletcher Jones Foundation Imprint in Humanities.

Being Christian in Vandal Africa

TRANSFORMATION OF THE CLASSICAL HERITAGE
Peter Brown, General Editor

I. *Art and Ceremony in Late Antiquity*, by Sabine G. MacCormack

II. *Synesius of Cyrene: Philosopher-Bishop*, by Jay Alan Bregman

III. *Theodosian Empresses: Women and Imperial Dominion in Late Antiquity*, by Kenneth G. Holum

IV. *John Chrysostom and the Jews: Rhetoric and Reality in the Late Fourth Century*, by Robert L. Wilken

V. *Biography in Late Antiquity: The Quest for the Holy Man*, by Patricia Cox

VI. *Pachomius: The Making of a Community in Fourth-Century Egypt*, by Philip Rousseau

VII. *Change in Byzantine Culture in the Eleventh and Twelfth Centuries*, by A. P. Kazhdan and Ann Wharton Epstein

VIII. *Leadership and Community in Late Antique Gaul*, by Raymond Van Dam

IX. *Homer the Theologian: Neoplatonist Allegorical Reading and the Growth of the Epic Tradition*, by Robert Lamberton

X. *Procopius and the Sixth Century*, by Averil Cameron

XI. *Guardians of Language: The Grammarian and Society in Late Antiquity*, by Robert A. Kaster

XII. *Civic Coins and Civic Politics in the Roman East, A.D. 180–275*, by Kenneth Harl

XIII. *Holy Women of the Syrian Orient*, introduced and translated by Sebastian P. Brock and Susan Ashbrook Harvey

XIV. *Gregory the Great: Perfection in Imperfection*, by Carole Straw

XV. *"Apex Omnium": Religion in the "Res gestae" of Ammianus*, by R. L. Rike

XVI. *Dioscorus of Aphrodito: His Work and His World*, by Leslie S. B. MacCoull

XVII. *On Roman Time: The Codex-Calendar of 354 and the Rhythms of Urban Life in Late Antiquity*, by Michele Renee Salzman

XVIII. *Asceticism and Society in Crisis: John of Ephesus and "The Lives of the Eastern Saints,"* by Susan Ashbrook Harvey

XIX. *Barbarians and Politics at the Court of Arcadius*, by Alan Cameron and Jacqueline Long, with a contribution by Lee Sherry

XX. *Basil of Caesarea*, by Philip Rousseau

XXI. *In Praise of Later Roman Emperors: The Panegyrici Latini*, introduction, translation, and historical commentary by C. E. V. Nixon and Barbara Saylor Rodgers

XXII. *Ambrose of Milan: Church and Court in a Christian Capital*, by Neil B. McLynn

XXIII. *Public Disputation, Power, and Social Order in Late Antiquity*, by Richard Lim

XXIV. *The Making of a Heretic: Gender, Authority, and the Priscillianist Controversy*, by Virginia Burrus

XXV. *Symeon the Holy Fool: Leontius's "Life" and the Late Antique City*, by Derek Krueger

XXVI. *The Shadows of Poetry: Vergil in the Mind of Augustine*, by Sabine MacCormack
XXVII. *Paulinus of Nola: Life, Letters, and Poems*, by Dennis E. Trout
XXVIII. *The Barbarian Plain: Saint Sergius between Rome and Iran*, by Elizabeth Key Fowden
XXIX. *The Private Orations of Themistius*, translated, annotated, and introduced by Robert J. Penella
XXX. *The Memory of the Eyes: Pilgrims to Living Saints in Christian Late Antiquity*, by Georgia Frank
XXXI. *Greek Biography and Panegyric in Late Antiquity*, edited by Tomas Hägg and Philip Rousseau
XXXII. *Subtle Bodies: Representing Angels in Byzantium*, by Glenn Peers
XXXIII. *Wandering, Begging Monks: Spiritual Authority and the Promotion of Monasticism in Late Antiquity*, by Daniel Caner
XXXIV. *Failure of Empire: Valens and the Roman State in the Fourth Century* A.D., by Noel Lenski
XXXV. *Merovingian Mortuary Archaeology and the Making of the Early Middle Ages*, by Bonnie Effros
XXXVI. *Quṣayr 'Amra: Art and the Umayyad Elite in Late Antique Syria*, by Garth Fowden
XXXVII. *Holy Bishops in Late Antiquity: The Nature of Christian Leadership in an Age of Transition*, by Claudia Rapp
XXXVIII. *Encountering the Sacred: The Debate on Christian Pilgrimage in Late Antiquity*, by Brouria Bitton-Ashkelony
XXXIX. *There Is No Crime for Those Who Have Christ: Religious Violence in the Christian Roman Empire*, by Michael Gaddis
XL. *The Legend of Mar Qardagh: Narrative and Christian Heroism in Late Antique Iraq*, by Joel Thomas Walker
XLI. *City and School in Late Antique Athens and Alexandria*, by Edward J. Watts
XLII. *Scenting Salvation: Ancient Christianity and the Olfactory Imagination*, by Susan Ashbrook Harvey
XLIII. *Man and the Word: The Orations of* Himerius, edited by Robert J. Penella
XLIV. *The Matter of the Gods*, by Clifford Ando
XLV. *The Two Eyes of the Earth: Art and Ritual of Kingship between Rome and Sasanian Iran*, by Matthew P. Canepa
XLVI. *Riot in Alexandria: Tradition and Group Dynamics in Late Antique Pagan and Christian Communities*, by Edward J. Watts
XLVII. *Peasant and Empire in Christian North Africa*, by Leslie Dossey
XLVIII. *Theodoret's People: Social Networks and Religious Conflict in Late Roman Syria*, by Adam M. Schor
XLIX. *Sons of Hellenism, Fathers of the Church: Emperor Julian, Gregory of Nazianzus, and the Vision of Rome*, by Susanna Elm

L. *Shenoute of Atripe and the Uses of Poverty: Rural Patronage, Religious Conflict, and Monasticism in Late Antique Egypt,* by Ariel G. López

LI. *Doctrine and Power: Theological Controversy and Christian Leadership in the Later Roman Empire,* by Carlos R. Galvão-Sobrinho

LII. *Crisis of Empire: Doctrine and Dissent at the End of Late Antiquity,* by Phil Booth

LIII. *The Final Pagan Generation,* by Edward J. Watts

LIV. *The Mirage of the Saracen: Christians and Nomads in the Sinai Peninsula in Late Antiquity,* by Walter D. Ward

LV. *Missionary Stories and the Formation of the Syriac Churches,* by Jeanne-Nicole Mellon Saint-Laurent

LVI. *A State of Mixture: Christians, Zoroastrians, and Iranian Political Culture in Late Antiquity,* by Richard E. Payne

LVII. *Constantine and the Captive Christians of Persia: Martyrdom and Religious Identity in Late Antiquity,* by Kyle Smith

LVIII. *In the Image of Origen: Eros, Virtue, and Constraint in the Early Christian Academy,* by David Satran

LVIX. *Being Christian in Vandal Africa: The Politics of Orthodoxy in the Post-Imperial West,* by Robin Whelan

Being Christian in Vandal Africa

The Politics of Orthodoxy in the Post-Imperial West

Robin Whelan

UNIVERSITY OF CALIFORNIA PRESS

University of California Press, one of the most distinguished university presses in the United States, enriches lives around the world by advancing scholarship in the humanities, social sciences, and natural sciences. Its activities are supported by the UC Press Foundation and by philanthropic contributions from individuals and institutions. For more information, visit www.ucpress.edu.

University of California Press
Oakland, California

© 2018 by The Regents of the University of California
First Paperback printing, 2024 | ISBN 9780520401433 (pbk)

Library of Congress Cataloging-in-Publication Data

Names: Whelan, Robin, author.
Title: Being Christian in Vandal Africa : the politics of orthodoxy in the Post-Imperial West / Robin Whelan.
Description: Oakland, California : University of California Press, [2018] | Includes bibliographical references and index. |
Identifiers: LCCN 2017033950 (print) | LCCN 2017037261 (ebook) | ISBN 9780520968684 () | ISBN 9780520295957 (cloth)
Subjects: LCSH: Christianity—Africa, North. | Christianity and politics—Africa, North. | Church history—Primitive and early church, ca. 30-600. | Africa, North—Church history. | Vandals—Africa, North—History.
Classification: LCC BR1369 (ebook) | LCC BR1369 .W44 2018 (print) | DDC 276.1/02 mdc23
LC record available at https://lccn.loc.gov/2017033950

25 24 23 22 21 20 19 18
10 9   8   7   6   5   4   3   2   1

CONTENTS

List of Illustrations and Tables	*ix*
Acknowledgments	*xi*
Time Line	*xiii*

Introduction	1

PART I. CONTESTING ORTHODOXY	27
1. African Churches	29
2. In Dialogue with Heresy: Christian Polemical Literature	55
3. "What They Are to Us, We Are to Them": Homoian Orthodoxy and Homoousian Heresy	85
4. Ecclesiastical Histories: Reinventing the Arians	109
PART II. ORTHODOXY AND SOCIETY	139
5. Exiles on Main Street: Nicene Bishops and the Vandal Court	143
6. Christianity, Ethnicity, and Society	165
7. Elite Christianity, Political Service, and Social Prestige	195
Epilogue: Homoian Christianity in the Post-Imperial West	219

Bibliography	*251*
Index	*293*

ILLUSTRATIONS AND TABLES

Map of Vandal Africa   *xv*

FIGURES

1. Ground plan of the Basilica of Melleus at Ammaedara (Haïdra)   *30*
2. Plan of Victorinus's privileged burial   *31*
3. Epitaph of the "Vandal boy" at Theveste (Tébessa)   *216*

TABLES

1. Known Homoian clerics and authors   *43*
2. Nicene bishops and clerics   *48*

ACKNOWLEDGMENTS

In writing this book, I have incurred more debts than I can adequately acknowledge here: to tutors, friends, colleagues, supervisors, librarians, faculty administrators, examiners, editors, readers, and students. If I've been unable to find space for many of those wonderful people in what follows, I can only apologize and trust that they'll claim a beverage of their choice next time I see them.

I am grateful to the Arts and Humanities Research Council, the Faculty of Classics and Corpus Christi College, Cambridge, and the Erasmus Exchange Programme for the grants which allowed me to undertake my PhD research, and to the Hulme Fund, the John Fell Fund, Brasenose College, Oxford, and the Oxford Research Centre in the Humanities for the postdoctoral fellowship which gave me the time I needed to revise my dissertation. I put the finishing touches to this book in the gaps between tutorials on early medieval history with enthusiastic students at Balliol College and St Peter's College, Oxford.

My particular thanks go to those who undertook to read the whole thing (some, heroically, more than once). Above all, I thank my doctoral supervisor, Christopher Kelly, who remains both my strictest reader and my most loyal champion; I continually appreciate both his criticism and his friendship. My examiners, Rosamond McKitterick and Caroline Humfress, gave many insightful suggestions for ways I might develop the thesis into a book, and my postdoctoral mentor, Chris Wickham, helped me to see my revisions through. At University of California Press, Eric Schmidt and Peter Brown gave me the impetus to make important changes to the manuscript; my peer reviewers were both incredibly generous and usefully pointed in their feedback. On that note, I thank Eric Schmidt, Maeve

Cornell-Taylor, and Cindy Fulton at the press and the copy editor Juliana Froggatt for their efficiency, their clarity, and their good-natured support throughout the publishing process.

Many others have provided crucial assistance of various sorts. Sam Cohen, Jonathan Conant, Richard Flower, Éric Fournier, Roland Steinacher, and Michael Williams sent me work in advance of publication. Pierre-Marie Hombert shared with me his edition of Vigilius's *Dialogue* ahead of publication, which helped me to sharpen my analysis and allowed me to cite his much superior text. Jonathan Conant, Rebecca Flemming, Éric Fournier, Erika Hermanowicz, Gerda Heydemann, Andy Merrills, and Michael Williams provided helpful comments on draft versions of various chapters. Andy also kindly supplied his map of Vandal Africa for my use, and Taher Ghalia provided the cover image. This book has also benefited from the many colleagues and friends with whom I've discussed all manner of things late ancient and early medieval—often taking time out of busy schedules to do so. I greatly appreciate their collective generosity.

Above all, though, I thank my family, whose love and fearsome support for my pursuit of an academic career never seem to diminish, no matter how obscure my work becomes. This book is for Ingrid, whose contribution I still cannot put into words.

Balliol College, Oxford
27 March 2017

TIME LINE

325	Council of Nicaea
357	Second Council of Sirmium
359–60	Councils of Rimini, Seleucia, and Constantinople
381	Councils of Constantinople and Aquileia
Early fifth century	Augustine of Hippo debates the Homoian count Pascentius in Carthage
405/6	Vandals and others cross the Rhine
406–9	Vandals in Gaul
409–28/29	Vandals in Spain
411	Conference of Carthage between Catholics and Donatists
412	Honorius's edict of unity against the Donatists
427/28	Augustine debates the Homoian bishop Maximinus in Hippo
428–77	Reign of Geiseric
428/29	Vandals cross into Africa
430	Siege of Hippo; death of Augustine
435	First treaty between Vandals and western empire; cession of the Mauretanias and part of Numidia
439	Capture of Carthage
Early 440s	Exile of Bishop Quodvultdeus and Carthaginian clergy
442	Second treaty between Vandals and western empire; cession of Proconsularis, Byzacena, and Numidia
454	Appointment of Deogratias as the bishop of Carthage

455	Vandal sack of Rome
474	Treaty of eternal peace between Geiseric and Zeno
477–84	Reign of Huneric
478/79	Appointment of Eugenius as the bishop of Carthage and grant of tolerance to Nicenes
c. 479–83?	Possible exile of Nicene bishops and clergy
20 May 483	Huneric's order convening the Conference of Carthage
February 484	Conference of Carthage between Nicenes and Homoians
24 February 484	Huneric's anti-Homoousian edict
Mid-484	Exile of Nicene episcopate; Habetdeum of Thamalluma visits court
484–96	Reign of Gunthamund
487	Eugenius of Carthage recalled from exile
494	Rest of Nicene bishops recalled; churches reopened
496–523	Reign of Thrasamund
mid-500s?	Exile of about sixty bishops to Sardinia
505?	Death of Eugenius in exile at Albi, Gaul
mid-510s?	Fulgentius of Ruspe recalled and then exiled again
523–30	Reign of Hilderic
523	Hilderic grants tolerance to Nicenes; appointment of Boniface as the bishop of Carthage
525	Council of Carthage
530–34	Reign of Gelimer
533–34	East Roman reconquest of Africa by Justinian and Belisarius

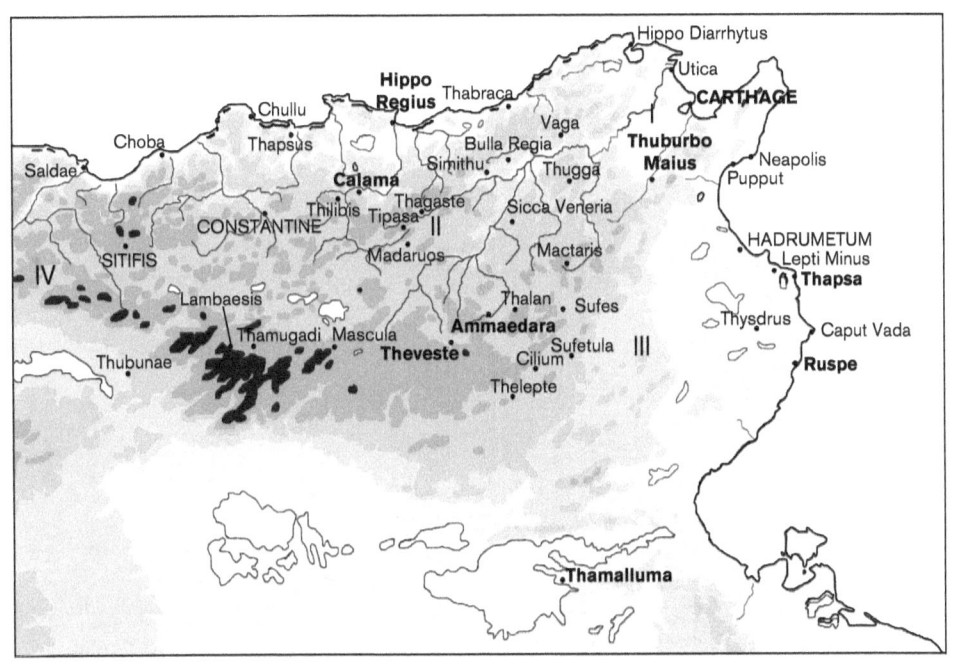

Map of Vandal Africa, reproduced and adapted with the kind permission of Andy Merrills.

Introduction

AUGUSTINE'S TEARS

[Augustine] died on 28 August 430 in his episcopal city of Hippo, while it was under siege by the Vandals, a few weeks before the surrender: what a symbol of the end of a world and—I say it once more!—of a culture.

—HENRI-IRÈNE MARROU, *SAINT AUGUSTIN ET LA FIN DE LA CULTURE ANTIQUE*

Sixty years on from the fourth edition of Henri-Irène Marrou's seminal *Saint Augustin et la fin de la culture antique*, the coincidence of Augustine of Hippo's death with the Vandal siege of his city remains a compelling symbol of discontinuity. The juxtaposition of the last days of the erudite late-antique exponent of classical civilization and the advent of a destructive military force perceived as its antithesis resonates profoundly. It sounds the end of Roman (North) Africa. Such a reading is encouraged above all by Augustine's biographer Possidius of Calama. His portrayal of these concurrent events is a brilliant evocation of the destruction of the world both he and his mentor shared. Augustine took the consequences of the invasion of Africa by the Vandal war band to heart: "More than ever tears were his bread day and night, as he led and endured those days of his life, now almost ended, which before all others were the most bitter and mournful of his old age."[1] Through those tear-filled eyes, the dying Augustine saw the whole of Romano-African society brought to naught: cities sacked; the aristocracy killed or put to flight; churches

---

Epigraph. Marrou (1958), 702: "[Augustin] est mort le 28 août 430 dans sa ville épiscopale d'Hippone, assiégée par les Vandales, quelques semaines avant la reddition: quel symbole de la fin d'un monde—d'une culture, a-t-on volontiers répété!"

1. Poss., *V. Aug.* 28.6 (ed. Bastiaensen: 206), adapting the translation by Weiskotten (1919), 113.

destroyed; bishops reduced to poverty; priests, monks, and virgins exiled; and all Africans facing a choice between death through torture or dishonorable subjugation.[2] Hindsight inevitably colors modern readings of the last chapters of the *Life of Augustine*. By 439, the Vandals had indeed taken over Augustine's Africa. They ruled it for the next century, until another invasion, by the armies of the Eastern Roman Empire in 533–34, resulted in another conquest of the African provinces and their subjection to Justinian's regime in Constantinople. As a consequence, few modern scholars have passed up the opportunity to summon the ailing Augustine as a tragic hero witnessing the destruction of all he held dear.[3]

Possidius's graphic amplification of the Vandal invasion has influenced both ancient authors and modern historians.[4] Its power as a piece of vivid writing is obvious; its historical merits as a description of the conquest, rather more dubious.[5] Still, even without Possidius's rhetorical violence, the mere coincidence of Augustine's death and the beginnings of Vandal Africa would instill a sense of rupture.[6] For the bishop of Hippo, more than any other writer, provides access to the minute detail of the Roman world that is said to have disappeared with his passing. Scholars have rightly lamented the lack of a Vandal Cassiodorus or Gregory of Tours, a historian willing to set events in the kingdom in a light sympathetic to its new rulers.[7] Yet this is to underestimate the importance of the unparalleled volume of sermons, letters, and tractates preserved by the bishop of Hippo's later admirers—and the richly textured accounts of late fourth- and early fifth-century Africa which they can support. What Vandal Africa truly lacks is an Augustine.

To all intents and purposes, Augustine is late-antique Africa. To describe and analyze social and political life in late Roman Africa, modern historians—in one way or another—must take in the view from Augustine's *cathedra*. As a consequence, conflict over the correct modes of religious observance—his recurrent concern—is formative for most accounts of the province. The most penetrating discussions of the age of Augustine stem from the literary traces of the Donatist schism, which split the African Church in the fourth and fifth centuries, since it is while detailing individual episodes of that ecclesiastical controversy that the bishop of Hippo (among others) provides the raw materials for a rather more secular sociology of (for example) urban and rural communities and hierarchies.[8] In

---

2. Poss., *V. Aug.* 28.4–31 (ed. Bastiaensen: 204–40).

3. E.g., P. Brown (2000), 428–30, though cf. now (2012), 400–402; Bonner (2002), 153–56; Chadwick (2009), 86–87; Evers (2010), 299; Shaw (2011), 805. For further references see Fournier (2008), 20–21; see also Vössing (2014), 43–44.

4. On the ancients see Courtois (1954), 70; Lancel (2002a), 19–20; Fournier (2008), 142–43.

5. See pp. 5–8.

6. Fournier (2008), 20–21.

7. E.g., Courtois (1955), 11–12; Clover (1986), 1; Shanzer (2004), 271. See too Merrills (2004b), 19–20.

8. See esp. Shaw (2011). See too Lepelley (1979–81), which also draws on the rich corpus of fourth-century epigraphic material; Dossey (2010); Magalhaes de Oliveira (2012).

such accounts, Augustine's death remains a pivotal chronological marker.⁹ Even Brent Shaw, a scholar committed to the sympathetic reappraisal of unfairly maligned historical actors, bookends his superlative recent book on "sacred violence" in late Roman Africa with appeals to Vandal destruction and "a social and religious world that disappeared in 430."[10] Historians of Roman Africa are seemingly so used to seeing the world through the eyes of Augustine that they too must look upon the Vandal conquest through his veil of tears.

In fact, the late-antique Africa that Augustine brings to life is still visible in the Vandal period. Sustained recent attention to its rich and diverse evidence has produced a very different vista to that which Possidius had his Augustine survey. Vandal Africa has profited from a belated integration into the broader revisionist project that has rewritten the transition from later Roman Empire to barbarian successor kingdoms as a "transformation of the Roman world."[11] It now appears as a world tantalizingly close to that of Augustine. An Africa still operating within a recognizably late Roman framework maintained its cultural, social, and economic complexity throughout the Vandal period. The overriding implication of the past generation of work is that any appeal to Possidius's decisive break risks being nothing more than an empty gesture.

Yet for historians looking back from the early medieval West, Vandal Africa retains a peculiarity that sets it apart from supposed post-imperial overachievers such as Theoderic's Italy or Clovis's Gaul, encouraging an equal and opposite sense of disjuncture. The Vandals' arrival provoked a conflict between groups that most surviving texts describe as Catholic and Arian Christians. The adherence of the Vandal kings and many of their followers to a form of Christianity understood by hostile contemporaries as "Arian heresy" was not unusual among barbarian rulers and groups. However, the occasional periods of hostility visible in other kingdoms contrast strikingly with the ongoing controversy in Africa. This Christian conflict has always been at the center of the problem with Vandal Africa. Scholars have conventionally made it emblematic of the kingdom's failure and its discontinuity with Roman Africa. The heresy of the new rulers (in this view) provoked discord with the Catholic population and prevented effective and stable government. As a result, Vandal Africa has traditionally been seen as a sort of "failed state" of the post-imperial West.[12] Recent reassessments, while convincingly asserting far greater political success, have tended (correspondingly) to downplay or to compartmentalize the

9. Dossey (2010) is a notable exception.
10. Shaw (2011), 1 (quote), 772–73, 802–6.
11. The title of the influential European Science Foundation project (1993-98) that resulted in a series of fourteen volumes published by Brill. On the absence of the Vandals from this project and their more recent fitting into its parameters, see Berndt (2007), 44–51; Merrills and Miles (2010), 20–22.
12. E.g., Courtois (1955), 153–271, 357; Geary (1999), 121–22; Collins (2010), 125; Kershaw (2011), 82. Cf. Heather (1999), 248.

effects both of Christian controversy and of Christianity in general. The Vandals have become effective successors to imperial rule almost in spite of their involvement in Christian politics. The historiographical irony is manifest. For scholars of late Roman Africa and the Donatist schism, the Vandal conquest is a fundamental break; for historians of Vandal Africa, the deep channels of continuity traversing the fifth century are choked by Christian conflict.

First and foremost, this book seeks to examine what it meant to be Christian in post-imperial Africa. It considers the implications of debates over the true Christian faith for the prominent social and political actors who shaped the kingdom and whose perspectives on their own religious affiliations are most visible: kings, aristocrats, and bishops. It proceeds on the basis that Vandal Africa's Trinitarian debates, like its structures of governance, are best understood with reference to their broader late-antique context.[13] The sophisticated culture of ecclesiastical disputation that had developed in late Roman Africa—and across the Mediterranean—continued in the Vandal kingdom.

The first part of this book uses a cache of understudied Christian polemical texts that preserve the efforts of contemporary churchmen to establish the legitimacy of their ecclesiastical institutions. These texts display the telltale signs of late-antique heresiology (that is, Christian writing about orthodoxy and heresy). They use arguments honed in previous controversies over correct Christian doctrine and practice. Christian controversialists in Vandal Africa drew on the history and heresiology of both the Donatist schism in Africa and the Arian controversy which had provoked so much conciliar wrangling throughout the fourth-century Mediterranean church (and continued to haunt its fifth-century agents). The textual traces of these debates (unsurprisingly) privilege one side over the other. Nonetheless, even from the polemic of the (so-called) Catholics, it is clear that the (so-called) Arians of post-imperial Africa could put forward a plausible claim to ecclesiastical legitimacy. This is, of course, part of the reason why so many texts were produced seeking to undermine that claim. At the root of Vandal Africa's new ecclesiastical controversy was a genuine contest over the identity of the true church, one often unnervingly like the Donatist schism that had preceded it. The resemblance is no coincidence: the consequences and cultural resources of that conflict helped to shape this new ecclesiastical controversy.[14]

The second part of this book evaluates the ramifications of these Christian debates for society and politics under the Vandals. It is underpinned by a sense of overriding continuities in the methods and modes of ecclesiastical controversy. These ongoing confrontations between churchmen cannot be firewalled from the

---

13. See esp. Fournier (2008), 269.

14. For discussions of specific influences from, consequences of, and similarities to the Donatist schism, see pp. 35–38, 96–98, 104–8, 130–34. For a synthetic account see Whelan (2014a).

rest of the transformation of late-antique Africa. Vandal Africa's ecclesiastical controversy retained the wide-ranging implications—both for the identities of individual Christians and for social and political life in the region—evident during the Donatist schism. These late Roman precedents should ward off any recurrence of earlier accounts of a dysfunctional polity riven with unbridgeable hostilities. Part 2 considers how the existence of two Christian communities influenced the formation of relationships among kings, bishops, and other elites. Drawing on recent work on ethnic and Christian identities in late antiquity and the early middle ages, its chapters show both how and why the demands of Christian uniformity and exclusivity might have been important to these influential social and political actors and, at the same time, how and why they might not. This was not simply a case of their Christianity being just one part of their identity (although there was that); there was also space for mutual recognition of Christian piety, authority, and prestige across (supposed) heresiological boundaries. The existence of this space allowed Vandal Africa's passionate ecclesiastical confrontations to fit into the functioning late-antique polity that has emerged in recent scholarship. All in all, this book argues that the kingdom's two Christian orthodoxies were key elements in its transformed but recognizably late Roman world, not catalysts for disastrous or disruptive change. It is my central contention that Vandal Africa, like the late Roman province it succeeded, was the site of a vibrant and often violent Christian conflict while remaining a viable political entity.

AFRICA UNDER THE VANDALS

The Vandal Africa that has emerged in recent years defies Possidius's bleak prognosis. Inspired by pathfinding work by Christian Courtois, a number of recent studies have rethought post-imperial Africa.[15] The region profited from the late Roman economy's "Indian summer" and maintained considerable prosperity well into the sixth century.[16] Various documentary texts show property rights, legal transactions, and practices of estate management upheld in the countryside.[17] Changes in Africa's cities closely paralleled those in other urban centers across the Mediterranean: the progressive abandonment of many traditional public spaces and monuments must be set alongside upkeep and commercial reuse.[18] At various sites, elegant townhouses were refitted with new

---

15. Courtois (1954); Courtois (1955); on his influence see, e.g., Merrills and Miles (2010), 20.
16. Wickham (2005), 708–12, 720–23; Leone (2007), 127–65; Von Rummel (2008), 164–73; Dossey (2010), 23–24, 62–97; Merrills and Miles (2010), 141–76 ("Indian summer" at 176); Conant (2012), 137–41; Bockmann (2013), 175–76, 242–45, though see also 238–40.
17. Conant (2004); Conant (2013); Merrills and Miles (2010), 159–62.
18. See esp. Ben Abed-Ben Khader and Duval (2000), 179–206; Wickham (2005), 635–44; Leone (2007), 134–65; Leone (2013), 98–99; Dossey (2010), 24; Merrills and Miles (2010), 152–55, 206–11; Conant (2012), 132–33; Bockmann (2013); Von Rummel (2016), 110–16.

mosaic floors, depicting scenes of hunting, villa life, and charioteers.[19] The extent of civic institutional continuity is difficult to evaluate; the numerous references to long-established offices and honorific titles are at least suggestive.[20] Contemporary literary activity similarly suggests a traditional patterning to elite civic life. Late fifth- and early sixth-century Africa saw an outpouring of classicizing texts, often characterized as a "Vandal renaissance."[21] African writers continued traditions of panegyric (now praising Vandal kings), epigram, and epic, as well as Christian poetry.[22] These texts show the persistence of a classical education system.[23] They extol opulent suburban villas and satirize the colorful urbanity of the Vandal capital. Certainly, the traditional lifestyle of the Romano-African elite did not perish in 430.

Awareness of the vitality of African society has gone hand in hand with reappraisal of the Vandals themselves.[24] Discussions have moved progressively further from their stereotypically destructive image.[25] The bleak picture of savage northern barbarians incompatible with Romano-African society has been jettisoned. The Vandals have benefited from new approaches to interactions between barbarians and Romans in late antiquity, symbolized above all by changing scholarly usage of the term *barbarian* itself.[26] It is now widely deployed—in lieu of a better replacement—as an apparently neutral term, without intentional reference to the ancient Greco-Roman discourse of barbarism.[27] Fierce debate persists on several issues, but most scholars emphasize the reciprocal interchanges across the frontiers

---

19. Clover (1982), 13–15; Leone (2007), 160–62; Merrills and Miles (2010), 211–12; Bockmann (2013), 76–82, 159–62, 170–72.

20. Overbeck (1973), 53–74 (with caution); Chastagnol and Duval (1974); N. Duval (1984); Merrills and Miles (2010), 78–81, 212–13; Conant (2012), 46.

21. Riché (1976), 37–39, with n. 142; Hays (2004); Hen (2007), 59–93, phrase at 74.

22. Courtois (1955), 228 n. 6; Clover (1982), 5–6, 10; Clover (1986), 8–10; Clover (1989), 62–69; George (2004); Hays (2004); Merrills (2004a); Miles (2005); Hen (2007), 71–72, 74–87; Merrills and Miles (2010), 213–27; Conant (2012), 146–48.

23. Conant (2004); Conant (2012), 133–36, 141; Hen (2007), 69–72; Merrills and Miles (2010), 213–19.

24. Important works include Clover (1993); Modéran (1998a); Modéran (2003); Modéran (2006); Liebeschuetz (2003); Berndt (2007); Howe (2007); Fournier (2008); Steinacher (2008); Steinacher (2011); Merrills and Miles (2010); Conant (2012); Bockmann (2013); Vössing (2014).

25. On this image see Bourgeois (1980); Merrills (2009).

26. See pp. 171–75, 183–84. Halsall (2007), 10–19, and Merrills and Miles (2010), 16–22, are succinct introductions.

27. The sense of *barbarian* implicit in recent scholarship remains somewhat problematic because of its ancient use as a subjective, extraordinarily flexible, and generally derogatory concept. It can cause confusion by naturalizing a far more fluid status. An individual like the Ostrogothic king Theoderic, who is a barbarian in modern scholarly terms, might or might not have been called or considered by specific contemporaries a barbarian in ancient terms. In this book, *barbarian* is generally used with the latter meaning. Where necessary, it is also deployed for the former; it should then be understood (rather like the similarly problematic *pagan*) as a word that "generates its own scare quotes": McLynn (2009b), 573; cf. Alan Cameron (2011), 25–32.

of the empire. A consensus has formed that barbarian groups were subject to considerable Roman influences both outside and inside the empire and used the Roman vocabulary of power and status to articulate their claims within it. An appropriately balanced synthesis would stress the real sense in which newcomers to the fifth-century West were accommodated and integrated, without ignoring the violence and upheaval inevitably part of this process.[28]

The Vandals fit this model well, as a heterogeneous war band whose collective identity formed in the provinces of Gaul, Spain, and Africa.[29] The military force that captured Carthage in 439 under the leadership of Geiseric was an amalgamation of elements of several groups. As well as the Hasding Vandals, from whose ruling dynasty Geiseric stemmed, it incorporated members of the Siling Vandal, Sueve, and Alan contingents who had also crossed the Rhine into imperial territory in 405/6 and had been the Hasdings' fellow travelers, though often as rivals, through Gaul (406–9) and into Spain (409–29). A series of unpredictable encounters with Roman armies, culminating in the defeat of the Roman general Castinus in 422, established the Hasding dynasty as the rulers of this diverse group. By the time Geiseric took his war band into Africa, it had also picked up some Goths and Hispano-Romans. As Guido Berndt has rightly stressed, whatever sense of group solidarity these Vandals had acquired by 439 was a product of those years on imperial soil. After the conquest, Geiseric's followers were settled on expropriated land, the much-disputed *sortes Vandalorum*. From then on, many leading Vandals seem to have adopted the lifestyles of late-antique Mediterranean aristocrats.[30]

The Vandal kings, once derided, have reemerged as plausibly legitimate political actors presiding over a viable late-antique polity.[31] Scholars grow ever more confident in attributing to Geiseric and his successors a combination of prudent continuity, intelligent innovation, and, above all, political success. The Vandal kings appropriated the norms of contemporary political culture and existing administrative structures (notably the legal system).[32] After initial conflict, the new rulers of Africa secured and maintained the support of the Vandal military elite and the remaining Romano-African aristocracy.[33] The political framework of aristocratic life in the region was reshaped: the African elite (both Vandal and

---

28. The most influential recent English-language contributions are Heather (2005); Heather (2009); Ward-Perkins (2005); Halsall (2007); Kulikowski (2007). Maas (2012) is a useful survey.

29. Heather (2005), 451–52; Berndt (2007); Berndt (2010); Merrills and Miles (2010), 27–55, at 47–50; cf. Modéran (2014), 43–130.

30. On the *sortes* see p. 173 n. 37; on these lifestyles, pp. 171–75.

31. See p. 6 n. 24.

32. On the administration see Jones (1964), 259–60; Barnwell (1992), 120–24; Aiello (2006); Merrills and Miles (2010), 77–81; Conant (2012), 45–46, 143–46. On the legal system see Merrills and Miles (2010), 218–19; Conant (2012), 137–39.

33. See esp. Merrills and Miles (2010), 56–82; Conant (2012), 142–59.

Romano-African) derived prestige from service in the court at Carthage and the broader royal administration. Geiseric's Hasding dynasty looks less and less like an aberrant exception in comparison with more celebrated barbarian rulers in Italy and Gaul. Moreover, the Vandal kings look ever more like their imperial contemporaries and predecessors. Nonetheless, their relationship with late Roman power was no simple *imitatio imperii*. Vandal kings exploited Roman means of representing power, but did so to distinguish themselves as the legitimate rulers of Africa, whether by introducing new dating eras that began with the conquest of Carthage and their individual accessions or by using ancient Carthaginian images on coins. Panegyrics delivered by court poets similarly tied the legitimacy of the Hasding dynasty to the flourishing of its capital city.[34] Vandal rule in Africa was based on a distinctive appropriation of the heritage of late Roman governance.

Finally, setting aside issues of confession, it is clear that African Christianity was not affected in the way Possidius stated. The vast quantity of ecclesiastical literature produced throughout the Vandal period defies his prognosis. These sermons, letters, doctrinal tractates, biblical *testimonia* collections, conciliar acta, psalms, poems, histories, and saints' lives demonstrate African Christianity's continued vigor. The evidence for destruction or abandonment of churches is extremely limited, and its connection to the Vandals is far from certain. Churches remained in use throughout the period.[35] It is more difficult to isolate contemporary building work, partly because prescientific archaeology removed the stratigraphic record at many sites. Nonetheless, refurbishments and new constructions have been identified amid the mass of undatable churches.[36] The most densely Christianized province of the Roman West—home to more than six hundred bishops in the early fifth century[37]—did not receive anything like Possidius's reversal until several centuries after the Vandal conquest.[38]

A HISTORY OF A PERSECUTION

A number of vocal contemporary observers struggled to leave aside issues of Christian doctrine. For one particularly outspoken commentator, the details of the

---

34. Chalon et al. (1985); Clover (1986), 8–10; Clover (1989), 62–69; Miles (2005); Berndt and Steinacher (2008b), 262, 270–71; Merrills and Miles (2010), 73, 168–75, 219–25; Conant (2012), 43–66, 142–59.

35. See, e.g., Ben Abed-Ben Khader and Duval (2000), 176–78; Baratte and Bejaoui (2001); Leone (2007), 148–57; Bejaoui (2008), 200–203; Von Rummel (2008), 156; Merrills and Miles (2010), 195–96; Conant (2012), 163–64.

36. Bockmann (2013), esp. 87–117, 163–66, 185–92, 200–214, 215–25, 227–35, 240–42. See also Leone (2007), 150–54, and Dossey (2010), 217 n. 96, for modern catalogues of church constructions attributed, sometimes rather dubiously, to the Vandal period.

37. Shaw (2011), 354, 807–11; cf. Dossey (2010), 125.

38. Handley (2004); Conant (2012), 362–70.

Trinitarian beliefs of the Hasding dynasty and of many other Christians in the kingdom outweighed any of the good they might have done. In the mid-480s, the Nicene ("Catholic")[39] priest Victor of Vita wrote the *History of the Persecution of the African Province* (*Historia persecutionis Africanae prouinciae*), covering events in the region from 429 to 484.[40] It is the only detailed contemporary African narrative of events in the kingdom, and, as a result, it is central to all histories of Vandal Africa. For Victor of Vita, the doctrinal affiliations of these kings colored everything: the continuities that modern historians have identified were overlooked or overturned as proof of the barbarity of the Vandals and the darkness into which Africa had plunged.

Victor's *History of the Persecution* is shaped by the intent signaled in its title. It begins with the end of Roman Africa, a Vandal conquest equally as brutal as that in the *Life of Augustine*.[41] Familiar modes of Christian apologetic discourse characterize ensuing events.[42] Victor's Vandal Africa is a world of black-and-white distinctions, populated by "Vandal" "Arian" "heretics"—"their people"—and "Roman" "Catholics"—"us."[43] The actions of Vandal kings and the Arian churchmen they backed are represented as a ruthless persecution of the true church; the kings, Geiseric (r. 428–77) and Huneric (r. 477–84), as illegitimate tyrants, who rival the stock hate figures of biblical and early Christian history. Their Catholic Roman subjects are the suffering martyrs and confessors of the true faith.[44] Victor's narrative culminates in the terrors of 484. Huneric called a conference between the two conflicting groups of churchmen, to take place in Carthage in February of that year. In the aftermath of this turbulent (and apparently inconclusive) meeting, the Vandal king promulgated an edict which proscribed Nicene Christians throughout the kingdom as heretics. He ordered all of his subjects to adhere to his favored form of Christianity, seen by Victor as Arian heresy, by 1 June or face severe punishments.[45] Much of the third book of Victor's *History* narrates, in gory detail, the experiences of recalcitrant Nicene bishops and laypeople in different cities of the kingdom as they were exposed to the enforcement of this law. The deployment of coercive force against African Nicene Christians is not the sole topic of the history. Victor does sometimes treat the broader politics of the kingdom, yet these episodes too are used to support his central thesis: Vandal rule was a persecution of the African provinces.[46]

---

39. See 10–12.
40. On the *Historia*'s date and Victor's known biography see (best) Howe (2007), 28–119; Vössing (2011), 11–16.
41. *HP* 1.1–12 (ed. Lancel: 97–102).
42. Fournier (2015).
43. Howe (2007), 120–55; Heather (1999), 245; Fournier (2008), 207; Conant (2012), 192.
44. Shanzer (2004); Howe (2007), 125–44, 255–63, 283–301; Fournier (2008), 164–211, 221–39; Steinacher (2008), 251; Merrills and Miles (2010), 184–92.
45. *HP* 2.38–3.14 (ed. Lancel: 139–81).
46. See esp. Merrills (2011).

The *History of the Persecution* has cast a long shadow over Vandal Africa. Early twentieth-century scholarship took its claims at face value. Vandal rule was characterized as a reign of terror: a monolithically Catholic population confronted "fanatical" Arian overlords.[47] More recently, a number of studies have demonstrated that Victor is a (deliberately) misleading guide to Vandal Africa.[48] Indeed, a close critique of the *History of the Persecution* has been crucial to the new consensus on the kingdom outlined above. These accounts also stress that Victor is deceptive in his discussions of the nature and consequences of Christian difference in the kingdom. Nevertheless, major aspects of the (apologetic) framework with which he presents these issues often remain in place, whether his use of heresiological terminology, his portrayal of the Hasding dynasty as persecutors, his conflation of the agency of Homoian churchmen with that of their royal supporters, or, perhaps most influential of all, his equation of ethnic and Christian communities. The rest of this Introduction seeks to reframe debates over orthodoxy and heresy in Vandal Africa, their connection to the policies of the Hasding dynasty and the identities of the Vandal war band, and the makeup of the two churches of the kingdom. The following sections take Victor's *History* as their point of departure, both because many of the same problems that his partiality poses affect most of the texts with which this book deals and because Victor remains, for better or worse, a necessary starting point for any account of Vandal Africa.

TWO ORTHODOXIES

Victor of Vita is insistent in calling the Vandal kings and their war band "Arian heretics." Throughout his *History*, Christian affiliation is the key criterion for classifying contemporaries in African society, whether they are Catholic Christians or followers of that heresy. Victor presents the designations "Catholic" and "Arian" without comment, as if simple descriptors; many other Christian writers of his ecclesiastical affiliation use the same terminology in that way. Yet these were far from neutral terms. Calling Christians "Arians" marked them out as followers (if at a distant remove) of the heresiarch Arius, the presbyter of Alexandria condemned at the Council of Nicaea (325).[49] Victor's *History* may not explicitly discuss Arius, but the mere use of the term was meant to suggest a link.

---

47. E.g., Courcelle (1964), 183–99; Van der Lof (1973). Modéran (2003), 21–23, has an excellent summary.

48. Shanzer (2004); Howe (2007); Fournier (2008); Fournier (2013); Fournier (2015); Merrills (2011); cf. Vössing (2011).

49. R. Williams (2001); Hanson (1988), 3–18, 129–78; Wiles (1993); Wiles (1996), 1–26; Ayres (2004), 15–20, 85–103; Lyman (2008), 237–46; Galvao-Sobrinho (2013), 35–124.

In late antiquity, such labels were powerful tools to delegitimize Christian opponents.[50] Both factions in late Roman Africa's ecclesiastical schism called each other similarly derived names. Those usually referred to as Catholics labeled their opponents Donatists after an influential bishop of Carthage, Donatus; in turn, they were called Caecilianists, from their support for Donatus's equally controversial rival, Caecilian.[51] Terms like *Arian*, *Donatist*, and *Caecilianist*—and, just as important, *Catholic*—must be used carefully. They are prejudicial, perpetuating the claims of one side of a Christian conflict. The relationships they suggest with the named founders of these "sects" are deeply misleading. Arians, Donatists, and Caecilianists would have neither seen their Christianity in this way nor called themselves by these names. They were Christians and, if further disambiguation was necessary, true, orthodox, or Catholic. The label *Arian* is particularly problematic, since a considerable gap separated the views of those so labeled in the Latin West and the teachings of Arius (whether in the hostile characterization of his contemporaries or what we know of his actual views).[52] The use of such terms in fifth-century texts like the *History of the Persecution* should not be ignored; it suggests one way that contemporaries could have viewed these Christians. Nevertheless, this does not mean that they can be allowed to stand without qualification. For the Donatist schism, there are no easy, neutral replacements.[53] For ease of comprehension, this book will use *Catholic* and *Donatist* when its argument casts back to late Roman Africa; the context will make clear whether the terms convey the heresiological force of ancient authors or the studied neutrality of modern scholarship. For Vandal Africa, less prejudicial replacements are available. Thus, *Catholic*, *Arian*, and other heresiological terminology will be used only when speaking from the perspectives of contemporaries like Victor of Vita.

If the Arian heresy attributed by Victor and others to the Vandals is problematic, so too is the Christian affiliation generally supposed to lie behind it. The Christianity of the Vandal war band is opaque. The precise context(s) of conversion are unknown: the sojourn in Gaul and Spain between 406 and 429 (and the influence of the Visigoths there) and their previous sphere of military activity in the late fourth-century Balkans (and its non-Nicene bishops) are often conjectured.[54] All

50. See 94–96, with n. 67.
51. On "Donatist" see (best) Shaw (1992), 5–14; (2011), 343–44. For "Caecilianist" see *Gesta con. Carth.* 3.30, 3.34, 3.123.8–9 (ed. Lancel: 187, 209).
52. Hanson (1988), 123–28; Wiles (1993), 39–41; Vaggione (2000), 41–43; Ayres (2004), 2, 13–14, 54–57; Gwynn (2007a), 7–8; Lyman (2008), 238.
53. See esp. Shaw (2011), 5–6 (on "African Christian" for "Donatist"); cf. O'Donnell (2006), 209–43 ("Caecilianist" for "Catholic").
54. For prudent caution see Liebeschuetz (2003), 79; Vössing (2008), 181; Vössing (2014), 31–33; Merrills and Miles (2010), 178–79. On Gaul and Spain see Heather (2007a), 143, using Orosius 7.41.8 (ed. Arnaud-Lindet: 3:122), but cf. Inglebert (1996), 567, on this passage. On the Balkans see, e.g., Jensen (2013), 277. For both conjectures see Zeiller (1918), 538–39; Castritius (2007), 73.

that can be said is that there were most likely Christians within the war band when it fought the Roman general Castinus in 422, and certainly when Geiseric took power in 428.⁵⁵ Given frequent references in ancient texts to Vandals as Arians en bloc, to their kings' support for Arianism, and to specific Arian Vandals, it seems likely that a considerable number of those within the war band, and the African elite that it became, were non-Nicene Christians of some sort. Nonetheless, the blanket designation of Geiseric's heterogeneous followers as Vandals—or, worse, barbarians—should provoke similar wariness in interpreting their sweeping characterization as Arians.⁵⁶

Greater precision regarding this non-Nicene Christianity is possible. The edict that Huneric promulgated in the aftermath of the Conference of Carthage in 484, preserved in full by Victor of Vita, defines true religion using the twin Councils of Rimini and Seleucia convoked by Constantius II in 359.⁵⁷ The creedal formulae agreed at those councils stated that God the Son was "like" (*similis* in Latin; ὅμοιος in Greek) God the Father and forbade the substance (οὐσία) language used in the formula of the Council of Nicaea, "of the same substance" (ὁμοούσιος).⁵⁸ Moreover, the contours of the polemic produced by "Catholic" churchmen in Vandal Africa— supporters of the Nicene formula—and wider late fourth- and early fifth-century historical developments suggest that the Arians they attacked were Homoians (in the modern scholarly terminology derived from the Greek).⁵⁹ Thus, *Homoian* and *Nicene* will be used to describe the competing churches of Vandal Africa.

Homoian Christianity was not new in Vandal Africa or the post-imperial West. As Huneric's citation of the twin councils of 359 suggests, this form of Christology had a long history, one to which churchmen and rulers in Vandal Africa turned to understand the present. In this regard, Victor of Vita is a rare example of a doctrinally engaged author who, in the main, wrote as if the arrival of the Vandals in 429 was the horizon for the relevant events of ecclesiastical history.⁶⁰ Homoian Christianity originally represented a compromise in a period of considerable debate (conveniently, if rather misleadingly, called the Arian controversy—even by me in

---

55. See Salv., *Gub. Dei* 7.11.46 (ed. Lagarrigue: 462) for a (perhaps implausible) story of Vandal biblical chanting before the battle in 422; Hyd., *Chron.* 79 (89) (ed. Burgess: 88–90) for Geiseric's supposed conversion from Catholic Christianity to Arian heresy in 428. On both passages, see the works in the previous note.

56. See p. 7.

57. *HP* 3.5, 3.12 (ed. Lancel: 176, 180).

58. On the councils' complicated proceedings and their creedal formulae (which, though modified, remained Homoian throughout), see Brennecke (1988), 5–86; Hanson (1988), 348–86; T. Barnes (1993), 144–51; D. Williams (1995), 11–37; Ayres (2004), 157–66.

59. See (best) Brennecke (2008b); Heil (2011), 251–76.

60. One exception is a reference to laws made by earlier Roman emperors, in response to Huneric's citation of them: *HP* 3.2 (ed. Lancel: 174–75).

this introduction) centered in particular on the validity of substance language for discussions of the Father-Son relationship in the godhead.[61] A number of militant supporters of the Creed of Nicaea—not at that time the generally revered document it would become—portrayed Homoian Christology as Arian, picking up a slur coined by disputants in the bitter Greek Christological arguments of the 330s and 340s.[62] But despite the vocal opposition of individuals like Athanasius of Alexandria, Hilary of Poitiers, and Lucifer of Cagliari, this Homoian creed remained a legitimate form of imperial orthodoxy in the following decades.[63] As a result of the campaigns of these and other hard-line Nicene bishops in both East and West, a broader turn to Nicaea within the Mediterranean church, and the antiheretical legislation of Theodosius I in the 380s, the label *Arian* stuck (in the minds of later Nicene churchmen at the very least).[64] Yet even if, from the last decades of the fourth century, the Nicene Creed became the touchstone for orthodoxy within the empire, various Christians across the Roman world continued to see Homoian Christology as Christian orthodoxy, and Homoian theology evolved.[65] The sparse evidence for these individuals, groups, and churches likely underrates their presence. Homoian Christianity was transported north of the frontiers through the missionary activity of (among others) Ulfila, the creator of the Gothic Bible. If the moments or contexts of their conversion are often unrecoverable, it is nonetheless evident that many Christians within several barbarian groups took up Homoian Christianity as correct doctrine and continued to affirm it well into the sixth century.[66] Just as important, Homoians can be seen in the fifth century in Constantinople, the Balkans, northern Italy, and, most relevant here, Africa.[67] Among his many other episcopal cares, Augustine of Hippo worried about the presence of

61. On the shape of the controversy see (best) Ayres (2004).

62. Ibid., 105–30; Parvis (2006), 180–81; Gwynn (2007a), 59–87.

63. Brennecke (1988), 87–242; Hanson (1988), 791–95; McLynn (1994), 22–31, 36–37; D. Williams (1995), 11–103; Ayres (2004), 222–43, 260. On those opponents see Flower (2013a).

64. On the turn to Nicaea in the late fourth-century church (often called "pro-Nicene" or "neo-Nicene"), see Markschies (1997); Gemeinhardt (1999); Ayres (2004), 133–269, esp. 167–68, 236–40, 260–67; M. Barnes (2007), 195–96; cf. D. Williams (1995), 12–18; Ulrich (1997). On the 380s as decisive (if only in retrospect), see Hanson (1988), 791–823; Leppin (2003), 66–86; Ayres (2004), 251–69; McLynn (2005); Hunt (2007).

65. See (best) Heil (2011), 251–76.

66. On Ulfila see Heather and Matthews (1991), 124–43; McLynn (2007). On Gothic conversions see Lenski (1995). For survey treatments see Schäferdiek (2007), 52–59; Brennecke (2008b), 134–43. On the contrasting ecclesiastical histories of the different barbarian groups, see now Berndt and Steinacher (2014a) and the forthcoming monograph by Yitzhak Hen with Cambridge University Press. On Homoian Christianity in the other successor kingdoms, see the epilogue.

67. On Constantinople see Greatrex (2001). On the Balkans and northern Italy see (with caution) the accounts of McLynn (1996), 479–84, and Amory (1997), 237–51; see too *HP* 2.24 (ed. Lancel: 132). For Africa see the next note.

these "Arians" and the self-confidence with which they professed their doctrine.[68] Indeed, Homoian Christians in Africa and elsewhere were convinced that their Nicene opponents were the real heretics: "Homoousians," defined by their wrongheaded belief that the Father, the Son, and the Holy Spirit were of the same substance (ὁμοούσιος).[69]

This book argues that the history of ongoing Christian debate over the definition of the true faith is the context in which ecclesiastical controversy in Vandal Africa should be located. There is a pervading sense that Christian disputes in the barbarian successor kingdoms were inherently different from what went before: a lingering trace of earlier views on the fifth century and its barbarian protagonists. Developments in post-imperial Africa tend to be detached from this earlier ecclesiastical history and the sophisticated culture of heresiological disputation that both developed from it and helped to sustain it. This detachment partly stems from the unusual framing of this ecclesiastical conflict in Victor of Vita's *History*, which stands free of the context of fourth-century controversies. Of course, debates over correct doctrine mattered to Victor and shaped the *History of the Persecution* to a greater degree than is sometimes appreciated.[70] Homoian Christians in Vandal Africa thought they were orthodox and sought to convince others. Both they and their Nicene opponents portrayed each other as heretics. Competing claims to the legitimacy that orthodoxy provided within the Christian community retained the same implications for Christian authority figures—and continued to concern rulers and their subordinates—for the same reasons they had in the later Roman Empire. Clerics seeking the validation of their church's and their own legitimacy used the same polemical tropes, strategies, tactics, and literary forms as earlier controversialists in Africa and elsewhere. Most crucially, these clerics appealed to the history and heresiology of fourth- and early fifth-century Nicene-Homoian disputes to claim exclusive possession of Christian truth. In setting out opposing camps of Catholic Christians and Arian heretics, Victor was contributing to the polemical campaigning of his own ecclesiastical faction.

VANDAL PERSECUTION

When seeking to establish their doctrinal definitions, and thus their own legitimacy, late-antique Christian factions often sought the backing of their rulers. Like

---

68. For overviews of Augustine and Arians see Mara (1986); M. Barnes (1993); McLynn (1996), 485–88; Lancel (2002b), 377–80; Sieben (2006); Brennecke (2007); Brennecke (2008a); Ayres (2010), 171–73; Whelan (2014b), 241–43.

69. See pp. 94–96.

70. See esp. Vössing (2011), 16–17, where the recent German translator of *HP* explains the omission from his work of *Liber fidei Catholicae*, a Nicene statement of correct doctrine that takes up forty-six chapters, *HP* 2.56–2.101 (ed. Lancel: 148–73).

the Donatist schism—and just about every other ecclesiastical controversy in late antiquity—conflict between Nicene and Homoian Christians in post-imperial Africa implicated the state. If it had not, we might know considerably less about the structures and ambitions of the Hasding regime in Africa. Victor of Vita's account of the coercive actions taken by Geiseric, Huneric, and their subordinates against Nicene Christians in the kingdom is crucial for the reconstruction of their governance in general. To salvage political calculus from violent intolerance, modern historians of Vandal Africa have put up convincing challenges to Victor's characterization of Hasding rule as persecution. To dispute his judgment—one echoed by contemporary Nicene texts—these historians have moved in several complementary directions. To begin with, they have limited the chronological and geographical extent of coercive interventions in ecclesiastical politics. In a series of important articles, Yves Modéran argued that the articulation and enforcement of anti-Nicene measures were at most intermittent and often restricted to the core Vandal province of Africa Proconsularis.[71] These measures found their broadest and strongest expression in the last years of Huneric, who sought the adherence of his entire kingdom to his Christian orthodoxy; not coincidentally, the execution of this policy is the culmination of Victor of Vita's History. However, while similar measures were taken from the first years of Vandal rule in Africa until Hilderic's grant of tolerance on his accession in 523, the religious coercion of 484 had a peculiar intensity.

Most narratives of religious politics in Vandal Africa reflect the changing attitudes and policies of different rulers (often exhibited, in Christian Courtois's elegant phrase, as a "gallery of kings," galerie des rois).[72] Royal interventions in Christian politics began early in Geiseric's reign and recurred at intervals throughout it. On a number of occasions—there are few precise chronological markers in the first book of the History—the king exiled Nicene bishops and clerics, banned services and new episcopal ordinations, confiscated churches and their property and transferred everything to the Homoians, and sought to enforce Homoian orthodoxy among royal servants. Huneric reissued some of his predecessor's enactments early in his reign before taking a more comprehensive approach, which included the exile of the whole Nicene episcopate (perhaps twice in consecutive years). A relative abatement seems to have followed under Gunthamund (r. 484–96), whose time in power is poorly served by contradictory ancient descriptions. Huneric's enactments seem to have remained in place—the Nicene bishops stayed in exile until 494—but enforcement seems to have become less proactive. Further measures were

71. Modéran (1993); (1998a); (2003); (2006). For these measures see (best) Conant (2012), 161–70. The succeeding narrative follows Merrills and Miles (2010), 177–203; Vössing (2011), 24–28.

72. Courtois (1955), 260–71; see Castritius (2006), 198–203; Merrills and Miles (2010), 57–60 (English translation at 57); Steinacher (2016), 235–98.

introduced during the reign of Thrasamund (496–523), though limited predominantly to the exile of bishops and the prevention of consecrations. Most notably, the entirety of the Nicene episcopate of Byzacena was expelled to Sardinia at some point in the first decade of the sixth century and remained there until the accession of Hilderic in 523.[73] This modified "history of the persecution" is, of course, only one side of the story. The reigns of all of these rulers saw cycles of greater and lesser activity and enforcement, including spells when the court made concessions.[74] Even Huneric, whose historical reputation has never recovered from his depiction by Victor as an archpersecutor, made moves to placate Nicene clerics early in his reign.[75] Coercive activity in favor of the Homoian and against the Nicene Church was far from ever-present.

This coercion has itself been recontextualized. Persecution is, of course, a deeply problematic concept. Any action prejudicial to "true" Christianity could be, and usually was, construed thus. Ascriptions of persecution to "orthodox" Christians by "heretical" Christians always bear two layers of subjectivity.[76] The same goes for the denunciation of "heretical" rulers as tyrants. Éric Fournier, in particular, has shown that Geiseric and Huneric followed late Roman precedents for punishing heretics in their anti-Nicene actions.[77] The high-water mark of religious coercion also represented the most intense engagement of any Vandal ruler with the imperial legacy. Huneric's ecclesiastical conference at Carthage in 484 between the Homoian and Nicene bishops was undoubtedly a reenactment of the Catholic-Donatist meeting of 411.[78] His edict from after the conference drew extensively and explicitly upon late Roman legislation and particularly Honorius's edict of unity (30 January 412), promulgated following the 411 conference.[79] Huneric's meticulous emulation and subversion of his imperial predecessors is particularly revealing of the ideology of a dynasty that saw its rule as God given.[80] Historians have convincingly read into the Hasdings' attested statements and actions the duty undertaken by emperors since Constantine—and pursued with a greater intensity beginning with Theodosius I—to ensure correct Christian belief among their sub-

---

73. *V. Fulg.* 13, 17, 25 (ed. Isola: 188–91, 197–99, 214).
74. See ch. 5.
75. See pp. 155–56.
76. Cf. Fournier (2008), 8–12.
77. Ibid., esp. 212–63; (2013).
78. For events around the conference (in two versions), see *HP* 2.38–3.14 (ed. Lancel: 139–81). On 411 see (best) Shaw (1992); Shaw (2011), 544–86; Hermanowicz (2008), 188–220. On 484 as reenactment see Howe (2007), 275–76; Fournier (2008), 113–15, 253–60; Fournier (2013).
79. *HP* 3.3–14 (ed. Lancel: 175–81). See Overbeck (1973), 77–79; Lancel (2002a), 175 n. 362, 177–79 nn. 372–80; Fournier (2008), 75 n. 3, 253–63; Fournier (2013); Conant (2012), 168–69, with n. 167. See also pp. 96–98.
80. Howe (2007), 259–63; Galli Milić (2009), 253–54; Merrills and Miles (2010), 71; Conant (2012), 183.

jects.⁸¹ Had Victor of Vita shared their version of the Christian faith, he might have praised the Vandal kings as worthy heirs to those renowned Christian emperors.⁸² As it is, royal interventions in ecclesiastical politics are better understood against this canvas than against the bloody backdrop of biblical and early Christian persecution he painted.

Finally, modern historians have stressed that these interventions were only one aspect of Vandal rule, and not necessarily fundamental to how all Africans perceived it. Royal ecclesiastical policies have been fruitfully, if often speculatively, set within Vandal power politics.⁸³ The kings' activities and self-presentation also represented far more than pious Christian rule. The near monomaniacal obsession with matters of Christian self-definition often attributed to them results from Victor of Vita's choice of events with which to construct his history.⁸⁴ Though these episodes of religious violence still necessarily provide the raw materials for narratives of Vandal Africa, the more thematic approach of recent historiography has yielded a greater sense of the multiple interests these kings had in ruling their kingdom. As already noted, a range of indices suggest that their claims to legitimate rule won considerable acceptance among their subjects.⁸⁵ Victor of Vita's complaints are thus less a reflection than a refraction of a broader African response, motivated by fears regarding the consequences of unqualified acquiescence. His hostility reveals the possibility of alternative responses.

Adopting a less chronological and more thematic approach to the politics of Vandal Africa has allowed recent commentators to play the *History of the Persecution* off against its author's contemporaries. Victor has become just one voice within a noisy (and not always harmonious) polyphony. This book adopts a similar approach, both to ecclesiastical controversy in the kingdom and to the *History of the Persecution*. The martyr and confessor stories of the *History* remain the best way to access the social dynamics of heresiology in Vandal Africa. But Victor's work requires careful handling. There is considerable reason to doubt that the episodes he describes unfolded as suggested. To make these stories meaningful, the historian fitted them to the categories, tropes, and cultural expectations of late-antique (and specifically African) Christian discourses of persecution and martyrdom.⁸⁶ Still, this does not permit us to explain away such episodes as simply authorial inventions.

---

81. For this imperial duty (and even echoes of Augustine's doctrine of *coge intrare*) in Vandal Africa, see Diesner (1966b), 40; Wickham (2005), 88–89; Howe (2007), 368; Löhr (2007), 45; Fournier (2008), esp. 214, 236–63; Merrills and Miles (2010), 189; Conant (2012), 183–84; Whelan (2014a), 516–19.

82. Cf. Fournier (2008), 3–5; Steinacher (2011), 54; Steinacher (2016), 112–13.

83. Heather (2007a); Steinacher (2008), 249–51; Steinacher (2011), 49–56; Merrills and Miles (2010), 181.

84. Cf. Courtois (1955), 264.

85. See pp. 7–8.

86. On the cult of martyrs in late-antique Africa, see now Dearn (2016); Moss (2016).

Rather, it invites a carefully differentiated approach. Victor had greater and lesser leeway to mold individual stories for his own purposes, depending on their proximity in time, their contexts, and the expectations of those audiences that had some familiarity with them. Much greater skepticism is permissible regarding the details of a private conversation between a Vandal king and an adviser from several decades prior to his writing than, say, for the public parading of scalped courtiers through the streets of Carthage a mere handful of years before.[87] Of course, the particular circumstances of even the more plausible events would not necessarily have been as written, given the apologetic purpose of Victor's work. Yet, for the purposes of this book, it is precisely that apologetic stance which makes his *History* valuable.[88] His accounts had to ring true for the African audiences that he hoped to persuade. It is in this sense that Victor's framing of these episodes can be particularly revealing. His accounts often engage (implicitly or explicitly) with alternative perspectives on the significance of these events. They also provide enough detail, in combination with contemporary texts, for modern observers to suggest plausible alternative readings. As a result, Victor's stories are valuable whatever their precise relationship to any "real" events, insofar as they can act as a basis for reconstructing differing contemporary views of the Vandal kings and the consequences of particular forms of Christian identity within African society.

VANDALS AND HOMOIANS

If critical reading of Victor of Vita and interrogation of his assumptions has produced much more sensitive readings of Hasding religious policies, close engagement with his *History* has a reciprocal implication for Vandal Africa's Christian controversy: it should not be tied too closely to the Vandals or their kings' political decisions. Homoian Christianity should be decoupled from both the Vandal war band and Vandal power. At the same time, the Christian identities of contemporary social actors, both Vandal and Romano-African, cannot simply be placed in confessional containers. The complex social world presupposed by Victor's *History* defies his ethnic and confessional dichotomies.

Homoian Christianity neither was nor was perceived as inherently barbarian or Vandal in fifth- and sixth-century Africa. The impression of coterminous ethnic and religious groups conveyed by Victor of Vita's *History* is an apologetic construct that the text itself undermines.[89] The Vandals were never the only Homoians in

---

87. For this private conversation see p. 176 n. 55; for the public scalping and parading, pp. 181–83.

88. For a similar approach to Gregory of Tours, using analysis of his highly rhetorical presentation of events to pursue alternative perspectives, see Reimitz (2015).

89. Heather (1999), 245, 248; Shanzer (2004), 286–87; Howe (2007), 120–82; Fournier (2008), 205–11; Conant (2012), 180–85.

Africa. There were Homoians among the Romano-African population even before their arrival (although Geiseric's war band contained the most prominent, and probably the largest, group of Homoians in 430s Africa).[90] Over the Vandal century, there is evidence for increasing adherence of Romano-Africans, both lay and clerical, to Homoian Christianity.[91] Victor's reference to Catholic Vandal confessors reinforces the point that confessional boundaries did not match up to ethnic ones, which were themselves blurred.[92] Of course, contemporary perceptions of group definition remain important even when misconceived. Yet even here Homoians and Vandals are normally distinguished. Vandal kings and Homoian clerics sought Romano-African adherents.[93] When Huneric's edict of 484 uses "us" and "them," it means "true Christians" and "Homoousian heretics," respectively, and not Vandals and Romans. It is plausible that Homoian Christianity represented for some Vandals an important element of their identity, but it does not follow that Vandalness was crucial to a Homoian Christian.[94] From the other side, only Victor makes Arianism fundamentally barbarian and Catholicism Roman. Other Nicene authors preserve confession and ethnicity as separate categories, and most discussions of Arian heresy do not even mention Vandals or barbarians.[95] For all parties in this Christian conflict, the matter at stake was the true Christian faith. Ethnicity or Roman identity might sometimes enter the equation, but the key term was *orthodoxy*.

The clear division of contemporary society into Nicene and Homoian Christians presupposed by Victor's *History* should in itself prompt caution. Recent work on religious identities in late antiquity stresses the recurring tendency for such dichotomies to dissolve on impact with real social situations.[96] For Christian authority figures, appropriate behavior and practice necessitated the social exclusion of members of other religious groups. Yet in the many interactions that made up their day-to-day lives in diverse communities, individual Christians often did not rate their religious identity as the most important aspect of who they were. Indeed, part of the point of Victor's history was to convince contemporaries who (to his mind) thought otherwise that their status as Catholic Christians had to be prioritized above good relations with the regime and potential social and political gain.[97] The "situational" approach to confessional identity that emerges from close reading of the *History of the Persecution* also suggests that a sharp contrast between

---

90. See pp. 13–14.
91. Modéran (2006); Merrills and Miles (2010), 195–200; Conant (2012), 172, for references.
92. *HP* 3.38 (ed. Lancel: 195); Howe (2007), 156–59. On blurring see ch. 6, esp. pp. 171–75.
93. Modéran (2003), esp. 36–42; Shanzer (2004), 286–88; Conant (2012), 166–70, 172.
94. E.g., Conant (2012), 180–84.
95. Howe (2007), 147–53, has a concise survey.
96. See ch. 6, esp. pp. 169–71.
97. See esp. *HP* 3.62 (ed. Lancel: 207–8).

the religious and the secular does not sufficiently capture the social interactions of elites in Vandal Africa. Christian identity could but did not have to be a source of conflict. The implications of ecclesiastical controversy might, on occasion, be ignored.

That controversy should be set at a similar remove from Vandal power. Victor of Vita and others depict a very close relationship between Arian churchmen and the Vandal court. These clerics are depicted as a royal coterie, and worldly power is adduced as a primary motive for adherence.[98] As a result, the Homoian Church sometimes becomes a "state" church for the kingdom in modern scholarship, if it is not ignored entirely. The broader late-antique and specifically African Christian inheritance renders the portrayals on which this conclusion is based intrinsically suspicious. In the Donatist schism, passions flared over instances of ecclesiastical negotiation with imperial agents, and intricate arguments were developed to justify or excoriate the religious coercion that ensued. As Michael Gaddis has shown in excellent syntheses, accusations of improper association with secular power were commonly used to undermine rival Christian groups across the late-antique Mediterranean.[99] Given the inevitable involvement of churches and bishops in politics, such insinuations were easily made. The Homoian Church of Vandal Africa was an autonomous institution throughout the Vandal period.[100] While some of its clerics possessed considerable political influence, this did not make them creatures of the king. This is not to deny that Homoian Christianity was an important political issue for Vandal kings, who set the conditions for ecclesiastical conflict.[101] Nevertheless, as Modéran forcefully argued, Vandal Africa's "guerre de réligion" was fought not between "un pouvoir et une Église" but between two churches.[102] It is on those terms that this conflict must be understood.

This book proceeds on the basis that Christian controversy in Vandal Africa is best approached, in the first instance, through the attested statements and actions of representatives of the Nicene and Homoian Churches. It seeks to avoid conflating the two ecclesiastical bodies with the Vandal political apparatus and the elites of the kingdom, since their interests diverged in important ways. Detaching these churches from power structures and specific elements within society permits a better understanding of the rationale behind Christian texts produced in this period. It also produces a more nuanced sense of the consequences of Christian orthodoxy upon politics and society, one that does not require overarching oppositional frameworks (Homoians and Nicenes, Vandals and Romano-Africans, the

---

98. See pp. 41–46.
99. Gaddis (2005); (2009).
100. Modéran (2003).
101. See pp. 96–103.
102. Modéran (2003), 23. This approach is also implicitly taken by Merrills and Miles (2010), 177–203; Conant (2012).

Christian and the secular). By adopting such an approach, this book attempts both to convey the sophistication of Vandal Africa's Christian controversy and to recapture the complexities of the role it played in social and political life in the kingdom.

BEING CHRISTIAN IN VANDAL AFRICA

Part 1 of this book argues that a culture of Christian disputation which had barely changed from that of the later Roman Empire flourished in Vandal Africa. It considers how clerics in the kingdom contested the definition of Christian truth and thus claimed to represent the true Christian Church. Chapter 1 sets the stakes of this controversy by presenting the extent and makeup of the Homoian and Nicene Churches in Vandal Africa. It pays heed to contemporary Nicene authors, worried that their more naïve congregants might worship in the "wrong" building, by arguing that these rival churches and clerics were not altogether different from each other. Homoian and Nicene churchmen were competing on the same basis. The Nicene Church likely had greater numbers, but various indices suggest that the two institutions were of a similar order of magnitude. Despite modern conceptions of a peculiarly Vandal Homoian Church, these two institutions also had similar cultures. References to non-Latin language use suggest that the constituent communities of both churches were linguistically and ethnically heterogeneous. The careers of Homoian clerics are difficult to access, but reading between the lines of Nicene attempts to portray their rivals as dependents of the Hasding regime—and their own bishops as saintly confessors—shows that the activities of both episcopates conformed to familiar late-antique norms. Perhaps surprisingly, Nicene bishops also suffer from the patchy survival of biographical information and the late-antique and early medieval tendency toward pseudepigraphy. That even the works of some of the best-known bishops of the period were preserved under the names of more famous ecclesiastical authors implies that other pseudonymous texts whose authors cannot be identified should not be dismissed. These thoroughgoing parallels suggest that Nicene and Homoian churchmen should be taken on the same terms.

Chapter 2 considers how those churchmen debated with one another. It introduces the heresiological literature produced in Vandal Africa and the vibrant culture of polemical Christian disputation that it embodies. These various tractates, florilegia, and dialogues have received little modern attention, in part because of their detachment from known authors but also because of their sometimes surreal formats: most notably, debates between long-dead church fathers and heretics. In fact, these literary forms were central to conflicts over religious authority, doctrine, and practice in late antiquity. Nicene and Homoian writers in Vandal Africa used them to stake their claims to orthodoxy and contest the arguments of their opponents, utilizing all the forms of persuasive rhetoric that had become the basic tools of the late-antique heresiologist. The "virtual" dialogue evident in this literature mirrored and modeled various forms of "real" debate between Nicene and Homoian authority figures. The striking resemblance between these texts and those written by earlier Christian controversialists was not merely a continuity of literary form. These works suggest that the practical implications of controversy for Christian clerics remained the same.

Chapter 3 argues that the balance of power in this ecclesiastical controversy has consistently been misunderstood. This chapter reconstructs the self-presentation of Homoian writers, who appropriated the legitimizing standards of the late-antique Christian community to portray themselves as members of the one, true Christian Church. Such entry-level assertions were reinforced by effective heresiology. Homoian writers painted their Nicene opponents as Homoousian heretics, deviants whose Christianity was called into question by use of an unscriptural term for the crucial relationship among the members of the Trinity. The Vandal court's antiheretical legislation supported this labeling. A corresponding shift in the balance of power can be traced in contemporary Nicene polemic, especially in the imaginary dialogue texts, which place renowned church fathers like Athanasius and Augustine in the role normally reserved for heretics. Homoian writers sought to push the Homoousians further beyond the limits of acceptable Christian belief and praxis by assimilation to worse heresies and paganism and by rebaptizing Homoousians who sought to join their Christian communities. The sophistication of this heresiology and the furious Nicene responses it received should force a rethinking of contemporary perceptions of the African Christian community. For at least some Christians in Vandal Africa, Homoian Christianity would have been orthodox; the Nicene Church, a heretical sect.

Chapter 4 examines the fundamental Nicene response to competing claims to Christian orthodoxy: making their opponents into Arians. This was not as straightforward as it might seem. A convincing depiction of contemporary Homoian Christians as Arians required considerable engagement with the history and heresiology of the church. To establish the crucial link between their contemporary opponents and the Arians of the past, Nicene authors imaginatively rewrote fourth-century ecclesiastical history. They reworked what they saw as an authoritative past to match the needs of the present. By portraying the ecclesiastical politics of Vandal Africa as a reenactment of earlier Catholic-Arian conflicts, Nicene clerics made their church into the descendant of a triumphant Catholic institution; that of the Homoians, the ongoing embodiment of the Arian sect. They also made themselves and their opponents the respective heirs of past heroes of Nicene orthodoxy and villains of Arian heresy. Homoian clerics shared this historical mind-set, deriving justification from their own versions of fourth-century ecclesiastical history. These were not the only narratives that both sides pressed into new service. The history of the Donatist schism in late Roman Africa also formed a crucial point of departure for heresiology in the kingdom. Nicene writers used anti-Donatist arguments to make their new opponents into heretics with whom their audiences would be more familiar. They did so, in part, because Homoians were also exploiting the history of church conflict in late Roman Africa to develop their own ecclesiological claims. Taken as a whole, part 1 reveals a controversy whose methods and substantive concerns were those of the Christian conflicts of the later Roman Empire.

This ecclesiastical conflict is important in itself. It shows that clerics continued to contest the definition of true Christian faith and to make distinctions between orthodoxy and heresy on specifically Christian terms: this was not a debate about barbarians and Romans or Hasding legitimacy. Nonetheless, Christian controversy cannot be partitioned from the broader range of social and political developments in post-imperial Africa. It had important consequences for the questions of identity and political formation that have dominated scholarship. Part 2 explores these consequences and suggests more nuanced models of interaction between the Vandal court, the Nicene and Homoian Churches, and the mixed elite of the kingdom, drawing on recent work on identity in late antiquity.

Chapter 5 reconsiders the relationship between the Vandal kings and the Nicene Church, which has often been seen as an obstacle to effective Vandal rule. Mutual recriminations between kings and bishops and the (at least partial) grounding of their respective legitimacies in conflicting versions of true Christianity have led to modern portrayals of inevitable conflict. In fact, partly because neither could ever fully undermine the other's authority, both had interests that could lead them to compromise. Even as they decried heretical Vandal tyranny, Nicene bishops petitioned their rulers to improve their church's lot, using obsequious courtly language and the appropriate bureaucratic channels to do so. Vandal kings sometimes granted these petitions; even when refused, these pleas were at least heard. The possibility of compromise was retained for as long as possible. The result was tacit or even explicit acknowledgment of the legitimacy of the other parties, whether as secular rulers or Christian authority figures.

The capacity of Nicene bishops and Vandal kings to escape the implications of the confessional distinctions they themselves encouraged suggests that the role of Christian controversy in shaping elite identities requires further reconsideration. When it comes to Christian self-identification, there remains an overwhelming tendency to see social identities in the post-imperial world as governed by ethnic affiliations. Time and again, Christian group membership is treated as subordinate or otherwise directly linked (as in "Vandal" or "barbarian" "Arianism" or "Roman" "Catholicism"). Chapter 6 reconsiders the interaction of Christian and ethnic identities in Vandal Africa. It emphasizes the fundamental implication of important recent theoretical discussions of identity: the situational nature of individual identity means that the relevance of any affiliation in any specific situation or broader social context cannot be taken for granted. As a result, neither confessional nor ethnic groups are constant contexts for individual action. The frequent exhortations of clerics and kings that (their) orthodox Christians avoid churchgoing, conversing, or even eating with heretics in fact suggest that Christians were traversing these (supposed) communal boundaries. Ethnic groups seem equally porous. Modern attempts to read profound statements of "Vandalness" or "Romanness" into the actions of contemporary aristocrats founder on the dearth of ethnic self-identification and discourse. As a number of recent studies argue, their actions are better understood as responses to the demands of social, not ethnic, distinction: the display of prestige and superiority within an elite culture shared by Vandals and Romano-Africans. The limits to the importance of each form of identity—and the variety of ways in which the demands of each could be interpreted—are multiplied when the two are combined. Ethnic identity was not especially relevant for clerics or kings when they sought to manage the boundaries of their orthodox Christian communities. On the rare occasions when these authority figures did construe a relationship between these two forms of identity, their depictions of the connection are much more subtle and varied than modern notions of "barbarian Arianism" suggest. In this regard, Nicene clerics could even be unexpectedly sensitive: discussing Vandals as simply another group of Christians seeking mercy from the one true God. Ethnicity was generally secondary even in these passages: of more consistent importance for both kings and clerics when policing their orthodox communities was the power and status of an individual Christian. The anti-Homoousian edicts of the Hasding dynasty targeted their political servants; Nicene anti-Arian polemic responded in kind, denouncing those who conformed as politically and economically motivated and detailing the dilemmas of Nicene officials. In that light, Vandal and Romano-African Christians—or Nicene and Homoian Vandals and Romano-Africans—should not be studied separately but rather taken together, as members of a mixed social elite.

Chapter 7 pushes this argument further, exploring the limits to the importance of heresiological distinctions in the kingdom's social and political life. If any particular group was singled out by those parties who sought to police their imagined Christian communities, it was the ruling elite of the kingdom (whatever their ethnicity). This chapter argues that elite individuals could nonetheless use their Christian piety to display their social status in spite of contemporary ecclesiastical controversy. Christianity was not a taboo subject in the Vandal kingdom; individuals could show loyalty to their kings without effacing the Christian aspects of their identities. Specific moments required a courtier or aristocrat to define their Christian faith more exactly, but otherwise the nature of courtly and aristocratic social interaction and the limits of government enforcement provided ample scope for artful dissimulation regarding doctrinal or ecclesiastical affiliation. The evidence of Christian martyrology, poetry, letters, and tombs is adduced to demonstrate that elite Christians, both Vandal and Romano-African, found ways to claim a determinedly Christian prestige that was nonetheless potentially acceptable to other members of the religiously heterogeneous elite. Overall, part 2 of this book suggests that controversy over the definition of Christian orthodoxy did indeed help to shape society and politics in Vandal Africa. The (potentially divisive) effects of this controversy were nonetheless crucially circumscribed, and thus eased, by the fact that Christianity—and a rigidly confessional Christianity at that—did not exclusively govern the identities of the kings, aristocrats, and clerics whose interactions worked to create and perpetuate the kingdom.

PART ONE

Contesting Orthodoxy

1

African Churches

"THEY ARE NOT THE CHURCHES OF GOD,
BUT THE CAVES OF BRIGANDS"

In a basilica in the episcopal complex of Ammaedara (modern-day Haïdra, Tunisia), a city in the south of the Roman province of Byzacena, stands a funerary notice advertising the burial of a Victorinus *episcopus* in an enclosure at the east end (see figures 1 and 2).[1] Had it remained in its original state, this inscription would simply have been added to the extensive catalogue of undated epitaphs for late-antique African bishops. Instead, in 568–69, some three and a half decades after the Byzantine reconquest of Africa, a bishop Melleus dedicated the church to Cyprian of Carthage, and the martyr's relics were placed beneath a new, western altar.[2] Ten years later Melleus was buried beside those relics, supplanting Victorinus through interment in a more prominent tomb.[3] Most likely at this time, an extra qualifier was added to Victorinus's epitaph: "VICTORINVS EPISC(OPVS) IN PACE *VANDALORVM*" (Victorinus, bishop *of the Vandals*, in peace). Engraved in a much cruder hand, the addition, *Vandalorum*, is a godsend, providing him a context: the period of Vandal rule. Given the common Byzantine association of Vandals and Arians in the mid-sixth century, it almost certainly

---

1. N. Duval and Prévot (1975), no. 58. This paragraph also draws on N. Duval (1981), 111–25, 165–207, at 184–87; Bockmann (2013), 202–7.

2. N. Duval and Prévot (1975), no. 1. Relics were also deposited under a new eastern altar, which was placed on top of the enclosure containing Victorinus's burial: ibid., no. 2, with N. Duval (1981), 120–25, 186.

3. N. Duval and Prévot (1975), no. 3.

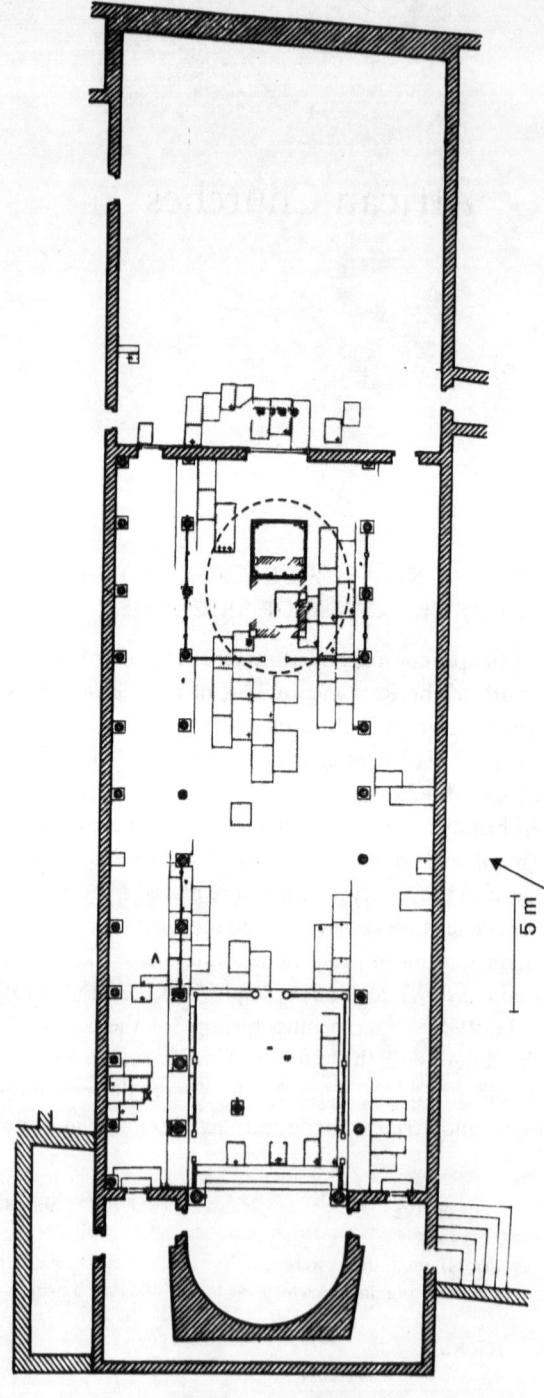

FIGURE 1. Ground plan of the Basilica of Melleus at Ammaedara (Haïdra, Tunisia), with ring indicating the location of Victorinus's burial and the eastern altar. From Bockmann (2013), plate 15, fig. 1, reproduced with kind permission of Reichert Verlag.

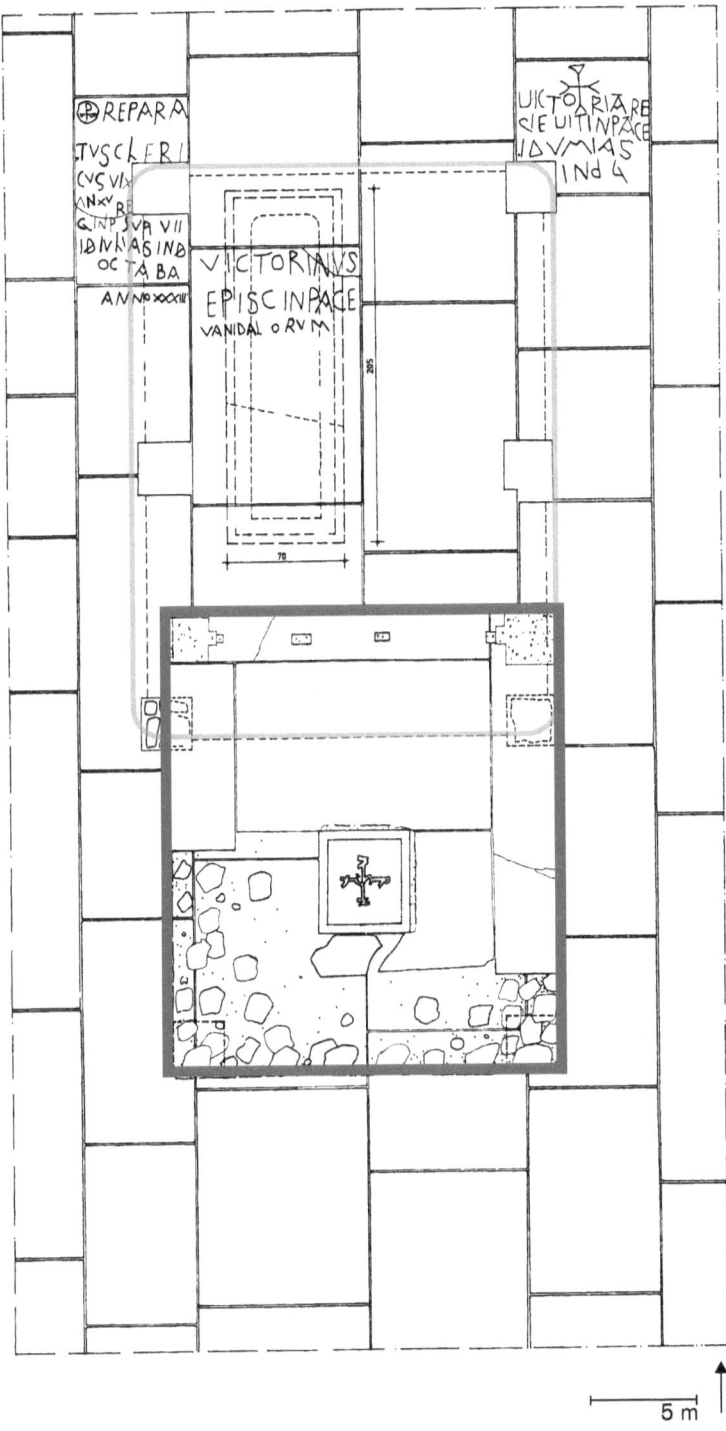

FIGURE 2. Plan of Victorinus's privileged burial next to the eastern altar of the Basilica of Melleus at Ammaedara (Haïdra). From Bockmann (2013), plate 15, fig. 2, reproduced with kind permission of Reichert Verlag.

identifies Victorinus as a Homoian bishop. The Nicene Melleus's inscription places a similarly telling emphasis on Catholic "unity": "MELLEVS, EP(IS)C(OPVS) VN(I)T(A)T(I)S, REQVIEBIT INP(A)C(E)" (Melleus, the bishop of unity, has found rest in peace). Melleus's project of refurbishment, rededication, and interment required careful distinction of his own status from that of the bishop who had already taken up posthumous residence in the church.

These privileged burials capture two African bishops (or their devotees) using familiar strategies of episcopal self-aggrandizement. They hold an important implication. The later Byzantine addition to Victorinus's epitaph at Ammaedara attempted to mark the Homoian bishop out as clearly "different" from his later Nicene counterpart. For modern observers it has the opposite effect, demonstrating the difficulty of distinguishing the activities and self-presentation of Nicene and Homoian bishops, or of their two ecclesiastical institutions. Here was an urban church in use in the Vandal period by a Homoian bishop. On his death, that Homoian bishop received a prominent burial within its walls of the sort that influential bishops in Africa and across the Mediterranean procured throughout the period. Were it not for a later polemical scrawl, Victorinus would be (at least to us) indistinguishable from hundreds of other ordinary African bishops. The identification of his church as one used by Homoians is equally exceptional. The doctrinal affiliation of churches in Vandal Africa (as elsewhere) can rarely be read from the material evidence, precisely because there were no major differences between them (at least as far we know).[4] Of course, there are fundamental limitations to the material record of late-antique African churches, due to both early prescientific archaeology and broader methodological problems of reading cultural meaning into material evidence. Yet the impression of a deep-rooted similarity that it provides may not be so misleading. Nicene and Homoian churches may not have looked all that different to contemporaries.

The degree to which these two sets of churches and communities might seem interchangeable worried Nicene churchmen from the beginnings of Vandal rule. Quodvultdeus, the Nicene bishop of Carthage during Geiseric's conquest of the city and its immediate aftermath, spent the conclusion of a sermon warning his congregation off his Arian rivals.[5] After evoking classic ecclesiological images of the church as the bride of Christ and mother of the faithful, Quodvultdeus contrasted his heretical opponents in equally traditional—and equally gendered—terms:

---

4. Leone (2007), 148; Von Rummel (2008), 156; Merrills and Miles (2010), 195–96; Bockmann (2013), 254; Bockmann (2014); see too the important remarks of Stevens (2012), 950. For similar problems in late Roman Africa see Lancel (1989), 150 n. 4, and Sears (2007), 34–37; in Ostrogothic Italy, Ward-Perkins (2010).

5. On Quodvultdeus see pp. 47–48, 51–53.

Do not let the strange, invented name seduce you from that mother, do not let the strange appearance of the church deceive you. The bride of Christ is not the one who does not know her husband. Disgraceful is she who contends to dishonor the appearance of such a husband with her words. In vain does she assign herself the name "church." I see you, O treacherous cave, deceiving, because you have been deceived. I see that you change your shape to the appearance of another. Why do you adorn yourself? Why do you embellish yourself so? Why do you spread your skirts? Why do you contend that you are equal, against the true bride? The bridegroom does not look upon you, because you are not the bride. But you say that you are beautiful, and you often glory in your gold and ornaments.[6]

Quodvultdeus used the trope of heretical church-as-prostitute to caution his congregation about the Homoian church in Carthage.[7] This church apparently looked deceptively similar to his own, to the extent that he feared members of his audience might attend it. This unnerving plausibility led Quodvultdeus to reconfigure its potential appeal as an illicit seduction. The Nicene bishop of Carthage's anxieties about the "appearance" (*species*) of this rival church, his repeated allusions to its embellishments and adornments, and his direct address to it as a physical space (*o spelunca subdola*) suggest he had an actual building in mind—perhaps one of several churches in the city moved into Homoian hands by Geiseric.[8] Who Quodvultdeus's Arians were is unknowable. They simply appear in his sermons as individuals professing a non-Nicene form of Trinitarian doctrine. It is unclear whether the Homoian ecclesiastics active in the first years of the Vandal kingdom were individuals who had traveled with the Vandal war band since Spain (or perhaps earlier), figures who were already present in Africa at the time of the conquest, or both (as seems most likely)[9]—and if both, when and how any shared institutional recognition developed between them. What is certain is that they posed no end of problems for the Nicene bishop of Carthage.

Quodvultdeus was not alone in feeling the need to prevent Nicene Christians from attending Homoian churches by slighting the buildings themselves. Almost a century later, Fulgentius, the Nicene bishop of Ruspe, a small town on the eastern coast of Byzacena, conveyed a similar message in the final stanza of a polemical psalm he wrote to educate contemporaries about Arian heresy: "Brothers, guard yourselves carefully, / that you might never enter their churches to pray. / They are not the churches of God, but the caves of brigands."[10] Both Quodvultdeus and Fulgentius sought to make Homoian churches into something decidedly other.

---

6. Quod., *C. Iud., pag. et Arr.* 22, quotation at 22.4–6 (ed. Braun: 256–58, at 257).
7. See Shaw (2011), 326–30, on this trope.
8. See Conant (2012), 163–64, with references.
9. See pp. 11–14.
10. Fulg., *ABC.* 294–96 (ed. Isola: 52). On Fulgentius see pp. 49, 160–63.

But in so doing, they implied that, from the perspective of individual Christian adherents, Nicene and Homoian cult sites, communities, and services did not look all that different. Such basic similarities required these two Nicene bishops and countless other contemporary Christian authority figures in Vandal Africa to emphasize that one church was the right place; the other, the wrong one.

Texts like Quodvultdeus's sermon and Fulgentius's psalm demonstrate that the Nicene and Homoian Churches of Vandal Africa were in direct competition for the loyalties of African Christians. They lay out in exquisite detail the intellectual basis for this competition: the many arguments used to justify the designation of one or the other as the true Christian institution and community in the kingdom. The next three chapters explore in depth these arguments and the debates they inspired. What these texts do not straightforwardly provide is a means to gauge the frequency and scope of that competition. Most of what can be known about Homoian churches is derived from Nicene polemical writings, which were not concerned to provide an accurate and detailed picture of the careers of their Homoian counterparts, nor of the size and structure of this rival institution. Quodvultdeus and Fulgentius do not locate the churches they discuss. Even the precious evidence of Victorinus's epitaph is, in effect, the result of Nicene polemical discourse. Somewhat more surprisingly, Nicene texts are patchy even in the coverage of their own institution. Few episcopal careers can be tracked in detail, and even texts written by influential Nicene bishops circulate under assumed names. As a result, it is not possible to assemble more than a superficial and somewhat misleading narrative of the two churches, their most prominent representatives, and the actions they took. At the same time it is vital to locate Nicene and Homoian clerics within fifth- and sixth-century Africa, to establish a framework in which the practical consequences of their competition might be understood.

This chapter pursues the implications of Victorinus's epitaph. It follows the lead of Quodvultdeus and Fulgentius's (supposedly) confused coreligionists in identifying basic similarities between the two ecclesiastical institutions of Vandal Africa. These two churches have often been portrayed as decidedly different in terms of size, profile, and personnel. The Homoian Church is generally seen as much smaller than its Nicene rival and its institutional formation as a reflection of dependence upon the Vandal war band and the Hasding regime. The following sections argue that Nicene defamation has led to these misleading portrayals. While it is likely that the Homoian Church could not rival the full strength of its Nicene opponent, the disparity between them was less pronounced than is generally assumed. Contemporary references to the liturgical use of some form of Vandalic language—the moments most likely to convey some sense of distinct ecclesiastical practice designed for Vandals—in fact show a diversity of languages and practices in both Homoian and Nicene Christian communities. The impression of

Homoian bishops as essentially secular political actors derives from their portrayal by the *History of the Persecution* and the *Life of Fulgentius* as Machiavellian "court bishops." Other episodes reveal a composite picture of Homoian churchmen performing the familiar roles of late-antique bishops. Once passages that describe the Homoian Church and its representatives are read in terms of the aims of their Nicene authors, that institution begins to look much less peculiar.

Ironically, the fragmentary attestation of the careers of Nicene bishops also makes their Homoian counterparts look less odd. For these bishops too it is rare to find a felicitous combination of texts and biographical contexts; their advantage lies in an absence of character assassination. This deficiency of lives (and *Lives*) thwarts the examination of the material consequences of Christian difference in one carefully delineated social environment, an approach taken in many studies of late-antique ecclesiastical politics. At the same time, it checks the unintended contrast that can form even in the most evenhanded treatments of (high-resolution) "orthodox" bishops and (fuzzy) "heretical" opponents. Moreover, it facilitates the integration of a set of anonymous and pseudonymous texts written in the kingdom that provide fascinating perspectives on this controversy and its concrete manifestations. All in all, probing the supposed differences between the Nicene and Homoian Churches of Vandal Africa provides a basis for taking these two institutions on equal terms.

THE NUMBERS GAME

Size mattered in late-antique ecclesiastical controversy. It also counted ideologically, as superior numbers justified ecclesiological claims within a Christian culture whose ideal was Catholic universality.[11] The spread and specific locations of rival ecclesiastical institutions were often crucial. On those terms, the Homoian Church has generally been seen as much weaker.[12] This is to some degree a commonsensical supposition, given that, on the eve of the Vandal conquest, the Nicene ecclesiastical body was theoretically in command of the resources and manpower of the Catholic and Donatist institutions merged by Emperor Honorius's edict of unity of 30 January 412.[13] Its continuing presence in the sees contested by those ecclesiastical factions is suggested by the *Register of the Provinces and Cities of Africa*, an African Nicene episcopal list produced in association with the ecclesiastical conference of

---

11. See, e.g., Bauer (1971), 190–94; Shaw (1992), 26–28; Shaw (2011), 557, 566–73; Wessel (2004), 178, 180, 259–60.
12. E.g., Liebeschuetz (2003), 78; Modéran (2003), 36.
13. See esp. Modéran (1998a), 248.

484. The *Register* names 459 Nicene bishops resident across all the provinces of the region in that year.[14]

Scant appearances of Homoian clerics and churches convey a similar geographical spread. Churches in Numidia and Mauretania Sitifensis (by 437), in Carthage (after 439), and then all across the Vandal kingdom (in 484) were supposed to have passed into the hands of Homoian clerics on royal orders. The framing of Hasding prohibitions of Nicene worship in the *sortes Vandalorum* (the province of Africa Proconsularis) similarly assumes Homoian communities beyond the capital.[15] Moreover, the terms of Huneric's edict of 24 February 484 suggest that his regime at least thought it plausible that Christians could participate in Homoian services all across the kingdom.[16] The problem is that there can be nothing like the same confidence in terms of the density of these communities and thus the size of the Homoian Church. Pinning down Homoian churchmen is difficult, especially as Nicene narratives normally present them at Hasding courts in Carthage.[17] Nevertheless, Homoian bishops can be seen at Ammaedara and Thamalluma in the far south of the kingdom (in southern Byzacena) and at Tipasa in the far west (in Mauretania Caesariensis, modern-day Tipaza in western Algeria).[18] A presbyter, Felix, was also active at the turn of the sixth century on the *fundus Gabardilla*, an estate on the provincial frontier between Proconsularis and Byzacena; it is unclear whether he was there as part of the formal Homoian ecclesiastical institution or operating in a more private capacity.[19] The only certain locations of church buildings used by Homoian clerics are in Carthage and Ammaedara.[20] As a result, it is unclear how common it was to have Homoian and Nicene bishops, churches, or congregations in the same city—in the manner so vividly attested for the Donatist

---

14. *Not. prov.*; see (best) Lancel (2002a), 223–48; Modéran (2006). The *Notitia* lists the Nicene bishops of each of the African provinces and Sardinia in order of seniority; many entries also list current place of exile. As Yves Modéran has suggested (2006, 168–69), it is evidently an apologetic text designed to show the superior numbers of a "Catholic" institution, perhaps intended to be presented at the Conference of Carthage (484) alongside the *Liber fidei Catholicae*, which it follows in the ninth-century Laon manuscript that preserves it (MS Laudunensis 113).

15. Conant (2012), 163–65. See Prosper, *Chron.* 1327, 1339 (ed. Mommsen: 475, 477); *HP* 1.9, 1.14–16, 3.3–14 (ed. Lancel: 100–101, 103–4, 175–81). Note too that Victor of Vita describes apparent acts of violence by Homoian mobs against illicit Nicene services at a number of sites in Africa Proconsularis: *HP* 1.41–42 (ed. Lancel: 115–16). On the *sortes* see p. 173 n. 37.

16. *HP* 3.12 (ed. Lancel: 180).

17. See pp. 42–44.

18. For Ammaedara see p. 29 nn. 1–3; Thamalluma, *HP* 3.43–46, 3.53 (ed. Lancel: 197–99, 203); Tipasa, *HP* 3.29 (ed. Lancel: 190–91).

19. *V. Fulg.* 6 (ed. Isola: 171–72). For bishops on private estates in late Roman Africa, see esp. Bowes (2008), 162–69; Dossey (2010), 125–42.

20. See Conant (2012), 163–64, with references; p. 29 nn. 1–3.

schism[21]—or if the norm was a church or churches solely occupied by one or the other. What can be said is that urban competition happened often enough for the politics of church use to be important: Nicene authors complain about Homoian possession of church buildings and celebrate their return.[22] Yet given the paucity of evidence for their presence, it seems unlikely that Homoian churchmen had the same tally or distribution as their Nicene rivals.

That said, the imbalance between the Homoian and Nicene churches should not be overplayed. It may not have been as great as the *Register* (an apologetic document) suggests.[23] The practical outcomes of both Honorius's edict and the transition to Vandal rule would have been more complicated than the continuing self-identification of the African "Catholic" Church implies. Catholic and Donatist congregations in some settlements combined as Honorius had prescribed, but in other places the status quo may have persisted until the Vandal conquest; certainly, ongoing tensions are evident into the 420s.[24] There is a jarring absence of evidence for Donatists from the 430s. Under Vandal rule, individuals and groups previously labeled Donatists could have assimilated to either side of the new conflict, on the basis of a host of potential factors (on the one hand, shared Trinitarian views, Homoian heresiological categorization, and possible coercion; on the other, shared hatred of the party of Caecilian and rebaptism of the members of that party).[25] Some, of course, may simply have refused to define themselves according to the terms of the new dispute and thus faded from view.[26] The same can be said more broadly. Other clerics and communities, whatever their communion, may have played little active role in ecclesiastical controversy, whether because the issues did not matter to them or because they were not closely connected to the other constituent communities.[27]

21. See esp. Shaw (2011), 569–80.
22. See pp. 32–34; Ps.-Victor, *Hom. Cyp.*; *Lat. reg. Vand. Alan.* (ed. Steinacher: 165–66); Carthage (525); *V. Fulg.* 25–26 (ed. Isola: 214–17).
23. See p. 36 n. 14.
24. See (best) Lancel (1989); for preexisting disunity within the African "Catholic" Church, McLynn (2016), 231–43.
25. For Donatists becoming Nicenes, see Frend (1952), 301; Markus (1997), 191–93; Conant (2012), 180, 184. For Donatists becoming Homoians, see Fournier (2008), 117–18, 154–63; (2012). Fournier stresses the role of rebaptism as a "ritual of [African] cultural integration," but note that many Christian communities across the Mediterranean adopted this practice (examples in E. Ferguson [2009], 451, 470, 575–76, 761), and it could just as easily divide as unite (if both parties saw each other as the heretics who lacked an efficacious baptism). For balanced views see Parsons (1994), 43, 56–60; Howe (2007), 263 n. 93; Pottier (2015); Conant (2016).
26. Shaw (1992), 33.
27. For a suggestive account of the regionalism of African episcopal networks in the early fifth century, see McLynn (2016); also Pottier (2015), 119, noting lack of Nicene self-regulation in the Vandal period.

Those bishops who did play an active role within the Nicene Church were not infrequently absent from their sees because of exile and prohibitions on ordination.[28] The province of Proconsularis was particularly badly hit, with a drop from 154 bishops in 457 to just 54 in 484; before a spate of new ordinations around 480, this tally may have been as low as three.[29] Byzacena similarly lost its entire episcopate to exile for most of Thrasamund's reign.[30] Yves Modéran's persuasive interpretation of a gnomic abbreviation in the *Register* of 484 suggests that eighty-eight African bishops transferred their allegiances to the Homoian side.[31] It may be telling that Nicene writers seeking to belittle their opponents emphasized their weakness outside Africa (a classic anti-Donatist argument) rather than inside the kingdom.[32] The Homoians were sufficiently numerous and widespread for their universalist claims to worry their opponents.[33] Whatever their physical spread and distribution, in the crucial battle to gain recognition as the kingdom's legitimate ecclesiastical institution, there is no good reason to suppose a significant disparity between these two African churches.

"I DO NOT KNOW LATIN"

On the first day of the Conference of Carthage in 484, called by Huneric to decide whether or not Nicene Christians held fast to Catholic doctrine, the Nicene delegates had a rude shock.[34] They entered the (unnamed) place of assembly to find Cyrila, a leading Homoian bishop from the city, seated on a throne. When they asked who would judge the case, a royal notary informed them, "The Patriarch Cyrila has said . . ." This reply is cut off in Victor of Vita's text by the ensuing tumult, as the throng of Nicene Christians gathered in the hall protested at Cyrila's use of the title *patriarch*, unnamed authorities sought to restrain them by ordering a beating by a hundred blows, and the bishop of Carthage, Eugenius, decried that order as persecutory.[35] Finally, the Nicenes asked Cyrila to set out his arrangements for the conference. His response baffles modern scholars as much as it did them: "I do not know Latin [*Nescio latine*]." Victor of Vita's Nicene bishops dismiss this answer as tactical: "We know that you have quite obviously always spoken

---

28. Conant (2012), 162–65, has a helpful collection of references.
29. *Not. prov.* 1.1–55 (ed. Lancel: 252–54); *HP* 1.29 (ed. Lancel: 110).
30. *V. Fulg.* 17–18, 25 (ed. Isola: 197–200, 213–14).
31. These Nicene bishops receive the note *prbt*, usually expanded to *peribit* = *periuit* (perished). Since a number demonstrably had not died by that time, Modéran (2006) convincingly suggested that the spiritual "death" of conversion to Homoian Christianity was meant.
32. Parsons (1994), 156; Modéran (2003), 36.
33. See ch. 3.
34. *HP* 2.52–55 (ed. Lancel: 145–47), quotations at 2.54, 2.55.
35. On Eugenius see pp. 48–49, 155–59.

Latin. You ought not to excuse yourself now, especially as you lit a fire under this matter [*huius rei incendium suscitasti*]." In Victor's account, the Homoian bishop finds other excuses to avoid giving the Nicenes a hearing, before they read out a pre-prepared statement of their doctrine, the *Book of the Catholic Faith* (reproduced in full by the historian). Cyrila's enigmatic statement receives no further attention.

This curious incident has occasioned much comment.[36] It has universally (and plausibly) been interpreted as evidence for use of a non-Latin language in Homoian circles in Vandal Africa, whether a specifically Vandalic language or a form of Gothic (perhaps related to the archaic ecclesiastical language of Ulfila's biblical translation and the commentaries used in Ostrogothic Italy).[37] It is difficult to say more. This has not stopped speculation that Cyrila's claim to non-Latinity was a statement of ethnic pride: an attempt to distinguish the Homoian Church as non-Latin, and thus non-Roman and Vandal.[38] This story has been used to frame the Homoian Church as an essentially Vandal institution, in a manner that would make it totally different from its Nicene rival.

A deliberate claim to ethnic distinction is not easily supported by the specific passage. Cyrila's statement is reported by an author generally hostile to him and with particular reason to attack the "patriarch" here. It cannot be ruled out that Victor invented these words; they are certainly reported in a manner calculated to make Cyrila look absurd, and thus illegitimate. Bishops in ecclesiastical meetings were supposed to be inspired by the Holy Spirit. Statements like this were often seized upon as uninspired speech.[39] Even if Cyrila's pronouncement was not a gaffe, it is difficult to turn it into the policy statement of an exclusively Vandal Homoian Church. The motive imputed by his Nicene opponents is more plausible.[40] Late-antique Christians did not like to be seen to have called in imperial or royal authorities against other Christians: it was all too easy for those who had been arraigned to attack the opponents who had had them brought there. The

---

36. Haubrichs (2012) provides a detailed summary.

37. Possibly a false distinction—debate continues over whether Vandalic was a separate language or a Gothic dialect: see (best) Reichert (2008); Reichert (2009); also Markey (1989); Tiefenbach (1991); Francovich Onesti (2002), 73–74, 85–87, 133–202; Francovich Onesti (2010); Steinacher (2008), 253–54; Haubrichs (2012). For ecclesiastical Gothic, its contrast to spoken language, and surviving texts, see Heather and Matthews (1991), 124–85; Amory (1997), 237–51; Burton (2002); Falluomini (2010). In the African ecclesiastical context, I will refer to this language as Vandalic for convenience.

38. Haubrichs (2012). It has even been suggested that Huneric must have condoned the move, since he left Cyrila in charge of the conference: ibid., 22, 27; cf. Lancel (2002a), 308 n. 229. Such suggestions underestimate the independence with which even bishops with close relationships to secular rulers could act on such occasions: see, e.g., McLynn (1994), 128–49; Wessel (2004), 138–80.

39. For inspired speech see Humfress (2007), 135–40; Gaddis (2009), 517–18. For verbal lapses see, e.g., McLynn (1994), 133–34; Lim (1995), 220; Humfress (2007), 261.

40. Cf. Fournier (2013), 407.

Carthaginian Conference of 411 (upon which this new conference was modeled) involved extensive wrangling over who was the plaintiff and who was the defendant: Catholics and Donatists alike argued that their opponents had sought adjudication first.[41] By demanding that Cyrila speak first—as plaintiffs in late Roman trials were supposed to do—the Nicenes set the Homoian bishop in this role. His tendentious response may have been, as they suggested, a way to avoid setting the debate's terms, so that his church did not seem like the one that had provoked it. In any case, although the Cyrila story provides a glimpse of alternative language use in Christian circles, it does not reveal an exclusively or distinctively Vandal Homoian Church. Instead, it suggests a plural linguistic and cultural milieu: Cyrila had often, perhaps even exclusively (*semper*), spoken in public in Latin.

In this regard, the confrontation over Cyrila's disavowal of Latinity is representative of references to Vandalic speech and Christianity in Africa. Far from supporting ethnic exclusivity, these passages suggest that different ethnicities and confessions shared forms of Christian praxis.[42] In 478 or 479, the eastern emperor Zeno sent an embassy to Carthage. As a result, Huneric promulgated an edict permitting the ordination of a new bishop of Carthage and freedom of worship for Nicene churches. At the same time, he demanded the following reciprocal concessions from Zeno for Homoian Christians in the East: "that the bishops of our religion, who are at Constantinople and in the other provinces of the East, [that] our bishops [*sic*], by his order, might have unimpeded authority [*liberum arbitrium*] in their churches to minister to the people in whichever languages they wish and to worship the Christian law."[43] Huneric's concern that Homoian bishops in the East be able to use "whichever languages they wish" has rightly been interpreted as ensuring that services conducted in Vandalic/Gothic were allowed, implying that a non-Latin language was used by at least some of his coreligionists in Africa.[44] At the same time, the king's use of the plural and stress on choice suggest that other options were also envisaged in both regions.[45] Equally revealing is the discourse on barbarian languages and worship given by the protagonist of a Nicene imaginary dialogue, the *Conference of Augustine with Pascentius*.[46] In an important passage discussed at length below, (Pseudo-)Augustine delivers a long speech to justify the use of ὁμοούσιος (of the same substance) in the Nicene Creed.[47] As part of his argument, Augustine provides evidence for use of Vandalic in the liturgy, citing the phrase "*Froia arme*, which is translated *Domine, miserere*." The context makes

---

41. See esp. Tilley (1991); Hermanowicz (2008), 200–212.
42. Schäferdiek (2007), 58.
43. *HP* 2.4 (ed. Lancel: 123–24).
44. See, e.g., Merrills and Miles (2010), 95.
45. Cf. Kitchen (2008), 146–48.
46. See pp. 73–75.
47. *Coll. Pasc.* 15 (ed. Müller, Weber, and Weidmann: 88–116); see also pp. 190–92.

clear that this Vandalic invocation is drawn from Nicene liturgy. The text frustrates any ascription of ethnic or even confessional exclusivity to this liturgical language. It explicitly states that Romans could attend services in Vandalic and beseech the Lord's mercy in that language; partly based on this passage, some have hypothesized bilingual masses.[48] The pseudonymous Nicene author's repeated stress on the validity of worship in the "barbarian" language implies that Homoian congregations did not have a monopoly on such services.

The *Conference of Augustine with Pascentius* gives a small but important nod toward the practical considerations that would, in any case, be suspected to break down a putative ethnic divide based on confession and language. The language politics of late-antique barbarian groups remain opaque. The best that can be said is that everything else known about the Vandals and their interactions in African society suggests extensive bilingualism (without even considering the problem of Punic, which is largely inaccessible in post-imperial Africa).[49] Certainly, this is the view taken as common sense by most recent commentators.[50] If they were indeed bilingual, those Vandals could have attended services conducted in Latin (whether Nicene or Homoian). When Christian services in Vandalic and the Christian observance of Vandals are set in the contexts that contemporaries allot them, they do not point toward an exclusively Vandal Homoian Church. Instead, they suggest that both Homoian and Nicene institutions were sites of ethnic and linguistic plurality.

HOMOIAN BISHOPS AND VANDAL REGIMES

Language use is not the only aspect of the Homoian Church in Vandal Africa that has led to its characterization as a peculiar ecclesiastical institution. In an influential article, Ralph Mathisen has strongly contrasted Homoian bishops in the post-imperial West with their Nicene counterparts.[51] For Mathisen, senior Homoian clerics were bishops of *gentes*, not cities, holding offices with characteristics derived from ad hoc arrangements for mobile armies. Thus, in all of the successor

---

48. Clover's (1982, 18) suggestion of bilingual masses partly stems from reading "which is translated" (*quod interpretatur*) as indicating what happened during the liturgy rather than as a textual gloss. Cf. Tiefenbach (1991), 255–56; Parsons (1994), 95–96; Falluomini (2010), 329–32.

49. On Punic in Vandal Africa, see Conant (2012), 186–89, with a useful bibliography for the late Roman period.

50. E.g., Francovich Onesti (2002), 87–91; (2010); Berndt (2007), 237; Hen (2007), 72–73; Merrills and Miles (2010), 95; Conant (2012), 63. On barbarian language politics see p. 39 n. 37. On Latin bilingualism in ancient society, Adams (2003) is fundamental, though less secure on "Germanic" (274–79, 447–50); see also Mullan (2011). On Latinity in Roman Africa more broadly see Adams (2007), 188–275, at 192–94 and 259–70, 573–76.

51. Mathisen (1997a), at 686–88 for Vandal Africa. For critique see Handley (2004), 293 n. 16; Heil (2011), 109–10.

kingdoms, these bishops formed coteries around the king and his close dependents. A number of scholars have echoed these conclusions. The African Homoian Church is labeled a "national" or "state" church;[52] Gideon Maier and Konrad Vössing have even argued that it functioned as a wing of the Vandal administration.[53] In this view the Homoian Church was an institution subordinate to its royal patrons; its bishops, mere creatures of the Hasding dynasty.

Modern depictions of a Homoian Church integrally linked to the Vandal regime are deeply problematic. The idea of a "state" or "national" church in late antiquity is itself highly contestable.[54] It unhelpfully elides the interests of two quite separate institutions and ignores a major current in Christian thought that found collaboration with secular authority profoundly unsettling.[55] Within late-antique Christian categories, the nearest equivalent to a "state" churchman is the caricature of the profane and ambitious "court" or "tyrant" bishop.[56] In fact, modern views on the character of Homoian bishops and their church are chiefly based on the use of this stereotype in Vandal Africa. As table 1 shows, most glimpses of Homoian clerics predictably come in Nicene texts: predominantly the *History of the Persecution* and the *Life of Fulgentius*.[57] They present the likes of Antonius, Cyrila, and Jucundus as overwhelmingly political figures largely active within Vandal courts at Carthage, as advisers to the king and to members of the Hasding dynasty. These clerics seem to have had intimate access to the royal family. Cyrila's predecessor as the Homoian patriarch, Jucundus, got in trouble early on in Huneric's reign for his frequent visits to the house of the king's brother, Theoderic; he was burned to death in public as part of a dynastic purge.[58] As a result of this familiarity, Victor of Vita often goes so far as to label these Homoian clerics as if they were personal attendants: the Arians were Geiseric's bishops ("episcopis ... suis"; also "sacerdotibus nostris" in direct speech); Jucundus was Theoderic's presbyter ("suo ... Iucundo presbytero"); Cyrila was Huneric's bishop ("Huniricum regem et Cyrilam episcopum eius").[59]

---

52. In, e.g., Francovich Onesti (2002), 42, 75; Maier (2005), 287–89; Castritius (2006), 194; Steinacher (2011), 53–55; cf. Courtois (1955), 225; Modéran (1998a) 264–66.

53. Maier (2005), 287–89; Vössing (2011), 26–27, 177 n. 217; Vössing (2014), 82, 96, 122, 129. See also Schmidt (1942), 97; Parsons (1994), 79.

54. For a nice statement, see Leppin (2003), 238.

55. See p. 20 n. 99.

56. Hunt (1989); Gaddis (2005), 75–79, 251–82.

57. *HP* 1.19–21, 1.43–44, 1.48, 2.8, 2.13, 2.16, 2.39, 2.51, 2.53–55, 3.1, 3.5, 3.14, 3.29–30, 3.38, 3.42–46, 3.48, 3.53–54 (ed. Lancel: 105–6, 116–17, 119, 125, 127, 139–40, 145, 146–47, 174, 176, 181, 190–91, 195, 197–98, 199–200, 203); *V. Fulg.* 6–7, 21 (ed. Isola: 171–77, 204–7).

58. *HP* 2.13 (ed. Lancel: 127). On that purge see Merrills (2010).

59. *HP* 1.19, 1.44, 2.22 (ed. Lancel: 105, 117, 132); cf. Modéran (2008), 219 n. 43.

TABLE 1 Known Homoian clerics and authors

Name	Date	References
Abragil, priest who asked Fulgentius a question about the Holy Spirit while in Carthage	Mid to late 510s?	*V. Fulg.* 21
Anduit, priest at Regia	484	*HP* 1.41
Anonymi 1, Homoian clerics at Carthage	Late 430s/440s	Numerous mentions in texts by Quodvultdeus
Anonymi 2 / Anonymous, author(s) of the sermons in the *Verona Collection*	Mid-fifth century, earlier than c. 500	African Homoian sermons in the *Collectio Veronensis*
Anonymi 3, Homoian clerics at court in the reigns of Geiseric and Huneric	c. 440s–480s	*HP* 1.19–21, 1.43, 2.8–9, 2.16, 2.51, 2.53–55, 3.1, 3.5, 3.14
Anonymous 3, notary for Cyrila, then bishop of Tipasa	484	*HP* 3.29
Anonymous 4, bishop, author of *Commentary on Job*	Early sixth century?	*Comm. in Iob*
Anonymous 5, bishop at Carthage, acquaintance of Fulgentius	Late fifth / early sixth century	*V. Fulg.* 7
Antonius, bishop of Thamalluma	484	*HP* 3.43–46, 3.53–54
Cyrila, bishop at Carthage	c. 477–84	*HP* 2.8, 2.22, 2.54–55, 3.29, 3.49; Greg. Tur., *DLH* 2.3
Fabianus, learned (cleric?) author of text against Fulgentius	c. 523–33	Fulg., *C. Fab.*; *V. Fulg.* 27
Fastidiosus, deacon, former Nicene monk	520s?	Fulg., *Ep.* 9
Felix, presbyter on the *fundus Gabardilla*	Late fifth / early sixth century	*V. Fulg.* 6–7
Jucundus, prominent cleric at Carthage	c. 457–81?	*HP* 1.44, 2.13
Marivadus/Varimadus, prominent deacon at Carthage	Mid-fifth century	*C. Var.* (probably 440s or 450s); *HP* 1.48 (latter part of Geiseric's reign)
Pinta, bishop refuted by Fulgentius at Carthage	Mid to late 510s?	*V. Fulg.* 21
Victorinus, bishop at Ammaedara	Vandal period	Funerary inscription

It would come as no surprise if the Hasding royal family had court chaplains who were Homoian clerics, but it would be wrong to take them as a microcosm of a whole ecclesiastical institution. The problem is that Victor of Vita and the author of the *Life of Fulgentius* place all Homoian priests present in Carthage—be they palace clerics of Vandal kings or princes, Homoian patriarchs, or other bishops temporarily resident in the city—into one lump category, the Arians at court. The third group, of "ordinary" bishops, is thus very difficult to distinguish. This is a familiar consequence of the "court bishop" stereotype. As is the case for fourth-century figures like Ursacius of Singidunum and Valens of Mursa, the absence of evidence for their activities beyond the court does not mean that they did not act as normal bishops alongside their entrenched involvement in the Christian politics that took place there.[60]

The most prominent aspects of royal patronage for Homoian churchmen themselves accord with the expected provision of support for a legitimate (and separate) ecclesiastical institution. On the one occasion when a Vandal king can be heard characterizing his material support, it is in a manner that presumes an autonomous institution. In his edict of 24 February 484, Huneric mandated the transfer of all of the churches, estates, and properties of Homoousian bishops to the "true worshipers of the divine majesty—that is, our [Homoian] bishops." He sought particularly to justify the reassignment of Nicene movables. "We do not doubt that that which is justly conferred to sacrosanct pontiffs will be of greater benefit for the support of the poor."[61] Homoian bishops were to be supported because they would make appropriate use of churches through the correct form of Christian worship, and the best use of ecclesiastical funds through their almsgiving. As Huneric's regime sought to portray it, royal patronage of the Homoian Church merely took the form of facilitating these righteous activities.

It is in this sense that Vandal regimes conditioned the actions of Homoian clerics. The patronage of Geiseric and Huneric (in particular) was instrumental in setting up a Homoian Church in Vandal Africa. Given the position of the Homoian clerics in Africa before the conquest, the standing that their institution achieved in the century of Vandal rule would have been simply inconceivable without the redistribution of churches and property which those kings enacted. For the same reason, maintenance of a good corporate relationship with Hasding dynasts would have been vital; what had been given to these clerics could potentially be returned. Nevertheless, as time went on, it is likely that the dependence of Homoian clerics on such good relations would have lessened, except insofar as the backing of late-antique regimes and their functionaries helped any clerics in securing their authority against ecclesiastical rivals. Over time, clerics like Victorinus would have put down roots in the communities where they had been established, a process helped by the resources afforded them.[62]

In the same measure, frequent episcopal presence at the center of secular and ecclesiastical power neither necessitates a structurally different Homoian Church nor marks out Homoian bishops from their contemporaries. Bishops went to

60. For the careers of Ursacius and Valens, decried by opponents as court bishops, see Hunt (1989); T. Barnes (1993), 6, 22–23, 71–81, 88–89, 97–100, 117, 129–35; D. Williams (1995), 2, 18–38, 71–72; Parvis (2006), 125. On Homoian bishops in the other successor kingdoms and a similar combination of "court bishop" polemic and evidence of a broader remit, see Epilogue.

61. *HP* 3.14 (ed. Lancel: 181). For Nicene polemic against Homoian charity see p. 45, with n. 68.

62. See esp. Heather (2007a), 144, for the suggestion that the Homoian Church "had come of age" by the late 450s.

court in late antiquity for lots of reasons.⁶³ In fact, by the mid-fifth century this practice was so common that it was normalized at Constantinople with the codification of the "home" synod (σύνοδος ἐνδημούσα), a rotating assembly incorporating the bishops resident in the capital at any given time.⁶⁴ It is notable that the survival of Nicene texts from the period similarly privileges Nicene bishops of Carthage and clerics who were particularly active in that city.⁶⁵ The appearance of a Homoian episcopal coterie at Carthage may simply reflect the skewed preservation of detailed information and, perhaps, the particular charge of controversy in the heart of both kingdom and African church.

Other Homoian clerics can be seen engaged in activities distant from the palace. Their attested actions provide a composite picture commensurate with the pastoral activities of any late-antique bishop. Repeated references are made to Homoian clerics debating with their Nicene rivals in public.⁶⁶ In the most basic terms, Homoian bishops wrote polemical doctrinal texts and preached.⁶⁷ As Yves Modéran and Danuta Shanzer have noted, complaints in texts by both Quodvultdeus and Fulgentius suggest that Homoian bishops were dispensing charity and amassing urban followings as a result.⁶⁸ A striking case from the *Life of Fulgentius* suggests that this patronage could extend much further.⁶⁹ The hagiographer narrates the beating that Felix, the Homoian presbyter on the *fundus Gabardilla*, gave to Fulgentius and a fellow monk, confusingly also named Felix. News of this injustice reached a "bishop of the Arians" who knew Fulgentius's parents and had esteemed Fulgentius greatly when he was still a layperson. He was thus "preparing to vindicate Fulgentius" if the latter so wished. This Homoian bishop, who had once moved in the highborn Fulgentius's social circle, is placed in the role of a patron, offering his influence to redress a wrong. Fulgentius refused, on the grounds that a Nicene monk being seen to accept the help of an Arian bishop could scandalize the faithful. The language of his refusal is illuminating: he did not seek the "judgment" of his Homoian acquaintance. Some sort of legal jurisdiction is implied here for this bishop, who can thus be seen playing two important episcopal roles at once: patron and provider of justice. When Homoian clerics are seen

---

63. Rapp (2005), 260–73.
64. Ibid., 266; Dagron (1974), 454–83; Papadakis (1991); Hall (2000), 738.
65. See pp. 41–45.
66. See pp. 71–72.
67. On Homoian texts see pp. 86–89. Gwynn (2012b), 885 nn. 81–84, has useful references for bishops as preachers.
68. Modéran (2003), 41–42; Shanzer (2004), 288; see also Conant (2012), 172. On bishops as urban patrons in late antiquity, see P. Brown (1992), 71–117, 148–50; P. Brown (2002), esp. 45–73; Lepelley (1998).
69. *V. Fulg.* 6–7 (ed. Isola: 171–77). On bishops as advocates and arbiters, see Harries (1999), 191–211; Rapp (2005), 242–52; Humfress (2007), 153–73; Humfress (2011).

in action outside of royal audiences, they fit an institutional profile much closer to that of their Nicene rivals than has been appreciated. They are best approached as independent ecclesiastical actors rather than as the simple clients of royal masters.

Homoian Christianity in Vandal Africa possessed a heterogeneity that can be noted but not extensively described. The partial evidence does not permit a clearer picture of the Homoian Church's structure, but the various grades of the priestly hierarchy are visible, including bishops, deacons, and presbyters.[70] Observance would have taken place in more or less public churches and the private chapels of kings and the elite;[71] services would have been conducted in Vandalic or Latin or both, by bishops, regular clergy, and chaplains, all of varying ethnicity.[72] These clerics participated in a sophisticated culture of Latin controversial and homiletic writing. No single Homoian churchmen can be picked out with real definition, but a composite picture of the activities of a number of them matches the purview of ordinary late-antique bishops. They would have served congregations varied in ethnic and social makeup. In theory, both Vandals and Romano-Africans could attend church services with any combination of Latin or Vandalic language and Nicene or Homoian confessional affiliation. Homoian rituals might have been the only option for Christians, one of two (as opposed to a licit or illicit Nicene community), or one of many, particularly in a major city like Carthage. This is without even beginning to explore the (by then largely invisible but doubtless still surviving) alternatives to Christian religious observance. These choices would not have been mutually exclusive. All in all, there is little to distinguish these Homoian churchmen from their Nicene rivals except for their receipt of royal patronage and the manner in which those rivals chose to represent it.

NICENE CAREERS AND TEXTS

Experience should condition most readers to expect that (supposedly) heretical clerics and communities will be difficult to locate and, where portrayed in the texts of their rivals, deformed by polemic. What is perhaps surprising about the church conflict in Vandal Africa is the difficulty in forming a profile of contemporary

---

70. Courtois (1955), 225; Heather (2007a), 138.

71. On public churches see pp. 36–37; for private royal chapels, pp. 42–43, on possible personal clerics of Hasding dynasty. On certain and possible private elite churches in Vandal Africa, see pp. 36, 204–5; on parallel arrangements in Burgundian Gaul (revealed by canons regarding the confiscation of Arian churches), Heil (2014b), 290–91; for the private arrangements of the late Roman elite, Bowes (2008), at 162–69 for Africa.

72. Attested Homoian clergy have both Latin names and "Vandal" ones: see table 1 and, e.g., Liebeschuetz (2003), 71. As ever, the relationship of such names to the ethnic self-ascription of the specific individual is uncertain (see p. 174, n. 42). What these names do suggest is the diversity of the cultural influences on the clerics in this church.

Nicene bishops. Information survives on the careers of individual bishops and clerics, but not on their writings.[73] Few texts are extant even of those whose inclusion in the handy *On Illustrious Men*—the who's who of late-antique Christian writers curated by Jerome's Gallic continuators, Gennadius of Marseille and Pseudo-Gennadius—would suggest a better chance of preservation.[74] Careers and surviving texts rarely connect. When they do, this seems to have resulted from a particular effort at postmortem preservation of an individual's literary legacy. Other figures were not as fortunate. Most extant Nicene Christian texts from the Vandal period are either pseudonymous or anonymous works attributed more often than not to Augustine[75] or texts that might as well be, since those who wrote them are attested at most once outside their own writings. Victor of Vita himself leaves scant trace beyond his *History*.[76] Any attempt to populate the Nicene Church with individual bishops is at the mercy of a handful of texts that provide rounded accounts of key individuals (see table 2).

Unsurprisingly, Nicene bishops of Carthage, the first see of the province of Africa and the capital of the new kingdom, are best attested. The bishopric's first occupant in the Vandal period, Quodvultdeus (c. 435–52), may be the same priest of Carthage who corresponded with Augustine and pestered the bishop of Hippo for his compendium *On Heresies*.[77] Geiseric expelled Quodvultdeus soon after capturing the city. In Victor of Vita's account, the bishop and a great number of Nicene clergy were "placed, naked and despoiled, on damaged ships."[78] Fortunately for Quodvultdeus and his clergy, divine providence took more care for their journey than had the king, guiding them into port at Naples. A sense of his participation in ecclesiastical controversy can be gained from the texts that modern editors have persuasively attributed to him. Highly polemical sermons illuminate Quodvultdeus's time in Carthage. Two sermons called *On Barbarian Times* were delivered during the Vandal conquest of the city. Three others titled *On the Creed* prepared baptismal candidates at Easter; alongside other sermons dedicated to the refutation of specific religious deviants, these texts refer to the presence and activ-

---

73. As an example, only two bishops mentioned in the entirety of *HP* have a text surviving independently under their own name: Eugenius of Carthage and Boniface of Gatiana.

74. See the short literary biographies in Genn. and Ps.-Genn., *Uir. inlust.* 74, 78–79, 96–98 (ed. Richardson: 87, 88, 95–96). The texts that survive with their attributions to these authors intact are the *Epistula* of Eugenius, Honoratus of Cirta's *Epistula ad Arcadium*, and the *Disputatio Cerealis contra Maximinum* (on which see pp. 75–77). Victor of Vita preserves the *Liber fidei Catholicae* (although without reference to Eugenius). Victor of Cartenna's *De paenitentia* survives under the name of Ambrose. See Dossey (2010), 154, 163–64, with notes.

75. Parsons (1994), 143.

76. On Victor's career, see (best) Howe (2007), 28–119; Vössing (2011), 11–16.

77. For the association (which remains controversial), see *PCBE I*, 947–49 (Quodvultdeus 5); Fournier (2008), 133 n. 43, for useful references.

78. *HP* 1.15 (ed. Lancel: 103). On the likely exaggeration here, see Fournier (2008), 180.

TABLE 2 Nicene bishops and clerics known to have written a text or mentioned more than once in texts other than the *Register* of 484

Name	Date	References (excepting own texts)
Boniface, bishop of Carthage	523–c. 535	Carthage (525); *Lat. reg. Vand. Alan.* s.a. 523; *V. Fulg.* 27
Boniface, bishop of Gatiana, primate of Byzacena	484, 517	*HP* 2.101; Carthage (525)
Cerealis, bishop of Castellum Ripense	484	*Cer. c. Max.*; date from *Not. prov.* 4.119
Deogratias, bishop of Carthage	c. 454–57	*HP* 1.24–27; Prosper, *Chron.* (*III. Continuatio codicis Reichenaviensis* 25)
Eugenius, bishop of Carthage	c. 478/79–c. 505	*HP* 2 and 3; *Lat. reg. Vand. Alan.* s.a. 487; Ps.-Genn., *Uir. inl.* 98; Vict. Tonn., *Chron.* 86; Greg. Tur., *DLH* 2.3
Ferrandus, deacon of Carthage, follower of Fulgentius	c. 523–46	
Fulgentius, bishop of Ruspe	c. 508–33	*V. Fulg.*
Habetdeum, bishop of Thamalluma	484	*HP* 3.45–46, 3.53–54
Honoratus, bishop of Cirta	430s	Ps.-Genn., *Uir. inl.* 96
Quodvultdeus, bishop of Carthage	c. 435–52	*HP* 1.15
Victor, bishop of Cartenna	430s/440s?	Genn., *Uir. inl.* 78
Victor, bishop of Vita	mid-480s	
Vigilius, bishop of Thapsa	484	

ities of contemporary Arians in Carthage. Quodvultdeus also produced a long apocalyptic treatise while in exile in Naples.[79] As far as can be told, he died there.

After a relaxation of Geiseric's ban on new Nicene bishops, Quodvultdeus was replaced by Deogratias (454–57), whose time in office Victor of Vita describes.[80] The *History of the Persecution* tells little of interventions by Deogratias in doctrinal controversy, barring his hounding by the city's Homoian clerics. It does pointedly commend the bishop's charity, particularly toward those taken captive in the sack of Rome of 455. The next Nicene bishop of Carthage, Eugenius (477/78–505?), is particularly well served by contemporary accounts. Much of books 2 and 3 of Victor of Vita's *History* revolve around Eugenius's actions in this period of his career. It is likely that Victor was a priest attached to the Carthaginian church in Eugenius's early episcopate and particularly close to him.[81] This bishop of Carthage also receives a significant chunk of book 2 of Gregory of Tours's *Ten Books of Histories*.[82] As Andrew Cain has suggested, Gregory most likely used an African hagiographi-

79. For all of these texts see Braun (1976).
80. *HP* 1.24–27 (ed. Lancel: 107–9).
81. Costanza (1980), 231–39; Lancel (2002a) 5–7, 22–27; Howe (2007), 57–58; Vössing (2011), 12–13.
82. Greg. Tur., *DLH* 2.3 (ed. Krusch and Levison: 40–45).

cal account of Eugenius's life.[83] Both Victor and Gregory preserve texts by Eugenius, and *On Illustrious Men* lists further (now lost) doctrinal works of his.[84] According to Gregory, Eugenius died in exile at Albi in Gaul; Victor of Tunnuna dates this event to 505, but his chronology is frequently unreliable, so this date is at best a placeholder.[85] The see of Carthage remained vacant until Hilderic lifted the prohibition of Nicene ordinations in 523, when Boniface (r. 523–c. 535) was appointed.[86] The acts of a Nicene Council of Carthage (525) attest to the efforts of the new bishop to reestablish ecclesiastical discipline—and establish his own authority—within the African Nicene Church.[87] Across the previous century, the frequent absences of bishops of Carthage had weakened the primate's position within the African Nicene ecclesiastical body; after the reconquest, the primate of Byzacena would petition Justinian to formalize the greater autonomy from Carthage that his office had gained.[88] Nevertheless, the prominence in the surviving literature of those bishops that the see did possess suggests that they were important and active, both in the organization of their own church and in controversy with their opponents.

The other Nicene ecclesiastical officeholder and controversialist whose career can be reconstructed in detail occupied a far more minor bishopric but also spent a significant portion of his career in Carthage. Fulgentius was a former government official who adopted an ascetic lifestyle from the last decade of the fifth century (at the latest). He was then the Nicene bishop of Ruspe in Byzacena from circa 508 to 533.[89] A *Life of Fulgentius* written shortly after his death by a member of his monastery at Ruspe furnishes the details of his colorful career, including various experiments in communal retreat, a visit to Rome, two periods of exile, and a sojourn in Carthage at the pleasure of Thrasamund.[90] Formidable quantities of the bishop's writings are extant, including eighteen letters on ascetic, moral, and doctrinal issues, eight sermons, and numerous Trinitarian and anti-Arian tractates. As already mentioned, he even wrote a polemical psalm; in imitation of an earlier literary effort by Augustine, its verses begin with consecutive letters of the alphabet, and thus it is titled the *Abecedarium* (or *ABCD*).[91]

---

83. Cain (2005).
84. *HP* 2.41–42 (ed. Lancel: 140–41); Greg. Tur., *DLH* 2.3 (ed. Krusch and Levison: 41–42); Genn., *Uir. inlust.* 98 (ed. Richardson: 96).
85. Vict. Tonn., *Chron.* 86 (ed. Cardelle de Hartmann: 27); see Modéran (1993), 154–55, for his chronological inaccuracies.
86. *V. Fulg.* 25 (ed. Isola: 214); Vict. Tonn., *Chron.* 106 (ed. Cardelle de Hartmann: 34).
87. Carthage (525) (ed. Munier).
88. Modéran (1998b) 703–5.
89. For more on Fulgentius's career, see pp. 160–63.
90. *V. Fulg.*; on the *Vita*, see Leyser (2007); Isola (2016).
91. Fulgentius's works are edited in *CCSL* 91–91A (ed. Fraipont); for the *Abecedarium* see Isola (1983).

When careers and texts converge in this way, as also in the case of Eugenius, it permits a closer analysis of how individuals approached problems of Christian difference and of the results of their activities. Eugenius and Fulgentius—or at least the personas that they and their supporters wished to advance—emerge with some clarity from their depiction in near-contemporary narratives and from their writings. This combination does not seem to be coincidental. The *Life of Fulgentius* frequently discusses the circumstances pertaining to specific texts and in places simply lists works that the bishop had written, as if the anonymous hagiographer had his subject's archive before him and was anxious to catalogue it for posterity.[92] The survival of two letters by Eugenius of Carthage presents an obvious parallel: they were each embedded in narratives.[93]

It is tempting to place the (partially overlapping) careers of Eugenius and Fulgentius at the center of the African Nicene episcopate under Vandal rule. Modern accounts of late-antique Christian controversies often use such figures as framing devices. Influential episcopal impresarios have provided the organizing principles for investigation of fourth- and fifth-century ecclesiastical politics.[94] Their centrality stems, in part, from their contemporary agency in forming and mobilizing broader networks of churchmen to ensure the acceptance or maintenance of specific doctrines or practices within an ecclesiastical institution and to counter the rival claims of factions with whom they did not share communion. Of course, as shrewd reviewers of recent studies of Athanasius of Alexandria and Theodoret of Cyrrhus have noted, it also results from the massive survival of their texts.[95] Collections of letters to and from and tractates by individual churchmen may be misleading in placing the unifying author at the center of conflicts and networks. In any case, the texts and biographical information available for Eugenius and Fulgentius are nowhere near sufficient to make them into linchpins like Athanasius and Theodoret.

There is enough to see that other figures were important in the Nicene Church, even if these glimpses do not pick those alternative agents out with any real definition. The literary biographies of the continuations of *On Illustrious Men* present various noteworthy African churchmen.[96] Particularly intriguing is one Victor, the bishop of Cartenna in Mauretania Caesariensis in the first decades of Vandal rule.

---

92. E.g., *V. Fulg.* 21, 25, 27 (ed. Isola: 206–8, 213–14, 221–22). These early efforts were carried forward by the considerable popularity of Fulgentius in the Carolingian period and later. On Fulgentius's medieval transmission and reception, see Hays (2010). For a useful discussion of the editing of Augustine's works by his followers (a parallel case), see Dolbeau (2006).

93. See p. 49, with n. 84.

94. E.g., Gwynn (2007a); Shaw (2011); Schor (2011). For an example of a series of individual bishops and episcopal factions as an organizing principle, see Hanson (1988).

95. Lyman (2009); Price (2012), 663–64.

96. Genn. and Ps.-Genn., *Uir. inlust.* 74, 78–79, 96–98 (ed. Richardson: 87, 88, 95–96).

Among other heresiological and moral texts, he is said to have written a work against Arianism (now lost), which he sent to Geiseric.[97] Not included in *On Illustrious Men* but better served by the vagaries of reception and transmission is Vigilius, the bishop of Thapsa in Byzacena in the latter decades of the fifth century. Vigilius wrote a number of important polemical doctrinal works, including an anti-Arian question-and-answer text and the *Dialogue against the Arians, Sabellians and Photinians*. Of his career, next to nothing is known.[98] Similarly, Boniface the bishop of Gatiana appears just twice in Nicene literature from Vandal Africa: first as one of the drafters of the *Book of the Catholic Faith*, the text read out by the Nicene delegates at the Conference of Carthage in 484; then, having assumed the primacy of Byzacena, as the author of a letter of 1 May 517 to a female monastery in his province, preserved in the acts of the Nicene Council of Carthage in 525.[99] He vanishes for the thirty-three years in between, but his prominent position in both 484 and 517 suggests much greater agency in the intervening period.

Privileging specific named bishops would also be to the detriment of a significant body of texts that directly address the institutional formation and self-identity of the Nicene Church under Vandal rule. An impressive set of pseudonymous and anonymous texts has emerged from decades of editorial work on obscure theological treatises.[100] For the most part, these works have been transmitted under the names of better-known individuals: in particular, Augustine of Hippo and Athanasius of Alexandria. The point at which the authors took on their assumed names is rarely possible to identify, since the earliest manuscript witnesses to the texts generally date to the Carolingian period.[101] The content of some texts suggests deliberate pseudepigraphy; other attributions contradict the authors' explicit statements. In either case, the absence of a securely attested individual does not devalue their importance. Indeed, in the absence of a totemic father figure, it is easier to approach the works of named and unnamed authors as equally valuable.

The contrast between attested and pseudonymous or anonymous authors is often fragile. The works of Quodvultdeus of Carthage are a case in point. By all rights, he must have been a household name within the African Christian community—and perhaps farther afield in the late Roman West—in the 440s and 450s. The bishop's name could have been impressed on the minds of his contemporaries in any number of ways: his (possible) association with Augustine; his dramatic and decidedly public expulsion; his status as the primate of Africa.[102]

---

97. Genn., *Uir. inlust.* 78 (ed. Richardson: 88); cf. Pottier (2015), 115–16.
98. See pp. 69–73.
99. *HP* 2.101 (ed. Lancel: 173); Carthage (525) (ed. Munier: 281). On the *Liber* see Lancel (2002a), 63–67.
100. See (with caution) Conant (2012), 170–79, using *CPL*.
101. For a rare exception see p. 53 n. 110.
102. *HP* 1.15 (ed. Lancel: 103).

Certainly, Quodvultdeus quickly became a revered figure in his unwillingly adopted Campanian home.[103] The preservation of his literary output (as reconstructed by modern scholars) seems, at first glance, to reflect such standing. As already noted, Quodvultdeus has been assigned twelve sermons, apparently produced during his tenure in Carthage, which deal primarily with heresiological themes;[104] he has also been judged the author of the apocalyptic *Book on the Promises and Predictions of God*, whose contents suggest that he wrote it during his exile in Italy.[105] Both the sermons and the *Book* were much copied and used in the early middle ages.[106]

For all this, the posthumous reputation of Quodvultdeus is illusory. The manuscript evidence does not give direct warrant to either attribution. In the early middle ages, the sermons circulated in two separate collections under the name of Augustine; the *Book* was consistently credited to either the bishop of Hippo or Prosper of Aquitaine. As a result, their reassignment to Quodvultdeus remains contested.[107] Whether or not this attribution is justified, the implication of the manuscript transmission of these works must be underlined. There are no texts extant under the name of Quodvultdeus. The remarkably early detachment of his likely works from his authorial persona should lead to a reassessment of the significance of other pseudonymous texts.

Christian literature from Vandal Africa can rarely be read in the light of specific and detailed external knowledge of its circumstances of creation. Yet for the purposes of exploring the Christian culture of the kingdom, absolute certainty regarding dates and named authors is not essential. Quodvultdeus's sermons are again salutary. Even if not the bishop of Carthage, the author(s) of these texts must correspond to the criteria by which he has been identified: an African Nicene cleric (or clerics) who preached sermons in Carthage during the transition from Roman to Vandal rule.[108] Likewise, the author of the *Book on the Promises and Predictions of God* must have been an African exile in Italy who had been present in Carthage at major political and ecclesiastical events in the first decades of the fifth century.[109] Not all of the pseudonymous Christian literature from this period drops such handy chronological markers in midflow. These texts can nonetheless be placed with confidence in the Vandal period. When even the probable writings of one of the most prominent African bishops of the period was already circulating anony-

---

103. Conant (2010), 1.
104. Braun (1976), 225–486.
105. Quod., *Lib. prom.* (ed. Braun).
106. Braun (1976), v–cvi, for transmission and justification of attribution.
107. Isola (1990), 10 n. 6; Parsons (1994), 135–36, 140, 162 n. 31, 164 n. 37; González Salinero (2002), 17–25; Van Slyke (2003), 48–63.
108. See esp. Quod., *DTB I* and *II* (ed. Braun: 421–37, 471–86).
109. See Quod., *Lib. prom.* 3.38.44, G.15, D.6.9–12 (ed. Braun: 185–86, 219–20, 196–98).

mously in the late sixth century alongside works both correctly and falsely attributed to Augustine,[110] it is clear that early-medieval pseudepigraphy should not be seen as a slight on his (now unknown) contemporaries.

CONCLUSION

Quodvultdeus and Fulgentius worried that African Christians might mistake Nicene and Homoian churches for each other. Quodvultdeus portrayed this mistaken impression as a result of too cursory an investigation of the "deceptive" similarities between the two. But even on closer inspection, these churches do not appear radically different. The Nicene Church was likely the larger of the two ecclesiastical institutions. All the same, the ambivalent results of the winding up of the Donatist Church, the impact of Hasding prohibitions on episcopal appointments, and the transfer of a substantial number of Nicene bishops suggest that this disparity should not be exaggerated. The same goes for their institutional makeup. Despite intermittent polemical innuendo, the Homoian Church was not defined by its relationship either to the Hasding dynasty or to the Vandal war band. Discussions of language use imply that the individual communities which made up these two institutions possessed similar heterogeneity. Perhaps the greatest underlying similarity between the two institutions is the fragmentary and disjointed preservation of texts and biographical information pertaining to individual clerics. Nicene and Homoian writers became part of the broader early-medieval trend toward pseudepigraphy.[111] It is difficult to see either episcopate in action, but a composite picture suggests, in both cases, bishops shaped by the norms of their distinctive late-antique leadership role. Beneath the alternative frameworks provided by hagiographical and heresiological accounts, the parallels between these two churches are obvious.

Quodvultdeus and Fulgentius may have had every right to be worried. The balance of power in ecclesiastical politics was delicate: a minority church supported by secular authority and gaining privileges, property, and converts confronted a church that had the advantage of a much more established presence in the communities of the African provinces but was suffering significant losses of material and personnel. This remained the state of play throughout the Vandal period in Africa. As a result, both Nicene and Homoian clerics had to deal with the uncertainty produced by "an uncomfortable multiplicity of authorities" (to quote Rebecca Lyman, writing on another context).[112] Of course, even in the apparently

---

110. See Braun (1976), xl, lxix, on the late sixth-century MS Torino, bibl. naz. univ. G.V.26 (most likely produced at Bobbio).

111. For Homoian texts and pseudepigraphy see pp. 87–88.

112. Lyman (2000), 153.

stable conditions provided by membership in an "established" church supported by the coercive force of the late Roman state, Christian churchmen never stopped worrying about their own authority and the competing claims of those they perceived as heretics. In the far less settled ecclesiastical climate of Vandal Africa, this project gained a redoubled urgency. Jonathan Conant has aptly characterized the history of post-imperial Africa as one of rulers and elites finding ways to "stay Roman."[113] For the two churches of Vandal Africa, it was just as much a struggle to become, or remain, orthodox.

---

113. Conant (2012).

2

In Dialogue with Heresy
Christian Polemical Literature

At some point in the mid-fifth century, an African Nicene exile in Naples wrote a text to refute the propositions of a Homoian deacon named Varimadus (or possibly Marivadus), which he had received through "a certain zealous and most religious man."[1] The preface to this lengthy, three-book refutation of contemporary Arian heresy communicates a vivid sense of urgency. "Now therefore with superfluous and unconnected words omitted, which are proffered by [the Arians] to subvert the faithful, we proceed now [*sic*] to refute those things, which we know to be put forward out of the zeal of those unfaithful people for the death of innocent spirits."[2] The anonymous author justified his refutation as a necessary response to Arian efforts to persuade contemporary Catholic Christians that their understanding of the Trinity was incorrect and to the dire consequences that could result. He was particularly concerned that ordinary Christians might be tricked by specious arguments from scripture:

> Looking out for the more humble and the slower of wit, thus with the help of the Holy Spirit, we have thus joined together our response to all of their objections in the manner of testimonies [*testimonialiter*], so that the one who reads it might be able to refute them not with mere words [*non nudis . . . uerbis*], as they are accustomed to object, but with legal documents, so that the guilty might be confounded on all sides, and reduced to naught, who struggle to construct such fictions on the "foundation of the prophets and apostles" [Eph. 2:20], the teachers.[3]

---

1. *C. Var.*, pref. 1–5, quotation at 3–4 (ed. Schwank: 9). On the text see Schwank (1961a); Schwank (1961b); McClure (1979), 194–95; Van Slyke (2003), 74–76; Humfress (2007), 231–32. On the likely association of this Varimadus with Victor of Vita and Vigilius of Thapsa's Marivadus, see p. 125 n. 86.
2. *C. Var.*, pref. 47–50 (ed. Schwank: 10).
3. Ibid., pref. 8–15 (9).

The anonymous author brought the (supposed) bankruptcy of the contentions made by Varimadus and his colleagues out into the open. Their teachings were not orthodox; they were made up.

Since no one called themselves a heretic in late antiquity, others did it for them.[4] Heresiological modes of argumentation necessarily permeated the writings of late-antique clerics. The legitimacy of Christian authority figures and the ecclesiastical institutions they represented always rested at least implicitly on a claim to accurately convey true Christian teachings. Given the reality of Christian diversity, these claims frequently conflicted; an explicit and convincing statement of orthodoxy then became a basic requirement. Once the mutual exclusivity of conflicting statements became apparent, the result, more often than not, was heresiological accusation and counteraccusation, as transpired once Varimadus's propositions had found their way into his opponent's hands. Claims regarding orthodoxy and heresy were intimately related: Rebecca Lyman fittingly defines heresiology as a "genre for asserting true Christian doctrine."[5]

Like many other Christian texts from Vandal Africa, *Against Varimadus* sets out, at length, a definition of correct doctrine and the heresies that diverged from it. More specifically, like other contemporary Christian writers, the anonymous author focused on issues pertaining to the relationship of the Trinity. Nicene clerics asserted the divine equality of a Trinity that was of one substance or essence (translating the Greek οὐσία) and emphasized the formula, recently promulgated at the Council of Chalcedon (451), of two natures in the one person of Christ. Homoian clerics, meanwhile, maintained a long-standing aversion to substance language and seem to have professed a very different Trinity, with Son subordinated to Father and Holy Spirit to Son.[6] Many modern commentators have thought that evaluations of the extent of the difference between these two positions convey how easy or difficult individuals who had received their Christian knowledge from Nicene clerics found it to accept Homoian claims to truth, and vice versa.[7] The basic problem is that the precise positioning and emphases of Homoian clerics' teachings are beyond reconstruction. They survive only in opponents' citations, which were selectively chosen and always mixed with stereotypical Arian statements. *Against Varimadus* is a case in point. Although supposedly based on a set of *propositiones* that the author had received through a Nicene inter-

---

4. On heretics (obviously) not calling themselves heretics, see, e.g., Shaw (1992), 8; Humfress (2007), 240; Av. Cameron (2008), 107. There are some exceptions: for abjurations by Christians on the point of conversion, see, e.g., Lim (1995), 99–102, and Millar (2004); for Christians playing the late Roman legal system, Humfress (2008), 134–35.

5. Lyman (2007), 296.

6. Brennecke (2008b) and Heil (2011), 251–69, are the best introductions. The two groups also differed importantly over baptism: see pp. 105–7.

7. See the excellent critique by Heil (2011), 266–69.

mediary, it includes responses to various arguments more likely taken from earlier Nicene polemic, such as the phrase "the Father is greater than me."[8] What Varimadus specifically taught is unrecoverable.

Such deformation of opposing views was the point. For late-antique churchmen, proving the truth of their doctrine was not an irenic exercise in biblical and patristic exegesis: it required (in Karen King's deliciously arch phrase) "the usual abuses of educated polemic."[9] In the quest to convince other Christians that their rivals were in error, little was off-limits. Writers could impugn the character of their opponents, connect them to earlier Christian deviants through (often dubious) genealogies, and argue that they could not be orthodox because they were few in number—to name just three common tactics used by Vandal-era controversialists.[10] By deploying these slippery and often disingenuous arguments, authors of polemical texts like *Against Varimadus* sought to encourage their readers to divide their Christian contemporaries into Catholic Christians and heretics. The massive corpus of heresiological literature produced by Christians beginning in the second century—with a particular proliferation from the fourth century onward—has received sustained critical scrutiny.[11] The signal implication of this work is that it is often more profitable to study how late-antique Christian writers made their arguments rather than what they argued was orthodoxy.

This chapter adopts that approach. It introduces the polemical Christian literature produced by Nicene and Homoian clerics in Vandal Africa.[12] These heresiological compendia, polemical tractates, biblical florilegia, and question-and-answer collections have only recently begun to attract attention.[13] But in their day they played crucial roles in polemical debates over doctrine. To borrow Averil Cameron's martial phrasing, once doctrinal controversy was "technologized" in

---

8. *C. Var.* 1.5 (ed. Schwank: 20).

9. King (2003), 30.

10. On character assassination, see, e.g., Lyman (2007), 297–98; Flower (2013a), 178–219. On the use of genealogies, see Flower (2011), 73–77; Eshleman (2012), 213–58. On genealogies as part of the rhetorical creation of Arianism, see Lyman (1993), esp. 46–47; McLynn (1994), 102–4, 128–37; D. Williams (1995), 145–47, 178; Wiles (1996), 5–6; Vaggione (2000), 41–43; Ayres (2004), 13–14, 56–57, 106–9; Gwynn (2007a), 7–8, 171–77, 224–25. On small numbers see pp. 35–38.

11. On heresiology, Le Boulluec (1985) is classic; see also King (2003), 20–52; Boyarin (2004). For introductions see Lyman (1993); Lyman (2007); Av. Cameron (2003); Av. Cameron (2008); Eshleman (2012), 149–76; Flower (2013b). For broader historiographical summaries and surveys of new approaches to "patristic" texts, see E. Clark (2004), 158–61; Graumann (2009), 539–41; Flower (2013a), 8–27.

12. Given the predominance of Nicene writers in the surviving Christian texts from this period and the more complicated textual histories of the works of their Homoian rivals, it will largely focus on the former. For a catalog of Homoian texts, see pp. 86–89.

13. See, e.g., Merrills and Miles (2010), 183–84, 196–200; Conant (2012), 173–75.

the post-Constantinian empire, texts such as these were used as "weapons."[14] Their production in Vandal Africa attests to fundamental continuities in the conduct and basic significance of Christian disputes over the identity of the true faith and its church. Like earlier controversialists, Christian polemicists in the Vandal kingdom adapted their heresiological rhetoric to persuade different audiences for specific ends. At the same time, they wrote these texts for a much wider audience of African Christians. This polemical literature was supposed to convince all Christians, whether or not they shared the author's confessional affiliation, that that author represented the legitimate ecclesiastical institution in post-imperial Africa.

These conflicting claims led Nicene and Homoian clerics into confrontations with one another. As the author of *Against Varimadus* foresaw, such altercations encompassed face-to-face exchanges of views. The second half of this chapter considers Christian debate and dialogue in Vandal Africa. Contemporary authors discussed numerous public debates and conversations between Nicene and Homoian Christians, but no genuine minutes survive. As a result, these sections instead focus on four remarkable dialogue texts that record face-to-face disputations between Nicene authorities and Arian heretics from the late Roman past. None of these were real debates; in all four cases, a Nicene author wrote the minutes. By the fifth century, imaginary dialogues against heretics and other religious deviants had developed into a distinct genre of Christian literature. The literary forms and stated aims that these invented debates share with texts used to contest the definition of correct doctrine against real-life opponents demonstrate their value as witnesses to ecclesiastical controversy. They also suggest that a strict distinction between "real" and "imaginary" late-antique Christian dialogue cannot be upheld. The manner in which the pretend disputants of these literary dialogues argue with one another reflects a broader culture of Christian disputation. The "virtual dialogue" characteristic of heresiological polemic continued to pattern the sermons, tractates, and florilegia written by Christians who were absorbed in the key problems of Christological and Trinitarian doctrine that divided these two ecclesiastical factions. Vandal Africa was full of polemical Christian debate.

CATALOGING ORTHODOXY

If they say: Why should the unity of the Trinity be taught from Holy Scripture [*diuinis lectionibus*], when three cannot be proved rightly to be one, nor one in three?

You respond: Listen, and recognize from these testimonies the unity of the Trinity, and cease to follow the depravity of the Arians [. . .] "Holy, holy, holy, Lord God Sabaoth" [Isaiah 6:1–3]. If there is not a Trinity, why did they say "holy" three times?

---

14. Av. Cameron (2007), 17; (1994). See also Av. Cameron (1999); Av. Cameron (2003); Av. Cameron (2008); similarly, Lim (1999).

And if there is not a unity, why did they say after that triple repetition that there is one Lord and God? If there is not a Trinity, why is it said in Genesis [Gen. 1:3, 7, 22]: "God said," "God did," and "God blessed"? If there is not a unity, why did it say "God" three times, and not commend "gods" with a plural number?[15]

In setting out what they considered correct doctrine, Christian writers were not afraid to produce compendious results. The opening chapter of *Against Varimadus* continues for some ninety-eight lines in this vein as the anonymous Nicene author derives evidence of both Trinity and unity from twenty-three biblical passages. In book 3 of the work, even this minimalist framing falls away as the author simply lists passages that support certain Nicene statements relating to the unity of the Trinity.

Against Varimadus blends two related, controversial genres. The framing of books 1 and 2 is that of a question-and-answer text: an *erotapokrisis*, to use the often-cited Byzantine Greek designation.[16] Two other surviving texts from Vandal Africa also take this form: the *Solutions to the Objections of the Arians* (possibly by Vigilius of Thapsa, a figure to whom this chapter will return) and the *Solutions to the Diverse Questions Objected by the Heretics* (by Pseudo-Augustine).[17] Like the quoted passage, these had a fairly standard format. A question, or "objection," is followed by an answer, or "solution" ("They say ... You respond ..."). Book 3 of *Against Varimadus*, meanwhile, is a testimonia collection: that is, a list of biblical proof texts. There are two further extant examples: Pseudo-Augustine's *Testimonies on the Father and the Son and the Holy Spirit*,[18] and the *Book on the Trinity*, a text wrongly attributed to Fulgentius of Ruspe in the seventeenth century, whose author is still called Pseudo-Fulgentius for convenience.[19] Each of these collections lists a set of heterogeneous passages underneath the heading it explains (e.g., "On the one God," "On the distinction of the persons of the Father and the Son and the Holy Spirit," "On the Holy Spirit").[20] Nothing further is provided, but that was the

---

15. *C. Var.* 1.1.1–17 (ed. Schwank: 11).

16. The classic study is Bardy (1932–33), published across six issues of the *Revue Biblique*; see also Dörrie and Dörries (1966); Volgers and Zamagni (2004); Papadoyannakis (2006); Papadoyannakis (2008); Papadoyannakis (2013); Bussières (2013).

17. Vig., *Solutiones* (ed. Hombert); for the plausible attribution, see Hombert (2010), 184–90; Ps.-Aug., *Solutiones* (ed. Schwank), with B. Fischer (1942).

18. *Test. Pat. Fil. et Spir. Sanct.* (ed. De Bruyne). This text survives in a sole MS (Fulda, Bonifatianus 2, second half of the eighth century). Its attribution to Vandal Africa is based on its shared linguistic features with other fifth-century African Old Latin Bible quotations and its likely use by Ps.-Fulgentius for his *Liber de Trinitate* (which would place it in the first decades of Vandal rule): see De Bruyne (1930).

19. Ps.-Fulg., *Trin.* (ed. Fraipont). Because of references to Donatists, Jonathan Parsons has attributed this text to a "transitional period" early in Geiseric's reign: see Parsons (1994), 45–46, followed by Fournier (2008), 156–57. As I suggest below (pp. 61–62), the contents of the text suggest a date in the reign of Huneric or his successor, Gunthamund.

20. *Test. Pat. Fil. et Spir. Sanct.* 1–3 (ed. De Bruyne: 227–29).

point: the absence of greater justification made the (sometimes controversial) interpretations of biblical passages seem natural.

To a modern reader, such lists may seem innocuous (and rather tedious). In fact, they reveal the undergirding of contemporary Christian disputation. The cataloging and deployment of authoritative quotations, whether drawn from scriptural, conciliar, or—increasingly from the fifth century—patristic texts, was a central strategy in late-antique disputes over the definition of orthodox doctrine.[21] Prominent doctrinal authorities across the late-antique Mediterranean assembled extensive collections of proof texts. Such florilegia acted as repositories of evidence for arguments made in the heat of debate, whether that polemical exegesis was deployed in texts or in oral statements made at church councils and public disputations.[22] Authors often sought to overwhelm their opponents (and their readers) with the sheer weight of scriptural passages, piled up one after another with little in the way of explanation to lighten the load. Classic proof texts were sometimes presented as if self-evidently useful, in spite of the often very different scriptural context from which they had been excerpted.[23] Such texts also increasingly stood alone as definitive statements, to the extent that debates at sixth- and seventh-century church councils centered on the veracity of their quotations.[24] In their cataloging of responses to heretical statements and of biblical passages that (apparently) support specific Trinitarian views, florilegia from Vandal Africa show the continued use of basic techniques of late-antique Christian controversy.

These texts were supposed to contribute to contemporary Christian conflict. Their purpose seems to have been twofold. The framing of question-and-answer texts as conversations between Arians and Catholics—with the imagined reader(s) standing in as the latter—suggests that these were designed to support putative Nicene Christian debaters in defending their faith. The preface to *Against Varimadus*, quoted above, makes clear that its anonymous exile author wrote with potentially vulnerable Nicene Christians in mind.[25] The ability to cite relevant biblical passages was crucial for the potential encounters he sought to draft; contemporary Christian writers, both Nicene and Homoian, frequently rattled them off to prove a point.[26] At the same time, these florilegia themselves act as definitive state-

---

21. The classic study is Av. Cameron (1994). On patristic citation (in particular), see Graumann (2002); (2009). See also Ayres (2004), 79–82.

22. On the use of patristic florilegia, see Gray (1989); Av. Cameron (1994); Richard (2011). Grillmeier (1987), 51–78, provides an extensive list; see too Lienhard (1999) on late-antique and early medieval Augustinian florilegia.

23. For a useful framing of this issue, see Wessel (2004), 126–37.

24. On this turn in ecclesiastical and conciliar debate, see esp. Gray (1989); Graumann (2012); Wessel (2012).

25. See pp. 55–56.

26. See, e.g., Van Slyke (2003), 74–78; Merrills and Miles (2010), 183–84.

ments of orthodoxy, not least by seeking a comprehensive response to all of the possible variations on particular Trinitarian themes—"against that which they say: how could the Son be equal to the Father?"; "against that which they say: the unbegotten Father and the begotten Son cannot be seen as equals"; "that the Son is equal to the Father."[27] It is noteworthy that all of these florilegia are closely related to the *Book of the Catholic Faith*, the statement read out by the Nicene bishops at the Conference of Carthage in 484. A number of Nicene bishops prepared this text in advance of the conference as a defense of the doctrine of consubstantiality. Like the florilegia on which it drew, the *Book* shows a marked tendency to list biblical testimonies to prove specific points of Nicene interpretation.[28]

Pseudo-Fulgentius's *Book on the Trinity* suggests an even tighter relationship to the consequences of contemporary ecclesiastical controversy. The biblical quotations on the titular theme (120–557) are followed by a Nicene profession of faith (558–616). They are also preceded by an extended polemical preface (1–119). In this introductory passage, Pseudo-Fulgentius rebuts a series of Homoian arguments about the identity of the true church, grappling with the relationship between the African Church in his own time and the same institution in the later Roman Empire and constructing a series of historical arguments based on the events of the fourth-century Arian controversy and the Donatist schism. He explicitly frames these arguments as responses to an unspecified *libellus*. This was most likely the anti-Nicene edict promulgated by Huneric on 24 February 484,[29] since Pseudo-Fulgentius tackles, point by point, the case made in that law for the criminalization of Nicene Christianity as Homoousian heresy.[30] Huneric justified his anti-Homoousian edict in three main ways: the Homoousians had failed to prove ὁμοούσιος from scripture at the Conference of Carthage, "one thousand or more" bishops had condemned this definitive term at the universal councils of Rimini and Seleucia in 359, and Homoousians had procured similar laws from sympathetic emperors against their own opponents.[31] The king's direct citation from Honorius's edict of 30 January 412 suggests that he had anti-Donatist legislation particularly in mind.[32] Pseudo-Fulgentius alludes to each argument and rebuts it. He cites someone who "has presumed that the worshipers of [the Catholic] faith must be called Homoousians" and an individual "who composed that *libellus* conceived with a savage mind [and] judged that the mass of divine testimonies as

27. Ps.-Aug., *Solutiones* 6, 15, 17 (ed. Schwank: 154–55, 162, 163).
28. *Liber fidei Catholicae* = HP 2.56–101 (ed. Lancel: 148–73). For the connections between the texts, see the studies of each in pp. 55 n. 1, 59 nn. 16–18. On the conference see p. 16 n. 78.
29. HP 3.3–14 (ed. Lancel: 175–81). H. Müller (2008), 35 n. 109, suggests that the text was a lost Homoian florilegium.
30. Chs. 3–4 further discuss the law and this response.
31. HP 3.5–7 (ed. Lancel: 176–77).
32. Ibid., 3.10 (178–79).

much from the New as the Old Testament must be opposed to homoousios"; he then seeks to justify ὁμοούσιος and undermine the heresiological term.[33] He notes the argument that Rimini's greater numbers made it a universal council of superior authority to Nicaea, and attacks it.[34] Although the number is different (830 at Rimini), this could still be a response to Huneric, as the 160 attendees at Seleucia roughly make up the difference.[35] Finally, Pseudo-Fulgentius refers to his church's earlier use of imperial legislation: "I see some about to produce contradictions, and to throw at us the persecutions of the Donatists, those people whose fury did violence to the laws, and who endured the laws to the full."[36] He attempts to shut down this line of criticism by finessing what constitutes genuine persecution.[37]

It is clear that this anonymous African Nicene author, writing in the last decades of the fifth century or early in the sixth, was responding either to the edict or to a text from the wider milieu of Homoian anti-Homoousian polemic in which the edict was framed. That a Nicene controversialist might see the collation of scriptural proof texts as an appropriate response to the criminalization of his form of Christianity, the exile of his church's bishops, and the confiscation of its property is an eloquent demonstration of the importance of basic techniques of doctrinal disputation in Vandal Africa. As such, the *Book on the Trinity* documents the need for representatives of Nicene and Homoian Christianity in Vandal Africa to prove their doctrine and to disprove that of their rivals. It indicates the contribution that contemporaries thought doctrinal polemic offered within those urgent debates. Making a convincing, and preferably exclusive, claim to orthodoxy was essential for these Christian controversialists in post-imperial Africa.

HERESIOLOGY AND PERSUASION

As the bald lists of proof texts in Nicene florilegia should already suggest, for Christian authority figures seeking to portray themselves as orthodox, simple assertion played a role. Before sympathetic audiences, clerics sometimes bypassed the arguments that proved them right and their opponents wrong. In so doing, they came closest to exposing the basis of all of their claims: a righteousness to be taken on trust.[38] In this regard, the robust statements of orthodoxy produced by marginalized Christians serve as powerful reminders that the assertions of the "Catholics" must not simply be accepted. Such claims to definition and judgment do not necessarily indicate wider assent or the author's capacity to enforce them;

33. Ps.-Fulg., *Trin.* 2.18–20 (ed. Fraipont: 239), 2.23–25 (240), 2.25–68 (240–41).
34. Ibid., 3.69–74 (241).
35. E.g., Ath., *De syn.* 12.1 (ed. Opitz: 239).
36. Ps.-Fulg., *Trin.* 4.113–15 (ed. Fraipont: 242–43).
37. Ibid., 4.115–19 (243).
38. Nicely evoked by Maxwell (2006), 120–21, 123–24.

they could just as easily reflect "fantasies of such power."[39] The efficacy of attempts to mark the boundaries of true Christianity (to use the language, taken from the work of the anthropologist Fredrik Barth, that suffuses recent studies of Christian group formation) must not be exaggerated.[40] If heresiologists sought, through boundary management, to strengthen communal cohesion, the social reality of religious diversity constantly eroded this solidarity. It was precisely the precariousness of their definitions of orthodoxy and heresy—amid competing claims to religious truth and everyday social relations between members of different Christian congregations and other religions[41]—that made late-antique Christian authority figures return to heresiology with such frequency and vehemence.

Many Christians seem to have taken a lot of convincing. The doctrinal controversies of the fourth century saw "the evolution of styles of or strategies for performance and narration of orthodoxy within different literary forms."[42] Such styles and strategies continued to evolve in the fifth and sixth centuries. These methods of "performance" and "narration," predominantly found and generally articulated in texts, were also implicated in the public actions of Christian controversialists. As Michel-Yves Perrin has nicely put it, a crucial goal for Christian clerics in late antiquity was the inculcation of a "heresiological ethos."[43] More than that, clerics needed to inculcate their own definitions of orthodoxy and heresy against those propounded by rivals.

The contested nature of such definitions required clerics to convince various audiences, in different registers, to more general and more specific ends. As a form of persuasive rhetoric, late-antique heresiology was impressively adaptable. Clerics implicated in the Donatist schism in late Roman Africa developed a particularly comprehensive approach.[44] Heresiology was used to persuade emperors and their courts to issue laws to criminalize opponents. It was deployed in communiqués to provincial officials requesting that those laws be applied to named individuals and churches and in letters to local magnates demanding enforcement on rural estates. It was used in books condemning opponents, whether to sway those heretics' followers or to bolster the writer's own community.[45] Densely argued letters and tractates were used to convince and reinforce bishops, priests, monks, and engaged laypersons. Sermons were delivered and simple polemical *libelli* written to exhort congregations

---

39. Iricinschi and Zellentin (2008b), 20.
40. Barth (1969). On boundaries see esp. Sandwell (2007), 4–5; Sizgorich (2009), 4–9. See also Lim (1999), 203; Boyarin (2004); Gaddis (2005), 73, 98; Jacobs (2007), 292; Kahlos (2007), 55–62; Iricinschi and Zellentin (2008b), 2, 18; Lyman (2007), 299; Conant (2012), 180.
41. See further pp. 169–70.
42. Ayres (2004), 81.
43. Perrin (2010).
44. Shaw (2011), 260–543.
45. See pp. 65–68.

and a wider Christian readership. Disputants in late Roman Africa modulated their message to suit specific audiences and situations. In writing to emperors and officials, controversialists might emphasize the heretics' threat to law and order or their liability to the provisions of specific existing legal prohibitions.[46] When engaged in "dialogue with the crowd," the same disputants played to the lowest common denominator, using lurid images of animalistic savagery and sexual depravity.[47] Their central message was not intended to lie dormant on the page; it was meant to have real effects on those involved in the contemporary African Church.

The coming of the Vandals did not alter the basic modus operandi of African clerics in Christian controversy. Ecclesiastical disputants wrote texts to persuade all of the audiences whose favor had been important in late Roman Africa and remained so in the new kingdom. Statements of the true faith were written at the request of Vandal kings or sent unsolicited as more or less hostile or conciliatory representations of the Nicene faction.[48] They were addressed to opponents in the form of a necessary corrective to errors and a rebuttal of attacks on the writer.[49] Tractates were also appended to or written as missives to coreligionists who needed guidance. The letters of Fulgentius of Ruspe are particularly full of apparent requests that he refute both individual Arian propositions and entire texts.[50] Histories were written that contextualized debates between Nicenes and Arians and the current state of the Nicene faction in post-imperial Africa.[51] Meanwhile, sermons such as *Against the Five Heresies* and *Against the Jews, Pagans and Arians*, delivered by Quodvultdeus of Carthage, attest the communication of heresiological categories of error to Christian congregations.[52] Few other Nicene sermons can be certainly pegged to the Vandal period, but there are at least a few plausible texts, which attack contemporary Arians.[53] Extant Homoian sermons similarly

---

46. On Donatists as threats to order see Hermanowicz (2008), 132–87; Shaw (2011), 517–39. On law and legal culture within late-antique debates over orthodoxy, see esp. Humfress (2007), 217–68; Hermanowicz (2008), 83–228.

47. Shaw (2011), 322–39. On preaching as "dialogues with the crowd," see P. Brown (2012), 339–41, citing Mandouze (1968), 591.

48. For Victor of Cartenna to Geiseric, see Genn., *Uir. inlust.* 78 (ed. Richardson: 88); Eugenius to Huneric, ibid., 98 (96), and *HP* 2.41–42 (ed. Lancel: 140–41); Habetdeum to Huneric, *HP* 3.53 (203); Fulgentius to Thrasamund, Fulg., *Dict. Tras.* and *Ad Tras.* (both ed. Fraipont). On these texts, see ch. 5.

49. E.g., Fulg., *C. Fab.* (ed. Fraipont).

50. E.g., Fulg., *De fide ad Petrum*; Fulg., *De Trin. ad Fel.*; Fulg., *Ad Mon.* (all ed. Fraipont). Though cf. Humfress (2012), 325–30, on the responsive controversialist.

51. On two polemical Nicene continuations of the chronicles of Jerome and Prosper (*Epit. Carth.* and *Lat. reg. Vand. Alan.*), see pp. 114–18.

52. Quod., *Adu. haer.*; Quod., *C. Iud., pag. et Arr.* (both ed. Braun). See also Fulg., *Serm. dub.* 2 (ed. Fraipont: 953–59).

53. Dossey (2010), 165–67, with detailed notes and bibliography. The fragility of such attributions is obvious. A rare exception is a collection of eighty sermons made by a Nicene bishop delegated to look

warn their audiences against the error of the Homoousians.⁵⁴ Just like any other heresiological writing from late antiquity, all of these texts were intended to persuade. Nicene and Homoian clerics in Vandal Africa took advantage of the literary forms and modes of argumentation that their predecessors had developed. The texts they produced were meant to play an active role in shaping contemporary perceptions of the African Church.

POLEMIC AND ITS AUDIENCES

Christian polemical texts from Vandal Africa were supposed to influence how African Christians thought. More than that, as two convoluted textual exchanges involving Fulgentius of Ruspe demonstrate, Nicene and Homoian writers sought to influence the same people. In his *Letter* 9, Fulgentius rebuts a sermon by a deacon Fastidiosus, a former Nicene monk and priest who had converted to Homoian Christianity.⁵⁵ Fastidiosus had preached on sin, the salvific effect of the Incarnation, and the obstinacy of the Donatist and Homoousian heretics who did not appropriately believe in that salvation.⁵⁶ His sermon came to Fulgentius's attention through a letter from a monk named Victor, who sought its refutation.⁵⁷ For much of his reply, Fulgentius takes Fastidiosus to task for his view of the Trinity; he nonetheless dedicates two paragraphs to personal abuse. Accusations of apparent sexual improprieties are used as psychological explanation for Fastidiosus's conversion to heresy. His "bodily fornication" led him into a "spiritual" one; he adopted a faith in which he did not believe so as to gain greater license to fulfill his sexual desires: all in all, "he took the members of Christ and made them the members of a prostitute."⁵⁸

---

after a colleague's diocese in his absence, most likely through exile: Ps.-Fulg., *Serm.* (*PL* 65: 855–954). The date of this collection—as of other, individual sermons—is suggested by references to barbarians and persecution, already limiting the utility of the sample. See, e.g., Ps.-Victor, *Hom. Cyp.* (*PL* 58: 265–68), on a barbarian takeover of Cyprian's cult sites; Ps.-Aug., *Serm. Mai* 42 (*PLS* 2: 1142–43), with anxieties about forced conversion in heretical captivity; Anon., *S. Morin* 1 (ed. Morin: 742–43), on persecution and possible martyrdom as present-day reality; cf. (in the same collection) Anon., *S. Morin* 27, 29 (ed. Morin: 814–17, 821–25), very brief anti-Arian polemic within creedal sermons; Anon., *H. Vind.* 5a (ed. Bogaert: 1911), comparison of devil's captivity to contemporary barbarian captivity. For further anti-Arian polemic (but with little to clarify a date), see Ps.-Aug., *S. spur.* 236.1–3, 246 (*PL* 39: 2181–82, 2198–200); Ps.-Aug., *Serm. Cai.* I.7.5 (ed. Caillau and Saint-Yves: 910–11).

54. See pp. 95–96.
55. Fulg., *Ep.* 9 (ed. Fraipont: 275–308); Fastidiosus, *Sermo* (ed. Fraipont).
56. See pp. 95, 104.
57. Fulg., *Ep.* 9, Victoris 3 (ed. Fraipont: 278), suggests that Fulgentius had encouraged Victor's adoption of a monastic life; Victor (and perhaps even Fastidiosus) may have been a member of one of Fulgentius's communities.
58. Fulg., *Ep.* 9.1, 9.21–22, quotations at 9.21.1 (ed. Fraipont: 283–84, 307–8, at 307); translation adapted from Eno (1997), 421.

Victor's letter, Fastidiosus's sermon, and Fulgentius's response are preserved as a dossier. To complicate matters further, Fulgentius accused Fastidiosus of pinching a section of anti-Donatist polemic from two letters (which Fulgentius attached to his letter to Victor for proof but are now lost) that the bishop of Ruspe had sent to one Stephania, "a religious daughter of the church."[59] This literary borrowing indicates that Fastidiosus and Fulgentius were plugged into the same networks of Christian intellectuals. The Homoian deacon shared Fulgentius's desire to persuade his African contemporaries; he had, after all, published this sermon, addressed to "most learned Christians."[60] Their shared readers were a key reason why these two clerics argued with each other.

Fastidiosus was not the only Homoian writer to trade barbs with the bishop of Ruspe. Fulgentius also wrote the ten-book treatise *Against Fabianus*, which survives only in fragments. This work responded to a lost work by Fabianus, some form of dialogue in which Fulgentius also played a role.[61] It is difficult to tell much about this Homoian Christian or his work from what survives of Fulgentius's quotations and paraphrases. As Leslie Dossey has noted, it is clear that Fabianus had a high level of grammatical training.[62] In refuting him, Fulgentius refers to scriptural passages in Greek on a number of occasions and quotes Vergil: neither are common features in his works. Noting Fabianus's claims to expertise in Latin, he chides the Homoian for conflating two verbs in his exegesis.[63] If such passages are a guide to the original work, they suggest one aimed at elite Christians: those who could afford to procure a classical education in late fifth- and early sixth-century Africa.

In evaluating the intended impact of texts like these, it is worth considering their specified recipients and purposes, since these helped to inspire their precise tone and structure. Such adaptations of basic heresiological messages can be revealing in themselves. At the same time, as the exchanges between Fulgentius and his Homoian opponents imply, it would be naïve to read such literature as if intended only for its addressee. Whether directed to a coreligionist, a rival, or an ambiguously positioned third party, polemical texts were always open letters. As Richard Miles and Jennifer Ebbeler have recently detailed, Christian literary exchanges often circulated far beyond the interested parties, whether as a result of deliberate planning or the vagaries of ancient methods of communication.[64] It is difficult to believe that Fabianus could have thought a dialogue involving Fulgentius would not find its way to the bishop of Ruspe eventually. Even when they

---

59. Fulg., *Ep.* 9.10 (ed. Fraipont: 295–96).
60. Fastidiosus, *Sermo* 2.21 (ed. Fraipont: 281).
61. See p. 83.
62. Dossey (2003), 115–16.
63. Fulg., *C. Fab.* 3.10 (ed. Fraipont: 770).
64. Miles (2008), 139–40; Ebbeler (2009), 270–71; Ebbeler (2012), esp. 75–189. See also Conybeare (2000), 41–48.

wrote for internal audiences, Nicene and Homoian writers in Vandal Africa had to bear in mind that texts could end up in opponents' hands. Third parties forwarded both Fastidiosus's sermon and Varimadus's propositions to Nicene churchmen.[65] The risk, or expectation, that a text could find its way to other readers always had to be taken into account.

Unnamed audiences were also intended. In the case of hostile missives, even if it is allowed that controversialists genuinely desired their opponents to change their ways, the efficacy of this correction required a public.[66] Consideration of an audience beyond those immediately addressed is also implied by the transcription and collation of Quodvultdeus's sermons and the later collection of Fulgentius's letters.[67] Individuals probably wrote and revised with later readers in mind.[68] The many polemical texts in Vandal Africa without identified addressees also presume this broader audience. Prefaces speak generically about the Christians (or, more rarely, the misguided heretics) intended as the recipients.[69] The common justifications that both sets of texts adduce are telling. Even when explicitly "for Felix" or "for Peter," "against Fabianus" or "against Varimadus," they were written for the African Christian community.

A more precise identification of this broader audience is unhelpful. Given the texts' stated aims and the social context of literary "publication" in late antiquity, a strong case can be made for a primarily internal audience, the position to which much recent scholarship on early Christian apologetic and polemic has leaned.[70] Again and again, the prefaces and even the titles of contemporary Nicene literature profess an intention to defend Catholic truth and fellow Catholics against the errors of Arian heretics and the questions or traps that they posed.[71] Even when it comes to texts explicitly directed to opponents, their belligerent tone makes it unlikely that the addressees were meant to feel persuaded and not simply harangued. Few of those who recognized that their doctrines and character were being impugned would have been amenable. The networks of contacts through which such writings circulated and the audiences to which they might be exposed

---

65. Fulg., *Ep.* 9 (ed. Fraipont: 277–308); *C. Var.*, pref. 1–5 (ed. Schwank: 9).

66. Ebbeler (2012), e.g., 50.

67. On the collation of the sermons attributed to Quodvultdeus into two principal collections, see Braun (1976), v–cvi; on the likely context of collation for Fulgentius's corpus, p. 50.

68. On African sermon collections see Dossey (2010), 147–72; Shaw (2011), 416–21. On letter collections see Ebbeler (2009), 271–72; Van Waarden (2010), 30–34, for a useful summary.

69. On benefitting fellow Catholics, see Vig., *Dial. I*, pref. I (ed. Hombert: 245); *C. Var.*, pref. (ed. Schwank: 9–10); Ps.-Fulg., *Trin.* 3.69, 3.73 (ed. Fraipont: 241); the full title of Ps.-Aug., *Solutiones* (ed. Schwank); *C. Fel.* 1 (*PL* 42: 1157). On benefitting heretics, see *C. Var.*, pref. 19–25 (ed. Schwank: 9).

70. E.g., Edwards et al. (1999b), 4–9; Rajak (1999), 61; Kahlos (2007), 56–57; Sandwell (2007), 76. For the bracketing together of apologetic and polemic, see esp. Av. Cameron (2002), 222–27.

71. See n. 69.

by public recital would also have been skewed towards individuals of shared ecclesiastical affiliation.[72] Direct and categorical denunciation tended to be for the benefit of others, not the recipient.

Still, it seems misguided to conceive of too exclusive an imagined audience. These writers' self-conception as Catholics meant that readers whom they considered part of their "mainstream" Christianity would, to their minds, have been the majority of African Christians. Especially when expressed in patronizing terms that exempted recipients from doctrinal responsibility, such as *imperiti* (inexperienced) or *stulti* (dull), this category could have included some within the churches of their rivals, reconceived as the dupes of heretical traps.[73] Above all, a precise division between missives intended for insiders and missives intended for outsiders fails to account for the necessarily hybrid tone of Christian polemical literature. Stated authorial purposes transcend the categories of modern scholars. A strict division between the pedagogic (intended to educate insiders) and the polemical (intended to refute outsiders) cannot be upheld. Heresiological polemic was fundamental to the process of teaching Christians what it was appropriate to believe.[74] At the same time, polemical attacks could be couched as salutary lessons for the inexperienced, to guard the writers against accusations of contentiousness.[75]

All of these texts were basically intended as rhetorically persuasive statements of the Christian faith. They could be articulated in subtly different ways, but their authors adopted the same methods to convince their readers, whatever their knowledge or ecclesiastical affiliation. In its many guises, heresiology informed all of the methods by which Nicene and Homoian clerics in Vandal Africa claimed the legitimacy that possession of Christian truth provided. Fundamentally, the writers of all of these texts sought to represent themselves as orthodox and their opponents as heretics, whether through explanation, rhetorical sleight of hand, or bald assertion. To return to the notion of boundary management: these writers could redraw the borders of their community to include members of "heretical" congregations. In any case, the distinction between Christians inside and outside their communities was less clear than is often thought. This was a boundary that these same Christian writers constantly sought to establish, not least through texts such as these.[76]

---

72. Schor (2011); Sotinel (2012).
73. On the early Christian trope of *imperitia*, see Lim (1995), 93–94, 102; Eshleman (2012), 91–124.
74. Perrin (2010).
75. Cf. Humfress (2012), 325–27.
76. See pp. 62–63, 169–70.

DIALOGUING WITH HERETICS

Arius said: Therefore, let the decrees of the Council of Nicaea be read out, and you will recognize that Athanasius or the authors of this [text] have corrupted what was the apostolic faith up to now by the addition of new words, so that, having used royal power, they could judge that those who adhered to the ancient doctrines of the fathers must be banished by fatal edicts.

Probus the judge said: If the reckoning of the present matter demands that the decree of the Council of Nicaea be recited, Athanasius should also order it in his declaration, so that it might be recited according to the will of both (if that is what is being offered).

Athanasius said: It fits the case that a full reading of those acts should not be prevented.

Probus the judge said: Therefore, as he desired, let the aforementioned decree of the faith of Nicaea be aired.

And thus it was read:

[The Nicene Creed is read out]

Arius said: You perceive, Probus, most distinguished of men, that the decrees of that council were composed in reproach of the apostolic faith with the daring of a reckless presumption. For what need was there that this new term, *homoousios*, should be inserted into the doctrine of ancient rules?[77]

Athanasius and Arius, the two great combatants of the Arian controversy, had been brought together at last. The setting was day one of a veritable "council of the sects," convened to identify the true faith. Another two infamous figures of Christian theological disputation, Sabellius and Photinus, had also been called before the judge, Probus, a recent convert from paganism who wished to discover correct Christian doctrine, and the assembled audience. However, it was obvious (even to the judge) that the main event would be a contest between Athanasius and Arius.[78] Therefore, the proceedings were conducted in a knockout format. Arius successfully refuted both Sabellius and Photinus—to disconcertingly warm approval from Athanasius—and then, in the quoted passage, attacked his archnemesis and the Nicene faith, focusing on the contentious consubstantiality (ὁμοούσιος) of Father and Son. Heated discussion continued into the evening and resumed the next day (book 2 of the surviving text) before the judge had heard enough. Probus ruled Athanasius's arguments clearly superior, despite Arius's grumbling about his opponent's tactics. Given the opportunity, Athanasius had finally beaten Arius, mano a mano.

---

77. Vig., *Dial. I* = *II* 1.18–19 (ed. Hombert: 285–87).
78. Ibid., 1.5 (261–62).

The text's authentic feel adds to the anticipation of a wonderful discovery for students of the early Arian controversy, if seemingly extant only in a Latin translation. It bears the hallmarks of the acta of a church council: the formatting of the stenographic record, the reading of a document and its entry into the minutes, the concern for correct protocol.[79] Even the strident tone of Arius's attack would not seem out of place in the stormier councils of the fourth and fifth centuries. Like any conciliar transcript, these acts are designed to reassure the reader of the validity of their contents: a properly conducted debate between Athanasius and Arius.

Before the textbooks of early Christianity are too hurriedly rewritten, it seems only right to mention a minor problem. This was not a real council, even if its author later reworked the debate to specify that it had taken place at a synod at Laodicea in 338/39, citing a (fictitious) rescript of Constantius II that had convoked it.[80] That author, Vigilius, a cleric who later became the bishop of Thapsa in Byzacena, exposes his artifice in a preface. He had sought a quick and entertaining means of rebutting the writings of contemporary heretics, and thus

> it appeared useful and very fitting, that I might introduce the character of each heretic with his own professed doctrines, who discuss with one another in person. And lest the arguments of each of them might cause doubt with no one examining them, I have made a certain judge, by the name of Probus, to carry out the office of judicial authority. Through his commendable discernment [*probabiliter discernente*] regarding each of them, the intention of impious depravity may be brought to naught. Therefore I have introduced Sabellius, Photinus, Arius, and, for our party, Athanasius, so that the truth, refined by the greatest contest of combatants, might reach the notice of all and, by the diversity of the characters and responses and interjections, the varied arrangement of this work might stop the readers from getting bored.[81]

Had he not shown his hand, eyebrows would doubtless have been raised at the presence of these chronologically disparate clerics in the same auditorium. The known activities of Sabellius (an early third-century priest) and Photinus (a mid-fourth-century bishop of Sirmium) do not overlap with their Alexandrian dialogue partners. In the second version of the text, Athanasius even communicates from beyond the grave. The Alexandrian bishop (d. 371) speaks approvingly of the Council of Aquileia (381) and cites his own rebuttals of one text written after the death of Ambrose of Milan (d. 397) and another written by Marivadus, a mid-fifth-century deacon.[82] In spite of its central conceit, the *Dialogue against the Arians, Sabellians and Photinians* is not part of the feverish doctrinal wrangling of the Constantinian Greek East. Rather, it belongs to the Vandal Africa of its author.

---

79. On conciliar stenography in late antiquity, see Teitler (1985), 1–15; Price and Gaddis (2005), 75.
80. Vig., *Dial. II*, pref. II (ed. Hombert: 246–52); see also Ficker (1897), 26–27, 32–33.
81. Vig., *Dial. I*, pref. I (ed. Hombert: 245).
82. Vig., *Dial. II* 3.27, 3.23 (ed. Hombert: 394–95, 387). On Marivadus see pp. 55 n. 1, 125 n. 86.

Specifically, this text must predate another work by Vigilius, probably written circa 470–82.[83] Vigilius is listed as the most recently consecrated bishop in the province of Byzacena in the *Register* of 484.[84] At some point soon after 484, the new bishop of Thapsa reworked the text of the *Dialogue*, adding the historical preface, a third book, which extends the head-to-head between Athanasius and Arius, and a judicial *sententia*, which summarizes all four debaters' arguments and hands the victory to the bishop of Alexandria.[85] This is an imaginary dialogue, drawing on the resources of past church conflicts to help its readership make sense of pressing present-day issues.

Historians of Vandal Africa have largely ignored Vigilius of Thapsa's extraordinary piece of literary invention; one of its few mentions dismisses it as irrelevant.[86] This is understandable: three books of fictitious debate between four long-dead Greek clerics do not easily fit into a historical narrative. Even putting to one side the alternative concerns of modern historiography on the successor kingdoms, the *Dialogue* may seem like an unusual text on which to focus inquiry into Christian debate in Vandal Africa. Such studies are normally framed around the minutes of the conciliar meetings through which ecclesiastical controversies were resolved or extended. Debates between Nicene and Homoian clerics in Vandal Africa do not leave such a paper trail: there is no extant transcript. The only remaining authentic ecclesiastical acta from the period are those of the Nicene Council of Carthage (525), which dealt with matters of internal ecclesiastical hierarchy and discipline.[87] This is not for want of public encounters between Nicene and Homoian Christians.[88] Alongside records of formal occasions like the Conference of Carthage in

---

83. The text is mentioned at Vig., *C. Eut.* 5.2 (PL 62: 136A); for details and dating see Ficker (1897), 10–42; Simonetti (1978), 506–8; Petri (2003), 28–39. Some have hypothesized an Eastern audience and career for Vigilius, since Theodulf of Orleans (d. 823), *De Spir. Sanct.* (PL 105: 273A), refers to a "Vigilius Africanus" writing against Eutyches in Constantinople: e.g., Lancel (2002a), 230; cf. Ficker (1897), 15–20; Guidi (2005), 8–10. Theodulf may have confused the author with his namesake, the sixth-century pope Vigilius, whose dubious Constantinopolitan sojourn during the Three Chapters controversy was well known: Sotinel (1992); (2005), 281–84. In any case, Theodulf says only that *Contra Eutychetem* was written there. The use of the *Dialogus* by the author of the *Liber fidei Catholicae* (see p. 72, with n. 93), the text's rewriting by Vigilius to take into account the events of 483–84, and its exclusively Latin and specifically North African patristic context—the views of its Athanasius are constructed from Latin Ps.-Athanasian texts, Ambrose, and Augustine (see Guidi [2005], 8–10, 22–43, and her notes on the text)—suggest an African milieu.

84. *Not. prov.* 3.109 (ed. Lancel: 264); Lancel (2002a), 227–30.

85. See pp. 122–27; for the dates and details of the two texts, see Hombert (forthcoming), 70–102. First edition: Vig., *Dial. I*; second edition: Vig., *Dial. II*.

86. Howe (2007), 22–23.

87. Carthage (525) (ed. Munier), with Merrills and Miles (2010), 200–203; see also pp. 49, 134–37.

88. H. Müller (2008), 33; Conant (2012), 173.

484,[89] there are references to Nicene Christians meeting Homoians and exchanging arguments (particularly in the reign of Thrasamund).[90] The provision of ready-made responses to heretical objections in florilegia, question-and-answer texts, and dialogues indicates that clerics thought such scenarios were all too common.[91] The *Dialogue against the Arians, Sabellians and Photinians* is the closest the Vandal kingdom comes to the sort of documentation that normally forms a first resort for studies of church conflicts in late antiquity.

Vigilius's *Dialogue* is of course much less (and much more) than a replacement for conciliar acts. It does not preserve the authentic, notarized statements of contemporary Christian rivals. What it does supply is a fascinating individual perspective on Christian polemical debate in Vandal Africa, written in a genre long beloved of controversial writers. As unusual as they may seem to modern eyes, imaginary dialogues were often used by early Christian writers to discuss controversial issues; their course of development coincided tellingly with that of heresiology. From the second century, Christian texts were written as two-handers with pagans, Jews, and Christian opponents.[92] In late antiquity, an impressive roll call of prominent ecclesiastical figures wrote (or translated) polemical dialogues with fictitious debaters: Jerome, Rufinus of Aquileia, Cyril of Alexandria, Nestorius, Theodoret of Cyrrhus.

More than that, the *Dialogue* spoke directly to the interests of Vigilius's ecclesiastical contemporaries. The doctrinal talking points of his Athanasius and Arius overlap extensively with those laid out in the *Book of the Catholic Faith* at the Conference of Carthage in 484. Vigilius's Athanasius and his Nicene contemporaries focused on the question of the Incarnation, arguing that Christ was not generated from anything external to God and that the divine power was unconstrained by "natural necessities" in that generation.[93] When called upon by Huneric to defend their faith against Homoian accusations of heresy, the bishops marshaled the same arguments that "Athanasius" used against "Arius." Given the similarities of both ver-

---

89. See p. 16.

90. For debates between Thrasamund and unnamed Nicene opponents, see *V. Fulg.* 20 (ed. Isola: 202–3). For discussions between Nicenes and unnamed Arians, see Fulg., *Ad Mon.* 2.2.1, 3.1 (ed. Fraipont: 34, 52–53); Fulg., *Ep.* 8.2 (ed. Fraipont: 258); Fulg., *De Trin. ad Fel.* 1.1 (ed. Fraipont: 633); *C. Var.*, pref. 1–5 (ed. Schwank: 9).

91. On prefaces see p. 67 n. 69; on *imperiti*, p. 68.

92. Useful surveys of early Christian dialogue are Bardy (1957); Voss (1970), esp. 135–74, 187–96, 293–98; P. Schmidt (1977).

93. *Liber fidei Catholicae* = *HP* 2.56–101 (ed. Lancel: 148–73). For concurrences see *HP* 2.57 (ed. Lancel: 148–49) = Vig., *Dial. I* = *II* 2.5 (ed. Hombert: 309–12); *HP* 2.58–62 (ed. Lancel: 149–52) = Vig., *Dial. I* and *II* throughout, esp. *I* = *II* 2.19 (ed. Hombert: 335–36); *HP* 2.63–64 (ed. Lancel: 152–53) = Vig., *Dial. I* = *II* 2.17–18 (ed. Hombert: 331–35); *HP* 2.65 (ed. Lancel: 153) = Vig., *Dial. II* 3.1 (ed. Hombert: 355–56); *HP* 2.66–74 (ed. Lancel: 153–58) = Vig., *Dial. I* = *II* 2.2–19 (ed. Hombert: 304–36); *HP* 2.75–98 (ed. Lancel: 158–72) = Vig., *Dial. II* 3.12–24 (ed. Hombert: 371–90). For a unique intertext see *HP* 2.65 (ed. Lancel: 153) = Vig., *Dial. II* 3.1.15, 3.2.5, 3.7.25–26 (ed. Hombert: 355, 356, 365).

sions of the *Dialogue*, a reciprocal relationship seems likely. The first edition, written perhaps only a few years before the conference, likely influenced the authors of the *Book*. Vigilius may have been present at the conference to hear it read out: his second edition, written a few years after, shows knowledge of the edict that resulted from the conference. The curiosity of the *Dialogue*'s origin and format should not obscure its significance. Vigilius's text acts, quite self-consciously, as a definitive statement of Nicene Christianity.

MINUTE BY MINUTE

In Vandal Africa, Vigilius was one of a number of authors to adopt the dialogue form to write Trinitarian polemic. A series of wonderfully inventive texts present themselves as the transcripts of historical debate encounters between a Nicene Christian and an Arian heretic. An anonymous author, identified as Pseudo-Augustine, created the *Conference of Augustine with Pascentius*, which purports to transmit the acts of a debate between the bishop of Hippo and a Homoian member of the late Roman elite, a count and man of senatorial status (*comes et uir spectabilis*).[94] Those two men had conducted a genuine disputation in Carthage at some point in the early fifth century. Details of its proceedings are preserved in the rancorous letters they exchanged in the aftermath as Augustine sought to publicly clarify the result.[95] Augustine's biographer Possidius built on them for a short description of the episode in his *Life of Augustine*.[96] No minutes were taken at the meeting; Pascentius had refused, to the chagrin of Augustine and Possidius.[97] The author of the *Conference* drew on the letters and the *Life* to rewrite this debate in transcript form but made a number of notable changes. The debate moves from Carthage to Hippo Regius and becomes a much more legally charged affair. Whereas the real confrontation took place on the spur of the moment in front of

---

94. *Coll. Pasc.* (ed. H. Müller, Weber, and Weidmann). On the text see Tiefenbach (1991); Heil (2007); H. Müller, Weber, and Weidmann (2008). The earliest manuscript witness (T: Torino, bibl. naz. univ. G. V. 26, most likely produced in Bobbio) provides a terminus ante quem of the second half of the sixth century. This collection is suggestive: the text of *Coll. Pasc.* is accompanied by two antiheretical sermons of Quodvultdeus (see p. 53 n. 110), the letters between Augustine and Pascentius, and Rufinus of Aquileia's *Expositio symboli*. Tiefenbach plausibly (but nonetheless speculatively) suggests that this manuscript copied an anti-Arian collection from Vandal Africa. The internal evidence of the text is more concrete: it contains local African detail (the debate happens in an otherwise unattested but plausibly genuine *domus Anicia* in Hippo Regius) and repeatedly refers to Africa, to barbarian Christian worship, and to legal circumstances specific to the kingdom (the criminalization of Homoousians). See Tiefenbach (1991), 253–56, 258–59; Heil (2007), 26; Vössing (2008), 173–74, 192–95; Weber (2008), 8, 18–19; Weidmann (2008), 44.

95. Aug., *Epp.* 238–41 (ed. Goldbacher: 4:533–62).

96. Poss., *V. Aug.* 17.1–6 (ed. Bastiaensen: 170–72).

97. Aug., *Ep.* 238.9 (ed. Goldbacher: 4:539); Poss., *V. Aug.* 17.2 (ed. Bastiaensen: 170–72).

an elite Carthaginian audience, a judge, Laurentius, presides in the *Conference*, conducting it as a *cognitio*, with an introduction setting out the case at hand, a judgment, and even a subscription ("I, Laurentius, *uir clarissimus*, have subscribed to these acts, held before me in the house of the Anicii in Hippo, with my own hand").[98] Laurentius arbitrates the discussion between Augustine and Pascentius, which focuses on the question of the legitimacy of the term ὁμοούσιος and, by logical extension, of the use of different languages for Christian worship.

The *Conference* begins with opening statements by the judge and the antagonists. It is made clear that Augustine and Pascentius were in conversation the day before: Laurentius expresses hope that their previous acrimonious discourse has been put aside and greater serenity will characterize the minuted conversation (*Coll. Pasc.* 1); Pascentius refers to a question Augustine had asked about Arius and Eunomius on the previous day (4). Augustine successfully convinces Laurentius that Pascentius should speak first and "declare the name of his faith" (2). Laurentius confirms that Pascentius had brought about this legal proceeding and should thus start things off (3). Pascentius's opening statement sets the tone for what follows:

> Pascentius the *uir spectabilis* said: That most prudent bishop of his faith, Augustine, who is present, could not deny that I am a Christian. I profess that I believe in the unbegotten Father, the begotten Son, and the Holy Spirit, but not that they are of one equal nature. And because yesterday, when I named Auxentius as a praiseworthy holy man of miraculous knowledge, and the same brother Augustine asked very scrupulously which of the two the same man had followed, whether Arius or Eunomius,[99] I did not hesitate to say anathema at once to the aforementioned Arius and Eunomius, demanding that he himself anathematise ὁμοούσιος, which is not to be found written in the Lord's books at all. He in no way consented to do this, by which he showed himself evidently, without doubt, to be a Homoousian. (*Coll. Pasc.* 4)

The Homoian count provides, in brief, his profession of faith as a (Homoian) Christian and describes his condemnation of Arius and Eunomius. Most strikingly, he notes that Augustine could not disavow his Christianity and accuses the bishop of Hippo of Homoousian heresy.[100] This accusation shapes the rest of the proceedings.

Laurentius seems convinced by Pascentius's statement, which he calls a "complete argument" (*integra prosecutio*; *Coll. Pasc.* 5), but Augustine prolongs the debate by previewing arguments developed later: Pascentius also uses unscriptural terminology, and ὁμοούσιος is simply a synonym for the biblical unity of Father and Son. When Laurentius does not quite take his point (7), Augustine reminds the judge of his need to keep his judicial superior (God) in mind (8). Laurentius

---

98. *Coll. Pasc.* 19 (ed. H. Müller, Weber, and Weidmann: 118).
99. In the real debate, Augustine's colleague Alypius asked this question: Aug., *Ep.* 238.4 (ed. Bastiaensen: 535).
100. On Homoian descriptions of Nicene Christians as Homoousian heretics, see pp. 94–96.

thus orders Pascentius to make a creedal statement (9). The Homoian count does so (10) and challenges Augustine to find unscriptural terms within it. If the bishop of Hippo can justify his use of ὁμοούσιος, Pascentius states, "even I myself will publicly proclaim that it was not established [*positum*] unjustly by them, and I will at once become an ally of their communion" (13). This provokes a long closing speech from Augustine (15), which dominates the extant text (215 lines in the critical edition). Augustine knits together a series of arguments to justify terms that do not appear in scripture, citing in particular the use of multiple languages by Christians. The resulting complications meant that terms absent from the biblical text were justified if the concept they signified was there. The *Conference*'s Augustine also argues against the idea that the Greekness or foreignness of the word ὁμοούσιος was itself part of the problem, quoting various other words derived from Greek (*Christ, Christian, abba, anathema, chrism*). The judge is convinced and finds in Augustine's favor (16). In spite of his earlier promise, Pascentius restates his denial of ὁμοούσιος as unscriptural (17), but Laurentius waves this aside in a short sentence in favor of its use (18).

The author of the *Conference* used Augustine's detailed account of the original proceedings and other works by Augustine, sometimes even quoting verbatim. The result is a convincing simulacrum both of Augustine's Trinitarian thought and of his public debates. Nevertheless, the setting of the reimagined dialogue is as much post-imperial Africa as Augustine's Hippo. The intrusion of the author's world is most obvious in (Pseudo-)Augustine's final peroration. In discussing language issues, this speech repeatedly references barbarians and their Christian worship.[101] The *Conference* cleverly repackages Augustine of Hippo's Trinitarian thought for the new ecclesiastical climate of post-imperial Africa.

A more straightforward Vandal context is the setting for another imaginary dialogue. The *Debate of Cerealis against Maximinus* claims to preserve the minutes of a debate between Cerealis, the Nicene bishop of Castellum, and Maximinus, "the bishop of the Ariomaniacs" (*episcopus Ariomanitarum*) before an unnamed Vandal king in Carthage.[102] This may be the same Cerealis attested as the second-most junior bishop of Mauretania Caesariensis in the episcopal list of 484.[103] The text's notice in a chapter added by a continuator of Gennadius of Marseille's own continuation of Jerome's *On Illustrious Men* sets a terminus ante quem of the death of Eugenius of Carthage (505?) for its composition.[104] This public debate has generally been

101. See pp. 190–92.
102. *Cer. c. Max.* (ed. Baise).
103. *Not. prov.* 4.119 (ed. Lancel: 269); on this association (and its fragility), see Fialon (2015), 138–40.
104. Eugenius is described as if still alive in Ps.-Genn., *Uir. inlustr.* 98 (ed. Richardson: 96). See Baise (2006), 234; see also Feder (1933), for the contents and likely date of Gennadius's work and of the pseudonymous additions to it.

associated with the conference of 484, but there is no reason to put it there[105] or even to think that it genuinely took place.[106] Although it is described as if it really happened in the Gallic continuation to *On Illustrious Men* and in Isidore's later compendium of the same name, these short entries show no awareness of any information beyond what the *Debate* supplies.[107] That text bookends the dialogue with narrative passages dressing it up as a real event. It begins with Cerealis traveling to Carthage from his see. His arrival does not go unnoticed among the heretics in the city ("those citizens who had plunged beneath the fury of God" [4–5]). Through them it comes to the attention of the (unnamed) king. A brief (and rather allusive) discussion between king and bishop quickly gives way to the appearance of Maximinus. The two churchmen exchange some cutting byplay: "Maximinus, the bishop of the Ariomaniacs, arrived and said to the bishop Cerealis, 'Do you see those sins that your people do? For that reason, God has abandoned you.' Holy Cerealis, elevated [*promotus*] by the truth, said, 'How has he deserted us and not you, who have butchered [*iugulatis*] spirits under cover of the Christian name [*sub Christiani nominis titulo*] and do not hold the true faith?'" (7–11) Maximinus challenges Cerealis to a debate, demanding two or three scriptural proofs in each response; Cerealis retorts that he will supply many. Cerealis proceeds to answer Maximinus's questions before setting out his own in turn. The narrative then resumes. Maximinus does not answer Cerealis's propositions ("putting it off from day to day" [533]; see Ecclesiastes 5:8) and so the bishop of Castellum addresses a complaint to the king. The king tells him that this failure to respond must reflect Maximinus's inability to do so. He orders Cerealis to return to his church and defers judgment of the debate to God.

Like Vigilius's *Dialogue* and the *Conference of Augustine with Pascentius*, the *Debate of Cerealis against Maximinus* provides a backstory for its dialogic encounter, setting the discussions (somewhat crudely) within the context of the Vandal court at Carthage. Despite its narrative frame, this is at its core an anti-Arian question-and-answer text. Maximinus enumerates twenty statements (18–45); Cerealis responds in numbered and headed chapters (1.46–20.453). These cannot represent an oral response: the format is too stilted. Nor do the questions ring true as the genuine words of a Homoian debater. Several begin, "That which they [the Arians] say" (*id quod dicunt*).[108] Historians have discussed whether this Maximinus could be the same bishop who faced Augustine in a public debate in 427/28.[109] The obviously textual quality of the exchanges counsels greater skepticism. This text is, at

---

105. Parsons (1994), 115 n. 115, with references; cf. Fialon (2015), 142–43.
106. For a very similar argument to that which follows, see Fialon (2015), 149–54.
107. Baise (2006), 234–35. All this: Cer. c. Max. 1–17, 532–41 (ed. Baise: 262, 285–86).
108. E.g., *Cer. c. Max.* 26–31, 39–44 (ed. Baise: 263–64). Compare the *elenchus capitolorum* of Ps.-Aug., *Solutiones* (ed. Schwank: 141–48).
109. Gryson (1980), 68; Parsons (1994), 80–81, 117 n. 120, with references; Mathisen (1999b), 195–96.

best, a heavily fictionalized write-up of some real encounter; more likely it is an imaginary dialogue that plays on Augustine's authority in a way similar to the *Conference of Augustine with Pascentius*.[110] Like that dialogue, the *Debate* author (whether Cerealis or an admirer) took an Arian opponent of Augustine and brought him into the Vandal period as a symbolic representative of that heresy.

Augustine reprises his role as protagonist in a fourth imaginary dialogue likely produced in Vandal Africa. The *Book on the Unity of the Trinity against Felicianus the Arian* is a fictitious debate between Augustine and an otherwise unattested Arian named Felicianus.[111] Their conversation receives little staging. In its preface, the anonymous author addresses a correspondent who had requested an antiheretical text. He justifies the *Book* as a means to protect the faithful from deception by heretics and explains that he will recount a conversation with a certain Felicianus. The text then segues into the debate, which starts off between "he" and "I" before abruptly adding names. The conversation has a fairly consistent rhythm. Felicianus presents short objections, which Augustine answers in depth; sometimes, Felicianus avers that he does not understand those responses, which allows the author to provide further explanation (e.g., "FEL: I should like you to elucidate your words to me with an easier example").[112] Specific issues of Christological and Trinitarian doctrine drive the discussion, often provoked by Felicianus's use of classic Arian formulations. Once again, the basis of proof is discussed, although on this occasion Augustine has to convince his Arian opponent that they should not simply argue logically, the opposite of the other Arian dialogue characters' stress on direct citations from scripture.[113] The text ends, like the *Conference of Augustine with Pascentius*, with a long, almost homiletic oration by Augustine; his final image is that of Christ separating the wheat and the tares.[114] As with the *Debate of Cerealis*, it is clear that a series of discrete Arian statements structure the work. On this occasion, they are more smoothly integrated into a dialogic structure and narrative.

---

110. For the suggestion that the use of "Maximinus" as the name of the Arian opponent was meant to characterize Cerealis as a new Augustine, see pp. 125–26.

111. *C. Fel.* (PL 42: 1155–72). See Ficker (1897), 77; Voss (1970), 366–68; Simonetti (1986), 42–43; Heil (2007), 25–27; Dossey (2010), 169–70, 279 n. 167; Hombert (2010), 197, with n. 59. *C. Fel.* shares many common themes with the imaginary dialogues securely dated to the Vandal period and is even attributed to Vigilius in one tenth-century manuscript. It is combined with Ps.-Fulgentius's *Book on the Trinity* (securely attested to the Vandal period: see pp. 61–62) in all bar two of the codices that transmit the latter (Fraipont [1961], 236), suggesting the association of the two texts from an early stage. Although caution is necessary, especially given the lack of a modern critical edition, this text plausibly stems from Vandal Africa.

112. *C. Fel.* 3 (PL 42: 1159).

113. Ibid., 2 (1157–58).

114. Ibid., 14–17 (1169–72).

HERESIOLOGICAL DIALOGUES IN LATE ANTIQUITY

In late antiquity, imaginary polemical dialogue written against other Christians developed into a distinctive literary form with its own conventions.[115] Vandal Africa's heresiological dialogues were part of this literary tradition. In the case of Vigilius of Thapsa, the chain of influence can be seen in specific texts. Alongside a collection of Latin anti-Arian dialogues that took Athanasius as their protagonist,[116] the principal model for the *Dialogue against the Arians, Sabellians and Photinians* was Rufinus's Latin translation of the Greek dialogue *On the Correct Faith in God* (whose textual history and authorial attribution are complicated).[117] *On the Correct Faith in God* similarly features an orthodox champion (the tellingly named Adamantius) taking on several characters representing different heretical views in a circumscribed field of Christian thought (various forms of Gnosticism). As in the *Dialogue*, the competitors present their arguments in front of a judge who is in the process of converting from paganism; Vigilius's "Probus" could be taken as a Latin translation of that judge's equally symbolic name, "Eutropius" (Of good morals).[118] Vigilius cribs numerous other features from that text and picks out several choice phrases: for instance, Adamantius and Athanasius are each described by their respective judge as an "able and faithful assertor" of the true faith.[119] Vigilius's prefatory justification may also have been inspired by Rufinus's stated aims for his translation. In the prologue to *On the Correct Faith*, the translator passes on to its dedicatee his approval of the "assertions of [Adamantius], through which he converted both the heretics to true doctrine [*dogmatum ueritatem*] and the gentiles to the faith."[120]

Vigilius's text stands in a long tradition of using dialogue to propagate Christian orthodoxy through the refutation and denunciation of opponents. Heresiological dialogues share many of the features common to all forms of Christian writing that seek to define authoritative teachings against those of others. As already noted, these dialogues bear a close resemblance to question-and-answer texts and other

---

115. See Whelan (2017).

116. Simonetti (1956), 8; Guidi (2005), 12–13.

117. For the surviving Greek text, see Bakhuyzen (1901); for Rufinus's translation, Buchheit (1966). On the possible identification of "Adamantius" with Origen and the greater faithfulness of Rufinus's Latin text to the original Greek compared with the surviving Greek text (which contains numerous much later neologisms and probable interpolations), see Ramelli (2012); (2013).

118. Each judge is described as *eruditus*: Ruf., *Lib. Adam. Orig. adu. haer.* 1.1 (ed. Buchheit: 2.15–16); Vig., *Dial. I = II* 1.2.2 (ed. Hombert: 255). For an earlier use of the *probus* pun for the praetorian prefect of that name, see Auson., *Ep.* 12.35–50 (ed. Evelyn-White: 36).

119. Ruf., *Lib. Adam. Orig. adu. haer.* 5.28 (ed. Buchheit: 99.19–20): "uiae autem ueritatis idoneus satis et fidelis assertor est"; Vig., *Dial. II*, sententia, 12.16–17 (ed. Hombert: 413): "ad uerum et rectum apostolicae fidei tramitem, cuius Athanasius idoneus et fidelis assertor exstitit" (and compare the closing judgments more generally).

120. For Vigilius's preface, see p. 70; Ruf., *Lib. Adam. Orig. adu. haer.*, prol. (ed. Buchheit: 1.13–15).

florilegia. If the common features of these different genres suggest a similar set of audiences and purposes, the explicit statements of their prefaces confirm them.[121] As Tessa Rajak has noted in a superlative study of an early example of Christian dialogue, Justin's *Dialogue with Trypho*, this genre was conducive to self-definition. It provided Christian writers with a means to communicate who they were and what they believed in contradistinction to their opponents.[122] The creators of such texts did not have entirely free rein to present their enemies as they desired; the potential for critical or even hostile audience response acted as a check on overly mischievous creativity. Still, in contrast to a real public encounter or even a written response to a theological treatise, dialogues provided authors with considerable latitude to characterize controversial debates as they wished. And unlike real-life debates, fictitious dialogues were easily controlled: the right side always won.

When viewed collectively, it is clear that late-antique heresiological dialogues have a particular repertoire of tropes, features, and "plots." The debt that authors in Vandal Africa owed to these generic traditions is obvious. At the same time, in formulating their texts, Vandal Africa's Nicene dialogue writers made distinctive choices that are significant for how they viewed contemporary ecclesiastical controversy (discussed at greater length over the next two chapters). Earlier authors sometimes used historical characters, but not always; they could also be content with fictitious representatives of specific heresies or stock characters named "The Orthodox" or "The Catholic" and "The Heretic" or "The Arian."[123] The repeated choice of past figures of Nicene Christianity and Arian heresy emphasizes the historical thinking of the writers who produced heresiological dialogues in Vandal Africa.[124] Like earlier adversarial imaginary discussions, these texts end in victory for the orthodox champion. Yet in no case does the defeated Arian recant his views; Arius and Pascentius even put their continued hostility on record. The choice to represent these deliberately qualified victories reflects the position of the Nicene ecclesiastical faction in Vandal Africa. Some earlier imaginary dialogues had judges, but they rarely displayed the pointed legalism of Vigilius's *Dialogue* or, most notably, the *Conference of Augustine with Pascentius*. Such marked concerns for procedure and legalese suggest a profoundly legalistic culture of Christian disputation.[125] In all of these ways, the imaginary debates that Vigilius and others scripted indicate something of the framework in which real altercations over orthodoxy were conducted.

121. See p. 67 n. 69.
122. Rajak (1999). See also Voss (1970), 172–74; Jacobs (2007), 291–98.
123. For references see Whelan (2017), 21, 28–31.
124. See pp. 112–14, 121–27.
125. See pp. 100–103.

While the generic traditions of imaginary Christian dialogue were important for the construction of imaginary anti-Arian debate texts in Vandal Africa, the literary history of real debate encounters was perhaps an even greater influence. Dialogue writers derived particular inspiration from the acts of Christian disputations held in late Roman Africa. As is self-evident, the authors of the *Conference of Augustine with Pascentius* and the *Debate of Cerealis against Maximinus* had read accounts of the specific Augustinian debates that they relocated. Stray echoes, like Probus's desire to avoid wasting time on "superfluous matters" or (Pseudo-)Augustine reminding the judge of the "tenor of our statement," suggest broader reading of the minutes of Augustine's confrontations.[126] Beyond specific tags, these authors reproduced the atmosphere of Christian polemical discussions through features like the mutual recriminations, so redolent of conciliar meetings, that Vigilius captured particularly neatly ("Arius said: You have used enough cunning and suspicious arguments"; "Athanasius said: Nothing more inept or absurd can ever have been found than the things that Arius takes pride in as if they were some invincible question").[127]

These dialogue writers did not just replicate the scrimmaging of public Christian confrontation; they also followed earlier authors in allowing its practical constraints to intrude. All four texts adopt the conceit that the imagined debaters were talking before the formal minuting began, a plot point in both invented and real debate transcripts.[128] References to the world beyond the dialogue can be elaborate. In his opening statement in book 2 of Vigilius's first version of the *Dialogue*, Athanasius refers to previous anti-Arian polemical texts (Athanasius's actual writings or an oblique reference to Vigilius's own texts?) whose contents he recapitulates for the benefit of the judge:

> Although for a long time I have frequently disputed about the unity of the substance without minutes [*citra acta*] and I have entrusted my disputations to writing, to which nothing more can be added in this disputation, nevertheless, because these things have been said at a distance with no opponent in range [*nullo eminus aduersante*], I hold it necessary to repeat these same things, and to convey them to this public examination [*in hoc publicae actionis examen emittere*], so that they might be able to strengthen the judgment of your justice.[129]

---

126. Vig., *Dial. I = II* 1.16.5 (ed. Hombert: 282): "in superfluis rebus necessarium tempus absumat"; Aug., *Coll. cum Max.* 8 (ed. Hombert: 390): "in rebus superfluis necessarium tempus absumis"; H. Müller (2008), 27, with n. 80, on "prosecutionis nostrae tenor[em]" in *Coll. Pasc.* (a verbatim intertext with *Gesta con. Carth.*).

127. Vig., *Dial. I = II* 2.4 (ed. Hombert: 307); *Dial. II* 3.2 (ed. Hombert: 357).

128. Vig., *Dial. I = II* 2.2 (ed. Hombert: 304); *Coll. Pasc.* 4 (ed. H. Müller, Weber, and Weidmann: 78); *Cer. c. Max.*, pref. 3–17 (ed. Baise: 262); *C. Fel.* 2 (PL 42: 1157). Earlier examples include invented cases, e.g., Hier., *Altercatio* 1 (ed. Canellis: 5–6); and genuine ones, e.g., *Acta conc. Aquil.* 2 (ed. Zelzer: 327); Aug., *Gesta cum Emerito* 1 (ed. Petschenig: 181–82); Aug., *Coll. cum Max.* 1 (ed. Hombert: 383–84).

129. Vig., *Dial. I = II* 2.2 (ed. Hombert: 304).

The pretense that time was passing as normal for the debaters—used by Vigilius in dividing his text into two "days" of debate—was also common to other authors, who equally made mention of their antagonists wearying and needing to break for the day.[130] Such devices add an extra sense of plausibility to contests that are, when it comes down to it, exercises in argument formulated by a single author.

The similarities between the fictive Christian debates of Vandal Africa and their genuine counterparts should not be treated as superficial. Recent work on dialogue in late antiquity has begun to rethink the relationship between real and imagined debate.[131] The uncanny plausibility of some imaginary dialogues from late antiquity means that, as Averil Cameron has noted, it is difficult to judge whether many "real" debates actually happened.[132] At the same time, aspects of "real" debates seem to have been inspired by traditions of (imaginary) early Christian dialogue. At the very least, the numerous tropes shared by genuine and fictive face-to-face Christian disputations make clear that both developed according to the same set of expectations.

If historians have begun to recognize the value of imaginary dialogues for the understanding of late-antique Christian controversies, it is partly as a result of greater skepticism regarding the impartiality of texts that preserve occasions when both sides of a conflict were able to represent themselves. In the first place, "real" face-to-face debates tended to be little less partisan than their virtual cousins. Respectful exchanges of views were rarely possible. As Richard Lim has persuasively argued, Christians found dialogue ideologically fraught because their claims to possess a single religious truth could sit awkwardly with open-ended discussion, and their oft-cited ideal of simple, unadorned speech could clash with the dialectical methods with which classical dialogue was conducted.[133] Debates were shaped by the desires of controversialists to gain public and potentially juridical victories over their rivals, exploiting the developed legal and political framework in place to support a single correct Christian faith. As a result, when Christians had the opportunity (or misfortune) to meet their opponents in person, they tended to debate not so much with that actual Christian and his views but with the heretical image of him they had constructed, both because of the agonistic character of such encounters and because this was the most direct means to assimilate him to available categories of heresy.[134] Particularly influential episcopal impresarios could orchestrate these public meetings almost as effectively as a writer

---

130. E.g., Theod., *Eranistes* 1, 2 (ed. Ettlinger: 111, 187–88); Hier., *Altercatio* 1 (ed. Canellis: 6); Vig., *Dial. I = II* 2.1 (ed. Hombert: 303).
131. Esp. Av. Cameron (2013); (2014).
132. Av. Cameron (2014), 18, 25, 27.
133. Lim (1995); (1999), 202–4; (2008).
134. Voss (1970), 297–98.

composing an imagined dialogue.[135] The status of the acts of councils and public debates as literary products and not simply naïve documentary accounts adds to the impression that similar skills went into the production of both "real" and "fictitious" acts. Making good their (self-proclaimed) "victories" in public disputations generally required participants to edit and publish a transcript of the meeting: they found various ways to shape it to their own apologetic purposes. Modern editions of the acts of major councils are often based upon transcripts and collections produced in accordance with partisan ancient editorial practices.[136]

The similar approaches of Christian controversialists to "real" and "imaginary" debate were rooted in rhetorical strategies basic to Christian polemical argument. Even outside notarized transcripts and their literary siblings, what Brent Shaw has described as "virtual dialogue" was central to Christian controversy over doctrine and practice.[137] Inspired by techniques learned during rhetorical schooling, disputants were prone to reinvent their rivals in the texts that they wrote against them.[138] The refutation of heretical opponents entailed imagining (and deviously mischaracterizing) their views, before delivering a response. Virtual dialogue was thus the essential mode of polemical exegesis: he/they say this (which is wrong); in response, I/we say that (which is right).

These modes of virtual dialogue found widespread use in Vandal Africa. Christians continued to debate by proxy textual means. This included refutations in dialogue form, where an opponent's words or questions were followed by the author's responses. So Eugenius of Carthage (478/79–505?) is said to have written debates (*altercationes*) with leading Homoians.[139] Fulgentius, meanwhile, having been recalled from exile by Thrasamund, responded to a (now lost) text written and sent to him by the king by cutting and pasting ten of its statements and offering responses.[140] Like Augustine of Hippo in his fictive dialogues with real opponents,[141] Fulgentius seems to have exploited the plentiful opportunity that such texts provided for mischaracterization in picking or even inventing the words of his unlucky interlocutor. Thrasamund was clearly not best pleased with this methodology; the next time he sent Fulgentius a text, his messenger demanded an immediate response. When Fulgentius refused, the messenger did not allow him to take the text for later perusal, but Fulgentius still wrote *To Thrasamund*.[142] Obviously, debating orthodoxy with a Vandal king at the Hasding court involved

---

135. McLynn (1994), 124–49, esp. 127–28; Graumann (2002), 357–409.
136. E.g., Schwartz (1934); Graumann (2002), 352–57; see too Lancel (1972–91), 1:353–57.
137. Shaw (2011), 12, 424. See too Jacobs (2007), 293.
138. See, e.g., Humfress (2012), 330.
139. Ps.-Genn., *Uir. inlust.* 98 (ed. Richardson: 96); see also pp. 156–57.
140. Fulg., *Dict. Tras.* (ed. Fraipont); with *V. Fulg.* 21 (ed. Isola: 204–5).
141. Lim (1995), 96–98; Miles (2008), 136–37; Humfress (2012), 329–30.
142. Fulg., *Ad Tras.* 1.1 (ed. Fraipont: 97).

different considerations from a skirmish with a fellow cleric. Yet if Fulgentius tellingly avoided direct polemic against his royal debating partner—something far from absent in his other works—he otherwise treated him like a fellow ecclesiastical disputant.[143] Fittingly, the bishop himself later became an unknowing participant in Fabianus's dialogue. Fulgentius's repeated complaints in the surviving fragments of the ten-book *Against Fabianus*—"for I neither thought nor said those things that you saw fit to put under my name in fake minutes [*falsis gestis*]"—would have struck a chord with the opponents of his hero Augustine.[144] Fabianus might even have written an imaginary dialogue in which Fulgentius took the role that Vigilius assigned to Arius.

Virtual dialogue was not just for the page: it could be performed. In late-antique sermons, virtuosic preachers conjured religious deviants and acted out their refutation, voicing both their own role and the speech of those imaginary opponents.[145] In Vandal Africa, Quodvultdeus of Carthage was particularly prone to ventriloquize various deviants. His Arian appeared on numerous occasions, including one extended dialogue on the "inheritance" of the church in which the preacher exhorted his opponent to solicit Christ as their *iudex ordinarius* (a provincial governor in his judicial role).[146] The dialogue begins with deceptive agreement between Quodvultdeus and his interlocutor:

> What do you say, Arian? I want you to respond to my questions.
> [. . .]
> So tell me what I ask you: Do you believe in the omnipotent God the Father?
> You say, "I believe."
> I ask, Do you also believe in Jesus Christ his Son, our God and Lord?
> You say, "I believe."
> I ask, Do you believe that he was God and man, born in the Holy Spirit from the Virgin Mary?
> You say, "I believe."
> You do well. [. . .] So if you are with me in all things, why do we quarrel?[147]

Yet the preacher soon reveals the Arian's true colors.

> What do you say, brother? Is the Son equal to the Father?
> You say, "He is equal."

---

143. On Fulgentius and Thrasamund see pp. 160–63.

144. Fulg., *C. Fab.*, 14.1 (ed. Fraipont: 783). On the text see p. 66; Dossey (2003), 111, 115–16; Merrills and Miles (2010), 199.

145. Three examples: Uthemann (1998), esp. 143–45, 164–71; Lunn-Rockliffe (2007), 63–86, at 70; H. Müller (2012), 301–2.

146. E.g., Quod., *Adu. haer.*, esp. 6 (ed. Braun: 279–92); Quod., *De sym. I* 4 (ed. Braun: 312–17); Quod., *C. Iud., pag. et Arr.* 7–8 (ed. Braun: 235–37); Quod., *De acc. ad grat. I* 12 (ed. Braun: 450–51).

147. Quod., *Adu. haer.* 6.6.18, 6.7.21–25, 6.10.34–35 (ed. Braun: 280–81).

Ha! Now see how what is hidden will be made manifest. How do you say that the Son is equal to the Father? In operation or origin? Power or eternity? Or perhaps both?

You say, "God forbid. He is equal in operation and power, but not eternity. For how could it be that the begotten is equal to the unbegotten?"

Oh, here it is, the grief appears that was hiding within him—he who was acting as if he was my coheir. He was thought to possess [the inheritance] with me, but he wants to divide it.[148]

When rendered in textual form and set out on the page, the similarity of these performances to the imaginary debate transcripts is obvious. Quodvultdeus acted out the condemnations that Vigilius and others sought to script.

CONCLUSION

Christian authority figures never stopped having to "perform" their orthodoxy. If the almost industrial quantities of heresiological polemic produced by posthumously revered "Fathers of the Church" indicate anything, it is the need that late-antique Christian practitioners felt to continually establish their legitimacy and that of the ecclesiastical institution they represented. Clerics in Vandal Africa took up this challenge with enthusiasm. They wrote in the polemical genres that controversialists had developed to prosecute doctrinal disputes. Through these texts, they sought to persuade African Christians of the rightness of their cause and the error of their opponents. These conflicting claims about orthodoxy and heresy led to polemical debate. Dialogue was also a particularly suitable form for setting out those claims in the first place, as Vigilius of Thapsa and others demonstrated. To be sure, Vandal Africa has no debate text to rival the *Gesta* of the Conference of Carthage (411) or the verbatim transcripts of Augustine's public confrontations with Donatists, Manichaeans, and Arians. The polemical debates between Nicene and Homoian clerics in Vandal Africa cannot but seem detached compared with Augustine's works, which were so obviously embedded in the rough-and-tumble of ecclesiastical politics in the Roman province. Yet in their own way, the many acts of "virtual" polemical debate produced by the kingdom's clerics are equally revealing. The parallels between the literary forms and rhetorical strategies of these debates and their late Roman predecessors indicate a common patterning of ecclesiastical controversy whose relevance went beyond strictly textual issues. A culture of Christian polemical disputation continued in Vandal Africa. The omnipresence of familiar modes of textual combat demonstrates not only that clerics fought over the definition of true Christianity—as they always had—but also that the potential consequences of success and failure in this endeavor remained the same.

---

148. Quod., *Adu. haer.* 6.14.53–6.16.61 (ed. Braun: 282).

3

"What They Are to Us, We Are to Them"

Homoian Orthodoxy and Homoousian Heresy

> *In short, according to us they are heretics, but according to them they are not. For they consider themselves to be Catholics to such an extent that they defame us with the label of a heretical name. What they are to us, we are to them.*
> —SALVIAN OF MARSEILLE, ON THE GOVERNMENT OF GOD

Early in the fifth book of his *On the Government of God*, Salvian of Marseille states the blindingly obvious: fifth-century Homoians thought that they were Catholic Christians. This was as true in Vandal Africa as it was in Salvian's Gaul.[1] The authors of the few surviving Homoian texts articulate a confident self-image as the only true Christians; the same image is also apparent in Nicene reports on encounters with Arian opponents and their characterizations of Arian heresy. Basic assertions of the truth of their teaching and the legitimacy of their church were bolstered by use of the criteria of late-antique Christian orthodoxy, including councils, creeds, fathers, and numbers. The considerable evidence for adherence to Homoian Christianity in Vandal Africa should not be viewed simply as a response to the employment of coercive force by Vandal kings.[2] Frequent references by Nicene writers to the unnerving plausibility of their opponents and corresponding attempts to gloss it as heretical deception suggest the potential effectiveness of this self-presentation.[3] The Arians of Vandal Africa could have been seen as its orthodox Christians.

Epigraph. Salv., *Gub. Dei* 5.2.9 (ed. Lagarrigue: 316).

1. On Salvian and his work see Maas (1992); Lambert (1999); Lambert (2000); P. Brown (2012), 433–53.
2. See p. 19 n. 91.
3. E.g., Quod., *Adu. haer.* 6.10–11 (ed. Braun: 281); Quod., *C. Iud., pag. et Arr.* 22 (ed. Braun: 256–58); Fulg., *ABC.* 294–97 (ed. Isola: 52).

This is only half the story. As Salvian of Marseille recognized when discussing Vandal and Gothic Christians, Homoian self-identification as orthodox came with concomitant denunciation of Nicene Christians as heretics. In staking a monopolizing claim to true Christianity, Homoian controversialists in Vandal Africa categorized their opponents as Homoousians (the sect of ὁμοούσιος), a term in use since the fourth century. The label *Homoousian* gained force from its inclusion in royal antiheretical legislation. Homoian disputants further pursued the demonization of their opponents by portraying Nicene Christianity as similar to other heresies and tantamount to paganism. By rebaptizing Nicene Christians who entered their communities, Homoian clerics suggested both that Nicene baptism was inefficacious and that its recipients were not truly Christians. Homoian authors drew upon the discursive strategies of late-antique doctrinal polemic to delegitimize their opponents and seek greater credence for their own teaching and church. With royal support, the Homoians acted out Salvian's dictum. What the Arians had been, and remained, to the Catholics, the Homoousians would be to them.

HOMOIAN TEXTS FROM VANDAL AFRICA

Few Homoian texts are extant from Vandal Africa (or more generally). The triumph of Nicene Christianity and the infamy of Arian heresy dissuaded later scribes from intentional copying. A far greater volume of Homoian literature was produced than has survived. Nicene texts from Vandal Africa refer to specific authors and writings now lost and to debate encounters with active disputants. Seemingly prominent Homoian controversialists appear fleetingly as the recipients of pieces of Nicene polemic (which are often themselves no longer extant).[4] Homoian doctrine was not only propounded by the writings of contemporaries. In his *Dialogue against the Arians, Sabellians and Photinians*, Vigilius refers the reader to his (now lost) refutation of Palladius of Rataria's attack on Ambrose of Milan (itself now either fragmentary or lost). The literary output of this late fourth-century Homoian luminary was evidently available to readers in Vandal Africa, as it was in the mid-fifth century to the Homoian bishop Maximinus—Augustine's debate opponent—when he produced his *scolia* on *Parisinus Latinus* 8907.[5] It is telling that Vigilius justifies his writing of the *Dialogue* with a need to refute the many tractates of his heretical opponents.[6] The great disparity in the survival of

---

4. See the table of Homoian clerics in ch. 1, at p. 43; for a comparable list of contemporary Homoians, Dossey (2003), 110-16. On these debates see pp. 71-72, with notes.

5. Vig., *Dial. II* 3.27 (ed. Hombert: 394-95), with Gryson (1980), 80-81; Bouhot (1981); D. Williams (1995), 151. For an excellent account of the *scolia*, see McLynn (1996).

6. Vig., *Dial. I*, pref. I (ed. Hombert: 245).

Nicene and Homoian texts is misleading.[7] Supporters of both Trinitarian positions were active participants in contemporary Christian debate.

Those Homoian texts that survive are preserved either within Nicene works that condemn them or under false attributions to less controversial writers. Vandal kings (at least nominally) wrote four of the texts from which a Homoian perspective can be reconstructed. Huneric's anti-Homoousian edict of 24 February 484, after the Conference of Carthage, and, to a lesser extent, those of 20 May 483 calling the conference and 18 June 478/79 granting concessions to the Nicene Church contain Homoian arguments. All three are transmitted in Victor of Vita's *History of the Persecution*.[8] As chapter 2 discusses, Homoian doctrinal pronouncements sent by Huneric's successor-but-one, Thrasamund, to the Nicene bishop Fulgentius of Ruspe are also extant, albeit in the cut-and-paste format in which Fulgentius responded.[9] All four texts must be set in the context of the rulers' interests in ecclesiastical politics, which were not coterminous with those of the Homoian Church, and the specific interactions between king and churches that produced them.[10] Huneric's edicts are first and foremost legislative statements; their specifically legal mind-set and implications are of great importance.[11] At the same time, all of these texts were shaped by the justifications of contemporary Homoian clerics, who were specifically cited by Huneric in the edict of 484 and generally influential in the formation of both kings' ecclesiastical policies.[12] Thus, these texts can be used to consider how Homoian Christians in Vandal Africa presented themselves and how they substantiated this self-representation.

As well as excerpts from Thrasamund, the Fulgentian corpus preserves a sermon of the deacon Fastidiosus (as part of *Letter* 9) and apparent quotations and extensive paraphrase of the learned Homoian named Fabianus (in the surviving fragments of the ten-book *Against Fabianus*).[13] Two similar texts have been preserved independent of Nicene polemic, although, partly for that reason, their dates and provenance remain controversial. The first is the anonymous three-volume *Commentary on Job*, falsely attributed to Origen.[14] It probably originated as a set of sermons, given its frequent use of direct address to its audience and

---

7. An unnamed *libellus* against ὁμοούσιος, attacked by Ps.-Fulg., *Trin.* 2.23–26 (ed. Fraipont: 240), could also be a lost Homoian text; given the content of Ps.-Fulgentius's riposte, it probably refers to Huneric's edict of 484. See pp. 61–62.

8. *HP* 2.3–4, 2.39, 3.3–14 (ed. Lancel: 123–24, 139–40, 175–81). On 478/79 as the date for the edict see Delmaire (1987).

9. Fulg., *Dict. Tras.* (ed. Fraipont); see p. 82.

10. See ch. 5.

11. See pp. 96–103.

12. See p. 91.

13. Fastidiosus, *Sermo*; Fulg., *C. Fab.* (both ed. Fraipont). See also pp. 65–66.

14. *Comm. in Iob* (ed. Steinhauser).

tendency to drive home each clause of the biblical text through repetition. The exegete derives predominantly moral lessons from Job, but he also uses one biblical phrase to launch a stinging attack on the Homoousian heresy. This polemical passage, alongside a paragraph praising the martyrdom of Lucian of Antioch, marks the text as the product of a Homoian author. The *Commentary* has been attributed to the reign of Hilderic, although its recent editor contests this date, suggesting 380s Milan.[15] Neither argument is entirely convincing; as both provenances seem equally plausible, I will use the *Commentary* sparingly, to support other evidence.

A more straightforwardly packaged group of sermons is preserved in the *Verona Collection*, a codex produced in the latter part of the fifth century in Italy (and most likely Verona, hence its modern designation).[16] The manuscript contains a number of Homoian texts, including a set of sermons on Christian festivals. One of the sermons is for Cyprian's martyr day; the African church father is frequently cited across the collection. As a result of these features, as well as exact verbal parallels in pseudonymous sermons attributed to Augustine and Fulgentius, the collection's editor, Roger Gryson, has suggested an African origin.[17] Once again, this attribution remains tentative: Cyprian was a revered patristic authority beyond Africa, used prominently by the Homoian bishop Maximinus in his *scolia*, and sermons attributed to Augustine rarely make for a firm basis for comparison. As the only certain context for the use of the festal sermons is a Homoian community in Italy in the late fifth century, I will also use them sparingly.[18]

All of these authors characterize the Christianity to which they adhered in familiar terms: as true, apostolic, and Catholic (among other adjectives used by

---

15. Leslie Dossey (2003) notes that the commentary's Old Latin Bible citations concur most often with African authors. Thus, she suggests that its author used an African *Vetus Latina* and wrote in Vandal Africa, citing his Homoian sympathies and the plausibly post-Roman social relations of his moral lessons. Recent scholarship has followed her (e.g., Steinacher [2008], 250; though cf. the more ambivalent Steinacher [2011], 53 n. 21; Merrills and Miles [2010], 198, with n. 130 [though sceptical on dating to Hilderic]; Conant [2012], 179 n. 234); so I do, albeit with reservations. The editor, Kenneth Steinhauser, disagrees, suggesting 380s Milan ([2006], 9–47). His arguments against a necessarily African *Vetus Latina* as biblical source are judicious; the concordances could derive from separate translations of a common Antiochene Greek text (25–32). Nevertheless, his rebuttals of a Vandal African context are unconvincing, showing little knowledge of the period or its Christian literature (38–40). There is no compelling evidence for 380s Milan over 520s Africa. The problem is that the author is simply a Greek-reading, late-antique Homoian exegete with a congregation. That individual could be Auxentius of Durostorum (41–47) or a bishop in Vandal Africa. There is little to choose between them.

16. *De solemn.* (ed. Gryson).

17. Gryson (1982b), xx; for the quotations of Cyprian and verbal parallels to pseudonymous sermons, see the notes to *De solemn.* (ed. Gryson).

18. The use of the sermons in this codex for bilingual services is evidenced by Gothic glosses identifying the appropriate biblical reading or summarizing the content: see Gryson (1982a), 77–92; for their implications for Ostrogothic Italy, pp. 239–40.

late-antique Christians to describe correct belief and membership in the legitimate Christian community). They are joined in this conviction by the assorted Arians, real and imagined, who populate Nicene polemical texts. These Arians owe as much to Nicene heresiological conceptions of their opponents as to the reality of contemporary Homoian Christians. Even reports on genuine encounters recast them to some degree according to Nicene expectations of Arian heresy. Nevertheless, polemicists have their Arian characters put forward statements and arguments that chime with those of contemporary Homoians. The Arian characters may represent a caricaturing of Homoian Christianity, but to be effective a caricature has, in some distorted fashion, to resemble aspects of what it portrays. With careful handling, their statements can be used to amplify and supplement Homoian Christians' self-presentation in Vandal Africa.

HOMOIAN ORTHODOXY

As a matter of course, Homoian authors described themselves and their church using terms connoting possession of the true Christian faith.[19] In the edict of 24 February 484, Huneric condemns Africa's Nicene Christians to a series of punishments "if they are not converted to the true religion which we venerate and worship."[20] The deacon Fastidiosus went further in his sermon.[21] Having laid out a bipartite conception of heretical error (of the Donatists and the Homoousians), he stated that "among them, the holy mother, the Catholic Church, knows how to sing with Davidic sound [*Davidico murmure*]."[22] Later in the sermon, he restated this conception of a true and universal Homoian Church, speaking of "the Catholic faith, fleeing the difficulties of each and every error."[23] These contentions did not go unnoticed. Fulgentius's correspondent Victor, who brought this sermon to the bishop's attention, emphasized, "[Fastidiosus] claimed Catholicity [*catholicam*] for himself."[24]

A strident claim to orthodox Christianity is evident from the terminology that Homoians used. It was also expressed through their self-presentation as holders of the authoritative standard by which correct faith should be judged. The first excerpt from Thrasamund's text to Fulgentius cites a passage from the *Book of the Catholic Faith*, the document produced by the Nicenes for the Conference of Carthage. Thrasamund then states, "They do not lack this response, because they

---

19. Cf. Moorhead (2010), 427–29.
20. *HP* 3.12 (ed. Lancel: 180).
21. See pp. 65–66.
22. Fastidiosus, *Sermo* 3.43–44 (ed. Fraipont: 281); translation adapting Eno (1997), 389.
23. Fastidiosus, *Sermo* 5.88–89 (ed. Fraipont: 282); translation adapting Eno (1997), 391.
24. Fulg., *Ep.* 9, Victoris 4.72–73 (ed. Fraipont: 279). See too *Comm. in Iob* 1.74.27–32 (ed. Steinhauser: 204–5).

agree with our faith."[25] The Nicenes are permitted the specified doctrine (Christ was born not extrinsically but from God) because it matches Homoian teaching. The conference itself invoked this conception of how orthodoxy could be proved. In its aftermath, Huneric stated that he had called it because some Nicenes had claimed to hold the true faith. They were thus summoned to Carthage to debate with "our bishops" (the Homoians) to see if some part of their doctrine could be justified.[26] The basic assumption was that the latter had nothing to prove and could be arbiters of orthodoxy and heresy; it was for the Nicenes to prove themselves by Homoian standards.[27]

The dense criteria of orthodox self-representation supported these doctrinal standards. The arguments of both Thrasamund and Fastidiosus are thick with scriptural citations, as are those of the imaginary dialogues' Arian characters. The importance of direct justification from the Bible is repeatedly stressed.[28] In his edict convoking the Conference of Carthage, Huneric orders the Nicenes to prove their faith "specifically from the divine scriptures, by which it might be recognized if you hold the entire faith."[29] The edict of 24 February 484 then reports that the Homoian bishops at the conference also made this demand.[30] Thrasamund posed a similar challenge, stating, "They who irrationally presume to say that the Son was born from the substance of the Father, ought nevertheless to show through the scriptures how it might not be a false profession of error."[31] These demands took as their point of departure Homoian possession of the correct interpretation of scripture, which their Nicene opponents had to share to be orthodox. In Nicene texts, real and imaginary Arians similarly accentuate biblical testimonia and proof texts.[32] Homoians claimed an authoritative understanding of scripture that could defeat the errors of others.

This focus on justification from scripture came with a self-identification as inheritors of the apostolic tradition.[33] Vigilius places an emphatic statement to this effect in the mouth of his Homoian Arius after a reading of the Nicene Creed.[34] For Arius, "the decrees of that council were composed in reproach of the apostolic

---

25. Fulg., *Dict. Tras.* 1–3 (ed. Fraipont: 71) = *HP* 2.66 (ed. Lancel: 153); quotation at Fulg., *Dict. Tras.* 4 (ed. Fraipont: 71).

26. *HP* 3.3–5 (ed. Lancel: 175–76); see also pp. 157–58.

27. See also *Cer. c. Max.* 12–14 (ed. Baise: 262).

28. On Homoians and scripture see Gryson (1980), 175–79; Hanson (1988), 559–61; Durst (1998), 149; though cf. Heil (2011), 268. On justification from scripture in Vandal Africa, see pp. 59–60.

29. *HP* 2.39 (ed. Lancel: 140).

30. Ibid., 3.5 (176).

31. Fulg., *Dict. Tras.* 325–27 (ed. Fraipont: 79).

32. *C. Var.*, pref. 6–15 (ed. Schwank: 9); *Cer. c. Max.* 14–15 (ed. Baise: 262); Vig., *Dial. I = II* 1.14, 2.20 (ed. Hombert: 279–80, 337–38); *Coll. Pasc.* 4 (ed. H. Müller, Weber, and Weidmann: 78–80).

33. Gryson (1980), 177–79; Vaggione (2000), 40–42.

34. See p. 69.

faith." The heresiarch then argues that if Christians have to profess ὁμοούσοις, "the preaching of the apostles is false," since they had never used it. For the apostolic faith to be true, the Nicene Creed has to be false.[35] Apostolic Christianity is made identical to an unchanging Homoian Christianity, an orthodoxy followed by "the apostles and their disciples and all their successors in order."[36] The real Homoian Fabianus similarly presented Homoian Christianity as apostolic when he used an African version of the Apostles' Creed to buttress Trinitarian arguments. In his response, Fulgentius appears distinctly unimpressed: "foolishly, it seemed fitting to you to try to twist [*uelle . . . retorquere*] the rectitude of the creed around to your meaning by misunderstanding." Yet Homoian citation of this widely respected document—the "perfect tenor" of the apostles' faith, in Fulgentius's words—would have been more of a threat than this dismissive rebuttal suggests.[37]

The Apostles' Creed was not the only statement of faith that Homoians in Vandal Africa used. Huneric's edict of 24 February 484 justifies Homoian orthodoxy with reference to a universal council and its creed. Twice, Rimini and Seleucia (359) are said to represent a statement of true religion.[38] The Homoian bishops at the conference had asked the Nicenes to prove the scriptural validity of ὁμοούσιος or to condemn "that which was rejected by the thousand or more bishops who came together from the whole world at the Council of Rimini and [*uel*] at Seleucia."[39] Similarly, when he proscribed the "Homoousian faith," Huneric adduced as justification that it was "already condemned in a council by the sum total [*cuncto numero*] of so many bishops."[40] Huneric and the Homoian bishops deployed the authority of a universal council to support their Christian faction. Like earlier ecclesiastical apologists, they cited the great number who approved that creed.[41] In the prologue to his collection of proof texts the *Book on the Trinity*, Pseudo-Fulgentius mentions a similar Homoian argument, although this time the head count is 830 for Rimini alone. These references to almost innumerable attendees gain particular force given contemporary depictions of the Council of Nicaea. Its attendees numbered (according to tradition) a comparatively paltry, if biblically symbolic, 318. Pseudo-Fulgentius noted the importance of the arithmetic. He complained about "that which they pretend . . . ought to be believed by many, rather than few, because the Council of Nicaea was celebrated by 318 fathers,

---

35. Vig., *Dial. I = II* 1.19 (ed. Hombert: 286, 288).
36. Vig., *Dial. I = II* 1.19 (ed. Hombert: 287).
37. Fulg., *C. Fab.* 36.2, 36.1 (ed. Fraipont: 854). On the Apostles' Creed see Westra (1997); (2002), 154–81, for North Africa.
38. On this creed and its reception see p. 12.
39. *HP* 3.5 (ed. Lancel: 176).
40. Ibid., 3.12 (180).
41. On superior numbers as an apologetic strategy, see p. 35, n. 11.

while indeed they boast that at Rimini 830 were congregated."[42] According to the Homoians, the fathers of Rimini massively outnumbered those of Nicaea. The creed they approved was thus authenticated as a standard against which to judge contemporaries.

Sheer head count was one way to represent Homoian Christianity as orthodox. Nicene authors also present Homoian appeals to patristic authority and the prestige of individual fathers.[43] Sometimes these names may not have resonated among African Christians. The "Pascentius" of the *Conference of Augustine with Pascentius*, in his opening statement, follows the genuine Pascentius in citing Auxentius (which of the two namesake Homoian bishops is not specified) as a marker of correct Christianity.[44] Vigilius's authorship of a text against Palladius of Ratiaria and Pseudo-Fulgentius's excoriation of Ambrose's Milanese predecessor, Auxentius, also suggest that leading fourth-century Homoians were used.[45] The difficulty is that, within these Nicene texts, genuine Homoian claims to patristic authority easily become entangled with portrayals of Arian heretical genealogy.[46] There is considerable reason to doubt that contemporary Homoians afforded Arius the significance that their opponents suggest.[47] The extent to which men like the two Auxentii and Palladius represented stereotypical Arian hate figures is harder to judge. Whether these authorities were introduced out of a Nicene conception of Arian genealogy or to counteract a real Homoian perspective on the transmission of orthodoxy must remain an open question. There are nonetheless signs that Homoians in Vandal Africa commandeered an appropriate figure also reverenced in the African and Nicene Christian traditions.

Cyprian was a figure of particular esteem among Latin Homoians, not least, as Yves-Marie Duval has argued, because his statements on Christology are notoriously vague and could be claimed by almost all fourth-century disputants.[48] Cyprian's views on the efficacy of heretical baptism were also fitting for a Christian faction committed to a policy of rebaptizing Christians who had received the mys-

---

42. Ps.-Fulg., *Trin.* 3.69–72 (ed. Fraipont: 241); on this text, see pp. 61–62, 128–32. The number at Rimini had clearly undergone inflation: e.g., Aug., *Coll. cum Max.* 2.5–8 (ed. Hombert: 384): says it was 330; Hil., *C. Aux.* 13 (*PL* 10: 617A) = Durst (1998), 161, says 600 at Rimini and Seleucia. For 318 as symbolic: see Aubineau (1966).

43. Vig., *Dial. I = II* 1.17 (ed. Hombert: 284). See too *C. Fel.* 3, 5, 6, 7, 13 (*PL* 42: 1158, 1160, 1161, 1162, 1167).

44. See p. 74.

45. Vig., *Dial. II* 3.27 (ed. Hombert: 394–95); Ps.-Fulg., *Trin.* 3.85–90 (ed. Fraipont: 242). See too the praise of Lucian of Antioch at *Comm. in Iob* 2.31 (ed. Steinhauser: 295–96).

46. See p. 113.

47. See pp. 10–11.

48. Y.-M. Duval (1974), 207–23, at 221. See also Gryson (1980), 178; Hanson (1988), 561, 828; Vaggione (2000), 41–42.

teries from Nicene clergy.[49] The third-century Carthaginian bishop is approved as a Homoian father and guarantor of orthodoxy in the mid-fifth-century *Dissertation* of the Homoian Maximinus.[50] As noted above, the African sermons copied out in the late fifth-century Italian Homoian *Verona Collection* repeatedly cite him as an authority; even outside direct quotation, they are imbued with his language.[51] Among the homilies on Christian festivals, there is a sermon for his martyr day.[52] The Homoian preacher—perhaps himself a bishop of Carthage—not only uses Cyprian as a model Christian but also suggests that his audience has a special relationship with him: Cyprian is "our martyr."[53] The source of such confident appropriation is obvious. Homoians in Vandal Africa harnessed Cyprian's legacy by taking over his basilicas outside Carthage[54] and with them, according to Procopius of Caesarea, the annual Cypriana festival. The historian reports a Vandal/Arian (from his Eastern perspective the categories are coterminous) view of the transfer: "they belong to the Arians."[55] Just as he had been a touchstone for Catholics and Donatists alike in Roman Africa, the great African martyr would have been used to lend his prestige to Homoian claims of orthodoxy;[56] their church too could be the church of Cyprian.

This use of the authority of an African church father shows the extent to which Homoians could adapt their claims to suit the Christian culture of Africa. Whatever the original contexts of the Homoian Christianity supported by the Vandal kings in Africa—*barbaricum*, the Balkans, Spain, or even the African province itself—Homoians in the kingdom presented their faith with reference to the standards demanded of Christians in the late-antique Mediterranean. They called themselves Catholics or holders of true religion. They asserted exclusive possession of doctrine that faithfully reflected the teachings of scripture, a universal council, and at least one revered father. It is notable that, of many polemical possibilities, Nicene writers chose to portray their opponents as convinced of their own orthodoxy (if

---

49. Fournier (2012). On Cyprian and (re)baptism see Lancel (2002b), 163–64, 279–82; Shaw (2011), 102–3. On rebaptism see pp. 105–8.

50. Max., *Diss.* 11 (ed. Gryson: 151–53).

51. I owe this observation to David Riggs, who has a forthcoming paper on these sermons. Direct citation of Cyprian occurs at, e.g., *De solemn.*, 15.5 (ed. Gryson: 90). See also *C. Iud.* and *C. pag.* (both ed. Gryson).

52. *De solemn.* 12 (ed. Gryson: 80–82), "de natale sancti Cypriani"; for "birthday" as describing a martyr day, see Sizgorich (2009), 306 n. 45.

53. *De solemn.* 12 (ed. Gryson: 80): "ui(n)demiarumque rubor ad cruore(m) martyris nostri concordat."

54. *HP* 1.16 (ed. Lancel: 104); see too Bockmann (2013), 96–100; for the complaints of an anonymous Nicene sermon on Cyprian's martyr day, p. 186.

55. Proc., *BV* 1.21.17–25, quotation at 1.21.20–21 (ed. Dewing: 180–84, at 182); translation adapted from Dewing. On the Cypriana, see Patout Burns and Jensen (2014), 535–36.

56. See, e.g., Tilley (1997), 104; P. Brown (2000), 209.

misguidedly) and credible in how they asserted it (if deceptively). Many of the specific elements that Homoian writers marshaled to make this case were not uncontroversial, drawing on a peculiar conception of the transmission of orthodoxy. Certainly, the authority of the Council of Rimini or a figure like Auxentius could (and indeed would) be contested.[57] Other aspects went to the heart of Christian, and specifically African Christian, self-identification. To convince the Christians of post-imperial Africa to adhere to their faith, Homoian writers set out a persuasive case that theirs was the true church in the Vandal kingdom.

THE HERESY OF THE HOMOOUSIANS

When openly contested, orthodoxy had to be presented as a monopolizing claim.[58] Two Catholic groups could not go into one church. A convincing case then became as much about denigrating competing claimants as about self-justification: being orthodox required turning others into heretics. Homoian Christians sought to do this to their Nicene opponents. They categorized them as a particular heretical sect, detached from the true Christian community: the Homoousians. This term appears widely in Vandal Africa. Like the members of previous heresies in late antiquity, the Homoousians were accorded legal status as a criminalized Christian group, a definition certainly operative from 483 and most likely introduced in the reign of Geiseric. The activities of Homoian clerics and the emphases of Nicene polemical literature corroborate the efficacy of this heresiological and legal categorization. The construction of the imaginary dialogue texts in particular suggests a shift in the power relations between the Homoian and Nicene factions. These intensely legal texts are framed as authenticated minutes of conciliar and judicial proceedings and portray symbolically charged Nicene authorities vindicating the term ὁμοούσιος and, in one case, themselves against the specific charge of being Homoousians. Such responses show Nicene writers processing the potential consequences of their criminalization. Those portrayed as heretics in late antiquity were often forced to confront their opponents' heresiological conception of them. As Caroline Humfress has put it, "An individual accused of being a 'Priscillianist' had to defend him or herself from this charge by engaging with a normative expectation of what a 'Priscillianist' was, regardless of what the defendant 'actually' was, or at least understood themselves to be."[59] As well as the familiar Catholic-Arian dichotomy, African Christians possessed an alternative framework, backed by legal and political authority, within which to understand contemporary events in their church: a conflict between true Christians and Homoousian heretics.

---

57. See ch. 4.
58. See pp. 56–57.
59. Humfress (2007), 241.

From the outset, Homoian Christianity had been intentionally defined to exclude substance (οὐσία) language and, in particular, the term "of the same substance" (ὁμοούσιος). For Homoian Christians, these were unscriptural terms and novel usages.[60] The Creed of Rimini (359), the touchstone for Latin Homoian orthodoxy, states, "The word οὐσία, because it was established naïvely by the fathers though it was unknown to the people, brought scandal, and because the scriptures do not contain it, it has been resolved that this be removed and there be absolutely no mention of οὐσία regarding God in the future, because the divine scriptures nowhere made mention of οὐσία concerning the Father and Son. We declare that the Son is like the Father in all things, as the holy scriptures declare and teach."[61] Rimini's orthodoxy was thus formulated to counteract substance-based creeds, especially the Nicene. Heresiological terminology evolved to reflect this state of affairs. Numerous late fourth- and early fifth-century texts show Homoians labeling their opponents Homoousians, the heretics of ὁμοούσιος. This coinage features both in Homoian texts and in the indignant rejoinders of Nicene anti-Arian polemic.[62] Nicenes were not the only Christians in Vandal Africa who could throw a time-honored heretical name at their opponents.

Homoians in Vandal Africa seem to have used this label frequently.[63] In his response to the Homoian Fastidiosus, Fulgentius refers to the term as the name that "the Arians are accustomed to call us."[64] Contemporary Homoian texts feature several references to Homoousians or attacks on ὁμοούσιος as definitive of Nicene error. In his sermon, Fastidiosus laid out a classic, bipartite conception of heresy, in which Homoian Christianity acted as a via media. Those heresies were "the Homoousians asserting the inseparable and individual Trinity, and that the Son was not less than the Father and the unbegotten Father was not the creator of his Son, and the Donatists also preaching that the good are polluted by communion with the bad."[65] The *Commentary on Job* also singles out the Nicene party for an extended attack. They were "the trinomial sect and heresy of the three gods," "called, in the Greek language, the triad, or *homoousios*."[66] To their opponents,

60. Hanson (1988), 559, 827 (with n. 15).
61. Full text (preserved only in Greek): Ath., *De syn.* 8.7 (ed. Opitz: 236).
62. "Letter of Auxentius" = Max., *Diss.* 26, 28, 29 (ed. Gryson: 161–62); *Serm. Arian.* 34 (ed. Hombert: 172); Aug., *C. serm. Arian.* 36 (ed. Hombert: 252–53); Aug., *C. Iul.* 1.75 (ed. Zelzer: 91–92); *Alt. Her.* (ed. Caspari: 145). See too *homousionista* in the early fifth-century Ps.-Ath., *De trin.* 3.225 (*PL* 62: 257B), with C. Müller (2012), 28 n. 38.
63. Parsons (1994), 99; Modéran (2003), 36; H. Müller (2008), 39; Weber (2008), 9. Merrills and Miles (2010) use it as a nonpejorative term in opposition to "Arian."
64. Fulg., *Ep.* 9.1.17–18 (ed. Fraipont: 284). See also Fulg., *Dict. Tras.* 657–59 (ed. Fraipont: 87); Ps.-Fulg., *Trin.* 2.18–20 (ed. Fraipont: 239).
65. Fastidiosus, *Sermo* 2.38–42 (ed. Fraipont: 281).
66. *Comm. in Iob* 1.75.2–3, 1.75.6–7 (ed. Steinhauser: 205). See also Fulg., *Dict. Tras.* 568–80 (ed. Fraipont: 85).

Nicene Christians represented a heretical sect, defined by their use of that unscriptural term.

The naming of a particular heresy was an important means of delegitimation.[67] The Homoians' use of the term *Homoousian* presented Nicene Christians as a sect that had splintered off from the main body by following something other than Christ. In this case it was a term rather than a man, as Pseudo-Fulgentius noted: "Assuredly, they judge a great crime to be attached to the Catholic faith, since they call its disciples Homoousians or One-Substantialists, as if *homoousios* or the substance of God contains the name of some man, just as the authors of diverse heresies ordain that the sect of their name must be preached to their disciples."[68] A comprehensive list of heresies follows, both ancient and recent, through which he labors his (rather pedantic) point. "Just as Simonians from Simon, Menandrians from Menander, Marcionites from Marcion, Valentinianists from Valens [Valentinus], Manichaeans from Mani,"[69] and ten more follow, so Homoousians from ὁμοούσιος. The primary intention of the pseudonymous author may have been to lampoon a supposed misapplication of heresiological rhetoric—who was this Homoousios, anyway?—but his thorough catalog also identifies the implications of this naming, which was not as ridiculous as he made it seem. The danger for Nicene Christians was that they could become yet another in a long line of heretical sects that had forsaken the path of true Christian doctrine. Through their labeling as Homoousians, their claim to be Christians was made illegitimate, in contradistinction to Homoian orthodoxy.

OLD LAWS FOR NEW HERETICS

Heresiological labeling was a potentially damning tool of defamation in late antiquity, but it was not always effective alone. To strengthen the capacity of this name-calling to shape the Christian community and the society in which it was embedded, Christian disputants often turned to the state.[70] Once made law, heresiological categories gained extra force. Edicts against named heretical sects gave Christian disputants leverage. When enforced, these laws generally resulted in the loss of public churches, exile for clerics, and civil disabilities for the laity.[71] Even if the original political will for enforcement had evaporated or had never truly been

---

67. The scholarship on heresiological terminology is voluminous. See esp. Shaw (1992), 5–14; Shaw (2011), 343–44; also Lyman (1993), 45–47; Wiles (1993), 40; Burrus (1995), 102–3; King (2003), 23–24; Ayres (2004), 2–3, 13; Gwynn (2007a), 5–7, 171; Humfress (2007), 222–23; Av. Cameron (2008), 105, 107; Iricinschi and Zellentin (2008b), 2.

68. Ps.-Fulg., *Trin.* 2.46–51 (ed. Fraipont: 240).

69. Ibid., 2.51–63 (240–41), for the full list.

70. On law and orthodoxy, see esp. Humfress (2007), 217–68.

71. For the provisions of late Roman legislation see Rougé and Delmaire (2005), 69–79.

there, the continued existence of such constitutions left the threat of prosecution dangling over the heads of those who could be defined as such. Controversialists could exploit their existence to threaten legal proceedings against individuals or whole communities. The potential mobilization of the coercive machinery of the late-antique state was a powerful disincentive. As a consequence, laws consistently shaped the power relations of ecclesiastical conflicts. Late Roman Africa supplies perhaps the definitive example. Catholic lobbying of the late Roman state in the 390s and 400s secured the application of the harsh terms of Theodosian antiheretical legislation to the Donatists. This process culminated in the Conference of Carthage (411) and an edict of unity that (at least theoretically) folded the Donatist Church into its Catholic rival. The law, in combination with continued imperial favor, tilted toward the Catholics what had previously been a broadly even balance of power.[72] Those intense negotiations and the previous century of interactions with the late Roman state shaped African Christian conceptions of secular authorities and their role (whether salutary or pernicious) in ecclesiastical affairs. In that sense, they cast the mold for the political agency of churchmen and the legislative interventions of kings in the new controversy.

Homoian categorization of their Nicene opponents as heretics received legal backing in Vandal Africa. While adopting Homoian Christianity as the legislated standard for orthodoxy in their realm, the Vandal rulers took their cue from Homoian heresiology to mark Nicene Christians out as Homoousian heretics. Just as with late Roman Africa's Donatist controversy, these efforts peaked with a conference in Carthage, followed by an antiheretical law.[73] Crucially, Huneric's two edicts regarding the Conference of Carthage address the Nicene bishops and their congregations as *omousiani*.[74] In the conference's aftermath, this group was suppressed and prescribed to join the true (Homoian) church, in the law of 24 February 484: "For this reason it is necessary for all Homoousians, who are well known to have held and continued to hold the substance of an evil persuasion of this kind, to be bound by these constitutions. . . . All those implicated in the errors of the abovementioned Homoousian faith, which has already been condemned in a council by the sum total of so many bishops, we order to abstain from every one of the aforementioned matters and undertakings."[75] For the purposes of the conference and the legislation that emerged from it, the Homoousians were a criminalized heretical sect defined by their use of the heterodox term ὁμοούσιος.

The edict's drafter was well aware of what this decision entailed. The text summarizes the content of later Roman emperors' antiheretical legislation and applies it

---

72. See (best) Hermanowicz (2008), 83–228; Shaw (2011), 490–586.
73. See p. 16 nn. 78–79.
74. *HP* 2.39, 3.4, 3.12 (ed. Lancel: 139–40, 175, 179–80).
75. Ibid., 3.12 (179–80); first part of translation adapted from Moorhead (1992b), 68.

to the Homoousians, even quoting a long schedule of fines verbatim from Honorius's 412 edict against the Donatists.⁷⁶ That this quotation came in a new edict of unity promulgated after a new Conference of Carthage itself suggests a desire to reenact the role reversal that Catholic lobbyists had previously achieved. If the close attention of the king and his agents to the minutiae of the earlier conference were not enough,⁷⁷ the edict provides explicit confirmation. Its prologue announces its theme: "It is approved that it is of the triumphal power of royal majesty to turn around evil designs against their authors."⁷⁸ The fifth paragraph clarifies its precise import: "Therefore it is necessary and most just to turn round against them that which is contained in those laws [*quod ipsarum legum continentia demonstratur*], which, since the emperors of various times were induced to error with them, happened then to be promulgated."⁷⁹ The Vandal king (or his drafter) knew how antiheretical laws were made and what they were supposed to achieve.

This specific legal categorization was in force not merely in the last two years of Huneric's reign. Huneric's edict of 20 May 483 convoking the conference implies that anti-Homoousian constitutions had existed under his predecessor, Geiseric: "Huneric, king of the Vandals and Alans, to all the Homoousian bishops. It is well known that not once but very often it has been forbidden that your priests should hold assemblies at all in the territories of the Vandals [*in sortibus Wandalorum*], lest by their seduction they might subvert Christian souls."⁸⁰ Victor of Vita's *History* makes it abundantly clear that the Nicene Church suffered proscription as a heretical sect at the very least within the principal area of Vandal settlement, the province of Africa Proconsularis, for much of Geiseric's reign.⁸¹ Following late Roman protocols for dealing with heretics, public worship was banned, new ordinations forbidden, a number of bishops sent into exile, and church property confiscated.⁸² Huneric's edict of 20 May 483 places those policies within the framework of legal actions against Homoousian heretics. Similarly, the edict of 484 portrays the conference as the result of an appeal by a heretical group (the Homoousians) against the orders of both Geiseric and Huneric.⁸³

Whether this is an accurate depiction of Geiseric's policies is an open question; no legislation survives. Victor of Vita merely states that "it had been forbidden

---

76. See p. 16 n. 79.
77. Cataloged by Fournier (2013).
78. *HP* 3.3 (ed. Lancel: 175).
79. Ibid., 3.7 (176–77); translation adapted from Moorhead (1992b), 66.
80. *HP* 2.39 (ed. Lancel: 139).
81. On this geographical delimitation (which did not always apply in practice), see p. 181.
82. See esp. Fournier (2008), 212–63; Merrills and Miles (2010), 180–81; Conant (2012), 161–70.
83. *HP* 3.3 (ed. Lancel: 175); see also pp. 157–58. Legal recognition of Homoian heresiological terminology could also be mirrored in the concern for the legality of the term ὁμοούσιος in Vigilius's dialogue: see pp. 100–103.

under King Geiseric that spiritual assemblies happen."[84] This vagueness might cast doubt upon the existence of a formal edict deploying specific heresiological terminology. However, Victor is not particularly forthcoming on the rest of Geiseric's legislative activity, referring only to the Vandal king's promulgating a decree appropriating movable wealth in the conquest's aftermath ("proponit decretum") and making orders ("praeceperat"/"praecepit").[85] It is unlikely that Victor, in portraying Vandal rule as illegitimate tyranny, would have wished to provide any more evidence of genuine lawgiving than was absolutely necessary.[86] Huneric's edicts for the conference were required for his narrative and would have been readily to hand in the mid-480s; Geiseric's were not necessary and perhaps were not easily accessible.[87] It remains possible that the edict of 20 May 483 saw Huneric recast his father's actions as precedent for his own. Huneric's edict could just as easily cite the precise legal formulation of Geiseric's policies. In either case, Nicene Christians were certainly defined and treated as heretics under Geiseric, according to late Roman legal standards, whether or not they were as yet specifically Homoousian heretics.

Nicene Christians were certainly proscribed as Homoousians in laws from 483–84 at the latest and remained categorized as such after Huneric's death. The particularly intense enforcement of Huneric's legislation may have eased, but these changing circumstances did not affect the potential force of the legal categorization. Those defined as sectaries in legal texts remained vulnerable even if the immediate political climate of their criminalization had shifted. The short historical text that Theodor Mommsen dubbed the *List of the Kings of the Vandals and Alans* records only that Gunthamund recalled first Eugenius of Carthage and, seven years later, the rest of the Nicene clergy, returning some churches to them.[88] These were acts of judicial clemency; there is nothing to say that the law was revoked. In any case, the reign of Thrasamund brought further coercive measures against Nicene Christians and was the context for many of the extant references to Homoousians. The edict of 484 and new laws that followed it would have continued to inhibit the Nicene faction at least until Hilderic, on his accession in 523, recalled exiled bishops, permitted new ordinations, and returned expropriated churches.[89] Even then the edict may not have been repealed; once more, this could have represented clemency regarding its application.

---

84. *HP* 2.1 (ed. Lancel: 122).
85. Ibid., 1.12, 1.43, 1.51 (102, 116, 121).
86. For Victor on Vandal tyranny see p. 9 n. 44.
87. For a similar point on Victor's preservation of laws, see Vössing (2014), 84.
88. *Lat. reg. Vand. Alan.*, s.a. 487, 494 (ed. Steinacher: 165–66), with Steinacher (2004), 177–78; see also Fournier (2008), esp. 212–63; Fournier (2013).
89. On Hilderic see pp. 163–64. For all of the details here, see Merrills and Miles (2010), 201–3.

DISPUTING THE LAW

Legal and political marginalization of Nicene Christians gives an extra bite to references to Homoousian heresy in Vandal Africa. When Homoian Christians slung this insult at opponents, they were not just appealing to a long-standing conception of what constituted heresy within their own Christian community. To label an individual or community Homoousian constituted a potential criminal accusation. The name bore an implied threat and alluded to compromising political circumstances. To present oneself in a way that could be inferred as Homoousian in either doctrinal writings or public debate risked incurring the harsh penalties laid out in Vandal legislation. Of course, laws do not work on their own. To have any impact on the way people act or think, they must be implemented, which in late-antique Africa meant that individuals had to be disposed to invoke them and representatives of the state had to be willing and able to enforce them (see chapter 7). Unfortunately, there is no direct evidence for the prosecution of a Homoousian in Vandal Africa. Many Nicene Christians were treated as heretics, but reports on that treatment do not allow a clear sense of whether judicial proceedings were involved and, if so, of what sort. From a number of references to judges, advocates, and legal culture, it is clear that secular courts were still available in the Vandal period.[90] Opportunities were there for individuals to seek the application of such laws in specific cases. Christian polemical literature implies that the potential invocation of these laws did affect the thinking of contemporaries and that the legal framing of the Homoousians as a proscribed sect had familiar consequences for ecclesiastical power relations in Africa.

The activities of Homoian clerics are suggestive. As Andy Merrills and Richard Miles have noted, those in early sixth-century Africa repeatedly adopted the demoralizing tactics used by earlier African Catholic controversialists: "Nicene opponents were to be directly engaged and challenged to public debate whenever possible."[91] Homoian clerics now had the position of supremacy that had served Catholic controversialists so well. Nicene disputants were in a double bind. When they sought to distinguish their orthodoxy from their opponents' heresy by presenting a consubstantial Trinity, they laid themselves open to a charge of heresy. If they stayed silent on that topic, it might appear that they could not respond or, worse, that they agreed with their opponents. This could be one of the reasons for the frequency with which Nicene texts from Vandal Africa were transmitted under assumed names.[92] Homoian controversialists could debate their rivals with such confidence precisely because of this legal support.

---

90. See p. 7, with n. 32 for references.
91. Merrills and Miles (2010), 199.
92. Cf. Parsons (1994), 422, which explains the tendency toward pseudepigraphy in terms of specifically political risks.

A number of features evident within Nicene polemical literature of the period similarly suggest the effects of proscription. Again and again, Nicene authors sought to prove the validity of ὁμοούσιος, or the consubstantiality and coequality it entailed, as an appropriate and indeed necessary expression of the relationship of the Trinity. They used various tactics. The weakness of ὁμοούσιος, and the problem that Homoian writers identified with it, had always been its absence from scripture. When not trafficking in (rather dubious) biblical texts using the word *substance*,[93] suggesting implausible translations,[94] or asserting that their opponents effectively professed three substances (τριούσιος),[95] Nicene authors sought to shift from solely scriptural proof to logical arguments. A recurring tactic was a demonstration that the Homoians were equally guilty of using unscriptural or novel terminology, be it "unbegotten," "Catholic," or even "Christian" itself. Once they felt that the Homoians had been hoist by their own petard, Nicene writers used a less literalist exegesis to argue that ὁμοούσιος alone conveyed the scriptural relationship between God the Father and God the Son.[96] Nicene concern to justify ὁμοούσιος with specific reference to the terms upon which their opponents contested its validity is striking. This was not an inevitable part of anti-Arian polemic; earlier Latin Nicene writers had been leery of discussing the Greek term.[97] The frequency with which African authors returned to it in the Vandal period must relate to its central role in their denunciation and legal proscription.

The fictitious legal proceedings of the *Conference of Augustine with Pascentius* and the two versions of Vigilius's *Dialogue* show Nicene writers challenging their heresiological categorization.[98] Within these imaginary dialogues, ὁμοούσιος is taken as definitive of Nicene Christianity; its legal vindication against Arian charges of unscriptural heterodoxy is necessary for that faith to be taken as Catholic.[99] In Vigilius's first edition, once Arius and Athanasius are one-on-one, Arius immediately has the Nicene Creed read out and attacks ὁμοούσιος as an unscriptural novelty. Discussion of Arius's demand that Athanasius show the term specifically written or placed ("proprie scriptum/positum") in the Bible takes up the

---

93. *HP* 2.58–59 (ed. Lancel: 149–50), with Lancel (2002a), 310 n. 243.

94. Ps.-Fulg., *Trin.* 2.28–43, 2.63–68 (ed. Fraipont: 240, 241), with the following quotation at 2.66–68: "ego et pater unum sumus; quod (ut dictum est) uerbum e uerbo translatum, homousion patres statuerunt."

95. Fulg., *Dict. Tras.* 657–60 (ed. Fraipont: 87); see also p. 105. This assertion is somewhat misleading, given that Rimini specifically banned substance language (see p. 95).

96. *HP* 2.56–57 (ed. Lancel: 148–49); Fulg., *Dict. Tras.* 642–66 (ed. Fraipont: 87–88); Vig., *Dial. I = II* 1–2 (ed. Hombert: 253–354); Vig., *Dial. II* 3 (ed. Hombert: 355–95); *Coll. Pasc.* 11–18 (ed. H. Müller, Weber, and Weidmann: 84–118).

97. H. Müller (2008), 39–40.

98. See pp. 69–75.

99. See also *C. Fel.* 3, 6 (*PL* 42: 1158, 1161).

rest of the first book until the judge, Probus, calls a stalemate, as Arius is equally guilty for his own (polemically constructed) belief in three substances (τριούσιος).[100] Most strikingly, the *Conference* all but puts Augustine of Hippo on trial for Homoousian heresy.[101] The judge, Laurentius, ends the *cognitio* by saying, "So then, even *homoousios*, which was called into doubt by your [Pascentius's] proposal, although it was not written, nevertheless that thing which lies hidden in the word is true. Let the unity be accorded due honor, lest injury should be done rashly to the Trinity."[102] The final and inevitable proof of Augustine's orthodoxy is based entirely on the legitimacy of ὁμοούσιος.

These texts act as commentaries on the criminalization of Nicene Christians as Homoousian heretics. Through alternative judicial proceedings, the authors sought to undermine the justifications given for their proscription. "Athanasius" and "Augustine" are both originally asked to prove their orthodoxy by showing that ὁμοούσιος was "written in the Bible": the precise demand that the Nicene delegates at the Conference of Carthage (484) faced and presumably the earlier rationale for the banning of Nicene Christianity.[103] These Nicene heroes' ability to prove their orthodoxy, when combined with the (in one case eponymous) probity of the judges, was meant to highlight a miscarriage of justice. Use of the Greek term should have resulted not in the categorization of Nicene Christianity as a heresy but rather in its recognition as Catholic. As Augustine puts it in his closing oration, "Far be it that we, being Catholics in the whole world, should blush that we are called by some people who do not understand the Greek word, because of the true faith of one and the same substance, Homoousians, because we rejoice that we are called, from the Greek name of Christ, Christians."[104] In these texts, proof of this Greek word's legitimacy brings victory to the Nicene avatars. For the reader, it was supposed to contrast pointedly with current circumstances. In lieu of a genuine judicial triumph in Vandal Africa, these courtroom dramas conveyed the unjust nature of Nicene proscription.

At the same time, the dialogues demonstrate the potential consequences of anti-Homoousian legislation and its effects on the ecclesiastical balance of power. Like Athanasius in the *Dialogue*, Nicene Christians (especially clerics) could be made to justify their profession of the Nicene Creed in judicial proceedings. Like Augustine in the *Conference*, they could face accusations of Homoousian heresy.

---

100. Vig., *Dial. I = II* 1.16–26 (ed. Hombert: 282–301); see also p. 123. "Proprie scriptum/positum" is at Vig., *Dial. I* 1.22.6, 1.23.12, with numerous variations in 1.19–26 (ed. Hombert: 286–301, at 294, 296).

101. See pp. 73–75.

102. *Coll. Pasc.* 18 (ed. H. Müller, Weber, and Weidmann: 118).

103. "Written in the Bible" ("scriptum in Lege"): ibid., 7, 15.83 (82, 98); "specifically from the divine scriptures" ("proprie de/ex diuinis scripturis"): *HP* 2.39, 3.5 (ed. Lancel: 140, 176); see also n. 101. For possible categorization as Homoousians under Geiseric, see pp. 98–99.

104. *Coll. Pasc.* 15.152–56 (ed. H. Müller, Weber, and Weidmann: 108).

Of course, as these texts reach their conclusions, they diverge from actual judicial procedure. The Nicene defendants succeed in proving Nicene Christianity to be the true faith, whereas in an actual legal case an individual accused of Homoousian heresy would have needed to prove his own individual orthodoxy against contemporary legal norms. The methods of proof in these imagined Christian courtrooms are also rather more exegetical than any real *uir clarissimus* would have permitted. Nonetheless, even the finales of these idealized Nicene victories could be seen as nods to contemporary circumstances. Athanasius and Augustine are vindicated, but they do not gain the total victory of some earlier imaginary disputants.[105] Minucius Felix, Adamantius, and Jerome awarded their protagonists the submission of their heretical interlocutors as disciples to their orthodox teaching.[106] More recently, the real Augustine had sought to make his debate opponents recant.[107] In the Vandal-era dialogues, the Arians remain recalcitrant. Arius even hints that he will appeal to the imperial court to have the sentence in Athanasius's favor overruled, a strategy that the judge Probus explicitly states he will seek to avert, partly by filing his own report to the emperor. Determined Homoian accusers would likely have had the same confidence in taking an appeal to the palace at Carthage.[108] The dialogue authors were not blind to the realities of their disfavor. The limits of what Nicene disputants could achieve conditioned even these ideal scenarios.

These judicial vindications were a far cry from the Nicene faction's genuine status in Vandal Africa. Unlike Augustine in the *Conference of Augustine with Pascentius*, Nicene Christians remained Homoousian heretics before the law. The significance of this development should not be underrated. It gave this Homoian category of Christian error, not unpersuasive in itself, the force of law. The extensive contemporary Nicene commentaries on ὁμοούσιος and the heresiological label derived from it—unusual in anti-Arian writing—make plain the results. To bolster their fellow Christians' identification of their church as Catholic, Nicene authors in Vandal Africa deliberately chose (to quote Humfress once more) to engage with the "normative expectation" of what a Homoousian was.[109] In so doing, they adopted the role normally forced upon a heretic. The elaborate legal scenarios of the imaginary dialogues show these Nicene clerics fully cognizant of the specific and dangerous implications of antiheretical laws. Those constitutions had the capacity to reduce Nicene Christianity to a heretical sect in the eyes of contemporaries, just as they had done in the past to the Donatists and, of course, the Arians.

---

105. H. Müller (2008), 36.
106. Voss (1970), 40–50, 135–48, 187–91.
107. See, e.g., Lim (1995), 99–102.
108. Vig., *Dial. I = II* 2.27–28 (ed. Hombert: 352–54).
109. Humfress (2007), 241.

GUILT BY ASSOCIATION

The designation of a Homoousian heresy divorced Nicene Christians from the church and pushed them to the margins of the Christian community. Disputants convinced of their church's universality were rarely content to permit their opponents even this uneasy liminality. As Rebecca Lyman has shown, polemicists often sought to assimilate an individual type of heterodoxy to more vilified heresies like Manichaeism and even non-Christian religions like paganism and Judaism.[110] The result was to congregate all these groups in one discursive space marked "error." At its most extreme, the elision of categories served to move a heretical group not merely to the margins but beyond the boundaries of Christian faith altogether. Heretics were robbed of their claim (already tenuous) to Christianity; in reality, they were (all but) pagans or Jews. Homoian Christians in Vandal Africa adopted this strategy against their Nicene opponents. Homoousian heresy was associated with other heresies; it was also presented as tantamount to paganism. Through guilt by association, Homoians sought to widen the gulf between their true Christianity and their opponents' error.

In his sermon to "most learned Christians," the Homoian deacon Fastidiosus fits the Homoousian and Donatist sects to the same psychological profile.[111] He argues that heretics are obstinate and self-harming, hurting themselves with the "life-giving words," the "surgical instruments" by which they could be saved.[112] Having sketched out this essential irrationality, Fastidiosus specifies that "for a long time now, a bipartite error has crept in": the teachings of the Homoousians and the Donatists. In spite of their doctrinal differences, these African heretics are made equivalent. This was a bold and far-reaching contention. Donatism remained a category of heresy attacked by Nicenes and Homoians alike in Africa, even if actual surviving communities have slipped out of the historical record.[113] For many in Africa this name would have remained a powerful symbol of wrongheaded Christian error. Fastidiosus's sermon tarred the Homoousians with the same brush.

The anonymous Homoian commentator on Job set Homoousian heresy in a much broader temporal and geographical context: the history of the world and of all previous heresies. The "three bands" of demons sent by the devil in the Book of Job, according to the commentator, fought against God from creation, through the era of the prophets and Christ's lifetime into the time of the apostles.[114] In the "most recent times," the devil fought not just with three bands but "in a thousand ways

---

110. Lyman (1993); (2007), 299. Such guilt by association was intimately related to the genealogical arguments that underpinned heresiological accusations: see p. 57 n. 10.
111. Fastidiosus, *Sermo* 2.21, 2.27–43 (ed. Fraipont: 281); see also pp. 65–66.
112. On such medical imagery see Gaddis (2005), 146–47.
113. On disappearing Donatists see p. 37 n. 25.
114. *Comm. in Iob* 1.73 (ed. Steinhauser: 203), glossing Job 1:17, "the horsemen made three bands."

and many different ways [sic]." He "contends and tempts, he plots, he seduces and subverts, through a multitude of heresies, through innumerable errors, through abundant seductions, through pseudo-Christs and pseudoteachers, of which this world is full, ... who ... while having the name of Christians and the appearance of piety, are full up of errors and impieties and seductions."[115] From these manifold iterations of non-Christian belief came one particular heresy in whose "type and figure" the devil had made the three bands in the first place: "the trinomial sect and heresy of the three gods, which has filled the whole world like a shadow."[116] In this passage, Homoousian heresy becomes the culmination of the devil's efforts to undermine the church. It is assimilated to the thousands of other heresies that populate the world, but it is not merely another of these. It is the very form and image of heresy and anti-Christianity itself. The Homoian commentator makes Homoousian heresy into the archetype of all non-Christian error.[117]

A more specific but no less harmful example of such heresiological elision is given by Thrasamund as part of his first text to Fulgentius. After citing biblical *testimonia* portraying Son and Holy Spirit as separate from the Father, he objects that the term ὁμοούσιος turned Christians into pagans: "Since attention is not paid to the divine laws and sacraments, people are made professors of paganism, those [i.e., pagans] who said *homoousios* before the arrival of the savior, of which also the heretics have been made professors, since they assert that the Father and Son and Holy Spirit are one God."[118] His objection neatly assimilates Homoousian heresy to paganism and presents it as fundamentally un-Christian. Ὁμοούσιος becomes part of pre-Christian pagan belief; the heretics who use it within their creed are said to have been turned into pagans. Homoousian heresy is ascribed a genealogy entirely separate from Christianity.

Homoian insinuation of the non-Christianity, and possible paganism, of Nicene adherents is implicit in their treatment of those who joined their congregations. Repeated complaints in polemical texts suggest that many Homoian clerics rebaptized Nicene Christians.[119] For Nicene disputants, this was a grave error that transgressed the scriptural injunction of "one God, one faith, one baptism" (Ephesians 4:5). According to the position set out by the see of Rome in the third century and adopted by African Catholics by the early fourth, Christians baptized by heretics required only the imposition of hands to become full members of a Catholic community. The term *rebaptism* is, of course, something of a misnomer, as those who

---

115. *Comm. in Iob* 1.74 (ed. Steinhauser: 203–4).

116. Ibid., 1.75 (205).

117. Note that the attribution of this text to Vandal Africa is contested: see pp. 87–88.

118. Fulg., *Dict. Tras.* 568–80, at 576–80 (ed. Fraipont: 85). The claim that ὁμοούσιος was a pagan term may stem from earlier polemic against οὐσία language as philosophical: see, e.g., Brennecke (2008b), 130.

119. See Parsons (1994), 156–57; Fournier (2012); Whelan (2014a), 515–16.

conducted it saw it as the sole true baptism of the Ephesian proof text; the recipient's previous initiation had not been efficacious.[120] The baptism of those previously baptized by heretics was a practice with a long history in the African province. For many African Christian communities it seems to have been a norm going back to the time of Cyprian (at least).[121] Its frequent use by Donatist clerics had been a particular bone of contention in the fourth and early fifth centuries,[122] and indeed the heretical nature of rebaptism formed a key part of the Catholic faction's successful campaign to have the Donatists subjected to the imperial court's antiheretical legislation.[123] The Donatists were not the only followers of this rite in late Roman Africa. Already in the late 420s, Augustine had heard rumors that Homoian clerics had rebaptized consecrated virgins in the entourage of Boniface the count of Africa and (perhaps as a result of this story) generalized it as a feature of Arian heresy in his *On Heresies*.[124] A number of other Christian communities across the late-antique Mediterranean adopted rebaptism as a means of stressing their church's exclusive possession of sacramental authority.[125]

The cultural baggage of this practice within African Christianity makes it difficult to assess whether the frequency of Nicene complaints accurately maps onto the emphasis that Homoian Christians placed upon it. The only secure reading of this polemic is that it stems from an African Nicene understanding of what constituted heresy.[126] It is nonetheless clear that many Homoian clerics did adopt this practice and used it for the same purposes of boundary management for which Donatists (and others) had previously deployed it. Only a single Homoian justification of rebaptism survives: Fabianus (as quoted or paraphrased by Fulgentius) asserted that Nicene baptism was of "no moment or substance."[127] This suggests that, like the Donatists before them, Homoian clerics considered their opponents' sacraments invalid. So for them, this so-called second baptism was really the single true baptism of Ephesians 4:5. The Homoousian faithful had not yet fully become Christians.

Rebaptism placed Nicene Christians in an awkward position vis-à-vis the broader Christian community. Homoian disputants could treat them as non-

---

120. See, e.g., Frend (1952), 136–37; Hermanowicz (2008), 144 n. 37.
121. On earlier African Christian debates over rebaptism and their influence on the Donatist schism, see Patout Burns (1993); Lancel (2002b), 172, 280–84; García Mac Gaw (2008).
122. Lancel (2002b), 172; Markus (2003), 322–25; García Mac Gaw (2008); Shaw (2011), 102–3.
123. Humfress (2007), 266–68; Buenacasa Pérez (2007); Hermanowicz (2008), 89, 97–155; García Mac Gaw (2008), 238; Shaw (2011), 532–39.
124. Aug., *Ep.* 220.4 (ed. Goldbacher: 4:433–34); Aug., *De haer.* 49 (ed. L. Müller: 98); see also Fournier (2012), 246–47.
125. See p. 37 n. 25.
126. See pp. 133–34.
127. Fulg., *C. Fab.* 29.12 (ed. Fraipont: 821).

Christians, since they had not been baptized.[128] The consequences of such an attitude can be read in angry Nicene responses. Quodvultdeus of Carthage draws attention to a version of this libel in his sermon *Against Five Heresies*. In the anti-Sabellian section, he segues into a denunciation of contemporary Arians and their practices. As he builds toward a rhetorical climax, he describes an imagined Arian rebaptism of a Catholic in the guise of a martyr act: "He builds a cave and strangles the Catholic there; he calls the Christian a pagan [*christianum uocat paganum*]; he forces a baptism upon the baptized, against that which is written, "He who has once been washed does not need to be washed again" [John 13:10]. The man shouts, 'I am a Christian [*christianus sum*]! Why do you tell me that I am not?'"[129] In his *Abecedarium*, Fulgentius of Ruspe again places an Arian accusation of paganism in the context of rebaptism: "In addition, they do not fear to repeat holy baptism, / and now compel the Catholic faithful to deny Christ, / and teach them to confess a falsehood if they wish to entangle some of them, / so that he who was a Christian might call himself a pagan, / and the baptism that he accepted when he was in the true faith, / having been seduced to perfidy, he might assert that he does not have, / so that he might perish with those rebels against God."[130] According to Fulgentius, converts to Homoian Christianity were taught to reinterpret their previous faith as a form of paganism rather than Christianity, just as they were convinced that their first baptism was nothing of the sort. Until they entered the Homoian Church, they were not Christians.

The resemblance to earlier Donatist accusations remains an important one. Attacks on opposing doctrines as showing the telltale signs of worse errors and on opposing Christians as cryptopagans were devices familiar to African Christian audiences.[131] They were part and parcel of effective heresiology, tarring heretics with an even more unpleasant brush. The assimilation of the Homoousian heresy to a broader category of heretical error was no less effective. In the hands of Fastidiosus, it attributed to the Homoousians the same deviant mental makeup as the Donatists. In the universal history of heresy constructed by the anonymous Job commentator, it makes these contemporary heretics the mold in which all heresy is cast. In all cases, the intended result was the same. The more unorthodox and

---

128. This was not an inevitable move; they could also treat them as catechumens, generally accorded status as Christians (if not *fideles*): Rebillard (2012b), 42–43; see too Sandwell (2007), 200–202. Compare Fulg., *De rem. pecc.* 1.22.1 (ed. Fraipont: 671), in which some Nicenes attend Homoian services "without the repetition of baptism."

129. Quod., *Adu. haer.* 7.38.153–39.157 (ed. Braun: 299). Compare Opt., *C. Parm.* 3.11, 5.3.8 (ed. Labrousse: 2:70–74, 124), with Donatists accusing baptized Catholics of paganism and an anti-Donatist gloss on John 13:10. The precise manner in which Quodvultdeus and Fulgentius (see next note) portray Arian rebaptism seems intended to evoke Donatism (see pp. 133–34).

130. Fulg., *ABC*. 67–73 (ed. Isola: 38).

131. See, e.g., Shaw (2011), 189, 272–82.

un-Christian the Nicene Church was made to look, the more plausibly Homoian Christianity could appear as the orthodox church of Africa.

CONCLUSION

The Homoian Christianity of the post-imperial West is often written off as a purely sectarian phenomenon. Writing on the successor kingdoms considers it primarily a matter of ethnic identity and solidarity. Meanwhile, patristic scholars cognizant of the loose ends of earlier conflicts rarely countenance the possibility of genuine doctrinal controversy in the post-imperial West—Gallic debates over Augustine's views on predestination and grace excepted. Their gaze turns eastward, to track the search for new answers about the Christian doctrine of God at Ephesus, Chalcedon, and Constantinople.

In Vandal Africa, newly ascendant Homoian Christians reopened old questions about the definition of orthodoxy. They portrayed themselves as the holders of the orthodox Christian faith and claimed to represent the true Christian Church. They also attacked their opponents using the quintessential modes of heresiological polemic: naming and shaming. The rhetoric of Homoian writers from this period is as sophisticated, devious, and brutal as that of any late-antique Christian disputant. It deserves to be taken seriously. Homoian Christians in Vandal Africa made a genuine claim to be its true and universal church. They were backed by the legal categorization of their Nicene opponents as adherents of a specific, criminalized heresy. The reaction of Nicene authors is telling. Their frequent attempts to throw off the Homoousian label bear witness to its power to discredit. The particular Nicene concern for the legal aspects and consequences of this term of abuse is similarly revealing. Homoian heresiology posed a serious threat to the Nicene Church's status in Africa. The Homoousian label challenged the validity of Nicene self-identification as the Catholic Church. It had the potential to alter perceptions of Christian conflict in Vandal Africa. The African ecclesiastical writers who dominate the surviving textual record with elaborate professions of Nicene orthodoxy and Arian heresy can mislead. For many, these Catholics were Vandal Africa's heretics.

4

Ecclesiastical Histories

Reinventing the Arians

The Homoian Christians of Vandal Africa were a self-evident problem for Nicene clerics. This alternative church was not a peripheral sect: it possessed clerics accomplished in the skill set of the Christian controversialist, who exploited their political favor to stake a convincing claim to orthodoxy. To maintain their Christian communities, Nicene clerics had to contest this claim and the depiction of their church as heretical, using the same heresiological strategies deployed by their opponents. Their response can be summarized briefly: they sought to turn Homoian Christians into Arian heretics. Accusations of Arianism against individuals, groups, doctrines, and churches surface across all manner of Christian literature. The label bore a heavy load of associations accrued over more than a century of polemical writing and public controversy. In their efforts to attribute heresy to their African rivals, Nicene polemicists had the weight of this history behind them. This chapter considers how they sought to establish the authority of this past and bring it to bear on a far less certain present.

Not every use of the term *Arian* in Vandal Africa necessarily made deliberate allusion to this thick polemical context. Nicene clerics encouraged Christians toward an instinctive mistrust of Arians by deploying stereotypes about heretics that had been drummed into Christian audiences in Africa and elsewhere for centuries.[1] These Arians were impious,[2] both excessively clever and excessively foolish,[3] and like

---

1. See pp. 63–64.
2. E.g., Fulg., *C. Fab.* 27.5, 32.1 (ed. Fraipont: 805, 831); Fulg., *Ep.* 9.4.1, 9.6.3 (ed. Fraipont: 287, 291–92); Quod., *Adu. haer.* 6.5 (ed. Braun: 280).
3. E.g., *C. Var.* 1.25 (ed. Schwank: 37); Fulg., *Ad Mon.* 3.1–3 (ed. Fraipont: 52–55).

animals.⁴ Through their subordination of Son and Holy Spirit, they worshiped multiple gods and were thus effectively pagan; their worship was idolatry.⁵ They committed violence⁶ and sexual improprieties⁷ and were betrayers of Christ, worse than Judas, the Jews, and Pontius Pilate's men.⁸ These barbed insults were naturally accompanied by basic assertions of the writers' own purity of faith, character, and reasoning and membership in a church that was orthodox, catholic, and apostolic. The generic nature of such attacks does not undermine their potential potency for audiences who knew a Christian deviant when they heard about one.⁹ Certainly, some Nicene Christians discerned the label's basic polarizing function even without understanding what Arianism entailed. A number of Fulgentius's correspondents avowed knowing that the Arians were wrong but not necessarily how or why.¹⁰ The standard, lurid profile of the heretic remained an important method of boundary management.

With all of these moves, Nicene clerics made their opponents into the sort of heretics to which their audiences had become accustomed. Nonetheless, as this chapter argues, Nicene accusations of Arianism against Homoian Christians in Vandal Africa were not merely insinuations of a generic heresy. The need to define and refute Homoians provoked an intense interest among Nicene clerics in the history and heresiology of the Arian controversy. They drew extensively upon earlier polemical arguments to remind the Christians of Africa who the Arians were, what they thought, and what they had done.

The history of the church in the later Roman Empire provided compelling resources for combating Arian opponents. However, Nicene writers had to more than simply re-create Arian heresy; they also had to convincingly apply it to contemporaries. To make this crucial connection, Nicene disputants went far beyond a simple identification of shared teachings. A late fifth-century history, the *Carthaginian Epitome*, created an ingenious genealogy to link the Arians of Vandal Africa back to their fourth-century forbears. Even more strikingly, its imaginary dialogues elide past and present, setting contemporary conflict in the world of earlier controversies, in part because it retrofitted that late Roman past to suit present concerns. Nicene writers attributed their faction's views to authoritative heroes like Athanasius, Ambrose, and Augustine and those of their opponents to Arius and men already condemned as his followers. These authors made it clear

---

4. E.g., Fulg., *ABC*. 26–28, 264–68 (ed. Isola: 36, 50); Ps.-Victor, *Hom. Cyp.* 2 (*PL* 58: 266B).
5. E.g., Fulg., *Ep.* 9.6.3 (ed. Fraipont: 291–92).
6. E.g., *HP* (ed. Lancel); *Passio beat. mart.* (ed. Lancel); Quod., *Adu. haer.* 7.38–45 (ed. Braun: 299–300).
7. E.g., Fulg., *Ep.* 9.21–22 (ed. Fraipont: 307–8); *HP* 2.24 (ed. Lancel: 132–33).
8. E.g., Quod., *Adu. haer.* 6.77 (ed. Braun: 292); Fulg., *ABC*. 256–63 (ed. Isola: 50).
9. Shaw (2011), 260–347.
10. See esp. Fulg., *Ep.* 8.1–2 (ed. Fraipont: 257–58); see also Fulg., *De Trin. ad Fel.* 1.1 (ed. Fraipont: 633); Fulg., *De fide ad Petrum* 1 (ed. Fraipont: 711).

that they and their contemporaries were reliving the doctrinal controversies of the past. This assertion was meant not only to lend authority to their church but also to benefit them personally. Vigilius of Thapsa and Cerealis of Castellum became the successors to great figures of Nicene Christianity; specific opponents like Marivadus and Huneric, heirs to infamous Arian heretics. As these Nicene clerics portrayed it, Vandal Africa was a new episode in the grand narrative of the Arian controversy, from which the Catholic Church's heroes would again emerge triumphant. This presentation of events did not go unchallenged. The preface to Pseudo-Fulgentius's *Book on the Trinity* acts as an important reminder that Homoian clerics used their own narratives of fourth-century history to claim present-day orthodoxy. Both churches presented themselves as fighting the battles of the fourth century. It was on these terms that Nicene disputants had to convince contemporaries that they were Catholic and their opponents Arian.

The history and cultural resources of conflicts between Catholics and Arians were not the only potential recourses for African Nicene writers concerned to preserve their authority. The debates of the Donatist schism also offered plentiful resources. As already noted, Homoians appropriated the African ecclesiastical heritage, eliding the Homoousians with the Donatists and turning their "persecution" of the latter against them.[11] Partly in response, Nicene writers assimilated their new opponents to their old ones, reusing arguments developed for the Donatists. They portrayed the Arians as African separatists, deploying classic arguments about Catholic universality. Moreover, in emphasizing that their rivals rebaptized, Nicene polemicists invoked a deviant practice that had helped to convince the imperial court to proscribe the Donatists as heretics.[12] Like appeals to impiety, betrayal, and "bad sex,"[13] the anti-Donatist tropes that Nicene writers used—and, for that matter, the anti-Caecilianist arguments that Homoians deployed—are best understood as appeals to shared notions of heresy within African Christianity. However they chose to denounce their opponents, it was through recourse to these ecclesiastical histories that Christian polemicists in Vandal Africa made their claims comprehensible and persuasive.

HISTORIA ARIANORUM

Nicene writers complemented their accusations against named Arian individuals and groups with detailed explanations of what this heresy was, why it was wrong,

---

11. See pp. 104–8.
12. Parsons (1994), 156–57; Modéran (2003), 36; (2006), 169; cf. Humfress (2007), 266–68; Hermanowicz (2008), 89, 97–155.
13. Shaw (2011), 326–32.

and how it could be defeated. Fulgentius's *Abecedarium* begins with a clear statement of these aims, which, though self-consciously pedagogical, were also inevitably polemical.[14] He asserts that earlier authorities, writing books on the faith and the Trinity, had cataloged almost one hundred heresies,[15] of which one was much worse than the others: "They called these Arians, providing the name from the founder [*auctor*], / who made different substances in the Trinity. / The sinful errors of those people I set out to report to you, / so that you might know more fully why you ought to shrink from them [*horrere*]."[16] Again and again, prefaces gesture toward Christians' need to learn how to defend Catholic truth and their adherence to it from contemporary Arian error.[17]

To that end, Nicene clerics sought aid from their predecessors. They collated encyclopedic lists of responses and proof texts that could refute Arian teachings.[18] These texts repeat the stereotypical statements of previous anti-Arian polemic.[19] Nicene writers also deployed the rhetorical strategies of earlier heresiological experts. By choosing Sabellius and Photinus as fellow contestants to Arius in his imaginary debate, Vigilius played to a tripartite conception of heresy asserted most forcefully at the beginning of Ambrose of Milan's *De fide*: Christianity was not the error of the pagans, the Jews, Sabellius, Photinus, or Arius.[20] Other authors used the traditional via media approach to orthodoxy, with Arianism and Sabellianism as opposite extremes.[21] Like earlier anti-Arian polemicists, these writers lumped together different forms of non-Nicene Christianity. They constantly portrayed the Homoian profession of likeness as if it hid more radical formulations, whether a Son "unlike" (*dissimilis*) the Father or a Trinity of three separate substances.[22] Specific accusations, such as comparison of the supposed Arian denial of Christ's divinity to that of the Jews, went back to Arianism's invention.[23] The

---

14. On pedagogy and polemic see pp. 67–68.
15. Most likely a reference to Aug., *De haer.*, which describes eighty-eight heresies.
16. Fulg., *ABC.* 31–40, quotation at 37–40 (ed. Isola: 36).
17. See p. 67 n. 69.
18. See pp. 55–62.
19. E.g., "There was a time when the Son did not exist," "before he was born he did not exist": Ps.-Aug., *Solutiones* 6.10–12 (ed. Schwank: 154); Fulg., *C. Fab.* 24.4.36–38 (ed. Fraipont: 800); Quod., *Adu. haer.* 6.40 (ed. Braun: 287); Vig., *Solutiones* 3.76–77 (ed. Hombert: 209); *C. Fel.* 5 (PL 42: 1160); "The one who sent is greater, the one sent is lesser": Quod., *Adu. haer.* 7.5 (ed. Braun: 293); cf. Ps.-Aug., *Solutiones* 40 (ed. Schwank: 184). See also Vig., *Solutiones* (ed. Hombert), with notes on precedents and parallels.
20. Vig., *Dial.*; Ambrose, *De fide* 1.1.6 (ed. Faller: 6–7).
21. E.g., Vig., *C. Eut.* 2.1–2 (PL 62: 103C–105B); Ps.-Fulg., *Trin.* 2.38–46 (ed. Fraipont: 240); *C. Var.* 1.16.34–41 (ed. Schwank: 31); Fulg., *De Trin. ad Fel.* 4 (ed. Fraipont: 636–38); Fulg., *Epp.* 8.21, 10.6, 14.38 (ed. Fraipont: 269, 316, 432); Fulg., *De rem. pecc.* 1.22.2 (ed. Fraipont: 671–72); Quod., *Adu. haer.* 6–7 (ed. Braun: 279–301).
22. See 101 n. 96, 102 n. 101.
23. Fulg., *De Trin. ad Fel.* 5.1 (ed. Fraipont: 638); see Gwynn (2007a), 172, for an earlier comparison.

Arians of Vandal Africa were characterized and refuted like those of the late Roman West.

This association was tied not only to the theological typology of their deviant beliefs. As Fulgentius's curt etymology suggests, by naming the name, Nicene writers implicated their opponents in Arius's error. Other authors also explicitly referred to the heresiarch. In his sermon *Against Five Heresies*, Quodvultdeus of Carthage performed a dialogue with an imaginary Arian opponent. Responding to a classic Arian maxim, "There was a time when the Son did not exist," which he argued violated a famous proof text, the preacher sarcastically asked, "When the Word was in the beginning, or when John was lying close to the breast of the Lord and learning from the Word of the Lord that 'in the beginning there was the Word, and the Word was God' [John 1:1], where was Arius?"[24] In another sermon, Quodvultdeus ridiculed the assertion made by Arians in Carthage that they were the true church, the bride of Christ; instead, their church was a prostitute whose integrity Arius had "snatched away."[25] For Nicene clerics, being Arian meant membership in the ill-begotten church of Arius.

It also meant participation in a sect whose long and checkered history was recorded in the writings of Nicene authorities. Vandal-era texts invoke a plethora of fourth- and early fifth-century Arian figures, councils, and creeds. Nicene authors name (among others) Eunomius of Cyzicus (the eponymous founder of the Eunomian heresy);[26] Auxentius of Milan and possibly his namesake from Durostorum;[27] another Ambrosian opponent, Palladius of Ratiaria, whose work was still circulating;[28] the Creed of Sirmium (357), nicknamed "the Blasphemy";[29] the Councils of Rimini and Seleucia (359) and their infamous "fraud";[30] and Augustine of Hippo's Arian debating partners Pascentius and Maximinus.[31] Nicene authors used their knowledge of these individuals, councils, and creeds to make arguments about present-day Arians.

All in all, Nicene clerics talked about and argued against contemporary Homoians as if they were the Arians of the past. They did so not only in general anti-Arian

---

24. Quod., *Adu. haer.* 6.40–45, at 6.44 (ed. Braun: 287).

25. Quod., *C. Iud., pag. et Arr.* 22.4–9, quotation at 22.9.34 (ed. Braun: 257).

26. Vig., *Dial. I = II* 1.22 (ed. Hombert: 293–94). On Eunomius see Hanson (1988), 611–36; T. Barnes (1993), 136–38; Vaggione (2000); Ayres (2004), 144–49.

27. Ps.-Fulg., *Trin.* 3.85–87 (ed. Fraipont: 242); *Coll. Pasc.* 4 (ed. H. Müller, Weber, and Weidmann: 78). On the Auxentii see McLynn (1994), 20–31, 183–85, 198–99, 204–6; D. Williams (1995), 76–83, 204–15; Flower (2013a), 207–17.

28. Vig., *Dial. II* 3.27 (ed. Hombert: 394–95). On Palladius see Hanson (1988), 595–96; McLynn (1991); McLynn (1994), 51–52, 112–18, 124–37, 146–48, 373–74; McLynn (1996).

29. Vig., *Dial. I* 1.21 (ed. Hombert: 292). On "the Blasphemy" see Hanson (1988), 343–47; Ayres (2004), 137–39, 179.

30. Vig., *Dial. II*, pref. II (ed. Hombert: 250); Ps.-Fulg., *Trin.* 3.69–84 (ed. Fraipont: 241–42).

31. See pp. 73–77.

tractates, where one might expect repetition of earlier heresiology, but also in responses to specific contemporaries. Homoian clerics in Vandal Africa traced their descent from their own fourth-century history and repeated the arguments and doctrinal emphases of earlier authorities.[32] These were the figures, events, and doctrines that Latin Nicene writers had denounced as Arian at that time. At one level, for fifth-century Nicene clerics to attribute Arianism to their opponents may have seemed only natural. Previous controversialists had done the heavy lifting, connecting Homoians of the Latin West like Ursacius and Valens, the Auxentii and Palladius back to the unfortunate presbyter of Alexandria as part of a demonic heretical succession. When Nicene clerics in Vandal Africa read Rufinus's carefully reworked narrative of the awkward events of the 330s[33] or Filastrius of Brescia's assertion that Arius believed the Son was like the Father,[34] they may have understood these as historical facts, unaware of their contentious origins. Yet even if it was obvious to them that their opponents in Vandal Africa, the Homoians of the late fourth-century West, and the many other forms of non-Nicene Christianity that emerged in the fourth-century empire shared a heresy originated by Arius, this does not mean that it was self-evident to their audiences. This was why Nicene writers expended so much energy on recapitulating and reframing the inherited wisdom of previous generations. The Homoians had to be made into Arians all over again.

MAKING THE CONNECTION

A thirteenth-century Spanish manuscript contains a little-known historical text from Vandal Africa. It is a revision of the chronicles of Jerome and Prosper of Aquitaine, falsely attributed to Isidore of Seville.[35] This history stops in 442 (before the end of Prosper's second, 445 edition) with a notice on the treaty between Geiseric and Valentinian III that ceded the core African provinces to the Vandals (quoted verbatim from Prosper). It can be dated to 496/97 by its final computation of 5,708 years "from the beginning of the world to the most recent year [*ad nouissimum annum*] of Thrasamund" and 5,652 years for the cumulative tally from creation to the Vandals' entry into Carthage.[36] Since it calculates various dates

---

32. See ch. 3.

33. Ruf., *HE* 10.12 (ed. Mommsen: 976–78), the source for Vig., *Dial. II*, pref. II (ed. Hombert: 246–52).

34. Fil., *Haer.* 66.1-2 (ed. Heylen: 244), a possible source for Vigilius's portrayal of a Homoian Arius: see p. 123.

35. Universidad Complutense de Madrid, Biblioteca Histórica MS 134, 42r–47v (available at http://alfama.sim.ucm.es/dioscorides/consulta_libro.asp?ref=B20920246&idioma=0).

36. $\overline{III}$CLXXXIIII + LXXXV + CCCCXX + XL + XXVII + CCLXXXVIII + XL + XL + CCCCLXXXV + DLXXXVII + XXXIII + CCCCXIII = 5,652: *Epit. Carth.* (ed. Mommsen: 497), with the chronological adjustment of Courtois (1955), 407–8.

using the regnal years of Vandal kings and most of its fifth-century material relates to the Vandals (both drawn from Prosper and added by the author), its provenance is clearly Vandal Africa and possibly Carthage: Theodor Mommsen, who produced a part edition, dubbed this text the *Carthaginian Epitome*.[37] The late date of the sole extant manuscript might normally cause concern, but its *indiculus* lists a number of fifth- and sixth-century African texts (by Augustine, Orosius, and Fulgentius) that were subsequently detached. The Madrid codex also contains a string of other late-antique chronicles, including the sole extant text of the Gallic Chronicler of 511 and one of the best witnesses to Hydatius of Chaves.[38] The *Epitome* is immediately followed in the Madrid codex by a version of what Mommsen called *List of the Kings of the Vandals and Alans*: a brief chronicle of Vandal history with a particular interest in the affairs of the Nicene Church and the coercive measures that Vandal kings took against it.[39]

The *Epitome* finds its place as one of the many fifth- and sixth-century imitators of Jerome whose geographical range contracted with the increasing political fragmentation of the late Roman West. The epitomator narrowed the vision of the universalizing Eusebius and Jerome to produce a largely African history from the second half of the 420s.[40] The *Epitome* nonetheless diverges in an important sense from other fifth- and sixth-century chronicles, epitomes, and *breuiaria*: it is not a continuation.[41] It ends a full fifty-four years before the author's own day, in stark contrast to the near contemporaneity of events described by Prosper, Hydatius,

---

37. Part edition: *Epit. Carth.* (ed. Mommsen).

38. On the manuscript see Burgess (1993), 17–18; Muhlberger (1990), 201; Cardelle de Hartmann (2001), 27*–38*; Steinacher (2001), 15–21; Steinacher (2004), 166–67.

39. *Lat. reg. Vand. Alan.* (ed. Steinacher); see also Steinacher (2001); (2004). The text's editor, Roland Steinacher, implies that the *Laterculus* and the *Epitome* formed a single original text and thus ascribes the same textual history to them ([2004], 172–74). However, this does not make sense, given the obvious break that separates them. The peace of 442 (the last event in the *Epitome* as separately edited by Mommsen) is followed by a computation to the most recent year of Thrasamund (496/97) before the narrative flow resumes (in what Mommsen considered the *Laterculus*) with a chronological marker for the duration of Geiseric's reign. The computation to 496/97 is completely out of place unless it is a closing computation with the date of the work, followed by a fresh start with the *Laterculus*. It seems much more likely that the *Laterculus* was later added as a continuation of the *Epitome*—by the same or a different author—in which form the two texts were transmitted. The final version of the *Laterculus* must postdate 534 because it includes the end of Gelimer's reign, while the wording of the computation at the year 523 suggests that a previous edition was written then.

40. On regional focus see Muhlberger (1990), 78, 148, 161–62; Croke (2001), 102–42; Burgess and Kulikowski (2013), 128–29. On the geographical specificity of supposedly "universalizing" Christian history, see Van Nuffelen (2010).

41. On naming issues see Burgess and Kulikowski (2013). With its intermittent chronological markers of imperial and Vandal regnal years, the *Epitome* falls most easily into their category of *breuiaria*.

and Cassiodorus.[42] Moreover, despite the regionalism of the text's final notices, specifically African or Vandal history is not the epitomator's overall concern. The period between Diocletian and Theodosius I receives the most extensive treatment of any between Abraham and Thrasamund: the years 303–95 take up six columns in the Madrid manuscript (45r–47v), to the one and a half devoted to 395–442 (47r–v). The epitomator's special interest is substantiated by the reintroduction of sections of Jerome that Prosper excised from his epitome (that is, assuming he was not working from a version of Prosper appended to a fuller version of Jerome).[43] The African epitomator also inserted information taken from Rufinus of Aquileia's *Ecclesiastical History* to supplement the more concise notices of the two chroniclers.[44] In contrast to its Gallic and Spanish siblings, the *Epitome* appears as an extremely thin account of the (by then rather distant) past of the historian's region. Instead, the heart of the work is a history of the later Roman Empire.

The *Carthaginian Epitome* is overwhelmingly concerned with the fourth century. This era had always been crucial for African Christians, but the old issues had faded: a single curt sentence dismisses Donatus and the Donatists.[45] Instead, this retelling of the fourth century is dedicated to the history of the Arian controversy. After a brief account of the Diocletianic persecution, the civil wars of the Tetrarchy, and the victory and conversion of Constantine, this key theme emerges for the first time:

> Peace is returned to the churches. But it did not remain for long. For that most ancient serpent sees the knowledge of Christ reaching right up to the apex of the kingdom. Since the idols were perishing and dying, the cunning enemy splits the unity of the church and the established doctrines of the apostles. He rouses priests [*sacerdotes*] against themselves. He disturbs the kings, all of the peoples, and the church. He finds [*inuenit*] a new question. Whence also the time is full of exile and rapine, and the whole world is at discord with itself. The author and inventor of this heretical depravity is Arius. (46r)

The epitomator's evocative portrayal of the universal impact of the teachings of Arius is reinforced in the shape of the following decades. The consequences of the controversy that the *Epitome* has Arius (and the devil) set in motion proceed to monopolize the narrative—barring notices of the deaths of emperors—until 361. The epitomator describes the events of Nicaea, Arius's ignoble death, and Constantius II's Arian conciliar activity, repeatedly referring to the subjection of

---

42. Prosper, *Chron.* (ed. Mommsen); Hyd., *Chron.* (ed. Burgess); Cass., *Chron.* (ed. Mommsen).

43. On Prosper's epitome and the alternative manuscript versions, see Muhlberger (1990), 55–73, at 55–56.

44. The Gallic Chronicler of 452 also used Rufinus for the reign of Theodosius but without the same level of detail in his account of Catholic-Arian conflict: ibid., 153, 167–69.

45. *Epit. Carth.* (ed. Mommsen: 495).

Nicene confessors to exiles and torments. The accession of Julian brings other subjects into the narrative, but the return of the Nicene exiles and their attempts to deal with the aftermath of Rimini remain to the fore. A brief reference to Julian's cruel pagan persecution swiftly gives way to further Nicene episcopal exile under Valens, followed by a long account of the career of Ambrose of Milan, using Rufinus to supplant Prosper's bland pen portrait of the bishop.[46] The *Epitome* takes in Ambrose's consecration and the basilica controversy with Valentinian II and Justin (intermingled with perfunctory notes on the defeat at Adrianople and Maximus's usurpation), ending with the victory of Theodosius I over Maximus, the destruction of paganism, and the banishment of the Arians.[47]

All of this may seem a familiar account lifted from Rufinus's *Ecclesiastical History*: the well-worn metanarrative of fourth-century church history retraced in all its Christian and specifically Nicene glory. Yet the epitomator does not simply reproduce this history of Nicene triumph; he subtly undercuts it. The Theodosian settlement is immediately sabotaged, in a manner that draws a straight line from Milan, and the Roman Empire, of the late fourth century to Vandal Carthage. After extensive discussion of Ambrose's dispute with the Arians at Milan, the epitomator directly quotes the *Ecclesiastical History*'s joyous celebration of Theodosius: "the worship of idols, which following the order of Constantine had begun to be neglected and destroyed, was ruined at his command [*eodem imperante conlapsus est*]."[48] This crucial moment is frustrated by the author's telling comment. In Theodosius's time, he states, the Antichrist had provoked doctrinal discord, and (Arian) priests supported by their rulers—the passage skips confusingly between nominatives singular and plural as it conflates their agency—"committed homicide, adultery, and many impious things publicly in church."[49]

> But, recognized and struck down in the Roman Empire [*regno Romano*][50] and not finding a place any longer, he [the Antichrist] transferred himself to the barbarian nations [*nationes*], as if proffering apostolic testimony: "We [the Arians] had been sent to the Romans, but because they judged themselves unworthy of the word of God, we turned [*conuersi sumus*] to the *gentes*. For you were worthy to receive the true faith." And transferring all the things about the calling of the gentiles [*de uocatione gentium*], of which the holy scriptures are full, to those persons, they occupied the souls of the barbarians. The enemy [the Antichrist] had his customary aid, that he might separate the Christian people who were subject to barbarian jurisdiction as

---

46. Prosper, *Chron.* 1173 (ed. Mommsen: 461).

47. Theodosius's triumph is conspicuously absent from Prosper, though not from the Gallic Chronicler of 452: Muhlberger (1990), 81–82, 88–89, 167–69.

48. *Epit. Carth.* 46v–47r, quote at 47r. Compare Ruf., *HE* 11.14–17, 11.19 (ed. Mommsen: 1020–24).

49. *Epit. Carth.* (ed. Mommsen: 496). On the ethnographic perspective of this passage, see pp. 189–90. See also Kitchen (2008), 61–62.

50. On this translation (and *regnum* as a term in the late fifth century), see Kitchen (2008), 58–59.

if converting them from Christ to him. And as they [the Arians] had bound [*deuinxissent*] the barbarians completely to themselves, they preached that there was "one God, one faith, one baptism" [Eph. 4:5] only among themselves and that they ought to repeat the baptism of those other people who were outside of their church [*ab eis foris*]. During the great discord in the Roman Empire up until Theodosius, by whom they were driven out from all the churches, they had not dared to commit this [repetition of baptism]. By this act today the enemy brings about those things to come: they are witnesses [*testes*] of the church, although their bodies are not butchered by the sword, but rather their spirits by water.[51]

More than a century may have passed between the Catholic-Arian conflicts in which Ambrose and Theodosius had triumphed and the time when the epitomator wrote. Yet those events remained of crucial relevance for this Nicene author. To his mind, the Arians of 380s Milan and 490s Carthage were engaged in the same nefarious deeds, attempting to deceive Catholic Christians, convert them to Arian heresy, and thus split the church. This similarity was neither a coincidence nor a case of mimesis. For, according to the epitomator, the fourth-century Arians and those of his day were the same people. Theodosius had forced them out of the empire's churches; they had gone to convert the barbarians, pretending to be true Christian missionaries; and now they had returned. The epitomator dreamed up an ingenious genealogy to characterize contemporary Homoians, a backstory that led them from Milan, via *barbaricum*, to Carthage. In his view, these circumstances were even worse than those of the dark days before Theodosius. The Arian bishops patronized by mid-fourth-century emperors may have done unspeakable things in the chaotic late Roman world created by Arius's demonic doctrinal intervention, but they had never dared to rebaptize Catholics.[52] Today (*hodie*) the Antichrist was doing so much worse through his Arian minions.

This parody of Christian missionary activity performs a crucial role in the *Epitome*'s narrative. It allows its author both to bring the fourth-century Arian controversy to Vandal Africa and to suggest that contemporary Arians outdid their predecessors. His narrative decision isolates the basic literary endeavor that Nicene clerics undertook in Vandal Africa. History could easily be on their side. The fourth century provided them with (to quote Peter Brown) a "facilitating narrative,"[53] in which were embedded multiple individual episodes of Catholic triumph over Arian opponents. The challenge was to make a convincing connection between that past and the present. Nicene writers responded to this test with imaginative answers.

---

51. *Epit. Carth.* (ed. Mommsen (496).
52. Ambrose would have disagreed: see Ambrose, *Ep.* 75A.37 (ed. Zelzer: 107); D. Williams (1995), 209.
53. P. Brown (1995), 4.

TYPOLOGY, REENACTMENT, AND NARRATIVE IDENTITY

Many Nicene authors in Vandal Africa explained present-day church conflict with reference to the history of the Arian controversy. The use of narratives to understand the world is, of course, not limited to Christians, Vandal Africa, or even late antiquity; their role in identity formation has provoked considerable discussion among theorists of various hues. In a rightly influential monograph, Thomas Sizgorich drew on such works of sociology, anthropology, and modern history to set out an elegant theoretical frame for the study of an almost omnipresent phenomenon in early Christianity. His formulation is worth quoting in detail: "For groups who understand their identity in primordialist terms, recalled events embedded in the defining narratives in accordance with which the group in question imagines its formative past often provide an interpretive grammar through which to make sense of contemporary events.... Individuals... understanding themselves to be 'emplotted' in large- and small-scale narratives most readily find other individuals and groups comprehensible as 'characters' within such narratives, with roles to play that are in large measure determined by such elements as the underlying 'themes' and 'plots' of the narratives in question."[54] Sizgorich used this model to explain the ubiquity of themes of martyrdom and persecution across late-antique Christian writings. Late-antique Christian identity was formed around a central narrative: the "Great Persecution" and its martyrs.[55] Contemporary events in the Christian empire, however divorced from those past incidents, were understood as new episodes in this unfolding narrative. Individual actors received a variety of well-worn costumes: true Christian or false believer, brave martyr or lapsed temporizer, pious emperor or pagan persecutor. The Nicene Church in Vandal Africa had its own iterations of this persecution narrative, most notably Victor of Vita's *History of the Persecution of the African Province*.[56] The recent past became a new Great Persecution; the Vandal kings were cast as persecuting Roman emperors and African Nicene Christians as martyrs and confessors. The decisions that an individual made assigned them a role in this ongoing story of Christian self-definition.

"Emplotting" events and individuals in this way required a reciprocal exchange with the past. Contemporary actors chose (or were perceived) to imitate past figures. Simultaneously, contemporary mimesis made individuals reinterpret those past actors and actions. By writing about both recent and distant events in a manner that elided past and present, late-antique Christians produced new versions of that past. Through selectivity and active rewriting—both, of course, normal

54. Sizgorich (2009), 9, also in general 1–143, esp. 21–80.
55. See also Gaddis (2005), 43–45.
56. *HP*; see also Shanzer (2004); Howe (2007), 183–318; Fournier (2008), which uses Sizgorich's work (199–200); Merrills and Miles (2010), 184–92.

features of constructing a narrative—they created versions of the past meaningful to their present-day concerns. Within the logic of a defining narrative, episodes took on a timeless character. The cast may have changed, but the plot, the characters, and the stage remained the same.

The theme of narrative identity has found especially fertile ground in late-antique Christianity because of a particular intellectual mind-set. Typology was fundamental to biblical exegesis and Christian reading practices. Late-antique Christians used this same method to make sense of their world.[57] This phenomenon can be ascribed a sharper heresiological intent. In a study of Christian invective of the mid-fourth century, Richard Flower examines how Christian writers used such portrayals of reenactment to authorize themselves and defame opponents. As he puts it, "By stating that enemies were combated by the same actions, or even the same words, as those used against the famous and paradigmatic biblical enemies of God, these authors presented contemporary events as re-enactments of events that their readers already knew and respected, and in which they could easily recognise who was on the side of righteousness."[58] In the middle decades of the fourth century, the familiar and authoritative story to which Christian writers appealed ran from biblical history to the age of persecutions. The recent past of the Christian empire was more treacherous ground, its interpretation marked by "uncertainty and confusion."[59] By the time Nicene clerics in Vandal Africa wrote, the ecclesiastical history of the fourth and fifth centuries had developed its own canonical narratives, further historical resources upon which Christian identity could be constructed and polemicists could draw.

The history of Christian orthodoxy and its vindication through the trials and tribulations of the fourth century was one such narrative. It played a crucial role in the self-identity of Nicene clerics across the Mediterranean. By the mid-fifth century, a grand narrative had coalesced that closed down much of the uncertainty of this "wavering century"[60]—if not the half century of continuing religious diversity and controversy that had followed it—with regard to both the Christianization of a pagan empire and the articulation of a single, universal statement of faith. This is not to suggest either a uniform Nicene interpretation of the fourth century or an absence of alternatives.[61] Still, this crucial period tends to take a particular shape

---

57. An abundant literature examines late-antique Christians' application of biblical typology, originally used to prove the unity of the Old and New Testaments, to their present day: e.g., Tilley (1997); M. Williams (2008), 1–24, esp. 9–16, with useful bibliography; Rapp (2010); Flower (2013a), 23–24, 180–82 (with n. 9). On pseudonymity and reenactment see Stang (2012), 41–55. For useful discussions of biblical reading practices see Ayres (2004), 31–40; Wessel (2004), 112–37.

58. Flower (2013a), 178–219, quotation at 218.

59. Ibid., 184.

60. P. Brown (1995), 4, citing Chuvin (1990), 36–56.

61. See Gardiner (2012), 15–50, on Socrates of Constantinople's distinctive treatment of the fourth century; see p. 128 n. 103 for non-Nicene alternatives.

in fifth-century histories, a narrative arc prefigured in the polemical writings of contemporaries like Hilary, Athanasius, and Ambrose. Fundamental Christian truth was articulated at Nicaea. The disputes of the half century before its triumph under Theodosius I were not, as modern interpreters might have it, the working out of difficult and previously unsolved theological issues in a charged political setting. Instead, they represented heretical attempts to pervert a preexisting truth. The fourth century gave Nicene Christians this facilitating narrative of Christian self-definition, heretical machination, and final Catholic vindication.[62]

At its heart was a sense of the timelessness of (current) Christian orthodoxy and the church that transmitted it. As Patrick Gray has noted, this portrayal of an unchanging faith inevitably required selective and even innovative historical reconstruction: "A monolithic vision of the patristic past required the excision of all that did not accommodate itself to that vision."[63] Nicene authors in Vandal Africa, contemporaries of the Chalcedonian and Miaphysite authors studied by Gray, used a similar historical vision to contextualize recent events. However, contrary to Gray's pessimistic pronouncements about unimaginative responses conditioned by a growing sense of historical closure, this "canonical" past remained open to adaptation. These Nicene clerics did not dully transmit an earlier version of history. They continued the dynamic process of reshaping it to suit their needs and create new precedents. They even wrote themselves into it, capturing the reflected luster of earlier heroes. In their writings, Nicene polemicists set up a dialogue between the ecclesiastical politics of the fourth-century empire and those of contemporary Africa. The new conflict became another episode in the metanarrative of disputes between Catholic Christians and Arian heretics.

DIALOGUES WITH THE PAST

The modus operandi of the imaginary dialogues from the Vandal period was in keeping with the processes of historical reconstruction central to narrative identity. Symbolically charged figures of the past debated the issues that split Catholic Christianity and Arian heresy both in their own time and in the present. With the creation of these surrogate fathers, Nicene authors lodged the ecclesiastical conflict of Vandal Africa in what they saw as an authoritative past. They and their Homoian rivals were written into old stories about Catholics defeating Arians. These texts

---

62. Promoted in the Latin West above all by the influential Ruf., *HE* (ed. Mommsen); cf. T. Ferguson (2005), 81–123. For a thumbnail version see Aug., *C. Max.* 2.14.3 (ed. Hombert: 572–75). This ancient metanarrative became the basis for most scholarly accounts of the Arian controversy but has now undergone significant revision: see Slusser (1993); D. Williams (1995), 7, 233; Wiles (1996); Ayres (2004), 11–12; Gwynn (2007a), 1–8.

63. Gray (1989), 34. See also Wessel (2012); the excellent Graumann (2012).

sought to inculcate a particular way of viewing contemporary Christianity. The Nicene Church was made into the church of Athanasius and Augustine; its rival, the heretical sect of Arius and Pascentius. The writers and their opponents were cast as the reenactors of famous Nicene Christian heroes and villains. By eliding past and present, these authors created (to return to Sizgorich) "an interpretive grammar" for Christians in Vandal Africa.[64]

Different writers chose different episodes of Catholic-Arian conflict, but all sought to produce convincing simulacra of their historical contexts. In the first version of his *Dialogue against the Arians, Sabellians and Photinians*, Vigilius of Thapsa returns to the controversy's early stages. In his final sentence, the judge Probus mentions Arius's attack on "what was recently found at Nicaea."[65] The heresiarch bitterly complains about the banishments brought about by the council.[66] This close proximity to Nicaea is made more plausible by the characterization of the dialogue's judge, Probus, as a recent convert from paganism. The creed that he professes quotes the statement that converted a learned philosopher in a legendary story set at the council.[67] Since Probus is said to be philosophically skilled,[68] it seems likely that he is supposed to recall this deeply symbolic figure. Vigilius drew on this legendary story, as elaborated by Rufinus in his *Ecclesiastical History*,[69] to produce a convincing setting in the years following Nicaea.

Of course, he then deliberately disrupted it with an explanatory preface, the introduction of Sabellius and Photinus, and further anachronisms. Heresiological reasoning governed this decision: this symbolic triad of Christological heretics allowed him to pinpoint particular differences between them and his own orthodoxy, an important consideration as contemporaries in Vandal Africa accused Nicene Christians of both Photinianism and Sabellianism.[70] Furthermore, it enabled Vigilius to argue that their heresies existed to prove Nicene orthodoxy. Each showed the importance of a quality by overemphasizing it: Sabellius clarified the "union of nature"; Photinus, Christ's humanity; Arius, the distinction of the per-

---

64. Sizgorich (2009), 9.
65. Vig., *Dial. II*, sententia, 4.11 (ed. Hombert: 401).
66. Vig., *Dial. I* = *II* 1.17 (ed. Hombert: 285).
67. Vig., *Dial. I* = *II* 1.1.4–5 (ed. Hombert: 253): "qui uniuersa quae uidentur et quae non uidentur, uirtute uerbi sui creauit." Compare Ruf., *HE* 10.3, esp. 10.3.18–21, for this creedal formula (ed. Mommsen: 962–63, at 962). On the story see Lim (1995), 182–216, esp. 191–99, on Rufinus's version.
68. Vig., *Dial. I* = *II* 1.2.1–2 (ed. Hombert: 255).
69. Ruf., *HE* 10.3 (ed. Mommsen: 961–63).
70. In Fulg., *Ad Mon.*, pref. (ed. Fraipont: 2), an unnamed "heretic" has accused Fulgentius's correspondent, Monimus, of "the error of Photinus." This heretic was presumably another Nicene Christian, since he cited Augustine and Jerome, although this is not certain. Homoian sermons happily coexist with passages from the two Nicene authorities in the late fifth-century Italian *Codex Veronensis*: see Gryson (1982a). Thrasamund implies that Nicene Christianity is Sabellian at Fulg., *Dict. Tras.* 748–58 (ed. Fraipont: 90).

sons. At the same time, Vigilius could refute each in turn, finding them guilty of (in a neat pun) "an error alike in all respects [*errore consimili*]," "for although they advanced through various paths of their own, nevertheless, they reached one crossroads."[71] The three heresiarchs may never really have met, but each had a crucial role to play in the revelation of Nicene orthodoxy.

This telescoping of time helped Vigilius to turn contemporary Homoians into the original Arians. In the *Dialogue*, Arius represents all Arians from his time to the present day. He professes multiple (contradictory) Trinitarian formulae and is held accountable for a superabundance of individuals, creeds, and doctrinal positions.[72] This characterization distills the polemic of fourth-century disputants, who depicted a monolithic Arian group by amalgamating diverse individuals, parties, and doctrines, which could be portrayed as simultaneously unchanging and multiplex, consistent and contradictory. Nonetheless, it is made clear that Arius's true profession is Homoian. As Athanasius states, "That the Son is like the Father [*similem patri filium*], you have established by the many and abundant decrees of your councils."[73] Arius's responsibility for these councils comes from a conception of a timeless Arian party, not historical reality; the major creedal statements of Homoian Christology were made in the 350s, well after Arius's death.[74] Athanasius asks that Arius show written in the scriptures "that the Father is unbegotten and unsuffering and that the Son is truly God from God, light from light, and like the Father." Again he demands, "Show it written, that the Son is like the Father, or profess him unlike."[75] For Vigilius, Arius is a Homoian, like contemporary Arians in Vandal Africa. By making Homoian Christianity the heresiarch's true Arianism, he strengthens the heresiological accusation against those African Christians. Their Christianity had always been Arianism, from the heresy's very beginnings. Vigilius also saddles contemporary Homoians with a more radical Arianism, since Arius is made to state more drastic subordinating formulae, like the Eunomian *dissimilis* and the three substances of the Trinity.[76] If Arius was a Homoian, a Eunomian, and a Triousian, so Homoians in Vandal Africa were Eunomians, Triousians, and, fundamentally, Arians.

Vigilius made clear that the first edition of his *Dialogue* was not intended as a forgery (although some later copyists transmitted it under Athanasius's name with other Athanasian texts).[77] The work records Christian history and subtly comments on it but does not purport to be a historical document. Vigilius later reworked this

71. Vig., *Dial. II*, sententia, 9–11, quotations at 10.9, 10.34, 11.13–15 (ed. Hombert: 408–13, at 410, 411, 412).
72. Vig., *Dial. I = II* 1.22–23, 2.19 (ed. Hombert: 293–97, 336).
73. Vig., *Dial. I = II* 1.22 (ed. Hombert: 293).
74. See, e.g., Ayres (2004), 133–66.
75. Vig., *Dial. I = II* 1.22 (ed. Hombert: 294, 295).
76. Vig., *Dial. I = II* 1.16, 1.25; *Dial. II*, sententia, 8 (ed. Hombert: 283–84, 298–99, 406–8).
77. Ficker (1897), 39–40; Hombert (2010), 185 n. 45.

text to try to make it exactly that, by adding a new, historical preface that announces its intent from its first words ("When, at the city of Nicaea...").[78] Drawing on Rufinus once more, he recounts the familiar narrative of Arius's excommunication and exile, the beguiling of Constantine through the intercession of Constantia and an Arian follower, the heresiarch's (ahistorical but apologetically convenient) outliving of the first Christian emperor, and the controlling of Constantius II by an Arian presbyter. Then the preface states that during grisly persecutions, Constantius ordered Probus to act as judge between Athanasius and Arius at Laodicea in the second year of his reign (i.e., 338/39). Vigilius effectively rewrites Christian history here, adding a new ecclesiastical council. Athanasius's defeat of Arius is made into a real event, a clear, early victory for Nicene orthodoxy over Homoian Arianism in the late 330s. A telling phrase reveals a specific polemical force. Constantius is said to have ordered Probus "before he congregated the bishops of the Lord from the whole world at Rimini and Seleucia by a ruse [*dolo*], desiring to make them all one." The manner in which Vigilius foreshortens historical time to make this point—the purported event took place a whole twenty years before the meetings of 359, with countless councils in between—adds to the sense of an argument being forced. This legal defeat predated the Councils of Rimini and Seleucia, which represented a crucial legitimating standard for African Homoians and a central plank of Huneric's edict against the Homoousians.[79] As a result of this historical creativity, Nicene Christians could justify themselves with a new precedent.

The elision of past and present in Vigilius's *Dialogue* works to associate Africa's churchmen with the Catholics and Arians of the past. The synchronization of contemporaries with historical figures could also be used for more personal purposes. It allowed Vigilius to commandeer Athanasius of Alexandria's authority. Athanasius's fifth-century reception as a Nicene hero is best known from Eastern controversies, but he had a similar reputation in the Latin West (and one less complicated by competing claims on his legacy).[80] Simply by writing as Athanasius, Vigilius asserts that he can accurately represent that father's doctrines and speak his words. These draw upon Latin Pseudo-Athanasian texts that Vigilius may well have thought authentic translations.[81] Yet he does not merely quote them; two books of dialogue required far greater creativity. The doctrine and exegesis that "Athanasius" professes are Vigilius's own.[82]

---

78. For what follows see Vig., *Dial. II*, pref. II (ed. Hombert: 246–52); on this text, pp. 70–71.

79. See pp. 91–92.

80. On Athanasius in the East, see Wessel (2004), 268; Graumann (2009), 551; in the West, C. Müller (2010); C. Müller (2012); also Gwynn (2012a), 173–84.

81. Guidi (2005), 13, 22–36, 91 n. 58, 116 n. 15, 123 n. 23, 173 n. 72; cf. Hombert (2010), 184–86.

82. For example, Vigilius uses two arguments identical to those of "Athanasius"—one heretic can be used to disprove another, and new heretics make necessary new doctrinal terminology—in *Contra Eutychetem*: see Vig., *Dial. I = II* 1.20–22 (ed. Hombert: 290–95); Vig., *C. Eut.* 3.2, 5.2 (*PL* 62: 111B-D, 135D-136A).

Moreover, on two occasions "Athanasius" refers the reader to texts that he had written against specific Arians for fuller discussions.[83] These lost works, written against a contemporary deacon named Marivadus and the late fourth-century bishop Palladius of Ratiaria respectively, must have been by Vigilius. By presenting these texts as Athanasian, Vigilius arrogated to himself the abilities of the bishop of Alexandria as a controversialist, an exegete, and an anti-Arian champion. Like Cyril of Alexandria during his conflict with Nestorius,[84] Vigilius set himself up as a new Athanasius.

Vigilius's attribution of his works to Athanasius also let him land a blow on an important contemporary opponent. The *History of the Persecution* portrays Marivadus as a favorite of Huneric's during Geiseric's reign.[85] In the midst of a long Trinitarian discourse in the *Dialogue*, Athanasius refers Arius to a detailed treatment of a particularly important Pauline passage, "confirming that the three are one God": "In the book which we have published against Marivadus, deacon of your impious heresy, it is evidently expressed most fully. Concerning this now, in this place, we have inserted a few select things. For, when he was objecting that a union would exclude equality from the Trinity and equality would exclude a union, among many other things I referred to this."[86] Vigilius not only has Athanasius accuse Marivadus of Arianism but also formulates the accusation as a personal relationship imputed within a conversation with the heresiarch himself. Marivadus's name arrives late in the dialogue, after many famous Arian individuals and creeds have been associated with Arius. Marivadus's placement within a catalog of condemned Arian heretics integrates him into this false succession. This potentially controversial contention about an influential opponent is all the more powerful for the subtlety with which it is made. No special reference is provided; Marivadus is treated just like Eunomius or Palladius. A useful comparison is Epiphanius's treatment of Origen in his *Panarion*.[87] The inclusion of an individual whose reputation was still in the making in a list of widely despised heretics slipped a contentious assertion under the radar. This slur is further strengthened by Athanasius/Vigilius's suggestion that he can simply lift his arguments against Marivadus to disprove the heresiarch, implying that Marivadus and Arius held identical views. Marivadus is not simply an Arian; he is the new Arius.

Another dialogue text, the *Debate of Cerealis against Maximinus*, similarly channels the authority of a Nicene father for its protagonist, who faces another earlier Arian heretic.[88] This time, Augustine is the obvious referent for the Nicene

---

83. Vig., *Dial. II* 3.23, 3.27 (ed. Hombert: 387, 394–95).
84. Wessel (2004), 73.
85. *HP* 1.48 (ed. Lancel: 119). For the two Marivadi as the same person, see Ficker (1897), 18, 44–50; Courtois (1955), 225 n. 3; Lancel (2002a), 293 n. 103; Guidi (2005), 17–20; H. Müller (2008), 34 n. 108.
86. Vig., *Dial. II* 3.23 (ed. Hombert: 387).
87. Flower (2011), 76–77.
88. See pp. 75–77; for a similar view of the text, see Fialon (2015), 149–54.

debater, Cerealis of Castellum, in his altercation with Maximinus. The narrative is set up so that Cerealis reenacts Augustine's defeat in 427/28 of an "Ariomaniac" bishop of the same name; the terms of his victory are identical. After his debate with Maximinus ended in stalemate, Augustine stated that he would send his opponent a refutation. The acts record Maximinus's reply, in his own hand: "Maximinus: When you have set forth this book and have sent it to me, if I should not give a response to everything then I will be guilty."[89] As far as can be told, he never replied (if he ever did receive *Against Maximinus*).[90] In the *Life of Augustine*, Possidius is careful to point this out.[91] After his supposed meeting with Cerealis too, Maximinus received a series of propositions to which he was supposed to reply. Again: "Maximinus the Ariomaniac bishop was unable to respond, putting it off from day to day [cf. Eccl. 5:8]."[92] The anonymous Vandal king makes the point clear: "Since Maximinus the bishop, convened by me, did not want to respond, thus it is understood that, when he was silent and did not want to respond to your propositions, he could not."[93] It is not certain that the author of the dialogue was Cerealis himself rather than a colleague or later admirer. Regardless, whoever wrote it made him a new Augustine, capable of defeating his Arian opponent in exactly the same way.

It was not only contemporary clerics who were burnished or tarnished by assimilation to historical Catholics and heretics. The debate proper in the second version of Vigilius's *Dialogue* begins with a fictitious *sacra* of Constantius II, providing orders to the judge Probus.[94] This edict makes a fair approximation of the titulature of the Constantinian dynasty ("Constantinus Constantius pious, perpetual, victor and triumphator, always Augustus");[95] the emperor's unifying goals in ecclesiastical politics, "having acquired our father's empire with divine support";[96] and the language and style of late Roman edicts on Christian religion. Crucially, to create his fictitious *sacra*, Vigilius took from a more recent edict: Huneric's laws convoking the Conference of Carthage (484) and proscribing the Homoousians. One obvious intertext signals their use;[97] there is also another

---

89. Aug., *Coll. cum Max.* 16.80–82 (ed. Hombert: 470).

90. McLynn (1996), 488 n. 61.

91. Poss., *V. Aug.* 17.9 (ed. Bastiaensen: 174).

92. *Cer. c. Max.* 532–33 (ed. Baise: 285).

93. Ibid., 538–40 (286).

94. Unless otherwise noted, all of the quotations in this paragraph are from Vig., *Dial. II*, pref. II, 63–85 (ed. Hombert: 251–52).

95. Compare, e.g., Constantius to the Italian bishops at Rimini in Hil., *Adu. Val.*, fr. 2.7 = A.8 (ed. Feder: 93).

96. On Constantius II's ecclesiastical politics, see the useful summary (with extensive bibliography) of Flower (2013a), 80–81.

97. Huneric twice justified convocation because "many have been found ... saying/asserting that they retained the whole rule of the (Christian) faith" ("plurimi reperti sunt / plurimos esse

significant verbal overlap.⁹⁸ The *sacra*'s purport more generally echoes Huneric's edicts. Both present Christian rulers, concerned for their subjects' spiritual well-being, asserting that the maintenance of orthodoxy is for them a primary duty. Of course, from a Nicene perspective, both rulers were also Arian tyrants whose misguided efforts to fulfill this responsibility meant that they enforced heresy and persecuted orthodox Christians. Specifically, it led both to produce edicts convoking conferences—one real and one imagined—that could be seen as prejudicial to the doctrinal discussion they ordered. Constantius II expresses outrage in the *Dialogue* that some have connected the substances of Father and Son, as unpropitious a starting point for a Nicene debater as Huneric's demand to "prove the faith of the Homoousians ... specifically from the divine scriptures."⁹⁹ Moreover, Constantius's conference occurs at the height of a persecution, as the preceding historical excursus declares, just as Nicene texts portray the context of Huneric's conference.¹⁰⁰ The author subtly introduces a parallel between a contemporary Arian ruler and an earlier one whose ecclesiastical interventions seemed of particular relevance. In a delicious inversion of the king's imperial pose, his invocation of Rimini and Seleucia, and his pretensions to a definitive statement of uniformity, Huneric's Christian policies are seeded in the distant past as the actions of an earlier Arian tyrant. Constantius II is Vandalized. He joins an African Christian landscape densely populated with figures from the history of the Arian controversy.

Christian orthodoxy had its own peculiar time. In the eyes of late-antique Christians, the true Christian faith had been made manifest and defended by certain individuals, in certain councils, and through certain creeds. Nonetheless, those historical contexts could not delimit this faith; it was the church's eternal teaching.¹⁰¹ This combination of the specific and the transcendent is exactly the approach of Vandal Africa's Nicene imaginary dialogues. They are simultaneously rooted in

---

repertos ... asserentes/dicentes se integram regulam Christianae fidei / fidei tenere/retinere"): *HP* 2.39, 3.4 (ed. Lancel: 139, 175). Compare Constantius II's justification of his conference between Athanasius and Arius: "nunc plerosque repperimus ... asserentes se integram fidei regulam retinere."

98. Vig., *Dial. II*, pref. II, 78–80 (ed. Hombert: 252): "*ne nostrae pietatis ac mansuetudinis praecepta*, solita temeritatis audacia *contemnentes, ad gravem nos prouocent iracundiam*"; *HP* 3.3 (ed. Lancel: 175): "qui *praeceptionem* inclitae recordationis patris nostri *uel mansuetudinis nostrae* crediderint esse temnendam censuram seueritatis adsumimus." Also compare Vig., *Dial. II*, pref. II, 72 (ed. Hombert: 251), "homines impia seductione fallentes," with *HP* 2.39 (ed. Lancel: 139), "ne sua seductione animas subuerterent Christianas." On these concordances and their implications, see Hombert (forthcoming), 93–97.

99. *HP* 2.39 (ed. Lancel: 140).

100. Ibid., 2.17–3.71 (129–212); Greg. Tur., *DLH* 2.3 (ed. Krusch and Levison: 40–45); see also *Epit. Carth.* 46r, which similarly characterizes Constantius II's reign as one of persecution of Catholics.

101. See (best) Graumann (2012).

acutely observed historical contexts and deliberately timeless. As a result, it is difficult to isolate one intended effect. The possibilities are multiform: As supposed historical documents, they could provide precedents, even quasi-legal ones. In their cleverly framed discussions of contemporary disputes, they subversively comment on Vandal Africa's ecclesiastical politics. They even trace a prospective narrative arc for those politics: if the Catholics had defeated the Arians in the past, they would do so again. Whichever conception is adopted, the manner in which these writers reproduced and retouched key moments and characters from the Christian past, and added some of their own, was clearly intended to shape their audiences' views about the uncertain situation within the African Church. At a basic level, these texts explained past incidence of Catholic-Arian controversy in a form that chimed with contemporary conflicts and their participants. For those with greater knowledge of this history, subtle allusions persuasively aligned the controversies of the past with the supposed Catholics and Arians of the present. Controversialists asserted their authority as equals of earlier Nicene champions and assimilated specific opponents to heretics already condemned. By characterizing themselves and their rivals as the heirs of historical figures, reenacting controversies whose meaning had already (to their own minds, at least) been demarcated, Nicene writers made a powerful statement about their respective statuses within the African Christian community. By planting their ecclesiastical conflict in the distant past, they reformulated its meaning in the present.

"WE SHOULD CONSULT THAT CITY OF RIMINI"

Nicene Christians did not have the freedom of the historical terrain of the Arian controversy. In fact, their concern to appropriate the history of the fourth-century church resulted from its continuing status as contested ground. Like other Christians less than enamored of Nicene triumphalism,[102] Homoians in Vandal Africa constructed alternative versions of this crucial period. As previously detailed, this historical perspective is best seen in Huneric's edict of 484 that set up the Councils of Rimini and Seleucia (359) as a crucial moment in the definition and transmission of orthodoxy.[103] Several of the texts already discussed in this chapter can be seen as attempts to rebut specific Homoian claims about this past, most notably Vigilius's reinvention of the 330s. Another author responded with a more tradi-

---

102. E.g., the "Eunomian" Philostorgius, *HE* (ed. Bidez); the historical sections of the anti-Nicene and anti-Macedonian fragments in a seventh-century MS from Bobbio, *Adu. orth. et Mac.*, esp. frs. 1–9 (ed. Gryson: 229–44), on which see pp. 240, 245 Maximinus's Homoian recasting of fourth-century ecclesiastical history, particularly regarding the Council of Aquileia: Max., *Diss.* (ed. Gryson). A lost late fourth-century Homoian historian has also been postulated; see (best) Brennecke (1988), 93–95, 114–41. For analysis of several versions of the fourth century, see T. Ferguson (2005).

103. See pp. 91–92.

tional form of historical argument. His text acts as an important reminder that fourth-century Christian history was contested in Vandal Africa as part of the definition of orthodoxy.

The preface to the *testimonia* collection the *Book on the Trinity* rebuts Homoian conceptions of the church and specifically their historical arguments.[104] The precise content makes clear that the anonymous Nicene author was responding either to Huneric's edict of 484 or to the wider milieu of Homoian anti-Homoousian polemic in which that edict was framed.[105] As already outlined, a key point of contest was the authority of Constantius II's twin councils of 359.[106] In this work, Pseudo-Fulgentius pours considerable polemical scorn on Homoian portrayal of Rimini and Seleucia as universal and authoritative.[107] After complaining about that which "they pretend, in the presence of the inexperienced [*imperitos*], ought to be believed by many, rather than a few," because more attended Rimini than Nicaea, he inverts the numerical contrast by setting the two councils in a different narrative. After Nicaea, adherence to ὁμοούσιος grew from the profession of a few bishops to encompass the whole world (3.74–76); "if later they met in such a multitude at Rimini, as they assert, the bishops of that sect would have multiplied through the world, their congregations would have grown, such a faith would even have occupied empires" (3.76–79). The acid test of a universal council was not merely the numbers present but the subsequent reception of its decisions. Nicaea was received as orthodox by the whole world. Rimini was not because "the cunning of that fraud was discovered through prudent and most righteous men" (3.80–81). Pseudo-Fulgentius makes reference to the central Nicene libel against Rimini, the so-called Arian *fraus* by which the church had been deceived.[108] For Pseudo-Fulgentius, this piece of sharp practice had been counterproductive. The council's subsequent lackluster support had merely made Nicaea's universality more obvious: "barely the remnants of Rimini have remained to prove the Catholics" (3.81–82). Comparative historical development was the proof of Nicaea's orthodoxy and Rimini's cunning heresy. A final sardonic remark puts the exclamation point on this argument: "We should consult that city of Rimini, where that act of fraud took place, or rather was inveigled [*concinnatum*], if it is agreeable. Whether it might have a bishop of that sect, I do not know" (3.83–85). The whole world became filled with adherents of Nicaea; probably not even Rimini itself had a bishop who professed its creed.

---

104. Ps.-Fulg., *Trin.* 1–4 (ed. Fraipont: 239–43).
105. See pp. 61–62.
106. See pp. 91–92.
107. Ps.-Fulg., *Trin.* 3.69–96 (ed. Fraipont: 241–42).
108. Meslin (1967), 287–88; Y.-M. Duval (1969); McLynn (1994), 22; D. Williams (1995), 28–34.

Pseudo-Fulgentius set Rimini within a familiar narrative of Nicene definition, Arian deception, and orthodox triumph. He did so to divorce it from any sense of universality or authority in the minds of the *imperiti* whom he saw his Arian opponents seeking to persuade.[109] To emphasize the consistent results of Catholic-Arian conflict, he extends his apologetic narrative to another episode: "Indeed I should talk more freely about Milan, where Auxentius as a cunning schemer [*artifex*] poured out the venom of his sect. His successor Ambrose, filled by the Holy Spirit, destroyed [Auxentius's] doctrine thus, that after death his name in that city would be scraped [*raderentur*] from the memory of the living and his name was considered just like some disease. Then, through this Ambrose, the faith was strengthened in the emperor Gratian and it increased in the bishops and they made it greater and greater in the people" (3.85–92). Rimini did not have an Arian bishop, but Milan had had one, and these were the results.[110] The Catholic father Ambrose had ensured that, after the Arian cunning of both Rimini and Auxentius, not just Milan but the whole empire was once again Nicene. The point of both stories is underlined: "For omnipotent God, who through all the scriptures promised increase for his church, would not renounce his promise, and permit falsity to grow" (3.92–95). Fourth-century events proved that the Nicene Church was the true church; the Arian, a heretical sect.

The competing arguments of the edict of 484 and the *Book on the Trinity* demonstrate that church history was contested in Vandal Africa. Homoians also justified themselves using fourth-century controversies, locating themselves within an alternative metanarrative of Christian self-definition. Huneric's edict suggests that the universal Councils of Rimini and Seleucia were a crucial episode within this facilitating narrative. Pseudo-Fulgentius removed them from this context, inserting them into a debilitating narrative of failed Arian trickery to make Homoian claims of Catholicity absurd. Of course, as Pseudo-Fulgentius is the "respondent" in this textual debate, it is easy to fall into the trap of reading his arguments as more cogent or convincing. As has already been detailed, Homoian Christians had their own potentially persuasive arguments about orthodoxy and heresy. It is in this context that Pseudo-Fulgentius should be read. By seeking to make those claims laughable, he implies that they were worryingly plausible.

THINKING WITH THE DONATISTS

Ecclesiastical history may have given Nicene writers cause for triumphalism, but they had to be careful. Excessive trumpeting of their historical success could

---

109. On the term see p. 68.

110. On Auxentius see p. 113 n. 28. On Ambrose and Gratian see McLynn (1994), 79–157; D. Williams (1995), 128–96.

encourage subversive reading of their present disfavor. As the preface of his *Book on the Trinity* continues, Pseudo-Fulgentius shows awareness of this danger. He immediately qualifies a statement on God's promised growth of the church:

> And lest it should move someone because we have said that the growth of the church had been promised through all the scriptures, and if they claim that it had been conceded through this oppression, they should know it is written in Jeremiah: "the partridge will cry out, it will gather what it did not bear, it will make them its own riches unjustly" [17:11]. And this is most certain evidence that the Catholic faith has never grown without tribulations and persecutions, so that it might be fulfilled what was said: "that through many tribulations and anguishes it will behoove us to see the kingdom of God" [Acts 14:21]. And the flourishing of that faith, the exile of innocents, and the proscriptions of miserable ones, and the torments and oppression of captives witnesses. (4.102–13)

The implication is that Homoian Christians could seize upon this statement as proof that their church was the true one. This potential rejoinder leads Pseudo-Fulgentius to essay a distinction between legitimate and illegitimate growth. The Homoians could not claim to be the church of the scriptures, since their recent increases "had been conceded through this oppression." The Nicene Church in Vandal Africa instead gained validation in this regard by contemporary maltreatment. The model of the persecuted church was often a refuge for late-antique Christian communities in political or social disfavor.[111] Like many other Nicene writers in Vandal Africa, it was a model to which Pseudo-Fulgentius turned.

Such a strategy could be exceedingly effective in explaining away adverse circumstances and maintaining communal cohesion. Yet this was not the end to Pseudo-Fulgentius's ecclesiological issues. Such a strategy also awakened the sleeping partner in any discussion of ecclesiastical legitimacy in Vandal Africa. Donatists in late Roman Africa deployed the ecclesiological model of the church of the martyrs to insist that their proscription and disenfranchisement were poor guides to their real ecclesiastical status. As Petilian put it during the Conference of Carthage in 411, "the true Catholic Church is with us: the one that suffers persecution, not the one that inflicts it."[112] Pseudo-Fulgentius again reacts quickly to snuff out this alternative perspective: "But I see some producing contradictions, and throwing at us the persecutions of the Donatists, whose fury did violence to the laws, and who endured the laws to the full. For if the Catholic mother received some from them to her pious bosom, without the injury of any baptism, without any quarrel, without any insult to the Holy Spirit, [it was] so that they who were converted willingly would grieve that Catholic charity had been hidden from them

---

111. Of many accounts, see Gaddis (2005), 68–130; Sizgorich (2009), 46–107; Shaw (2011), 66–194; Flower (2013a), 127–77.

112. *Gesta con. Carth.* 3.22 (ed. Lancel: 184).

for so long" (4.113–19). Lasting African memories of the use of the state by the party of Caecilian in suppressing the Donatists could align the Nicene Church uncomfortably with the Arians whom they sought to denounce as persecutors. Further qualification was thus necessary. Pseudo-Fulgentius's response was to dismiss the comparison out of hand. For the anonymous Nicene cleric, the two cases were fundamentally different: in each one the true church played a different role, whether rightful dispenser of salutary coercion or proved sufferer of persecution.[113] The identity of the church did not change, even if its circumstances did. Pseudo-Fulgentius artfully calibrated his ecclesiology to explain the activities of the Catholics in both the old Donatist schism and the new Arian controversy.

The continuing relevance of arguments from the Donatist schism is obvious from Pseudo-Fulgentius's close argumentation. It is also evident from the text to which he may well have been responding. In his edict of 24 February 484 proscribing the Nicenes as Homoousian heretics, Huneric not only quotes verbatim from Honorius's anti-Donatist law of 30 January 412 but also problematizes his appropriation of such legislation. For Huneric (or his drafter), the Homoousians were deserving of these punishments because they had sought to inflict them upon others by inducing emperors into error with them. In effect, (illegitimate) Catholic exploitation of imperial legal channels to persecute the Donatists acted as justification for (legitimate) Homoian recourse to Vandal power to proscribe the Homoousians. In the context of such an argument from the past, it is easy to see why Pseudo-Fulgentius would feel the need to restate a Nicene "Catholic" view of the anti-Donatist lobbying of the 390s, 400s, and 410s. Homoian use of the ecclesiastical politics of late Roman Africa did not end with Huneric's edict of unity. Fastidiosus also drew on this legacy to associate the Homoousians and Donatists as likeminded heretics. The inheritance of the Donatist schism was available not only to Nicene writers like Pseudo-Fulgentius: Homoian writers also took it up to make subtle ecclesiastical arguments. Both in response to Homoian attempts to appropriate this history and as a result of their own church's decades of engagement in anti-Donatist lobbying and polemic, African Nicene authors often wrote as if their current ecclesiastical conflict were the same as the previous one. They replayed arguments from that schism in a manner that elided the Homoians with the Donatists. In so doing, they made these supposed Arians into heretics more familiar to their African Christian audiences.

One particularly prevalent justification was that the geographical spread of the Catholic Church had to correspond to the universality of its name. Since the Donatists were almost exclusively congregated in Africa, they could not be that

---

113. An echo of Augustine on true and false persecution: see Gaddis (2005), 139; Fournier (2008), 236–39; Sizgorich (2009), 62–64, 75–77.

church, which was "spread throughout the world."[114] This "transmarine" argument was redeployed in Vandal Africa, overlaid upon a Christian group that, like the Donatists, could plausibly claim ecclesiastical ascendancy only in Africa.[115] Quodvultdeus of Carthage frequently used it to attack contemporary Arians.[116] In his third sermon titled *On the Creed*, the preacher addresses an imaginary opponent, "How is it that you exult, Arian, that you hold the truth, when an evil error, separating you from Catholic doctrine, testifying that you are a heretic, and separating you from the communion of the whole world, condemns you to one corner?"[117] At the other end of the Vandal period, Fulgentius of Ruspe received a request for guidance from an otherwise unknown correspondent called Felix on how to defend the Catholic faith. In his *Book on the Trinity to Felix*, Fulgentius uses this query as a springboard for a developed statement of "the faith . . . that hitherto the holy church holds throughout the whole world."[118] This faith was preached from the apostolic sees of Rome, Antioch, Alexandria, Ephesus, and Jerusalem. "Therefore, compel the Arians, Donatists, Nestorians, Eutychians, Manichaeans, and remaining heretical plagues to communicate with these churches. . . . For they do not agree with them, because through the perversity of their faith they want to be divided off from the unity of the church in one part."[119] In Nicene polemic, the Arians had joined the Donatists as African separatists.

Nicene polemicists also repurposed another key strand of earlier African Catholic polemic: they made repetition of baptism a major feature of Arian heresy.[120] Victor of Vita and Quodvultdeus both highlight the practice as one of the worst Arian characteristics and portray its enactment as a form of martyrdom.[121] Most strikingly (as quoted above), the *Carthaginian Epitome* singles out rebaptism as the reason that contemporary Arians were worse than their fourth-century

---

114. Doyle (2005), esp. 233–40; see also Frend (1952), 206, 323–24; Markus (1970), 113–14; Lancel (2002b), 283; Hermanowicz (2008), 84.

115. Cf. Modéran (2003), 36; (2006), 169.

116. Quod., *C. Iud, pag. et Ar.* 20.1 (ed. Braun: 255); Quod., *De sym. III* 13.4 (ed. Braun: 363); Quod., *Lib. prom.* D.5.7 (ed. Braun: 194–95).

117. Quod., *De sym. III* 9.9.23–26 (ed. Braun: 361).

118. Fulg., *De Trin. ad Fel.* 1.2 (ed. Fraipont: 633).

119. Ibid., 1.3 (633). See also *HP* 2.41, 2.101 (ed. Lancel: 141, 173); *Coll. Pasc.* 15.152–56 (ed. H. Müller, Weber, and Weidmann: 108).

120. See pp. 105 n. 120, 106 n. 121–24.

121. *HP* 1.19–21, 1.30–33, 2.29, 3.23, 3.27, 3.36, 3.45–52 (ed. Lancel: 105–6, 110–12, 134–35, 185–86, 188–89, 193–94, 198–202); Quod., *Lib. prom.* 1.36.50, 2.19.35. D.8.16, D.14.23 (ed. Braun: 58, 105, 201, 208); Quod., *C. Iud., pag. et Arr.* 19 (ed. Braun: 254–55); Quod., *Adu. haer.* 7.38–46 (ed. Braun: 299–300); Quod., *De sym. I* 13.6–8 (ed. Braun: 334); Quod., *De ult. quart. fer.* 6.15–24 (ed. Braun: 404–5); Quod., *De acc. ad grat. II* 12.6 (ed. Braun: 469); Quod., *DTB I* 8.4–13 (ed. Braun: 436); Quod., *DTB II* 14.3–4 (ed. Braun: 486).

predecessors.[122] When Catholics censured Arian rebaptism, they did so as if arguing against Donatists. As Jonathan Parsons has noted, the scriptural passages Ephesians 4:5 ("one God, one faith, one baptism") and John 13:10 ("he who has been washed once does not need to be washed again") were again brandished as proof texts.[123] Fulgentius uses these arguments in the *Abecedarium*, a text whose very literary form makes the Donatists a referent for African Arians; it seeks to imitate Augustine's polemical *Psalm against the Party of Donatus*, another ABC.[124] The Homoians' baptismal practices aligned them with a previous enemy of Africa's Nicene faction. Nicene writers did not hesitate to exploit the resemblance.

Whether an analogy between the two heretical groups was always intended is unclear. In his book for Felix, Fulgentius makes the connection explicit, asking, "What do the unhappy people say who, cut off from the church of God and impenitent in their hearts, contradict the church, and since they try to split that same church, which is the seamless tunic of the lord, are themselves torn more easily?"[125] After this richly ambiguous rhetorical question—are these schismatic-sounding individuals Arians or Donatists?—Fulgentius clarifies: he is referring to both: "That man says that he is redeemed by the blood of Christ. So was the blood of Christ shed solely for the Arians or only for the Donatists?"[126] Others, however, kept this relationship implicit. What can be said is that Nicene portrayals of Homoians as Arians appealed to a lexicon of heretical characteristics that had been drummed into their African congregations in the decades prior to the Vandal conquest. Even if the reader was not supposed to think that the Arians were Donatists, he was to understand them as alike, and thus similarly deviant. If both Nicenes and Homoians kept using arguments developed during the Donatist schism, it was because that was one of the best ways to claim ecclesiastical legitimacy within the African Christian community.

NICAEA AND ITS LEGACY

On 5 February 525, Bishop Boniface of Carthage (r. 523–c. 535) opened the African Nicene Church's first provincial council for almost a century.[127] The meeting's minutes pass over the previous decades lightly. Allusive references are made to "the yoke of grave tribulation" endured by the African Church and the "renewed

---

122. See p. 118.
123. Parsons (1994), 156–57.
124. Fulg., *ABC*. 67–73 (ed. Isola: 38); Aug., *Psalm*. (ed. Anastasi). On the relationship between these texts see Isola (1983), 20–22; Shaw (2011), 482 (with nn. 138–39), 475–89 for a sympathetic reappraisal of Augustine's psalm.
125. Fulg., *De trin. ad Fel.* 1.5.52–55 (ed. Fraipont: 634).
126. Ibid., 1.5.56–6.58 (634).
127. Carthage (525) (ed. Munier).

liberty" provided by Hilderic's grant of tolerance in 523.[128] Arianism barely figures in proceedings concerned with the reestablishment of canonical discipline and Carthage's primacy (seemingly a necessary project, given the meager attendance).[129] Nonetheless, the assembled African "Catholic" bishops make clear their status as heirs to the Nicene fathers, just as Vigilius, Fulgentius, and Pseudo-Fulgentius do in their anti-Arian writings. Before turning to disciplinary matters, Boniface attends to one final piece of procedural housekeeping, a confession of shared doctrine: "Indeed this is the true and Catholic faith, which, once it was written down at the Nicene council by the 318 convened bishops through the revelation of the Holy Spirit, was diffused through the whole world everywhere, and received by the whole church." The assembly gives its unanimous assent; the creed is read out and entered into the acta. All present subscribe to the text: "By all the bishops, it was said: this is the faith that we taught and teach; anyone who is reluctant or avoids subscribing to it denies that he is a Catholic."[130]

Through their acclamation of the Nicene Creed, the gathered bishops claimed descent not only from the 318 fathers of Nicaea but also from the African Catholic Church in late Roman Africa. Several of the annual councils of the 390s and 400s began with a ceremonial subscription to the Nicene Creed or its Trinitarian doctrine.[131] Boniface explicitly sought to revive the protocol of these earlier meetings (and not only because this justified his assumption of the role of preeminent authority in the African Church, which his distant predecessor Aurelius of Carthage had been accorded within them).[132] Through long quotations of earlier acta and canons, the council of 525 produced an institutional statement that derives its authority from African "Catholic" precedent. In this context, the reiteration of Nicaea's ceremonial reading is revealing. When afforded the opportunity to meet in council once more, the African Nicene Church placed itself in the line of the ecclesiastical body that had met in a spirit of inspired collective decision making both at Nicaea in 325 and at Carthage in the age of Aurelius and Augustine.

Boniface's reenactment of the councils of the early fifth century is yet another example of the crucial role that the accumulated weight of specifically Nicene historical precedent played for the African Nicene Church. This profound sense of the definitive power of distant historical events was shared by its Homoian rival, which looked back to Rimini and Seleucia and denigrated Nicaea. As a result, although the conflict between the Nicene and Homoian Churches under the

128. Carthage (525), 1.54–58 (ed. Munier: 256); see also 1.12–16, 1.28–31, 1.126, 1.156–61, 1.245–50 (255–60).
129. Merrills and Miles (2010), 201–2.
130. Carthage (525), 1.304–51, quotations at 1.311–15, 1.349–51 (ed. Munier: 262–63).
131. Carthage (390), 6–24 (ed. Munier: 12); *Breu. Hipp.* (ed. Munier: 30), with Munier (1974) xx–xxii, 53; Lancel (2002b), 159–60; Carthage (419), 19–27 (ed. Munier: 89–90).
132. Carthage (525), 1.253–307 (ed. Munier: 260–62); though see McLynn (2016), 234–37, noting the similarly limited geographical scope of the attendees of earlier Carthaginian councils.

Vandals was in many ways new to late-antique Africa, contemporaries understood it, wrote about it, and argued about it within a thick context of earlier cultural associations. This does not mean that these churchmen were stuck in the past. It was precisely when seeking to establish the legitimacy of their church in the present day and to subject contemporary events, figures, and texts to the glorifying or eviscerating treatment that worked to divide orthodox from heretic that writers turned to the historical resources and heresiological tools that earlier conflicts provided.

For Nicene clerics, this historical turn may have been particularly attractive because they lacked recent favorable rulings. An African Nicene Church that had become used to the regular production of persuasive documentation had to adapt its modus operandi in the absence of the regular conciliar meetings whose procedure Boniface adopted. Their imaginary transcripts rewriting earlier conflicts might plausibly be read as surrogates for the institutional clout of real acta. At the same time, it was in the nature of ecclesiastical controversies that their participants turned to formative pasts to make their arguments. Miaphysite writers in the fifth-, sixth-, and seventh-century East rewrote ever more intricate versions of events surrounding the Council of Chalcedon to strengthen communal cohesion against their Chalcedonian rivals.[133] For the Catholics and Donatists at the Conference of Carthage in 411, the issues of *traditio* and the *causa Caeciliani* from a century earlier remained the key topics of discussion. Both parties assembled extensive apologetic dossiers to prove that their versions of the schism's origins were correct and thus that their current claims to Catholicity were valid.[134] To contest Christian orthodoxy was often to fight over a distant past whose implications for the present required careful clarification. For Nicene clerics in Vandal Africa, this meant using earlier histories and heresiologies of the Arian controversy to produce new anti-Arian dossiers to frame contemporary ecclesiastical conflict.

Contesting that past also meant dealing with the consequences of the Donatist schism. The Theodosian nostalgia of the Council of Carthage in 525 inevitably touched on a central aspect of the age of Augustine. That era had seen a step change in the "Catholic" faction's campaign against their Donatist rivals. The yearly councils of the 390s and 400s were themselves inaugurated, in part, as a means to tackle the problem of that alternative ecclesiastical hierarchy.[135] The meetings in Carthage represented a chance for the party of Caecilian to decide policies and set the agenda for embassies to the court in Ravenna. In seeking to reestablish ecclesiastical discipline in 525, the assembled bishops turned to the canons of these councils,

---

133. Watts (2013) has a neat encapsulation.
134. Hermanowicz (2008), 203–20; Shaw (2011), 66–83, 146–94.
135. For the annual provision see Lancel (2002b), 159–60. On these councils see Merdinger (1997); McLynn (2016), 234–37.

many of which had been formulated in the context of campaigns against and then final reconciliation with the Donatist Church.[136] The African Nicene Church, as momentarily reconstituted by Boniface, harked back to an institution that had sought to define itself as both anti-Arian and anti-Donatist. In this way, the council of 525 reflected a broader concern of controversialists in Vandal Africa with the ecclesiastical debates of late Roman Africa. The legacy of the Donatist schism lived on in Vandal Africa, if not in open conflict between those claiming descent from the ecclesiastical hierarchies formed around rival bishops of Carthage in the early fourth century, then in the use of the same arguments and strategies to contest the status of the true church in a new ecclesiastical controversy.

If both Nicene and Homoian writers could turn to the church conflicts of late Roman Africa for justification, other fourth-century controversies also remained up for grabs. Nicene clerics certainly saw their own ecclesiastical histories as canonical treatments of the past. The characters, events, councils, and creeds involved were, for them, strong foundations upon which to base their legitimacy as Christian authority figures. Yet not all would have agreed. Homoian clerics would likely have demurred, as the Nicenes' own contemptuous discussions of Homoian historical arguments testify. Moreover, it cannot be assumed that Christians affiliated with a Nicene church or cleric would automatically have given greater or lesser credence to an individual because they taught like Athanasius, could defeat Maximinus, or ruled like Constantius II. This is why Nicene writers went to such lengths to explicate the nature and history of Arianism; it is also why they attributed familiar characteristics of both generic and specifically African heresy to their rivals. All the same, the presence of more recondite allusions indicates that they expected at least some of the audience to be in on the joke. By displaying their detailed knowledge of earlier Catholic victories and assimilating themselves to the Nicene champions involved, Nicene churchmen sought additional respect from fellow members of their ecclesiastical institution. Through their many acts of historical re-creation, explanation, and conflation, Nicene clerics conveyed to all of these readers the nature of the Arian heresy that confronted Catholic Christianity in Vandal Africa. The desired outcome was clear: that African Christians would recognize the true faith, "of which Athanasius"—and now Vigilius—"was an able and faithful champion."[137]

---

136. See esp. Carthage (525), 1.389–615 (ed. Munier: 264–70).
137. Vig., *Dial. II*, sententia, 12.16–17 (ed. Hombert: 413).

PART TWO

Orthodoxy and Society

Christian orthodoxy mattered in Vandal Africa. It mattered to its kings, who promulgated antiheretical edicts and used methods up to and including coercion and state violence to police religious uniformity. It was self-evidently important to the kingdom's clerics, who, as part 1 has demonstrated, contested its definition in literary and public confrontations using heresiological tools honed over centuries of Christian disputation. It was also significant for the Vandal and Romano-African aristocrats of post-imperial Africa, not only because of the potential enforcement of legislation that excluded heretics from court and administrative service but also because the personal convictions of individual Christians could impact their ability to participate politically and interact with other members of the religiously heterogeneous elite.

Still, ecclesiastical controversy was far from everything in Vandal Africa. Excellent revisionist work has highlighted alternative perspectives that effectively ignored contemporary doctrinal disputes.[1] Emphasis has been laid on the more secular aspects of Vandal rule and its portrayal by courtiers, above and beyond the often vituperative perspectives of clerics.[2] The result is a better-balanced reassessment of post-imperial Africa and particularly its kings, whose concerns were far broader than their oft-repeated representation as tyrannical persecutors suggests.[3] Vandal Africa has been rescued from its misleading depiction in Victor of

---

1. See p. 6 n. 24.
2. Esp. Miles (2005); Merrills and Miles (2010), 225–27. For alternative versions of the same contrast, see Clover (1989), 59–60, 68–69; Liebeschuetz (2003), 83; Conant (2012), 130–95, esp. 159, 193–95.
3. See pp. 5–8, 17–18.

Vita's *History of the Persecution*. It is no longer seen as a dysfunctional kingdom where "relations between the indigenous inhabitants and the conquerors were consistently poor."[4]

Recent scholarship has provided a salutary reminder that Christian conflict was only one aspect of the Vandal kingdom, and one that could be of greatly reduced importance for some of its most influential figures. This necessary move away from an apologetic Christian narrative has, however, produced a tendency to unhelpfully compartmentalize Christianity in post-imperial Africa. In its sharpest formulations, this contrast between the secular and the Christian effectively evacuates elite society and the Vandal court of Christian characteristics, which persist only within unambiguously ecclesiastical circles. Even when construed more moderately, such a contrast marginalizes both the "secular" interests of Christian bishops and the effects that Christian affiliation had upon the identities not only of aristocrats but also of kings, who presented their rule as divinely sanctioned.[5] As it is, these nuanced versions of a Vandal polity underwritten by a secular modus vivendi remain the most sophisticated approaches to the results of Christian controversy, insofar as they consider the divergent interests of kings, aristocrats, and clerics. Other accounts still perpetuate Victor of Vita's image of a society fundamentally split on confessional grounds, often by subsuming doctrinal differences within an alternative dimorphic schema: an African society divided on ethnic lines.[6] In more or less complex configurations, each framework gives an impression of parallel worlds, whether those separate spheres were inhabited by clerics and secular elites, Nicenes and Homoians, or Romano-Africans and Vandals. Such models of division simply cannot be upheld. All of these individuals were participating in the same society and polity: a kingdom in which the influence of Christianity was manifest.

Vandal Africa's Christian politics cannot be compartmentalized. They had consequences for individual social and political actors, from the court in Carthage out into the far reaches of Vandal power. This should not, however, signal a return to earlier versions of Vandal Africa that make Christian conflict the leitmotif of a "failed state." For these consequences were circumscribed in practice, not only by the routine limits of bureaucratic or ecclesiastical enforcement in the premodern world but also by the broader range of interests and affiliations held by the powerful individuals whose activities were, in effect, the kingdom's politics. Kings, aristocrats, and even bishops had other concerns, which shaped their subtly different emphases when it came to the maintenance, display, or enforcement of orthodoxy.

4. Collins (2010), 125.
5. On kings and bishops see ch. 5; on elites, chs. 6–7.
6. See p. 166 n. 7.

These concerns sometimes countervailed, and potentially overrode, the expectations of a determinedly orthodox Christianity. Recent work on ethnic, Christian, and other social identities in late antiquity provides a means to consider how the demands posed by adherence to the true Christian faith, in a context of ecclesiastical conflict over its definition, affected social and political life in Vandal Africa. Such an approach permits refined elite sociability and bitter Christological controversy to coexist: not as parallel worlds but as inseparable aspects of the same polity. The result is a better appreciation of the degree to which Christian orthodoxy influenced the relationships among the Vandal kings, the ruling elite, and the twin churches of the kingdom.

5

Exiles on Main Street

Nicene Bishops and the Vandal Court

In the summer of 484, the Vandal court at Carthage received an unexpected visitor.[1] Habetdeum, the Nicene bishop of Thamalluma in Byzacena, came out of penal exile to approach Huneric. He escaped the clutches of his minder, a notorious Homoian bishop named Antonius, and undertook an arduous journey to deliver a polemical tome (*libellus*) in person. In the extract of the tome paraphrased by Victor of Vita, Habetdeum lambasts Huneric for the consequences of the anti-Homoousian edict promulgated that year: exile, confiscation of property, and the rebaptism of Nicene Christians. After quoting Cicero's famous exclamation "O tempora, o mores" (O the times! O the customs!), he demands, "If what you have is called faith, why do you disturb the members of the true faith with such persecutions?"[2]

According to Victor of Vita, personal experience lay behind Habetdeum's righteous indignation. Earlier in the third book of his *History*, Victor describes Habetdeum's forced rebaptism while in exile not far from his home city. Habetdeum, of course, triumphed over this tribulation. Though his chained body succumbed to the water, his mind held out. His retort, as reported by Victor, punned subversively on the idea of God as emperor of heaven: "But after you bound me in chains and blocked up the door of my mouth, in the palace of my heart, with angels taking dictation, I composed a report [*gesta*] of my violation and sent it for my emperor to read."[3] In

---

1. For this story see *HP* 3.53–54 (ed. Lancel: 202–3).
2. The full extract is at ibid., 3.53 (203). Translation adapted from Moorhead (1992b), 86.
3. *HP* 3.45–46 (ed. Lancel: 198–99), quotation at 3.46 (199), location at 3.43 (197), with Lancel (2002a), 197 n. 457; Conant (2012), 177.

these two stories, Victor presents a persecuted Nicene bishop, sent, in his own account, to the margins of African society,[4] pouring invective in a set-piece confrontation upon a Vandal king to whom he felt no loyalty.

As is so often the case with the polished rhetoric of a Christian apologist, all is not quite as it seems.[5] On arrival in Carthage, Habetdeum had to secure access to Huneric to present his book. Success in staging this coup de theatre would have required the connivance of influential contacts within the court, rather undermining the bishop's claim to utter marginalization, "cast away from the sight of all the peoples."[6] The Vandal king not only granted an audience but heard out this rebarbative polemic. The expected violent retribution was not forthcoming: the "wicked tyrant" merely pointed out that the matter was under the Homoian bishops' jurisdiction. Even Huneric's referral of the case cannot have been binding, for Habetdeum simply returned to exile, satisfied to have exercised his conscience.

These elements of Victor's story could be read as working against his intended moral: further holes to be picked in his highly tendentious account of Vandal persecution. More sympathetically, they could be seen as reflecting a long-standing tension in Christian accounts of exemplary figures like martyrs and holy men. Victor (and presumably Habetdeum) was far from the first late-antique Christian authority figure to struggle with the correct balance between otherworldly detachment from and confrontational engagement with hostile secular forces. This curiously inconclusive confessor story dramatizes a central paradox in late-antique discourses of martyrdom and persecution.[7] Throughout late antiquity, churches in political disfavor played a double game: loudly demanding, "What has the emperor got to do with the church?" while seeking to negotiate a better position from that very secular authority. "Dissident" churches like the African Donatists and Syrian and Egyptian anti-Chalcedonians are well known for valuing ecclesiastical purity and secular renunciation. Recent work has also shown their persistent and astute exploitation of late Roman courts and local authorities.[8] Individual bishops too

---

4. See Habetdeum's statement in the next paragraph. He was in fact in exile close to his home city in the southern fringes of the province of Byzacena. To be fair to his characterization, this put him at the edge of the desert and thus at the farthest reaches of royal authority.

5. For Victor as an apologist see pp. 9–10. For a bemused response to the Habetdeum story see Lancel (2002a), 329 nn. 480–81, 329–30 n. 484, 330 n. 485.

6. HP 3.53 (ed. Lancel: 203); translation adapted from Moorhead (1992b), 86. On accessing power see Millar (2006), 192–234, esp. 224–34; Kelly (2013a), 47–51.

7. On the vexed issue of whether individuals should "seek" martyrdom, see Gaddis (2005), 160–68; de Ste. Croix (2006), 153–64; Fournier (2008), 59–60.

8. On the Donatists see Opt., C. Parm. 3.33 (ed. Labrousse: 2:20–22), also for that famous quotation, with similar discussion at 1.22 (1:220–22) and criticism of perceived hypocrisy on these terms; see also Drake (2000), 216; Fournier (2008), 50–66, 115; Hermanowicz (2008), 83–220; Shaw (2011), 508–20. On the Syrians see Van Rompay (2005), 239–52, 261–62; P. Wood (2010), 163–256, esp. 164–74, 194–95, 210–12. On the Egyptians see Watts (2010), 216–53.

can be caught in this act, even Nicene "Catholics."[9] It was only through the cultivation of influence in elite circles, in their cities and at the center of power, that bishops could pursue the implications of Christian exclusivity. Paradoxically, this could require them to be at their most flexible regarding Christian affiliation.[10]

Habetdeum manipulated the structures of Vandal power to broadcast his disengagement from them. His visit can hardly be construed as a failure. Whatever inside track Habetdeum had, he used it to risk open criticism and a public profession of faith before a king who had made clear his commitment to the punishment of Homoousian heretics, through retributive violence if necessary.[11] Confronted by this provocation, the king declined to take more stringent action—both he and his predecessor, Geiseric, may have been aware of the dangers of making martyrs[12]— but neither did he choose to show mercy and grant concrete concessions. The actions taken and the opportunities spurned by both protagonists, as reported by Victor, show the range of options on the table for Nicene bishops and Vandal regimes in their interactions.

This peculiar encounter is valuable precisely because it gestures toward but nonetheless eludes any simplistic reading as a meeting of confessor and persecutor (or, for that matter, Catholic king and heretical bishop). In this sense, it is an apt illustration of the complex relationship between Nicene bishops and their Vandal rulers. The incompatibility of their claims to an authority grounded in correct Christianity seems inescapable. Vandal kings could be pious patrons of the true church only if Nicene claims were swept aside; Nicene bishops had to repudiate the jurisdiction of kings whose enactments painted them as criminalized sectaries. To maintain their personal authority and communal integrity, those bishops could both denigrate Vandal power and affect a detachment from worldly politics, modeling themselves on heroic martyrs and confessors. As a result of the hostile stances that both parties often adopted, historians have generally portrayed the Nicene bishops of Africa as an opposition group mutually estranged from an unsympathetic Vandal court.[13]

---

9. See, e.g., T. Barnes (1993) and Gwynn (2007a), esp. 166, on Athanasius of Alexandria; McLynn (1994), 79–219, 291–360, esp. 170–219, on Ambrose of Milan; Wessel (2004), 90–103, 256–67, on Cyril of Alexandria and Theodosius II; Schor (2011), esp. 90, 174–79, on Theodoret of Cyrrhus and Theodosius II.

10. E.g., Theodoret's petitioning of the "Arian" general Aspar in 448: see Lee (2007), 160; Schor (2011), 178.

11. See, e.g., the scalping of Nicene courtiers earlier in Huneric's reign: pp. 181–83.

12. HP 1.44, 1.47 (ed. Lancel: 117–19), with Fournier (2008), 241–42, 249–50. This may simply reflect the addition of yet another trope of persecution by Victor. Cf. Gaddis (2005), 90–92; de Ste. Croix (2006), 180 n. 84: Julian as persecutor because of his refusal to create martyrs.

13. See esp. Modéran (1993), 186–88, followed by Hen (2007), 91–92; also Gil Egea (1998), 434; Nicolaye (2011), 481 n. 18; Conant (2012), 159.

This characterization has had major implications. Recent work draws a sharp contrast between ecclesiastical opposition and elite integration into the realm's power structures. As a neat framing device, the praise of Vandal kings by classicizing poets is juxtaposed to the invective of Nicene bishops like Victor and Habetdeum.[14] The social and political detachment suggested by the bishops' outsider personas has enabled scholars to extricate the polity from narratives of persecution and tyranny and to present rounded Vandal rulers whose concerns went beyond questions of ecclesiastical jurisdiction.[15] The cost has been an excessive downplaying both of the distinctly Christian presentation of Vandal kingship and of the influence of contemporary Nicene bishops—not to mention their Homoian counterparts, often ignored almost entirely. Episcopal officeholders were not always so usefully peripheral; as Habetdeum's day at court demonstrates, they were in a position to move to center stage. Bishops were not marginal figures in Vandal Africa. They must be written back into the history of Vandal rule.

This chapter reconsiders the interactions of Vandal kings and Nicene bishops. The former presented their government as a pious enactment of divine will, a stance that often committed them to tangible support for the clerics whom they perceived as orthodox. At the same time, it is not hard to identify factors that might have led them toward greater compromises: not least, the continuing influence of Nicene bishops. Given their successful integration of other elites into their government, it would seem incongruous if the Vandal kings made no effort to conciliate a Nicene episcopate that had attained a decidedly elite status within late Roman Africa. It would be equally curious if an African Church that spent the first decades of the fifth century continually, and often innovatively, petitioning political authorities abandoned this strategy for the next century[16]—and in stark contrast to the contemporary Romano-African aristocracy. The strident oppositional rhetoric of African Nicene bishops does not tell the whole story. Bishops like Habetdeum were embedded within the elite social and political networks of the kingdom. Few episcopal careers can be tracked, but isolated texts and episodes provide glimpses of alternative Nicene approaches to Vandal power. These possibilities can be seen most clearly through the better-attested activities of two high-profile Nicene bishops: Eugenius of Carthage and Fulgentius of Ruspe. In spite of their calls for the faithful to spurn their earthly king in favor of the King of Kings, Eugenius and Fulgentius were in frequent contact with Vandal rulers in efforts to win concessions or even, perhaps, their conversion. For their part, Vandal kings continued to listen to Nicene bishops and on occasion proved sympathetic to their cause.

---

14. See p. 139 n. 2.
15. See pp. 14–18.
16. For studies of African Catholic petitions to the late Roman state, see p. 97 n. 72.

COMPROMISING UNIFORMITY

The results of royal antiheretical legislation seem robustly straightforward. The terms of Vandal edicts labeled the Nicene Church heretical, forbade its worship, and confiscated its property, threatening both its institutional legitimacy and its material basis. On various occasions, Nicene bishops and clerics were physically removed from their sees, both individually and en masse, and either relocated to the kingdom's fringes (normally the desert south or Sardinia) or held in the vicinity of their home city.[17] In their place, Vandal kings provided support to the Homoian churchmen whom they characterized as "sacrosanct pontiffs."[18] Beyond legal backing for their form of doctrine, those clerics received churches and property taken from Nicene clerics and Romano-African aristocrats.

These enactments might seem, at first glance, to confine Vandal rulers and the Nicene episcopate to a less than conciliatory relationship. They touched directly on how kings and bishops alike sought to legitimate their authority. Through their antiheretical legislation, Hasding dynasts staged themselves, in familiar imperial terms, as divinely sanctioned rulers.[19] Few genuine pronouncements of these rulers survive; those that do harp on this key theme in the representation of late-antique rulership. More than once, Huneric described his territories as God given.[20] Writing in Justinian's Constantinople, Procopius and Jordanes recounted stories that suggest Geiseric claimed the same divine favor.[21] Even the polemic of African Nicenes against their kings as persecuting tyrants and instruments of the devil can be seen as implicit engagement with those kings' claims of piety and providential government. Indeed, the rigid stance against Nicene Christians that Victor of Vita and others decried as diabolical cruelty was presented as part of this ruler ideal by Huneric in his edict of 24 February 484:

> It is approved that it is of the triumphal power of royal majesty to turn around evil designs against their authors. For whoever invents something depraved is to blame for what he incurs. In this way, our clemency has followed the will of the divine judge, which treats each person just as their deeds have merited, whether those are good or perhaps the opposite: either it makes them pay or it happens that they should be rewarded. This is why for those appealing [to us] / provoking [the conference][22] [i.e., Nicene Christians], who thought that the precept of our father of noble memory, or that of our mildness, should be disdained, we assume a severe judgment.[23]

---

17. Conant (2012), 161–66.
18. *HP* 3.14 (ed. Lancel: 181).
19. For modern accounts that discuss these same passages from Victor of Vita, Procopius, and Jordanes, see p. 16 n. 80.
20. *HP* 2.39, 3.14 (ed. Lancel: 139, 181).
21. Proc., *BV* 1.5.24–25 (ed. Dewing: 52–54); Iord., *Get.* 33.169 (ed. Giunta and Grillone: 72).
22. On the translation of *prouocantibus*, see p. 157, with n. 71.
23. *HP* 3.3 (ed. Lancel: 175).

In Huneric's view, his punishments of Nicene Christians were guided by and indeed in imitation of the equity of divine justice. The meting out of "severe judgment" was a necessary part of the portfolio of a king whose rule was ideally marked by "clemency" and "mildness."[24] Benevolence was not due to all suppliants; heretical sectaries were supposed to receive what was fitting. In his anti-Homoousian edict, Huneric argues that the adoption of this austere aspect allows him to declare divine support for his actions.

In response to such assertions—and their material consequences—many Nicene bishops denounced the Vandal kings as illegitimate. To protect the cohesion of their congregations, they exhorted their audiences to consider the decisions and coercive capacities of the tyrannical heretics currently in power and of transient secular rulers in general as nothing compared with the real terrors of the Last Judgment. As well as directly attacking the legitimacy of secular authority, Nicene bishops recommended the renunciation of the worldly, something they themselves claimed to practice.[25] Bishops exploited hostile legal enactments to depict themselves as pious outsiders who had cut themselves off from earthly politics and advantages, like the martyrs and confessors of old. They sought to turn a position of weakness into one of strength by casting themselves as representatives of the true Christian Church, whose faith "the exile of innocents, and the proscriptions of miserable ones, and the torments and oppression of captives witnesses."[26] To defend their legitimacy, Nicene bishops often adopted positions that set them on a collision course with their rulers.

Historians have largely accepted such representations of unyielding royal opposition to Homoousian heretics and intractable Nicene opposition to Vandal power as reflective of political reality. The not infrequent grants of concessions to Nicene Christianity within the kingdom give the lie to a relationship of unremitting hostility. In 454, 478/79, and 523, Vandal kings permitted the appointment of Nicene bishops in Carthage, in Africa Proconsularis, and across the whole kingdom respectively. They returned confiscated churches in Carthage and elsewhere in 494 and 523. Huneric and Thrasamund provided Nicene bishops the opportunity to

---

24. On tensions between clemency and equity in late-antique Christian ideals of rule, see Gardiner (2013).

25. Conant (2012), 176–79, usefully collects references; the following are supplementary. For pointed metaphors of celestial rule and justice: see Quod., *Adu. haer.* 2, 6.27 (ed. Braun: 262–64, 284); Quod., *C. Iud., pag. et Arr.* 21.5 (ed. Braun: 256); *C. Var.*, pref. 22–25 (ed. Schwank: 9); *Coll. Pasc.* 2 (ed. H. Müller, Weber, and Weidmann: 74–76); Ps.-Victor, *Hom. Cyp.* 2 (*PL* 58: 266B–267A); *V. Fulg.* 6 (ed. Isola: 173); also p. 45. For worldly and heavenly rewards: see Fulg., *De rem. pecc.* 1.21.5–22.1 (ed. Fraipont: 670–71); Quod., *C. Iud., pag. et Arr.* 7 (ed. Braun: 235–36); *V. Fulg.* 9, 20 (ed. Isola: 181–83, 204).

26. Ps.-Fulg., *Trin.* 4.111–13 (ed. Fraipont: 242).

make their case by debating correct doctrine publicly.²⁷ It should not be a surprise that these kings did not maintain the strict equity that Huneric had set out as characteristic of a divinely inspired royal judge. As some contemporary Christian readers of his edict might have noted, even God could be expected to be merciful, if his suppliant was penitent. Vandal kings were periodically amenable to the granting of concessions. As a result, the question is not so much whether or not the Hasding dynasty was willing to compromise. Rather, it is how to characterize those compromises and where their origins lay.

SHUTTLE DIPLOMACY

Vandal kings did compromise on the strict implications of late-antique ideals of religious uniformity. The oppositional stance articulated (in particular) by Nicene bishops has meant that discussions of the royal orders which benefited them—and Christian politics in Vandal Africa more broadly—have sought underlying causes beyond Africa. On the one hand, scholars have turned to Ravenna, Rome, and Constantinople for the African Nicene Church's residual political loyalties.²⁸ On the other, improvements in the lot of Nicene Christians are normally associated with the pragmatic demands of Vandal foreign relations.²⁹ This approach has some justification. As Jonathan Conant has demonstrated, kings and clerics alike were part of Mediterranean-wide social and political constellations.³⁰ The African Nicene Church had contacts that pushed its case at Ravenna and Constantinople. The Vandal kings were equally concerned to establish beneficial relationships with other Mediterranean powers, especially the two imperial courts. This made them inclined to grant concessions when prompted by prestigious embassies.³¹

---

27. On permission for appointments see p. 156, with n. 59, and p. 163, with n. 105; on the return of confiscated churches, p. 159, with n. 80, and p. 163, with n. 105; on invitations to debate, pp. 157–58, with n. 72, and pp. 160–61, with n. 88.

28. E.g., Courtois (1955), 245–46, 288–89; Parsons (1994), 89; Francovich Onesti (2002), 75; Maier (2005), 78. See esp. suggestions of a foreign audience for Victor of Vita; discussion and references are in Howe (2007), 52, 361–65; Vössing (2011), 17–20.

29. In, e.g., Parsons (1994), 100; Modéran (1998a), 257–58; Castritius (2006), 193; Löhr (2007), 45–46. Cf. Courtois (1955), 292–93.

30. Conant (2012), 67–129.

31. The appointment of new Nicene bishops of Carthage in 454 and 478/79 and an edict of tolerance in the latter year coincided with such initiatives: ibid., 29–36, 164–65; on the latter, see also Delmaire (1987). Hilderic's similar, if longer-lasting, concessions on his accession in 523 may also have been associated with his close relationship, as a guest friend (ξένος), to the stridently Chalcedonian Justin and Justinian: Conant (2012), 170, 313; Proc., *BV* 1.9.5 (ed. Dewing: 84). Nicene embassies also sought to harness the influence of the bishop of Rome, appropriating his authority for their efforts to preserve ecclesiastical discipline: Conant (2012), 83–84, 104.

At the same time, there were severe limitations to imperial agency in African ecclesiastical politics. Direct intervention was not possible. Emperors could not dictate terms to Vandal kings. Imperial success in pressuring Vandal regimes depended on the balance of power in the Mediterranean at the time, the stability of those regimes, and whether they were expansionary or conciliatory. Realpolitik as much as the conditions of African Nicene Christians had to be part of Constantinopolitan interests. Eastern emperors had many calls upon their energies, and in a century that saw widening ecclesiastical divisions in the Eastern provinces over Christological doctrine and sometimes rancorous relations among Constantinople, Alexandria, Antioch, and Rome, the controversy (or persecution) in Africa cannot even be said to have been a priority in church politics. Sometimes, favorable conditions enabled the securing of concessions. Yet there was little that emperors or their ambassadors could do if the political calculus altered at the Vandal court, as seems to have happened quite quickly after those concessions were made.[32]

Nicene Christians were aware of this problem. Victor of Vita describes the hubris of an ambassador from the emperor Zeno who arrived in Carthage in mid-484 trumpeting his capacity to defend Nicene churches. In what Victor portrays as a calculated snub, Huneric had Nicene Christians tortured on the routes that the ambassador took to and from the palace.[33] Whether or not this characterization is accurate, it demonstrates that a Nicene bishop understood that imperial influence in Vandal Carthage had drastically attenuated. Like other members of the African elite, Nicene bishops quickly realized after the conquest that it was the Hasding dynasty—and not the Theodosian—that now produced their earthly rulers (with all the baggage that wielders of secular power carried for African Christians).[34] As a result, when they sought the involvement of secular authority in ecclesiastical politics, it was more often than not Hasding dynasts—rather than emperors in Ravenna or Constantinople—to whom they turned.

THE INTERESTS OF COMPROMISE

Shuttle diplomacy was far from the only means of contact between Nicene bishops and Vandal kings. Hasding moves to conciliate Nicene churchmen were not simply a result of external leverage exerted by the rewards of imperial recognition and the threat of imperial invasion. It would be odd if kings capable of adapting their religious policies to appease external powers were oblivious to the appeals of some of their more prominent subjects. It would be equally strange if Nicene clerics sought in no way to influence kings whom they saw cave to Constantinopolitan

---

32. E.g., *HP* 1.24 (ed. Lancel: 107–8).
33. Ibid., 3.32 (192).
34. See esp. Conant (2012), 156–59.

senators.³⁵ As this chapter discusses in greater detail below, Nicene bishops did approach Vandal rulers on a number of occasions. As in the Habetdeum story that begins this chapter, such contacts sometimes involved petitions for specific concessions, which were sometimes granted. These episodes suggest an additional set of considerations for Hasding dynasts and Nicene episcopate beyond the strict enforcement of Christian orthodoxy. If mutual hostility characterized many of their actions and pronouncements, neither party was locked into this course of action. Both had pragmatic interests in compromising that could be reconciled with their broader claims to authority.

If this flexibility has been overlooked, it is partly because of common modern misconceptions about royal support for Homoian churchmen as reflecting a "state" or "national" church. As chapter 1 discusses, the Homoian Church was not an organ of the Vandal state, nor were Homoian churchmen simply court bishops.³⁶ The static proprietary or bureaucratic models imposed on the relationship between these particular rulers and bishops do not account for the dynamic character of their interactions, which were always subject to the fluctuations inherent in a court polity.³⁷ For individual clerics and ecclesiastical factions, just as much as for aristocrats, bureaucrats, and generals, success at the center of power required the cultivation of influence and favor. Individual Homoian clerics may have been influential at court, but they did not have an incontrovertible call on this favor; some even paid the ultimate price for backing the wrong candidate for the throne.³⁸ Vandal kings were not yoked to total and unconditional support. As a result, their regimes had leeway to pursue more refined approaches to ecclesiastical politics.

Likewise, conciliation of the Nicene Church need not always have been ideologically fraught for Vandal rulers. Only a small sample of actual royal pronouncements survives. Most were selected by the Nicene polemicists whose vituperative works amplify modern accounts of Vandal royal self-representation (like this one). If we could hear more of Vandal kings speaking in their own voice—or at least that of their legal advisers—alternative visions of their Christian kingship might emerge. Pending the unlikely uncovering of previously undiscovered Vandal legislation, Huneric's emphasis on his clemency and mercy in a law framed by the concept of salutary retribution hints that different permutations of royal virtue could have been deployed at other times. Numerous *comparanda* from elsewhere in the post-imperial West certainly suggest ways to reconcile the granting of concessions to heretics with pious posturing.³⁹

---

35. On prestigious embassies see Conant (2012), 29–36.
36. See pp. 41–46.
37. Cf., e.g., P. Brown (1992), 15–17; Kelly (2004), 180–81; Hermanowicz (2008), 156–87.
38. *HP* 2.13, 2.16 (ed. Lancel: 127, 129); see also p. 42.
39. See pp. 229–32.

There were also important reasons why such concessions might have been seen as necessary. The influence that bishops had attained within their communities and their prestige in late-antique African society made them figures that rulers had to take seriously.[40] Rounded biographies of specific officeholders are rarely achievable, but individually attested actions demonstrate, at the very least, that some Nicene bishops still had the capital, both social and financial, to maintain their communal roles.[41] Vandal recognition of Nicene episcopal authority was already implied by their attempts to challenge this influence and status, continuing late-imperial norms regarding the punishments of heretics that worked to undermine clerics by confiscating their resources and removing them from their cities. Similar motives seem to have conditioned the extralegal punishments that Nicene bishops received from Vandal officials (at least according to their apologists). Andy Merrills has argued convincingly for Victor of Vita's obsessive concern with a form of "social martyrdom" involving the humiliation of Nicene bishops through the subversion of markers of their status.[42] The precise impact of these measures cannot be quantified. Certain roles were probably more difficult to play for Nicene bishops than for their predecessors, their contemporaries elsewhere in the West, or even their Homoian rivals. An early attempt to mediate with Geiseric, for example, seems to have failed.[43] Nonetheless, it is extremely improbable that the Vandal kings could ever have completed the project of unmaking Nicene episcopal authority (if, that is, they ever undertook it on such terms). In all likelihood, the Vandal kings had to reckon with an episcopate that had both the platform to encourage dissent toward royal authority and the capability to disrupt the smooth functioning of royal governance in individual communities. In certain circumstances, Nicene bishops would have had to be conciliated.

The possible openness of Vandal kings to the conciliation of their most influential subjects can be matched up to the desires of Nicene bishops to pursue such concessions. The only remaining traces of most of these individuals are heresiological tractates. As a result, it is all too easy to sketch African Nicene bishops as two-dimensional

---

40. Cf. Heather (2007a), 137. On bishops as elites in late antiquity, see, e.g., Rapp (2000). On bishops in late Roman Africa, their influence, and its limits, see Dossey (2010), 125–41; Shaw (2011), 195–206, 348–440, 490–543.

41. The clearest evidence comes from church building and refurbishment: see 8, n. 36; some of these initiatives can be identified as definitely episcopal or clerical: see *V. Fulg.* 27 (ed. Isola: 221–22); Poinssot (1926), on Furnos Maius; Raynal (2005), A.7, at 433, on Uppenna, and Ben Abed-Ben Khader et al. (2004), 89–93, on Aradi, with Stevens (2007). Uppenna and Aradi could, of course, equally be the burial sites of Homoian, Nicene, or other clerics. See also evidence of Nicene charity in *HP* 1.25–26, 2.33 (ed. Lancel: 108–9, 136–37); evidence of Nicene resources in the fuller biographies of Eugenius and Fulgentius: pp. 155–63.

42. Merrills (2011).

43. *HP* 1.17–18 (ed. Lancel: 104–5).

figures whose crude hostility to those whom they considered heretical can be taken for granted. The persona that bishops adopted when seeking to construct a group identity was only one among many registers they needed to master. Individual late-antique officeholders whose textual corpora have benefited from greater postmortem preservation permit a better sense of this enforced omnicompetence and pragmatic flexibility.[44] Authority and social prestige did not come automatically with a see.[45] They had to be cultivated through competent handling of the demands of various communities and institutional contexts: the churchman's own congregation, wider urban (or rural) community, and broader ecclesiastical and social networks, ideally populated with like-minded bishops and clerics, major landowners and grandees, and representatives of local and central authorities. Faced with the expectations of these constituencies, a bishop was unlikely to get away with a one-note performance as an otherworldly confessor or committed heresiologist. If other episcopal guises tend to be obscured in Vandal Africa, they should not be ignored.

Nicene bishops had to live in the polity that the Vandal kings ruled. As a result, like earlier ecclesiastical "dissidents," they had to invoke secular power in certain circumstances.[46] Such mundane necessities can occasionally be glimpsed. The acts for the second day of the Council of Carthage in 525 provide a precious trace of pragmatic engagement.[47] The penultimate document read at the council was a letter from Boniface the bishop of Gatiana (location unknown) and primate of Byzacena to the nuns of the *monasterium Bagaulianense* (another unlocated toponym). It confirms their license to select a presbyter to conduct the liturgy. What matters for the present discussion is how Boniface signed off on his decision. The letter ends with a formula dating it to 1 May 517: "given on the kalends of May in the twenty-first year of the most glorious King Thrasamund."[48] At a time when the bishops of Byzacena—Boniface included—were in exile in Sardinia, the primate called the king who had sent him there "the most glorious."

---

44. The varying approaches (and efforts at self-fashioning) evident in the voluminous surviving writings of Augustine provide the best illustration. Taking only the most recent English-language contributions to a vast scholarly literature—and reducing complex and context-specific performances to broad "roles"—contrast, e.g., Augustine the preacher (Rebillard [2012a], 61–79, 88–91; H. Müller [2012]; P. Brown [2012], 339–41) with Augustine the petitioner (McLynn [1999]; Hermanowicz [2008], 83–187; Shaw [2011], 490–543; Shaw [2015]) and Augustine the theological consultant (e.g., Conybeare [2005]; Vessey [2005]; Kurdock [2007], 206–14; Humfress [2012]).

45. Modern treatments of even the most outwardly successful bishops highlight teething problems, which could overwhelm the less capable: McLynn (1994), 53–78; Rousseau (1994), 145–89, esp. 150–51; P. Brown (2000), 188–90, 198–200; M. Williams (2011), 89–90; Wessel (2004), 15–73. See too accounts of bishops gone bad: Gaddis (2005), 251–82; and of the ideals that they were expected to live up to: Lizzi Testa (2009), 533–36.

46. Cf. Shaw (2011), 515–16.

47. Carthage (525), 2 (ed. Munier: 273–82, letter at 281).

48. Ibid., 2.370–71 (281). On Boniface see *PCBE I* 156–57 (Bonifatius 18); Lancel (2002a), 313 n. 358.

He did so for a simple and practical reason. Legally valid documents had to be dated. If the monastery wished to defend this privilege in future, it needed authenticated proof. As with other contemporary legal documents, this meant adopting the official and widely used Vandal systems of dating: in this instance, "in the Xth year of (the most glorious) King Y."[49] In spite of his position as an exiled bishop of questionable status in the eyes of the political center, Boniface appropriated the validating force of the Vandal king's name. In so doing, the primate unavoidably recognized Vandal jurisdiction and Thrasamund's legitimacy. Boniface's signature is a reminder that, like it or not, Nicene bishops had to construct their authority within the political and legal framework that those kings engendered. Nicene bishops had to involve themselves in patronage networks inevitably shaped by the king and his court. As Habetdeum of Thamalluma's royal visit at the beginning of this chapter shows, working against the king's interests required one to be embedded within the structures of Vandal governance.[50] Even outright rejection of Vandal power was, in a sense, a form of engagement (however hostile) with it.

The denigration of Vandal legitimacy provided a means to account for their disfavor, but it was not the only way that Nicene clerics formulated their relationship to Vandal power.[51] One anonymous Nicene author writing at the latest in the first decade of the sixth century imagined the possibility of royal support for his church. The *Debate of Cerealis against Maximinus* (as chapter 2 discusses) takes place at the royal capital.[52] On his arrival in Carthage, the Nicene protagonist, Cerealis of Castellum, comes to the attention of the (unnamed) Vandal king character. After a stilted debate with Maximinus, a prominent Arian bishop, Cerealis and his church receive tacit royal backing.[53] When Maximinus does not respond at the end of the text, the Nicene bishop seeks a judgment. The king answers, "Go into your own church. Since Maximinus the bishop, convened by me, did not want to respond, thus it is understood that, when he was silent and did not want to respond to your propositions, he could not. Now God judges between you."[54] For this imagined Vandal king, the bishop of Castellum and his church deserve a con-

---

49. Conant (2004), 201–2; (2013), 37–40. On Vandal dating formulae see Clover (2003), 49–59; Conant (2012), 148–59.
50. See pp. 143–45.
51. Cf. Courtois (1955), 244–45; Diesner (1968), 14.
52. See pp. 75–77.
53. *Cer. c. Max.*, 532–41 (ed. Baise: 285–86).
54. Ibid., 538–41 (286). Fialon (2015), 149, suggests that the character who delivers this judgment is an arbiter appointed by the king. The key phrase is "cui erat iniunctum," which could equally be translated as "the one who had been ordered [by the king]"—i.e., a royal appointee—or "the one by whom it had been ordered"—i.e., the king. Since an additional arbiter character does not otherwise feature in the text, I choose the latter translation. In any case, the first reading still suggests a concern for a favorable decision by a representative of the Vandal state.

tinued existence in parallel to Maximinus and his institution. This rapprochement may take place in a rather abstract Vandal court, but it is not so detached from reality. In an important concession to the politically possible, the Vandal king offers not a complete volte-face—this is no conversion narrative—but rather a grant of tolerance with the hint of something more substantial.[55] The *Debate of Cerealis against Maximinus* suggests that, in an ideal world, royal favor—or at least royal license—would be something Nicene clerics might wish to acquire.

This section has been necessarily tentative regarding the possible interests of Vandal kings and Nicene bishops in more conciliatory modes of interaction. Without a Vandal law code, it is rarely possible to see how kings responded to petitions that tested the limits of their laws or justified the caving to special interests that was a routine part of late-antique governance.[56] In the absence of an extensive episcopal letter collection, like that of Augustine or Theodoret, it is difficult to gain more than glimpses of the regular interaction with central and civic officialdom necessary for bishops to achieve their goals in both ecclesiastical politics and their wider remit.[57] When only two African Nicene episcopal careers can be reconstructed in detail, discussion of the social and political engagement of the broader episcopate in the Vandal period must remain piecemeal and somewhat speculative. The rest of this chapter will examines the tenures of those two bishops, Eugenius of Carthage and Fulgentius of Ruspe. By excluding these two high-profile figures from the preceding discussion, this section has sought to show how less prominent Nicene bishops had to mine a vein of sociopolitical pragmatism. The careers of Eugenius and Fulgentius provide a more substantial sense of the possibilities of sustained pragmatic engagement between Nicene bishops and the Vandal court hinted at by Habetdeum's visit, Boniface's letter, and Cerealis's debate. As their actions amply demonstrate, the cultivation and manipulation of social influence and political clout were far from incompatible with the oppositional rhetoric of a confessor suffering under persecuting tyrants. While they called on their congregations to renounce the world, these bishops sought a better place for their church within it.

EUGENIUS, HUNERIC, AND GUNTHAMUND

Huneric's reign began propitiously for the Nicene Church. The new king permitted Nicene services once more and put in place harsh anti-Manichaean measures to prove his bona fides (although, for Victor of Vita, these moves retrospectively

---

55. For this denouement in the context of other late-antique dialogue texts, see p. 103.
56. On the routineness of this caving see esp. Kelly (2004), 229–30.
57. See esp. Shaw (2011), 195–259, 490–543; Schor (2011), 133–79.

became manifestations of the king's barbarian subtlety).[58] Victor's bitter portrayal of a false dawn makes clear the high hopes that Nicene clerics once had. Huneric's conciliatory turn also led, in the wake of an embassy from Constantinople, to the appointment of a new bishop of Carthage in 478/79: Eugenius filled a see that had been vacant for more than twenty years since the death of its last incumbent, Deogratias. The new bishop quickly set about making his mark. According to Victor, he secured a flood of donations, which he gave out as charity; the money apparently never stayed in his treasury more than a day, and, in the historian's words, he provided "such almsgiving that it might seem incredible that he was spending such amounts."[59] Both Victor and Gregory of Tours also preserve independent accounts of the bishop healing blind men before large urban crowds.[60] The miraculous aspects of both sets of undertakings might be questioned, but the impression remains of a bishop performing highly visible activities designed to win an urban power base. He certainly attracted members of the Vandal court to church.[61]

Perhaps as a result of these activities, Eugenius had a turbulent tenure. His Nicene faction was defeated by its Homoian opponents at the Conference of Carthage in 484, proscribed in the aftermath, and sent into exile (perhaps twice) in the course of that year. Eugenius was recalled in 487, only to be sent away again in the later 490s or 500s, dying at Albi in Gaul sometime in the first decades of the sixth century.[62] Yet Eugenius's position of influence may also explain why his relations with the Vandal court always retained the promise of Huneric's early years. These relations provide a neat illustration of the dual strategy of Nicene bishops in Vandal Africa. Like other members of his ecclesiastical faction, Eugenius exhorted his congregation to renounce worldly things, setting profession of the true faith in opposition to an illegitimate and tyrannical earthly power.[63] At the same time, the bishop of Carthage was in frequent contact with the court and exploited connections there to try to further his aims.

Like his comrade Habetdeum of Thamalluma—and an earlier African Nicene bishop, Victor of Cartenna—Eugenius gave his Vandal king an unsolicited doctrinal tract.[64] An addition to Gennadius of Marseille's own continuation of Jerome's *On*

---

58. *HP* 2.1–2 (ed. Lancel: 122); Merrills (2010), 143–44.

59. *HP* 2.2–7, quotation at 2.7 (ed. Lancel: 123–25 at 125).

60. Ibid., 2.47–51 (143–45); Greg. Tur., *DLH* 2.3 (ed. Krusch and Levison: 42–44). For Gregory on Eugenius see Cain (2005).

61. *HP* 2.8–9 (ed. Lancel: 125–26); see also pp. 181–83.

62. *HP* 2.53–3.20, 3.34, 3.43–44 (ed. Lancel: 146–84, 192–93, 197–98); *Lat. reg. Vand. Alan.*, s.a. 487 (ed. Steinacher: 165); Greg. Tur., *DLH* 2.3 (ed. Krusch and Levison: 44); Vict. Tonn., *Chron.* 86 (ed. Cardelle de Hartmann: 27).

63. Greg. Tur., *DLH* 2.3 (ed. Krusch and Levison: 41–42).

64. Victor of Cartenna sent a (lost) long book, *Aduersum Arianos*, to Geiseric: Genn., *Uir. inlust.* 78 (ed. Richardson: 88).

Illustrious Men refers to debates (*altercationes*) that Eugenius conducted through intermediaries "with the prelates of the Arians" (*cum Arianorum praesulibus*) and sent to Huneric for his perusal.[65] Eugenius's *Debates* is now lost, making it difficult to identify precise motives for its presentation. Theological statements sent to "heretical" late-antique rulers varied widely in tone and import. They ranged from subtle, even obsequious efforts that genuinely sought to persuade to volleys of brutal invective intended rather to reinforce the author's disfavored community and to advertise his confessorial persona.[66] The extant passage of Habetdeum's book certainly conforms more to the latter model, but the format of Eugenius's text and the nature of its presentation suggest, however tentatively, something closer to the former. Demonstrations of victory in debates with Homoian opponents could represent a quasi-legal case for the superiority of Nicene orthodoxy and thus an effort to persuade Huneric to legislate in its support.[67] Equally important is the manner in which Huneric received this case for Nicene superiority: "through the mayor of his palace" (*per maiorem domus eius*). In post-imperial polities, the mayor of the palace was an influential courtier who often controlled access to the king, acting as the intermediary for subjects' petitions.[68] In using this high-ranking court official as the conduit for his pro-Nicene document, Eugenius was exploiting the correct administrative channels to seek a favorable royal response.

Eugenius's engagement with the court seems to have earned a result, if not quite the one he intended. His submission of the *Debates*, and the broader Nicene campaigning it implies, could have been associated with Huneric's decision in 483 to call the following year's Conference of Carthage.[69] Huneric's edict against the Homoousian heresy promulgated in the conference's aftermath explains his original rationale for its convocation. As quoted above,[70] Huneric describes the Nicenes as "provoking [the conference]" or perhaps "appealing [to him]" (*prouocantibus*),[71] and he portrays the assembly as resulting from Nicene pleas of mitigation of a preexisting interdiction preventing their church services: "When we saw this was being disregarded and that there were to be found many among them saying that they retained the whole rule of the faith, presently it was decided that all be ordered

---

65. Ps.-Genn., *Uir inlust.* 98 (ed. Richardson: 96); on the additions to Gennadius, see Baise (2006), 234.

66. Compare, e.g., Hil., *Ad Const.* (ed. Feder), and Hil., *In Const.* (ed. Rocher), written in short succession. For episcopal invective against heretical rulers, see Flower (2013a), 78–126.

67. See p. 64, n. 46.

68. See Barnwell (1992), 121–22, with 88–89, 102–3, 141–42, which suggests that this *maior* could be Obadus (see next page) because this office is similar to *praepositus regni;* but cf. Jones (1964), 259–61, and Aiello (2006), 25–26, 28, where they are separate.

69. The presence of Reginus, an Eastern envoy, at the promulgation of the edict of convocation implies that opinion at Constantinople was also a factor: *HP* 2.38 (ed. Lancel: 139).

70. See p. 147.

71. *HP* 3.3 (ed. Lancel: 175); cf. Lancel (2002a), 314 n. 363.

... to convene."[72] This explanation is in sharp contrast to that of Victor of Vita, who presents the order of convocation as the commencement of a new round of persecution.[73] Of course, the terms of the conference—proof of the term ὁμοούσιος solely from scripture—were prejudicial to Nicene Christianity and likely to end in its condemnation. However, this on its own does not justify the devious motives that Victor ascribes to Huneric. From the perspective of the Vandal king, it was only natural that the Nicene bishops had to prove their orthodoxy on Homoian terms.[74] Nicene attempts to reroute Vandal policy had not gone unnoticed and had even won a concession: the king had agreed to reconsider Nicene proscription. The problem for the Nicenes was that this concession did not go quite far enough.

Eugenius's efforts to persuade Huneric did not end with the *Debates*. After the king sent out the order to convene, Eugenius first had an informal conversation with the royal notary, Vitarit, who had read it out publicly. He then entered into an extended dialogue with the king and the chamberlain (*praepositus*), Obadus, to try to change the conference's terms to better suit the Nicene faction.[75] His first letter to Huneric through Obadus is striking in its tone.[76] In seeking to persuade the king to make the conference universal—thus allowing the Nicene faction to call upon their superior Mediterranean numbers—Eugenius displays a studious politeness, using the correct deferential forms of address for his earthly ruler. He humbly entreats Obadus's "magnificence" to convey his petition "to the ears of the lord and most clement king," who is asked to act "according to the benevolence that makes him so great [*benignitate qua tantus est*] and the justice of his wisdom."[77] For his petition to have a chance of success, Eugenius had to frame it in a manner befitting a request to a legitimate monarch. If doing so could protect the earthly interests of the Nicene Church, even a supposed heretical tyrant like Huneric could be praised with the virtues of an ideal ruler.

That attempt at persuasion failed. The terms of the conference remained the same and its proceedings ended in acrimony. A general law against Homoousian

---

72. *HP* 3.4 (ed. Lancel: 175).
73. Ibid., 2.40 (140).
74. See pp. 89–90.
75. *HP* 2.40–45 (ed. Lancel: 140–43). Victor preserves the text of Eugenius's first letter to Huneric; a series of often hostile oral exchanges between Eugenius and Obadus follows. These read rather like a stereotypical dialogue between a confessor and a persecuting magistrate, part of Victor's broader pro-Nicene apologetic purpose; naturally, there is no way of judging their relationship to any genuine conversations between the two. See a parallel problem with Athanasius's *Historia Arianorum*: T. Barnes (1993), 130–31; Gwynn (2007a), 40 n. 91.
76. *HP* 2.41–42 (ed. Lancel: 140–41); cf. Overbeck (1973), 70.
77. *HP* 2.42 (ed. Lancel: 141). Cf. Gil Egea (1998), 277; Maier (2005), 168; Steinacher (2016), 171. It is worth noting that Huneric uses similar language in the prologue to his edict the following year: see pp. 147–48. This may suggest that Eugenius was playing on themes common in the king's self-representation or that Huneric was responding to a theme from Nicene petitions.

heresy across the Vandal kingdom followed. The Nicene attendees, including Eugenius, were to be sent off into exile, but not before (in Victor's telling) a strange episode that hints, once again, at their political importance. Huneric apparently ordered the defeated Nicene bishops to assemble at the Temple of Memory (an important if poorly understood landmark in the city of Carthage) to swear an oath in favor of a change to the succession: if they pledged allegiance to his son, Hilderic, as heir, the king would return them to their churches.[78] According to Victor, this was a trap. All were sent into exile, whether or not they swore: those who did not, because they had disobeyed the king's will; those who did, because they had violated the Gospel prohibition on oaths. The absurd cruelty of this move in Victor's telling—if Huneric's desire for their support was sincere, why send them all into exile? If not, what need did he have of another charge against proved heretics?— renders it pretty much impervious to readings other than that which the historian sets out: the persecutory abuse of a deranged tyrant.[79] Whatever was in the minds of Huneric and his agents in requiring the oath, this odd sequel to the conference again suggests that they saw those bishops as important political actors in the kingdom, whose approval might help to secure a difficult transition of power. At the very least, those Nicene bishops who swore had bought into the idea that the king might truly seek their support for his heir.

Huneric may have sent the Nicene bishops into exile, but Eugenius's persistent efforts to wield influence at court bore fruit under the king's successor, Gunthamund. (Huneric's attempt to allow Hilderic to jump the dynastic queue evidently failed.) According to the *List of the Kings of the Vandals and Alans*, Eugenius earned a recall in 487. In 494, Gunthamund brought back the rest of the exiles and had Nicene churches reopened, "at the request of Eugenius the bishop of Carthage" (*petente Eugenio Carthaginense episcopo*).[80] The petitions of Nicenes could be answered; their status, improved. Of course, Eugenius's subsequent return to exile shows that his astute political maneuverings were only so effective. Nonetheless, his continued seeking of concessions for his church remains important. Eugenius's persistence suggests that the hostility of Vandal policymakers to the Nicene faction was by no means seen as a foregone conclusion. Huneric and Gunthamund were not simply there to be reviled; they could also, potentially, be persuaded.

78. *HP* 3.17–20 (ed. Lancel: 182–84). On the *aedes Memoriae*, see Leone (2007), 155, with references.
79. On the difficulty of interpreting this story, see Lancel (2002a), 318–19 n. 399; Fournier (2008), 260–62. For more sympathetic readings of Huneric's sincerity, see Howe (2007), 276–78; Merrills (2010), 143–48; but cf. Conant (2012), 178.
80. *Lat. reg. Vand. Alan.*, s.a. 487, 494 (ed. Steinacher: 165–66), with Steinacher (2004), 177–78; on this text, see p. 115, n. 40.

FULGENTIUS AND THRASAMUND

Perhaps even better placed than Eugenius to be a player in Vandal politics was Fulgentius, the bishop of Ruspe circa 508–33.[81] A well-educated aristocrat of senatorial lineage, the young Fulgentius had quickly been snapped up by "higher powers" (*sublimiores potestates*) to serve as a procurator, a tax official in Gunthamund's administration.[82] Like his role model Augustine, Fulgentius abandoned a burgeoning civil service career first for monastic retreat and then for the episcopate.[83] His *Life* portrays him as a charismatic forgoer of worldly ties. Yet he retained powerful connections within the kingdom, including a family acquaintance who was an influential Homoian bishop and offered to pursue redress when Fulgentius took a beating from a Homoian presbyter, and Silvester, the "good Christian and leading man [*primarius*] of the province of Byzacena" who gave him land for a monastery.[84] The anonymous hagiographer, a Nicene monk and close associate who wrote the *Life* after Fulgentius's death (c. 533), provides an account of the bishop's election to the see of Ruspe that is striking for its indications of the potential interpenetration of Vandal administration and Nicene Church.[85] Fulgentius was not the only prominent social actor involved; his competitor was a worldly deacon whose brother had tried to use the influence of a friend, another royal procurator, to procure the see. The hagiographer stresses that Fulgentius's monastic humility saw him appointed. This apparent "reluctance to power" and the contrast it made with the worldly *ambitor* whose attentions the community of Ruspe spurned represent a textbook piece of moralizing.[86] Whether or not Fulgentius was as humble—or the deacon as ambitious—as the *Life* suggests, a fundamental point stands. The Nicene bishopric of even a small coastal town carried sufficient cachet to attract the involvement of two alumni of the Vandal administration.

Soon after his appointment, one of many carried out by the primate of Byzacena in contravention of a kingdomwide ban, Fulgentius was among the roughly sixty bishops whom Thrasamund sent into exile on Sardinia.[87] He then emerged as the leader of the Nicene faction in exile. This might explain why, when Thrasamund sought to recall a Nicene bishop to debate orthodoxy, Fulgentius was his choice; then again, his bureaucratic background and social connections might also have been factors. At least judging by his *Life*, it seems Fulgentius spent

---

81. Modéran (1993), 135–62; Hen (2007), 87–91; Leyser (2007); Merrills and Miles (2010), 196–203.
82. *V. Fulg.* 1 (ed. Isola: 160). On the office and Fulgentius's tax collection duties, see Jones (1964) 260; Merrills and Miles (2010), 164; Conant (2012), 143–45, 376.
83. *V. Fulg.*, esp. 1–4, 14–15 (ed. Isola: 158–67, 191–95).
84. Ibid., 7, 10 (176–77, 184); *PLRE* 2:1012; on Fulgentius's social circle see Stevens (1982).
85. *V. Fulg.* 14 (ed. Isola: 191–94); Saumagne (1962), 425; Rapp (2005), 202. On the author see Leyser (2007), 177–78, and now Isola (2016), 7–25.
86. Leyser (2007), 176.
87. *V. Fulg.* 17–18 (ed. Isola: 197–200); Merrills and Miles (2010), 196.

considerable time at Carthage, rallying the Nicene congregation and debating Homoian opponents.[88] On two occasions he was required to respond to Thrasamund on doctrinal matters.[89] The first time round, the king put forward a doctrinal statement that Fulgentius was to answer.[90] The bishop repackaged this document as a series of statements which he answers one by one. Intriguingly, Fulgentius begins the text with Thrasamund's approving citation of a passage from the *Book of the Catholic Faith*, the document submitted by the Nicene party to the Conference of Carthage in 484. The Vandal king had put forward a shared point of reference, which Fulgentius chose to emphasize.[91] In this way, Thrasamund held out hope that he could be convinced by his Nicene interlocutor; his indeterminate stance also lent extra weight to his harsh criticism of Nicene doctrine.[92]

When Thrasamund next sent a theological statement, Fulgentius was supposed to respond immediately, but he refused: always a wise decision in late-antique doctrinal controversy, which frequently seized upon unguarded statements.[93] Instead, he took his time over a three-book treatise that both answered the king and entreated his conversion to true, Nicene Christianity.[94] The text opens with Fulgentius's explanation for disobeying the king's orders, followed by a defense of its content: the bishop must not deny Christ before men (1.1). He then tacks a steady course, emphasizing biblical precepts of doing honor to both temporal kings and God, the sempiternal King of Kings (1.2). The model of the Old Testament prophet speaking truth to an earthly ruler provides Fulgentius with a safety net as he walks the tightrope between competing expectations of courtly politesse and antiheretical polemic.[95] Strikingly, the text then moves into a quasi-panegyrical passage.[96] Thrasamund (already "most clement king," *clementissimus rex*, "most pious king," *piissimus rex*, and "your mildness," *tua mansuetudo*) is praised for his wisdom and learning, especially in Christian terms, and particularly as a barbarian king "constantly occupied by the numerous cares of rule";[97] such things are expected more of the leisured or Roman. These studies are lauded for the good example they provide to his people. Thrasamund is applauded for ruling Africa with moderation:

---

88. *V. Fulg.* 20–21 (ed. Isola: 202–8). Eno (1997), xvii, suggests that Fulgentius was in Carthage in 516/17–18/19—followed by Merrills and Miles (2010), 196–97—but supplies no justification. See Modéran (1993), 156.
89. See pp. 82–83.
90. Fulg., *Dict. Tras.* (ed. Fraipont); *V. Fulg.* 21 (ed. Isola: 204–5).
91. Fulg., *Dict. Tras.* 1–4 (ed. Fraipont: 71).
92. See esp. Fulg., *Dict. Tras.* 568–80 (ed. Fraipont: 85).
93. See p. 39 n. 39.
94. Fulg., *Ad Tras.* (ed. Fraipont).
95. On Fulgentius's biblical models see Parsons (1994), 335–36.
96. Cf. Isola (1994–95); Diesner (1966b), 38.
97. Fulg., *Ad Tras.* 1.2.2.95–96 (ed. Fraipont: 99).

rightly, he is more interested in broadening the extent of his spirit than that of his kingdom.[98] This is praise to bear comparison with the encomiastic verse of contemporary African court poets and commensurate with the acceptable means of addressing a ruler.[99] Thrasamund's decision to recall Fulgentius was rewarded with an elaborate public statement of his virtues delivered by this prominent Nicene bishop.

Indeed, this Thrasamund is an ideal Christian monarch: clement, mild, tireless in his governance, pious, biblically learned, and seeking spiritual successes over martial victories. Like any good panegyrist, Fulgentius both conveys these expectations and shows his subject's realization of them. Of course, there is an edge to this depiction, as becomes clear in the text's postscript.[100] If Thrasamund does indeed represent this Christian ideal, he will naturally want to recognize the truth: that is, Nicene Christianity. Fulgentius ends with a prayer, that Thrasamund should honor Christ as he honors God the Father. Vandal dynastic politics too find a carefully judged place: "for this is deserved by you, so that you might profess him, who made you better than your father, to be equal to his Father according to the divine nature." One final gambit is offered seeking Thrasamund's conversion: "I beg, glorious king, that you might consider in yourself the largesse of divine tribute and not diminish the power of the giver, so that he who gave you a temporal kingdom might also give you the sempiternal one."[101]

Without knowing the original text to which Fulgentius was responding, it is difficult to know what to make of this plea. Still, it is hard not to suspect that Fulgentius somewhat reinterpreted his brief, especially as Ambrose had done something very similar in the late 370s with his *De fide*, taking an order to defend his theological views as a royal request for doctrinal instruction.[102] Nevertheless, however disingenuous Fulgentius's portrayal of a king on the point of conversion was, the tone of the text remains important. Rather than being explicitly polemical, the tract maintains its conceit of a theological primer throughout, explaining Christ's two natures, his eternity, and his passion. The early chapters categorize numerous heresies, but Arians are never mentioned by name,[103] nor is an Arian Christology consistently in the back of Fulgentius's mind as he delineates the Nicene view. Direct heresiological accusations against the king or his Homoian subjects are

---

98. Cf. Fulg., *De uerit. praed.* 2.39 (ed. Fraipont: 516–17), for a similar conception of ideal rulership but in more generic terms.

99. See p. 8 n. 34; esp. Chalon et al. (1985), 249–50.

100. Fulg., *Ad Tras.* 3.36 (ed. Fraipont: 184–85).

101. Ibid., 3.36.2 (185).

102. Ambrose, *De fide* (ed. Faller); McLynn (1994), 79–106, 111–19.

103. Fulg., *Ad Tras.* 1.4 (heresy in general and Jews), 1.5 (Manichaeans), 1.6 (Photinians and Sabellians), 1.7 (those who deny that the Son was born substantially from the Father, with no reference to Arians) (ed. Fraipont: 100–104).

entirely absent. In fact, the most strident denunciation of a heretical group comes at the beginning of the third book, with an attack on those who thought the Son's divine nature suffered on the cross: a clear reference to contemporary Eastern doctrinal disputes.[104]

Fulgentius took pains to find an acceptable and nonconfrontational (or at least more subtly confrontational) means to present the Nicene case to the king. His effort failed; he was sent back into exile. Yet his sojourn in Carthage remains revealing: like contemporary panegyrists, he could acclaim Thrasamund as a legitimate king; he also felt it worthwhile to produce a sustained and exhaustive argument in an attempt at conversion. Thrasamund, for his part, not only recalled Fulgentius from exile but afforded him the oxygen of publicity and was rewarded with the customary praise befitting a ruling monarch. The former royal official put in a deft courtly performance, reminding Nicene attendants how to order their loyalties. The king presented himself as a learned exegete and a conciliatory figure in ecclesiastical politics. Both parties emerged from the encounter with credit, their legitimacy as political actors tacitly accepted.

On Thrasamund's death in 523, the king's cousin Hilderic took power. One of his first acts was to grant major concessions to Nicene Christians. On his orders, episcopal exiles were recalled, churches reopened, and a new bishop of Carthage consecrated. This was no one-off. Hilderic upheld a policy of tolerance toward the Nicene Church throughout his seven-year reign. Across the kingdom, the primates of the African provinces ordained new bishops and called synods to restore order to a fractured institution.[105]

No text explicitly states that Nicene lobbying was behind Hilderic's clemency. Foreign policy may have entered the equation, as when Huneric permitted the consecration of Eugenius, since Hilderic pursued a close relationship with Constantinople.[106] It is still difficult to see how the new king could have taken this momentous step without any contact with his kingdom's Nicene episcopate. His cousin is said to have known his sympathies in advance, binding him by oath not to restore Nicene privileges.[107] Some prominent figure or figures at Thrasamund's court might have persuaded the heir apparent that tolerance was the right course of action. However the decision came about, its result—a boost to Vandal legitimacy in Nicene circles—is clear from the *Life of Fulgentius*. Thrasamund's death

---

104. Fulg. *Ad Tras.* 3.1 (ed. Fraipont: 147–48); Diesner (1966b), 39.
105. Merrills and Miles (2010), 201–3.
106. See p. 149 n. 31.
107. Vict. Tonn., *Chron.* 106 (ed. Cardelle de Hartmann: 34); though cf. Modéran (1993), 154, on Victor of Tunnuna's sometimes questionable reliability.

and Hilderic's succession are made a turning point. Hilderic is praised for his "miraculous goodness," having used his "most clement authority" to restore liberty to the church.[108] This was one Vandal judgment whose validity Nicene clerics would not question.

Hilderic's decision diverged from the frequent impulses of Vandal kings to portray themselves as committed defenders of orthodoxy. Yet his grant of concessions should not be disconnected from the previous eight decades of Vandal rule in Africa nor emplotted as a revolutionary break. It had precedents in Habetdeum's audience with Huneric, Gunthamund's concessions, and, not least, the irenic stance of the *Debate of Cerealis against Maximinus*'s imaginary "Vandal king." It must also be set in the context of Eugenius's shrewd political scheming and Fulgentius's deft panegyrical prose. Nicene bishops and Vandal kings spent a century locked in an awkward embrace. Nicene declamations of Vandal tyranny coexisted with tacit acceptance of Vandal legitimacy. Bishops sought the ear of the king in attempts to counteract their position of political disfavor. They found routes to him: hardly surprising, given the presence of numerous Nicene Christians at court, in spite of Vandal orders preventing Nicene officeholding.[109] Vandal kings, for their part, seem to have permitted and even occasionally encouraged these audiences and entreaties; sometimes, they granted their interlocutors' requests. Even when met with failure, these contacts kept the lines of communication open and offered a means of usefully obscuring a relationship that could become all too clear-cut in its basic antagonism.

The reason that Vandal kings and Nicene bishops stayed in touch in spite of their fundamental doctrinal hostility is simple. Both sides needed some form of recognition from the other: bishops had to petition rulers they saw as heretical persecutors to temper or evade the coercive powers of the state; kings had to engage with bishops whom they legislated against as heretics because of the elite status of bishops in African society and the significant Christian constituency that this elite sought to represent. Neither could simply ignore the other party nor easily circumvent its interests. This is not to whitewash the relations between Vandal kings and Nicene bishops. Certainly, not all bishops were able to wield the influence of Fulgentius or Eugenius; even those two prominent exiles were not always treated with courtesy by their rulers. There was conflict, recrimination, abuse, and violence, both judicial and extrajudicial. This chapter has not set out to deny their significance. Rather, it has been an attempt to understand how the kings and the Nicene Church coexisted in Africa for ninety-five years of Vandal rule. A century of unyielding ideological intransigence was neither desirable nor feasible.

---

108. *V. Fulg.* 25 (ed. Isola: 214).
109. See pp. 199–210.

6

Christianity, Ethnicity, and Society

If barbarian ferocity sought to debate the faith with us and if Arian heresy could dispute rationally—but when has it been rational, when it separates God the Son, the savior, from God the Father?—why did they do it with tricks and machinations, and why did they want to turn everything upside down, with the storm of their fury like the gale of a tempest?
—VICTOR OF VITA, HISTORY OF THE PERSECUTION

As its final excursus demonstrates, Victor of Vita's *History of the Persecution* is the most strident statement of barbarian Arianism produced in late antiquity. Where earlier authors made scattered and suggestive references to collusion between Arians and barbarians, the barbaric nature of Arianism, or the heretical irrationality of barbarians, Victor systematized them. He incessantly collapsed the distinction between Vandal/barbarian and Arian/heretic—and between the normative categories, Roman and Catholic, to which they were polar opposites.[1] Descriptions of Vandals and Arians in the *History* are almost indistinguishable. Barbarism and heresy combine to make those people different from, and worse than, the Romano-African population.

Victor's double negative is often taken as the default (Roman and/or Nicene) interpretation of the relationship among barbarians, Arians, and Christianity not just in Vandal Africa but across late antiquity.[2] An inverse relationship is similarly taken for granted. It has long been almost axiomatic that the Christianity of the

Epigraph. HP 3.63 (ed. Lancel: 208): "si disputare nitebatur de fide nobiscum barbara ferocitas et heresis Arriana rationabiliter disputaret—sed quando tenuit rationem quae a patre deo deum filium separat saluatorem?—quare dolis et calumniis egerunt, et uelut spiritu tempestatis procella sui furoris totum subuertere uoluerent?" Translation adapted from Moorhead (1992b), 90. It is worth noting the collocation of *barbara ferocitas et heresis Arriana*—difficult to capture in English translation—and the slippery manner in which these two substantives become one "they" doing violence to both Christian faith and social order.

1. Heather (1999), 245, 248; Howe (2007), 120–82, 302–18; Fournier (2008), 207; Conant (2012), 180.

2. On the actual diversity of such views, see pp. 183–93.

various groups that entered the fifth-century empire acted as a form of ethnic solidarity.³ These groups' seemingly prevalent adherence to Homoian Christianity has been seen in terms of what an influential discussion has called "strategies of distinction,"⁴ insofar as it made these groups different from the normatively Nicene populations of the territories that their kings came to rule. Being a (Homoian) Christian was part of being, for example, a Goth.⁵ Vandal Africa is sometimes recognized as an exception, given its royals' attempts to make Homoian doctrine the Christian orthodoxy of all of their subjects.⁶ More frequently, though, this form of Christianity is portrayed as essentially Vandal in fifth- and sixth-century Africa and a means for those Vandals to distinguish themselves or even to deliberately avoid assimilation into the Romano-African population.⁷ Recent work has rightly questioned the premises upon which such views are based.⁸ Nevertheless, ethnic divisions tend to be retained when it comes to Christianity, while Christian affiliations are often bypassed in discussions of aspects of elite culture common to Vandals and Romano-Africans.⁹ As Ralph Mathisen recently put it (and he is far from alone in this view), "At a time when ethnic identity still mattered . . . and when other kinds of identifying marks, such as language, dress, and personal grooming, simply were not good indicators of ethnicity, it may be that identification as an adherent of Rimini or Nicaea[,] something that could

---

3. The classic statement is Zeiller (1918), 582–87. See also Thompson (1966), 109–10; Liebeschuetz (1990), 153; Moorhead (1992a), 94–95; Geary (1999), 121–27; Lim (1999), 197; Maier (2005), 18, 82; Mitchell (2007), 289; Brennecke (2008a), 179; Lyman (2008), 252; Inglebert (2012), 18; Maas (2012), 63. On ethnicity and ecclesiastical affiliation in the other kingdoms, see pp. 233–37.

4. Pohl and Reimitz (1998).

5. Thompson (1969), 40; Van der Lof (1973), 148; Burns (1984), 159–60; Moorhead (1992a), 95; Snee (1998), 180; Heather (2000), 449; P. Brown (2013), 105–6; references in T. Brown (2007), 417–18. Cf. Sumruld (1994), 27–31, for the (unhelpful) opposite; Amory (1997), 236–76, for a refreshingly revisionist (but not entirely successful) view.

6. Schäferdiek (1978), 508; Geary (1999), 121–22; Heather (2000), 449; P. Brown (2013), 105–6; now cf. P. Brown (2012), 400–402; Lyman (2008), 252–53.

7. Parsons (1994), 79, 99–100; Amory (1997), 144, 308; Francovich Onesti (2002), 82–83; Liebeschuetz (2003), 77–81; Aiello (2005), 553–54, 565; Spielvogel (2005), 201, 221; Berndt (2007), 216–17; Brennecke (2007), 209; Castritius (2007), 12; Mitchell (2007), 289; Reichert (2008), 169; Vössing (2008), 183 (at least early in the Vandal period); Vössing (2011), 25; Vössing (2014), 29–31, 42–43, 94–95; Nicolaye (2011), 480; Haubrichs (2012), 42; Inglebert (2012), 18. Cf. Courtois (1955), 223–27.

8. E.g., there is nothing specifically "Germanic" about Homoian doctrine: Brennecke (2008b); (2014). On the absence of a uniform "Vandal" culture distinct from that of Romano-African contemporaries, see pp. 171–75.

9. Slippery terminological issues also persist: all too often, Vandal and Homoian are made synonymous or deployed as an ambiguous compound, "Vandal Homoian (or Arian)," which implies a specifically or exclusively Vandal form of Christianity: see, e.g., Heather (2007a), 138; Nicolaye (2011), 477–78; Fournier (2012). On the ambiguities of the multiple scholarly meanings of *Vandal* (ethnic, political, chronological): see Von Rummel (2002), 131 n. 1.

be concretely determined, served primarily as a means of establishing or declaring ethnic identity."[10]

This chapter reassesses the degree to which ethnicity influenced the social environment in which Christian identities were articulated, by interrogating the perspectives of the authority figures who sought to define and police orthodox Christian communities. It argues that the dominant paradigm of dual ethnic and Christian affiliations—of an inevitable connection between Nicenes and Romans, and Homoians and Vandals—does justice neither to the variety and subtlety of contemporary perspectives nor to the insights of recent critical work on group identities in late antiquity. This chapter takes as its starting point the proposition that ethnic and Christian affiliations were not always relevant for individuals in their social interactions. Individual identity is multifaceted and situational, in the sense that the manner in which it manifests itself depends to an important degree on the specific situation in which it does so.[11] This means that what (for example) their "Vandalness" or "Catholicity" meant to an individual—or to those with whom they interacted—was constantly changing. More than that, those ethnic and Christian identities themselves varied in their "salience" (to use a now standard sociological term).[12] "Vandalness" or "Catholicity" was just one aspect of a person's selfhood; it did not govern all the other facets of who they were (for example, gender, social status, occupation, familial roles). As a result, texts like Victor of Vita's *History* that discuss the implications of particular forms of identity cannot be treated simply as reflections of wider cultural norms. They are better read as attempts to shape them while confronting (and thus revealing) much greater variety in actual social practice.

In sharp contrast to Victor, this chapter begins by taking Christian and ethnic identities separately. It suggests that both of these forms of group identity were of at most intermittent relevance for contemporaries. Neither Christian nor ethnic communities were stable or bounded groups. Exhortations in sermons, tractates, and royal pronouncements document a multitude of ways in which Christians were not supposed to traverse the boundaries of their confessional community: such exhortations imply that Christians probably did, as a result of alternative conceptions of what it meant to be properly Christian. While numerous texts attest Christian authority figures worrying about Christians *not* worrying about heresiological exclusivity—about being Nicene or Homoian—there is little evidence of parallel concerns for ethnic distinction. Practices once read as means of ethnic self-identification are better understood as ways to display social superiority. Far from participating in separate ethnic communities, Vandal and Romano-African

---

10. Mathisen (2014), 190.
11. The classic study is Geary (1983).
12. For the best concise summary of this point see Rebillard (2012a), 4–5.

aristocrats shared a common elite culture, which they used to compete with one another in displays of their prestige.

What can be said for Christian and ethnic forms of identity in isolation counts doubly in their intersection. Among their strictures upon what it meant to be properly part of Christian groups, neither Vandal kings nor clerics (whether Homoian, Vandal, or Nicene) can be seen to rate ethnic affiliation as an important criterion for church membership. There is no clear surviving evidence that kings or clerics made doctrinal difference into ethnic distinction: they evince a generic concern for orthodoxy. All of these figures focused on powerful Christians, not Vandal or Roman ones. Edicts aimed to ensure the Homoian orthodoxy of anyone in royal service, whatever their ethnicity. Nicene polemic inverted those demands by denouncing the political power and worldly gain associated with a heretical confession; its authors aimed to persuade elite actors to prioritize orthodoxy over social status and political loyalty. In this sense, the policing of orthodoxy reflected the courtly and aristocratic milieu shared by elite Vandals and Romano-Africans. When imagining communities of orthodox Christians, kings and clerics rarely thought about a particular ethnic group. Instead, they concentrated upon the ruling elite, both Vandal and Romano-African, within the kingdom.

The role of ethnicity in these efforts at Christian group formation was much more circumscribed than has often been thought. Ethnic group formation and ethnographic perspectives nonetheless influenced how visions of an ideal orthodox (imagined) community were translated into concrete action. However, contemporary understanding of these two forms of identity was much more subtle and varied than Victor of Vita's portrayal of barbarian Arianism—or modern conceptions of Vandal Homoian Christianity—allows. Individual kings and clerics held differing conceptions of Vandal identity, how it related to Christian affiliation, and how that relationship pertained to concrete situations. Both Vandal kings and Nicene clerics had a surprisingly flexible approach to the intersection of ethnicity and Christianity. To be sure, on a number of occasions, Nicene clerics hinted at a connection between ethnic and Christian communities and alluded to the negative characteristics of barbarians, Arians, or barbarian Arians. Such allusions suggest that feelings of dual ethnic/confessional hostility were present among their congregations, ready to be invoked if necessary. Still, when it came to discussions of Vandal Christians, Nicene writers could be unexpectedly sympathetic. Passages in the *Carthaginian Epitome* and the *Conference of Augustine with Pascentius* suggest that, when Nicene writers were not seeking to explain away their current earthly tribulations, Vandal Christians could be treated like their Romano-African counterparts. Even Victor makes an exception: a pair of Nicene Vandal confessors who are exempted from his cultural stereotyping.[13] Nicene authors recognized that

---

13. See pp. 188–89.

the intersection of ethnicity and confession was complex; it had to be discussed carefully so as to meet the needs of particular situations. No other contemporary African writer felt the need to make the relationship between these two forms of identity so clear cut. In this sense, Victor of Vita's *History* is an anomaly.

BOUNDARY MANAGEMENT

A central matter at stake in this chapter is how far Christians in Vandal Africa always saw adherence to a specifically orthodox (in the sense of Nicene or Homoian) Christianity as determining their actions, even when it cut against the normal pattern of social relations—and specifically with fellow Christians. A particularly clear example of such everyday sociability comes in the preface to one of Fulgentius of Ruspe's many works of doctrinal troubleshooting: the *Book on the Trinity to Felix*.[14] The eponymous addressee, a zealous Nicene Christian, had repeatedly requested a book setting out "how to believe concerning the holy Trinity." Felix had particular reason to make this request for consultation, which Fulgentius recounts: "You earnestly enquire . . . how you might be able to defend the Catholic and orthodox faith against the errors of heretics, particularly those whose society you enjoy [*praesertim quorum societate frueris*]." This Nicene Christian was in regular contact with Homoians, with whom he discussed doctrine (seemingly among other things). Notably, Fulgentius moves on to fulfill his acquaintance's request without passing comment on the ethics of the social interactions that motivated it. Neither the bishop nor this particularly pious layman seems (at least on this occasion) to have thought that such contacts were a problem in themselves, perhaps an indication of just how commonplace they were. Of course, both Fulgentius and Felix were careful to mark out the heresiological boundaries between Felix and his Arian acquaintances, even as he "crossed" them by seeking out the Arians' company. Yet there is no guarantee that all Christians would have been so cognizant of this dividing line.

Felix's experience ties in with the findings of numerous recent studies of Christian identity in late antiquity (although such work generally focuses on putative dichotomies between Christians and pagans or Jews). Late-antique Christian communities did not exist in the world simply as distinct social groups. Whatever latent group solidarity they possessed had to be mobilized, whether through physical gatherings of people or, more subtly, through the inculcation of particular attitudes and habits within group members. This was not an easy task. Among others, Jaclyn Maxwell and Bella Sandwell (on John Chrysostom in Antioch) and Éric Rebillard (on Augustine in Hippo) have convincingly used the evidence of sermons to show the gulf between the rigidly normative and prescriptive statements

14. Fulg., *De Trin. ad Fel.* 1.1.1 (ed. Fraipont: 633).

of preachers and the plurality of beliefs and practices among their congregations.[15] It might be suggested that the difficulties of late-antique Christian clerics in getting their congregations to live as Christians according to their definitions, and to respect the boundaries they drew regarding what that entailed, were even greater when (as here) those boundaries divided Christians.[16] Just as John Chrysostom and Augustine struggled to impose a logic of religious exclusivity upon the social decisions of their congregants, so the normative statements of Nicene and Homoian clerics in Vandal Africa confronted communities of Christians whose identities as social actors and Christians were far from wholly shaped by the polarizing effects of heresiological rhetoric. After all, as the previous chapter discusses, even those clerics could be flexible in their sociability.

As in Chrysostom's Antioch or Augustine's Hippo, effort was expended in Vandal Africa to make religious differences a meaningful part of Christians' social interactions. Clerics drew the boundaries of their communities with respect to doctrinal affiliation.[17] Both Nicene and Homoian writers used heresiology to claim that they alone represented the true church and to persuade African Christians of this.[18] They sought to ensure that their readers and congregations respected the dividing line between orthodoxy and heresy in various aspects of their sociability, a concern that Vandal kings also shared. Nicene clerics told their audiences to avoid the churches of their opponents;[19] they were to accept neither their charity nor their promises of advancement;[20] even conversation with Arian heretics was potentially perilous.[21] By giving a new baptism to Homoousians who entered their congregations, Homoian clerics sought to clearly distinguish the two churches and make the true Christian community exclusive of the heretics.[22] Beyond having expected social implications, the antiheretical legislation of Vandal kings forbade potentially unruly dialogue between the two parties and may even have sought to prevent orthodox Christians from eating with heretics.[23]

---

15. Maxwell (2006); Sandwell (2007); Rebillard (2012a); Rebillard (2012b). See too the excellent Kahlos (2007); Sizgorich (2009), 21–80. Markus (1990) remains the classic account of the problem.

16. On the language of boundary management, see p. 63.

17. Cf. Fournier (2008), 205–11, for a slightly different conception of this group definition.

18. See pt. 1.

19. Quod., *C. Iud., pag. et Arr.* 22 (ed. Braun: 256–58); Fulg., *ABC.* 294–97 (ed. Isola: 52); also Fulg., *De rem. pecc.* 1.22.1 (ed. Fraipont: 671).

20. Quod., *De sym. I* 13.4–10 (ed. Braun: 334); Quod., *Adu. haer.* 7.37, 7.39–41 (ed. Braun: 299); Quod., *DTB I* 1.5–6 (ed. Braun: 423), with Conant (2012), 172; Fulg., *De rem. pecc.* 1.21–23 (ed. Fraipont: 668–72); Fulg., *ABC.* 235–63 (ed. Isola: 48–50); Quod., *Lib. prom.* D.5.7 (ed. Braun: 194).

21. *C. Var.*, pref. (ed. Schwank: 9–10); Fulg., *Ep.* 8.2 (ed. Fraipont: 258); Fulg., *Ad Mon.* 2.2, 3.1 (ed. Fraipont: 34, 52–53).

22. See pp. 105–7.

23. *HP* 2.39, 2.46 (ed. Lancel: 139, 143), with Fournier (2008), 255, on *scandalum*.

These prescriptions demonstrate that, in certain contexts, some figures saw these practices as problematic. Of course, they also suggest that such activities were in fact taking place and that—as in the case of Felix—members of these imagined communities did not see problems with crossing those (supposed) boundaries, which pertained not only to social interaction and political activity but also to public acts of religious worship.[24] Prohibitions on conversation and shared dining point to mundane sociability between members of the two different Christian groups; likewise, suggestions of possible secular advancement hint at social contacts between elite individuals of different confessions. Most strikingly, individuals were attending both Nicene and Homoian church services. Multiple attendance would certainly have been possible in Carthage, and individual Christians may well have been able to shop around in other urban centers across the kingdom.[25] These are precisely the sorts of interactions between Christians that parallel contexts would lead us to expect. For clerics in their polemic and kings in their legislation, differences in Christological and Trinitarian doctrine were of overwhelming importance when defining Christians. It cannot be assumed that all Christians in Vandal Africa made doctrinal differences into meaningful social distinctions.

Similar comments could be made about apparent ethnic differences, partly because modern research into ethnic and Christian forms of identity in late antiquity has drawn on the same critical literature.[26] "Vandals" and "Romano-Africans" were no more "natural" as social groups than "Christians," "pagans," or "Jews." There is now a broad consensus that late-antique ethnic groups were not based on innate genetic, biological, or cultural criteria but rather were heterogeneous communities united by a common sense of belonging to that group and thus represent a question of individual and collective perceptions rather than objective realities.[27] Ethnic identities were social/cultural constructs: they were not innate, uniform, or fixed. Nor did they necessarily inhere in any particular set of practices or outward markers (that is, "cultural stuff").[28] Above all, they were just one aspect of the identities of individuals in this (and any) period; ethnic communities, like Christian

---

24. See Merrills and Miles (2010), 192–96, a compatible approach.

25. See pp. 36, n. 19, 37 nn. 20–21.

26. For modern theories of ethnicity used for late-antique religious identities: see esp. Sandwell (2007); Sizgorich (2009), 5–12, 48–51; Rebillard (2012a); M. Williams (2017) 13–57. For points of convergence: see esp. Buell (2005); A. Johnson (2006).

27. Compare, e.g., Halsall (2007), 35–62, with Heather (2009), 12–26, which are far more compatible on ethnic identity than their authors have suggested (although now acknowledged by Heather [2015]); see now the superb Pohl (2013b); also Pohl (1998a); Pohl (1998b); Pohl (2002); Pohl (2005); Pohl (2013a); Pohl, Gantner, and Payne (2012), esp. Wickham's contribution; Brather (2004), 97–117; Kulikowski (2007), 52–70; Gillett (2009); the (unhelpfully polemical) critiques of ethnogenesis in Gillett (2002b). I have found useful the recent theoretical work of Brubaker (2002); Jenkins (2008).

28. On "cultural stuff" see Jenkins (2008), 12.

ones, only intermittently represented distinct social groups. Work on the Vandals has responded with particular vigor to efforts to rethink the importance of ethnicity and ethnic groups in the late and post-Roman West.[29]

This turn stems, at least in part, from the particular scarcity of ethnic and ethnographic discourse in post-imperial Africa.[30] There are notably fewer examples of the relevant ethnic identifications in contemporary African texts than in works from the other kingdoms. Jonathan Conant has pointed to the absence of elite Romano-African individuals self-identifying as Roman.[31] At the same time, individuals specifically labeled Vandals in texts are most often members of the ruling family,[32] and the lump term *barbarian* is employed rather more widely.[33] This limited use of ethnic terminology might reflect the reduced salience of such affiliations in Africa; it could also be misleading. It may be that, as Conant suggests, Roman identity was seen as politically charged for elite actors and Africanness provided a less perilous and more integrative form of self-identification; the significance of Romanness would thus be important because, not in spite, of contemporary silence.[34] Even in that sense, though, the infrequency with which fifth- and sixth-century African writers explicitly state that being Roman or Vandal was at stake is salutary.[35]

Of course, public expressions of a particular ethnic affiliation would have been important in certain contexts. The Vandals were given land in Africa explicitly linked to their identity as Vandals, "the lots of the Vandals" (*sortes Vandalorum*). In other kingdoms, such privileges proffered a set of concrete and specific contexts for the performance of particular ethnic identities. Royal legislation promulgated, to all intents and purposes, in response to specific cases highlights the significance of an individual's status as (say) a Burgundian in interactions with the agents of the fisc, in the context of demands for military service, and in the working out of land

---

29. Esp. Von Rummel (2007), 183–91, 231–45, 270–323, 337–42; Von Rummel (2008), 157–64; Berndt (2007); Berndt (2010); Steinacher (2008); Steinacher (2011), 66–73; Merrills and Miles (2010), 83–108; Conant (2012), 43–66, 130–95.

30. Such moves have also been easier to make because of the Vandals' marginality in early to mid-twentieth-century debates about barbarian groups (see p. 3 n. 11); they thus carry fewer assumptions than groups that better served national or nationalist agendas (e.g., Franks, Anglo-Saxons) or became crucial for particular models (e.g., the Goths for ethnogenesis).

31. Conant (2012), 186–93, esp. 186.

32. Something similar can be said for Ostrogothic Italy: Amory (1997), 464–65.

33. For a partial survey see Howe (2007), 147–48.

34. Conant (2012), 186.

35. The unmatched pair of "Vandal" ("ethnic") and "Roman" (possibly "ethnic" but also "cultural"/"universal"/"imperial") identity further complicates this issue. The degree to which specific individuals would have seen Vandal ethnicity and Roman identity as compatible or incompatible remains an open question, but one significantly problematized by the reemergence of strong local/provincial identities in the fifth century: see, e.g., Mathisen (1993), 17–26; Amory (1997), esp. 277–313; Gillett (2009), 393–96. For a preliminary exploration of some aspects of this intractable issue, see Pohl (2014).

disputes.[36] That the same might be said for Vandal Africa is plausible in this comparative context, especially given Procopius's suggestion that these lands were tax exempt from the original settlement and the wider sense from contemporary texts of Vandals as "servants of the king." It is difficult to say more given the absence in the African material of laws comparable to those surviving from fifth- and sixth-century Gaul and Italy.[37] Contexts that required or encouraged an outward claim to or expression of status as a Vandal must have existed, but they remain inaccessible to modern observers.

The commonalities between Vandals and Romano-Africans are what seem most obvious from contemporary texts and material culture. On the one hand, there is the considerable evidence for Vandal adoption of (what have been seen as) Roman customs, lifestyle choices, and modes of expression, such as villas, bathing, rhetorical education, and literary patronage.[38] Late fifth- and early sixth-century African poets present particularly nice examples of these prestigious activities, whether it is Luxorius's descriptions of pleasure gardens and a hunting scene incorporated into their elegant residences by Vandal dynasts and aristocrats or Dracontius's recollection of barbarians attending Latin grammar classes (that crucial stage in the life course of an elite Roman male).[39] On the other hand, many cultural signifiers once seen as inherently Vandal—particularly dress and appearance—have been shown to be common to a broader late-antique Mediterranean military culture in which the elite of the empire also participated.[40] As a result, the practices of contemporary elites are more easily read as elements of a common culture than as sites of ethnic differentiation. In Conant's words, "from the vantage point of the twenty-first century their ways of life are virtually indistinguishable."[41]

---

36. Innes (2006); Halsall (2007), 422–54 (445 for Africa).

37. For the most comprehensive recent accounts of the *sortes*, see Tedesco (2012); Modéran (2014), 155–79; Steinacher (2016), 151–66. On their tax-exempt status, see Proc., *BV* 1.5.11–15 (ed. Dewing: 50); Merrills and Miles (2010), 66–68; Conant (2012), 47–48; see also *HP* 1.22 (ed. Lancel: 106–7), with Von Rummel (2011), 26; Modéran (2014), 166–67. On Vandal identity and military/political service see pp. 180–83. The precise significance of the *sortes* for Vandal identity was essentially linked to the ongoing conditions of this landholding and tax exemption, for which there is no evidence from Africa. For a putative connection to ongoing military or political service, see, e.g., Tedesco (2012), 205–211, 222–23; Steinacher (2016), 165–66. Comparative evidence gets us only so far, given the need to differentiate between processes of settlement in different kingdoms: see Wickham (2005), 86; Halsall (2007), 436; Steinacher (2016), 157–58; cf. Innes (2006), 48.

38. Miles (2005); Merrills and Miles (2010), 97–102, 204–27; Conant (2012), 43–58, 65–66; cf. Halsall (2007), 496–97.

39. *AL* 299, 327, 364 (ed. Shackleton-Bailey: 246–47, 262–63, 283); Drac., *Rom.* 1, pref. 12–15 (ed. Bouquet and Wolff: 1:134). On grammarians and life course, Kaster (1988) is fundamental.

40. Von Rummel (2007); Merrills and Miles (2010), 83, 97–102. See also Swift (2006), on the Rhine-Danube frontier.

41. Conant (2012), 66.

This does not mean that aspects of this common elite culture could not have been used to manifest ethnic distinctions. Nor does it show that a Vandal and a Romano-African necessarily were, saw themselves, or were seen as the same. Other indices, like names and language, display greater differences.[42] More to the point, contemporaries could and did distinguish Romans and barbarians.[43] These contemporaries were Romano-Africans, but even definitions made by outsiders are important.[44] The point is that these distinctions—whoever made them—do not have any visibly consistent basis. Certain criteria could be taken as signs of Vandalness or Romanness by some but not others. The cultural stuff of these ethnic identities was not uniformly defined.[45] This means that we cannot impose ethnic ascriptions that contemporaries did not make.[46] Like the doctrinal differences that (supposedly) divided Christians, observable differences such as names and language were not necessarily made into significant distinctions. They could be ignored or even interpreted as if shared. At the same time, things held in common could be made into distinguishing features.[47] Our ability to tell the difference between Vandals, Romano-Africans, and individuals with a multitude of other ethnic affiliations is considerably circumscribed and almost entirely dependent upon explicit statements in extant texts: statements that may be misleading as to the intentions of a given individual in a particular situation. From the (admittedly partial) surviving evidence, ethnic self-identification does not seem to have been a primary agenda.

The activities and modes of self-identification adopted in Vandal Africa have convincingly been explained as means to express not ethnic but rather social distinction (to reappropriate a concept drawn from the work of Pierre Bourdieu).[48] What was important for all of these actors within African society was to convey and reinforce elite status against social inferiors. It has been plausibly suggested that this was a more consistent concern than the expression of, say, Vandalness against Romanness.[49] These behaviors could profitably be interpreted in terms of

---

42. Francovich Onesti (2002), 133–202; Reichert (2008); Merrills and Miles (2010), 93–96; Conant (2012), 58–64; though cf. Steinacher (2008), 253–54; Von Rummel (2008), 157–58; esp. Handley (2011), 24 n. 7.

43. Merrills and Miles (2010), 92; Conant (2012), 58–59.

44. See, e.g., Halsall (2007), 40–42; Kulikowski (2007), 69–70; Jenkins (2008), 11, 14, 23, 57, 64, 74–76; Heather (2009), 24; Pohl (2013b), 26.

45. On "cultural stuff" see p. 171, n. 28.

46. See Kulikowski (2007), 61–62, on the Goths.

47. For important general discussions, see Pohl (1998b), at 20–22; Brather (2002), 171–72; Heather (2009), 14.

48. Von Rummel (2007), 191, 323, 342; Von Rummel (2008), 157–64; Merrills and Miles (2010), 92–93; Steinacher (2011), 66–73; Conant (2012), 52. This turn from ethnic to social distinction reverses the adoption of the phrase "strategies of distinction" by Pohl and Reimitz (1998), taken from Bourdieu (1984), 66, about *social* distinction. See Pohl (1998a), 5–6, with criticism of Gillett (2002a), 16 n. 26.

49. Merrills and Miles (2010), 92–93.

an elite habitus (using another term elaborated upon by Bourdieu, which, perhaps surprisingly, has been more popular in accounts of late-antique religious identities than ethnic ones).[50] In that light, Vandals and Romano-Africans would both have been acting according to a shared cultural sense of how elites should behave. This best explains the common signifiers that both sets of individuals used: they acted as effective means of communicating this status to one another and to the rest of society. High-status individuals of all ethnicities in the Vandal kingdom operated in the same sociopolitical setting and—whatever the implications of specific property rights or tax status—with similar requirements, expectations, and possibilities.[51] As Andy Merrills and Richard Miles put it, within an astute analysis of Vandal identity, "The Vandals adopted the trappings of African elite lifestyles, not because they wanted to be Romans, but because they wanted to be elites; this offered them a means of establishing their own identity in a meaningful form in the post-Roman world."[52]

ORTHODOXY, ETHNICITY, AND STATUS

Up to this point, this chapter has considered the Christian and ethnic identities of individuals in Vandal Africa in parallel. It has invoked the problems associated with a maximalist view of their implications, both broadly theoretical and specifically provoked by textual and material evidence from fifth- and sixth-century Africa. Alternative concerns like everyday sociability and the display of prestige seem, for many, to have been of more consistent importance. Christian and ethnic affiliations cannot be assumed as the most significant aspects of an individual's sense of self; as a result, Christian and ethnic groups were at most intermittent contexts for action. What being a Catholic Christian or a Vandal meant was a result of a complex interplay between self-identity and the perceptions of others. Of course, as Victor of Vita's dual ethnic/religious dichotomy suggests, to understand these forms of identity also requires consideration of their intersection. In this regard, Victor is rare in his pervasive assumption that particular Christian and ethnic affiliations were—indeed, should be—connected.

Within the efforts at Christian boundary management discussed above, ethnicity was at best peripheral.[53] The martyr and confessor stories of the *History of the Persecution* demonstrate that royal legislation on Christian orthodoxy was

---

50. I owe this suggestion to Caroline Humfress. On habitus and late-antique religious identity, see esp. Sandwell (2007).
51. Conant (2012), 53; Bockmann (2013), 19–20.
52. Merrills and Miles (2010), 93. See also Von Rummel (2008), 162–64.
53. The next section discusses those occasions when ethnicity did intrude on these efforts.

enforced regardless of ethnic identity.[54] Ethnicity does not seem to have assumed particular importance for Homoian clerics in constructing their orthodox community. The statements made in extant Homoian texts, even in the polemical representations of their Nicene opponents, are ethnically neutral.[55] There is a corresponding scarcity of ethnography in Nicene discussions of the effects of the same policies. As noted earlier, Victor of Vita alone explicitly addressed himself to Romano-Africans.[56] Other Nicene writers, on the face of it, show concern for all Catholic Christians and seek to prevent any of them from converting to Arianism (and from doing so for less than acceptable reasons). Given the manner in which the Hasding dynasty sought to ensure the orthodoxy of all its subjects, there is every reason to think that at least some of these writers were also concerned with the souls of individuals that they (or we) might think of as Vandals.

Kings and clerics policed correct Christianity without obvious reference to ethnic affiliation. Moreover, the manner in which contemporaries sought to ensure the orthodoxy of specific individuals and the integrity of Christian groups fits well with the demands of aristocratic sociability set out in the previous section. The most obvious thread running through these efforts at boundary management is the social status of those targeted as possible transgressors. Kings and clerics alike zeroed in on the elites of the kingdom, both Vandal and Romano-African. As in the later Roman Empire, royal efforts to enforce correct religious observance focused on the court and those in administrative service.[57] On a number of occasions, Vandal rulers decreed that their courtiers in particular or officeholders more broadly had to adhere to orthodoxy. Those who did not were either to be stripped of their payments in cash and kind (*stipendium* and *annona*) or banned from serving altogether; they were also liable to the enforcement of antiheretical legislation.[58] Concern for the orthodoxy of their attendants and administrators also

---

54. Merrills (2011); Conant (2012), 166–69, for references.

55. Victor of Vita provides the only two exceptions. In an episode set under Geiseric, he has the priest Jucundus dissuade the king's son Theoderic from executing a Nicene confessor by saying, "The Romans will begin to preach that he is a martyr" (*HP* 1.44 [ed. Lancel: 117]). This equation of Nicene and Roman cannot be separated from Victor's view of coterminous ethnic and confessional groups (considered further at pp. 183–85, 188–89). It is particularly suspect given the leeway the historian had for this piece of invented speech, framed as private counsel from decades earlier. Victor also has "the bishops of the Arians" advise Huneric to take measures to stop Christians in "barbarian clothes" from entering Nicene churches, but the import of this decision involved a definition of Vandal identity wide enough to encompass all of those in royal service; Victor's precise phrasing also destabilizes the connection between external appearance and self-identification (see pp. 181–83).

56. See p. 19.

57. Rougé and Delmaire (2005), 78; Fournier (2008), 229; Humfress (2008), 134.

58. On laws and implementation see (best) Fournier (2008); Conant (2012), 166–70, 180–84. For Geiseric see *HP* 1.43 (ed. Lancel: 116); Huneric, ibid., 2.23, 3.3–14 (132, 175–81); see also ibid., 2.10 (126), for Nicene courtiers deprived of *annona* and *stipendium*. For Thrasamund see Fulg., *ABC.* 249 (ed.

seems to have influenced royal patronage. Both the *Life of Fulgentius* and Procopius's *History of the Wars* suggest that Homoian adherence could lead to advancement under Thrasamund.[59] Given the paucity of surviving texts, it is difficult to reconstruct the emphases of Homoian clerics. Nevertheless, it is noticeable that Fastidiosus's sermon addresses "most learned Christians": perhaps mere praise for correct doctrine but also possibly an indication of their social background.[60] If the anonymous *Commentary on Job* was written in Vandal Africa,[61] it too could evince a Homoian bishop who shared the concerns of the Vandal kings regarding the ruling elite's Christianity. Again and again, the exegete stresses the status, wealth, and administrative duties of Job and his companions.[62] Nicene clerics similarly wrote with this elite in mind, although theirs was an inverse perspective. Like their earthly rulers, Nicene authors coupled privilege and political advancement with Homoian Christianity. Yet whereas Vandal kings sought a close link between membership in the ruling elite and profession of their Christian orthodoxy, Nicene clerics decried the connection between power and Arian heresy. Their texts reflect anxieties over the intersection of political power, social status, and Christian confession.

Nicene polemic often portrays the Arians of Vandal Africa as powerful, and commensurately dangerous, individuals.[63] These heresiological accusations of inappropriate worldliness tend to frustrate the identification of these powerful Arians, be they kings, clerics, or lay elite. It was not in the authors' interests to use the lump term with greater specificity.[64] Nevertheless, Nicene fulminations in general and the frequent references in particular to the perils of persuasion or coercion by those in the political ascendancy had obvious relevance for elite actors. Their Christian affiliation was the most strictly policed, and they had the most to gain or lose from the results. Nicene authors recognized that political circumstances were such as to support Arian heresy and to provide easy lures, in the form of opportunities for power and wealth, to those who adhered, and loss of standing

---

Isola: 50), where Nicene Christians are forbidden from serving (*militare*); Conant (2012), 168, interprets this as military service. For *militia* as any service in late-antique governmental jargon, see Kelly (2004), 20, 134; see also *militaret* at *HP* 2.23 (ed. Lancel: 132).

59. *V. Fulg.* 20 (ed. Isola: 202); Proc., *BV* 1.8.9 (ed. Dewing: 74–76).
60. Fastidiosus, *Sermo* 2.21 (ed. Fraipont: 281).
61. On the problems of location and date, see p. 88, n. 15.
62. *Comm. in Iob* 1.9, 1.17, 1.46, 2.32–33, 2.46, 3.4, 3.6, 3.10, 3.15–17, 3.39 (ed. Steinhauser: 101, 115–16, 158, 296–300, 320–21, 349–50, 352–53, 357–58, 365–68, 401); see also 3.27 (automatic damnation of pagans and heretics) (382–83); cf. Dossey (2003), 107–110, 116–21.
63. These references have often been interpreted as depictions of Vandals—e.g., Isola (1990), 60–65; Inglebert (1996), 620, with n. 126—but given the absence of ethnography and the mixed ethnic composition of the ruling elite (see pp. 171–75), this seems a misstep.
64. Sometimes the activities described suggest Homoian clerics, in particular rebaptism and (false) charity: see pp. 45 n. 68, 133–34.

and potential physical harm to those who did not.[65] It was more or (usually) less subtly implied that those who shared the Christian faith of the earthly ruler did so because they had not ordered their priorities correctly. They were Arians not because they thought this made them members of the true Christian Church but because, as an act of obedience to the king, it made them powerful in Vandal Africa.[66] By contrasting the worldly with the divine, Nicene authors sought both to persuade prominent figures not to take this bait and to explain away the actions of those who did.

Elite political actors were also explicitly discussed. Whether the protagonists were named contemporary aristocrats or invented late Roman officials, they were used to show the correct Christian response to conflicting loyalties. The best studied of these morality tales are the martyr and confessor stories in the *History of the Persecution*.[67] Again and again, prominent members of the court and notables from the kingdom's cities are presented with the classic martyr's dilemma: fidelity to state, family, and social position—and conversion to Arianism—or preservation of their spotless faith. Less noted but equally important are the ideal (and less than ideal) political figures of contemporary heresiological dialogues.[68] The officials who judge each case face similar quandaries. In the *Conference of Augustine with Pascentius*, the judge, a *uir clarissimus* named Laurentius, appears to have been suborned by the powerful Pascentius, an Arian count, *uir spectabilis*, and *nobilissimus*, to bring a charge of Homoousian heresy against Augustine.[69] Pascentius's titles suggest something of the pressure (it was imagined) that he could bring to bear: both men had senatorial status, but he outranked the judge. Laurentius has to be reminded by the bishop that God, a higher judge, is in his presence. By the end of the text, the judge has belatedly set his priorities in order: "I choose, *uir nobilissimus*, [to incur guilt] in your eyes, rather than incur the guilt of a perennial charge in the eyes of God."[70]

The judge in Vigilius's *Dialogue against the Arians, Sabellians and Photinians*, Probus, shows this model behavior throughout, living up to his name. The debate effectively catechizes Probus, who announces his recent recantation of paganism and desire for Christian truth at the outset;[71] his final judgment is a Nicene confession of faith.[72] Nevertheless, his choice of this doctrine is presented as if it resulted

---

65. Quod., *C. Iud., pag. et Arr.* 7.38–42 (ed. Braun: 299); Quod., *Lib. prom.* D.5.7, cf. D.13.22 (ed. Braun: 194, 207); Fulg., *ABC.* 290–92 (ed. Isola: 52).
66. E.g., *C. Var.*, pref. 22–25 (ed. Schwank: 9); see too the references in p. 148 n. 25.
67. See pp. 199–206.
68. On these texts see pp. 69–77.
69. *Coll. Pasc.* 3, 5, 7–8 (ed. H. Müller, Weber, and Weidmann: 76–78, 80–82).
70. Ibid., 16 (116).
71. Vig., *Dial. I = II* 1.1 (ed. Hombert: 253–55).
72. Vig., *Dial. II*, sententia, esp. 11 (ed. Hombert: 411–13).

solely from Athanasius's superior argumentation; Probus retains a punctilious obsession with correct procedure.[73] In this dialogue, Probus shows that, at least in an ideal world, the performance of administrative duties could coexist with adherence to true Christianity, a point that the preface to the second version of the text emphasizes.[74] The judge receives a backstory as a man who had proved himself faithful during Constantius's reign (though whether to the emperor or to Christ is unclear from the syntax). His response to Constantius's decision to appoint him to judge Athanasius and Arius is salutary: "He, with all public cares banished far off, preferred to carry out his own orders with all speed, that he might both comply with the imperial orders and prove the most true faith by his own examination." When forced to choose between his dual loyalties, Probus adopts a third way. Laurentius and Probus represent models for elite action with special resonance for Nicene clerics, given that senior officeholders could well have acted as judges in cases against Homoousian heretics.[75] Victor of Vita, Pseudo-Augustine, and Vigilius of Thapsa were concerned to ensure that Christian officials not only avoided conversion or adherence to Arian heresy but also made sure in their conduct to value the orthodox faith above the worldly influence of prominent Arians. While they did not rule out legitimate service to the Vandal state, Nicene authors desired the ruling elite to prioritize adherence to correct Christianity above all other factors. Whether these texts and sermons had elite audiences, and how receptive these audiences might have been to this message, is not known. Nevertheless, they plausibly reflect concerns that would have informed Nicene clerics in their dealings with members of the Christian communities of Africa.

In all of this, the potential salience of ethnicity cannot be entirely ruled out. Its absence from surviving texts does not preclude the occurrence of individual social situations in which it could have been invoked. What is clear is that there is no particular reason to read ethnicity into these passages. The manner in which kings and clerics policed correct Christianity in Vandal Africa reflects broader late-antique cultural norms. The correct religious observance of their political servants was always of particular concern for rulers, who tended to associate religious deviance with disloyalty and subversion. Elite figures were similarly important for clerics because of the influence they projected, both through officeholding and, just as important, through landed property: elite actors could shape the religious observance of their dependents and tenants. The continued centrality of such issues in discussions of Christian conformity and deviance in the kingdom also reflects the shape of post-imperial African society. As far as can be seen, Vandal and Romano-

---

73. Vig., *Dial. I = II* 1.5, 2.10, 2.27 (ed. Hombert: 261–62, 320, 352); *Dial. II* 3.10, 3.11 (ed. Hombert: 368, 370–71).

74. For what follows, see Vig., *Dial. II*, pref. II (ed. Hombert: 250).

75. On the continued operations of the lawcourts in Vandal Africa, see p. 7 n. 32.

African aristocrats seem to have inhabited the same political, cultural, and social space. As a result, when kings or clerics sought to make their definitions of correct Christianity a meaningful part of contemporary social practice, it was only natural that they would take individuals from both ethnic groups together. In approaching the problem of orthodoxy in this way, they also would have reinforced the sense that this mixed elite formed a corporate entity defined by office and status.

COURTIERS DRESSED AS VANDALS

Ethnicity was peripheral to the politics of Christian affiliation. Nevertheless, it features in conjunction with confessional identity in a number of passages and episodes described in African Christian texts. Such passages have (perhaps inevitably) received a great deal of commentary for the insights they might bring to the study of ethnic identity. They have often been taken as reflections of a concerted initiative on the part of Vandal kings and Nicene and Homoian clerics to define and police the boundaries of exclusive ethnic groups through religious affiliation, and even as representative of much wider cultural notions and prejudices.[76] The infrequency with which this form of identity crops up in heresiological literature suggests otherwise. The relationship of these discussions of ethnic and confessional identities to wider cultural attitudes cannot be taken for granted.[77] To be sure, to gain wider acceptance, authors had to take into account the perspectives of their audiences and possibly—in the case of historical narratives—the views of the individuals described, insofar as they were aware of them.[78] Nonetheless, like all statements about the makeup and nature of groups, these passages must be understood, in the first place, as reflections of the views of their authors. In any case, the attested statements and actions of Homoian and Nicene clerics and Vandal kings themselves suggest plural understandings of the relationship between ethnic and Christian affiliations and multiple ways in which ethnicity and ethnography could be deployed for specific Christian arguments. This multitude of possible interfaces between ethnicity and Christianity further fragmented as authority figures sought to translate them into concrete action. Unsurprisingly, the various interested parties conceived of the importance that ethnic affiliations possessed for Christian group membership in ways related to their own interests. Texts from Vandal Africa that discuss ethnicity and Christianity provide insights into ways in which specific individuals in specific situations could comprehend, use, and

---

76. See the references in p. 166 n. 7; also Liebeschuetz (2003), 77–81; Howe (2007), 279–82; Fournier (2008), 206–7; Haubrichs (2012), 42. See also Conant (2012), 182, for "Arianism" as "central . . . to the royal construction of Vandal identity" (though with excellent general remarks at 180–84).

77. See, e.g., Gillett (2009), 397–403.

78. This approach is partly inspired by that used by Reimitz (2015), 51–123, to study the *Decem libri historiarum* of Gregory of Tours.

manipulate the available means of construing a relationship between them. They are best read as attempts to account for ethnic differences and harness ethnographic prejudices as part of the maintenance of orthodox Christian communities.

The role that "Vandalness" played in the Hasding dynasty's policing of orthodox Christianity is a case in point. Vandal identity seems to have mattered in antiheretical legislation in proportion to its importance in individual regimes' conceptions of their rule in Africa.[79] The territorial distribution of the measures that Geiseric enacted to prevent Nicene worship and episcopal ordination implies ethnic considerations of this sort.[80] These prohibitions were limited to Africa Proconsularis, where Geiseric had granted the Vandal war band hereditary parcels of land.[81] When looking back to his father's orders, Huneric explicitly mentioned the banning of Nicene services within the *sortes Vandalorum*.[82] There is no other extant legislation or reported non-Christian decision of a general applicability from Geiseric or the early years of Huneric with which to compare this one explicit reference to the *sortes* and previous laws limited to the proconsular province. Nevertheless, this geographical concentration seems to relate less to a vision, held by Geiseric and Huneric, of an orthodox Christian community framed around their Vandal followers, and more to their conceptions of the extent of their power and the nature of their kingship.[83] Nothing else known about these laws connects them to the Vandals or their Christianity: they applied to all the Vandal kings' subjects in that province.[84] Yves Modéran has plausibly suggested that, in this period, the term *sortes Vandalorum* connoted not only the estates given to individual warriors but also, through a semantic drift, the kingdom itself.[85] In the first decades after its establishment in Africa (at the very least), leadership of the Vandal war band remained a central part of royal authority. These laws reflect an understanding that Hasding power in the middle decades of the fifth century was concentrated in the lands where that war band had been settled.

A much-cited story, supplied by Victor of Vita, of exemplary violence in Carthage during the reign of Huneric also associates correct Christianity with Vandal identity, but in the sense that being a Vandal could be taken as broadly

---

79. A vexed question, and discussion has centered on the royal title: see, e.g., Gillett (2002c); Steinacher (2013).
80. See esp. Modéran (2002), 109.
81. See p. 15 n. 71.
82. *HP* 1.29, 2.39, 3.4 (ed. Lancel: 110, 139, 175).
83. A problem generally approached from the other direction (anti-Nicene measures as reflecting the extent and conception of Vandal power): see (best) Steinacher (2008), 246–49; cf. Modéran (2002), 107–10; Merrills and Miles (2010), 66–68; Bockmann (2013), 130–31.
84. Conant (2012), 181–83.
85. Modéran (2002).

synonymous with service to the king.⁸⁶ Soon after Eugenius was appointed the bishop of Carthage and Nicene services permitted again, "the bishops of the Arians" advised Huneric to order him (in Victor's words) to "prohibit from entering the church whomever he should see in barbarian clothes [*in habitu barbaro*], whether men or women." After quoting Eugenius's rejection of this demand, Victor provides a helpful gloss: "[he did so] particularly because there was a great multitude of our Catholics who were entering [church] in the clothing of those people [the barbarians], because of the fact that they were serving the royal house." To make an example of these heretical courtiers, Huneric placed torturers outside the church doors, who scalped them; the women were then paraded in the streets, in case anyone had missed the point. Like all of Victor's Nicene martyr stories, this grisly tale cannot be taken entirely at face value (although its gruesome spectacle would not have been out of keeping with the exemplary character of much Roman justice).⁸⁷ Still, given that it purports to describe a public event that took place less than a decade before the historian was writing, it can hardly be dismissed.⁸⁸

The extent to which Victor—rarely keen to make fine distinctions regarding an individual's status as a Roman or a barbarian—nuances the role of ethnicity is revealing.⁸⁹ At first glance, Huneric's demand suggests that Vandalness was one of his concerns in enforcing orthodox Christianity in his capital. The Nicene congregants' "barbarian" clothing causes his anxiety. However, in Victor's own wording, Huneric targeted "men or women in barbarian clothes," not "barbarians" or "Vandals," and the historian explained that these individuals wore "barbarian" clothing because they were courtiers. As Philipp von Rummel has convincingly argued, this "barbarian" clothing was not only a possible courtly costume for anyone in Vandal service but also an aristocratic fashion shared by Vandals and Romano-Africans.⁹⁰ The orthodoxy at stake here was indeed that of Vandal courtiers, but only insofar as anyone who served the Vandal king and dressed like a Vandal was a Vandal courtier. Victor himself hints that this was not the only way in which their identity could be understood. Throughout this episode, the historian refrains from referring to these courtiers as barbarians, consistently using circumlocutions about courtiers adopting barbarian or Vandal dress and appearance. In this way, Victor destabilizes the connection between outward appearance and self-identity. He had good reason to do so: if his "great crowd of our Catholics" were made into Vandals or barbarians, this would have caused problems for his depiction of Catholic

---

86. *HP* 2.8–9 (ed. Lancel: 125–26). The best readings are Von Rummel (2007), 183–91; Merrills and Miles (2010), 102–4; Merrills (2011), 111.

87. On exemplary Roman justice see Shaw (2003).

88. The precise date is unclear from the text: the implication is that it took place within a couple of years of the appointment of Eugenius in 478/79.

89. See p. 9.

90. Von Rummel (2007), 183–91.

Christianity as the defining feature of civilized Roman life. Nevertheless, that he has Huneric preserve this same distinction between identity and appearance in the specific wording of his order suggests that this is not merely an artful side step.[91]

The scalping of the Nicene courtiers provides an excellent case study of the difficulties in reconciling external definition and outward appearance (not to mention cultural stuff) with self-identification. It may well be (as Von Rummel suggests) that Vandal identity in the kingdom was essentially performed through outward markers: the adoption of military modes of aristocratic self-expression and participation at court and in the military or administration.[92] Whether this meant that the Romano-African individuals who "performed" that identity saw themselves as Vandals is another matter altogether. Certainly, contemporary observers like Victor of Vita could perceive them in other ways. In any case, to serve at court, one did not need to be or become Vandal, whether simply by assuming military dress and lifestyle or, less tangibly but more crucially, by adopting the specific ethnic self-identification.[93] What this suggests is that one possible way for Hasding rulers and others at their court to view their political servants, despite their diversity, was as Vandals, rather as it had been for the heterogeneous individuals within their war band in the 420s and 430s.[94] Nevertheless, this remained just one of many ways of understanding the identity of those political servants. No extant edict names Vandals (or Romans) as the target of antiheretical legislation; even those paraphrased instead speak of courtiers and officeholders. Ethnicity remained a subsidiary element in Hasding political ideology and the conceptions of Christian community that both were inspired by and themselves influenced that rulership.

BARBARISM AND HERESY

Close reading of Victor's *History of the Persecution* suggests a number of ways in which Vandal kings understood and portrayed Christian, ethnic, and social identities. Setting it within the broad array of contemporary texts reveals a similar plurality of Nicene Christian perspectives. As already noted, Victor's fundamental equation of ethnic and confessional identity has often been taken as not only the typical view of Nicene Christians in Vandal Africa but also representative of a

---

91. Had he wished to, Victor could easily have portrayed Huneric's order as relating straightforwardly to Vandals (/barbarians), thus suggesting that the king had mistaken the courtiers' ethnic identity as Vandal (/barbarian) because of their appearance. This would have provided him the opportunity to trumpet their continued Romanness as a result of their adherence to true Christianity. His spurning of this narrative possibility seems telling.

92. Von Rummel (2002), 132–33; (2008), 162–63.

93. See Merrills and Miles (2010), 219–27, on contemporary court poets.

94. See p. 7.

dominant strand of thought in late antiquity. In fact, like the broader classical and late-antique image of the barbarian, barbarian Christianity had always been pegged in numerous ways, depending on the specific point—often only tangentially related—that an author wanted to make.[95] It could be, as in the *History of the Persecution*, a double inversion of the norms of Roman Christian society: barbaric and heretical.[96] The distinction between these abnormal forms of behavior could be collapsed further by using the same tropes to describe both (madness, anger, lack of control).[97] This dual stereotype could be used to encourage antagonism toward heretics as barbaric, barbarians as heretics—and both at the same time. Yet the differences caused by either or both dichotomies could also be put to one side, played down, or even inverted. The barbarians' pious observance and Christian actions could be emphasized over doctrinal differences.[98] The categories themselves could be ignored: baptism was, after all, supposed to transform Christians by removing them from their ancestral traditions.[99] Being Christian could transcend Roman or barbarian origins; Christians from both sides of this perceived divide could be considered on the same terms. Individual late-antique authors portray barbarian Christians variously across their works and even within individual texts. A range of possibilities was available to individual Nicene clerics when thinking about, interacting with, or responding to barbarian Christians.

Hostile presentation of an integral relationship between barbarism and Arianism was only one way of thinking about Christian Goths, Vandals, and Burgundians in late antiquity. The same goes for post-imperial Africa. Outsiders and later authors certainly conveyed an impression of a specifically Vandal Arianism.[100] However, as Tankred Howe has noted, statements that make Arianism explicitly Vandal or barbarian—or even refer explicitly to Vandals or barbarians as Arians—are vanishingly rare in Vandal Africa itself. Likewise, only Victor makes a clear equation of Romanness and Catholicity.[101] Nicene authors wrote both ethno-

---

95. G. Clark (2011); see also P. Wood (2010), 21–37; Maas (2012); Van Nuffelen (2012), 176–85; Heydemann (2013), 179–97. On the flexibility of "the barbarian", see esp. Amory (1997), 18–25; Halsall (2007), 56–57; Steinacher (2008), 249; see also Heather (1999), 241. On the diversity of Christian views, see Inglebert (1996); Chauvot (1998), 429–59, 481.

96. Ambrose of Milan provides numerous examples: see McLynn (1994), 182; Chauvot (1998), 280–81; Liebeschuetz (2005), 226 nn. 4–6; Von Rummel (2007), 128–43; Humphries (2010a), 54–55; G. Clark (2011), 38.

97. Howe (2007), 120–41, 183–227; also P. Wood (2011), 433–34; Maas (2012), 68. On bestial imagery to describe heretics, see Flower (2011), 82–86; Shaw (2011), 333–34.

98. Orosius and Salvian are prominent examples: Inglebert (1996), 566–67; G. Clark (2011), 35–38; Van Nuffelen (2012), 176–85; Maas (1992); Lambert (2000); P. Brown (2012), 444–47.

99. Chauvot (1998), 432, 446, 459, 481; Maas (2003a); Maas (2012), 67; Kitchen (2008), 29–30; P. Wood (2010), 28–37; Heydemann (2013), 196; cf. Sandwell (2007), 67, 195.

100. References (with caution) in Conant (2012), 159 n. 119.

101. Howe (2007), 147–55, 217–27. See also Conant (2012), 190–92.

graphic and heresiological polemic, but the two rarely converged in this way.[102] So, in the *Life of Augustine*, Possidius of Calama portrays a Vandal destruction of Africa during invasion but never once alludes to the doctrinal affiliation (or even the Christianity) of the war band, nor does he ever accuse them of persecution.[103] Similarly, Quodvultdeus of Carthage's two sermons titled *On Barbarian Times*,[104] delivered during the Vandal conquest of Carthage, do not mention heresy, while, in his other sermons, his repeated attacks on the Arians at work in the city after its capture never connect their actions to Vandals or barbarians.

Authors did juxtapose these two forms of stereotyping, and it would be misleading to suggest that Christian polemic against barbarians destructively hostile to the true church held no potential heresiological resonances, especially in the light of the shared uncivilized characteristics of barbarians and heretics. Still, it is important to note that authors other than Victor of Vita made such juxtapositions more allusively. The relationship between barbarism and heresy is rarely given more concrete expression than suggestive insinuation. Quodvultdeus's *Book on the Promises and Predictions of God*, written in exile in southern Italy, is representative. It shares the anti-Vandal and anti-Arian hostility of Victor's *History*, but these two types of animus run in parallel. Quodvultdeus repeatedly figures the Vandals as impious Old Testament characters who had destroyed sacred vessels and prevented worship in the Temple, clearly alluding to the actions taken against Nicene property and church services.[105] Yet this typology is never tied to the abundant antiheretical and anti-Arian polemic of the work.[106] The closest the two come is presence in the same sentence in the apocalyptic section on the "half times" (*dimidium temporis*). Quodvultdeus writes (after an unfortunate lacuna), "... as is thought by the heretics and particularly the Arians who will then have the greatest power. Gog and Magog, as some have said, are the Goths and Moors, the Getae and Massagetae, through whose savagery the devil himself now devastates the church and will then persecute more widely, and even make them cease the continual sacrifice."[107] The Vandals (called Goths to facilitate figuration as Gog from Revelation)[108] are persecutors, but they are not the same as the "heretics, and particularly the Arians," who also appear in this inventory of apocalyptic happenings. Quodvultdeus's works are certainly not favorable to the Vandals or to the form of

---

102. Something similar can be said for the other successor kingdoms, especially Italy: see pp. 236–37.
103. Poss., *V. Aug.* 28.4–13 (ed. Bastiaensen: 204–10); Fournier (2008), 142–44.
104. Quod., *DTB I* and *II* (ed. Braun).
105. Quod., *Lib. prom.* 2.24.50–51, 2.33.72, 2.34.76 (ed. Braun: 118–20, 138, 142).
106. Ibid., 2.6.10–11, 2.19.35, 2.21.41, 2.27.57, 2.28.60, 2.31.69, 2.34.73, 3.38.41, D.5.7, D.8.15–16, D.14.23 (80–82, 105, 110–11, 125–26, 127–28, 135, 139, 183, 194–95, 200–201, 208).
107. Ibid., D.13.22 (207).
108. Inglebert (1996), 620; Van Slyke (2003), 128–29; see too Humphries (2010a).

Christianity their kings supported. While hinting at a connection between the Vandals and the Arians, they preserve an outward distinction between them.

Two anonymous Nicene sermons from the Vandal period hint more strongly at a connection, but still without going beyond innuendo.[109] The *Homily on the Bishop and Martyr Saint Cyprian* is a short sermon, delivered on Cyprian's martyr day, that has often been attributed to Victor of Vita, given the overlap in subject matter and argument with the *History of the Persecution*.[110] It bemoans the loss of Cyprian's see and the persecution of his Christians before describing Cyprian in heaven petitioning God for his people with startling parrhesia (1–2). After the account of this persecution, barbarians and Arians again rub shoulders in the same sentence: "Let the barbarian be destroyed, because the city that he holds is destroyed [*ciuis habetur exstinctus*], and do not let the perfidious hold the altars, from which the faithful are excluded and mourn" (1). The implication is that the persecution of the true church, the apparent destruction of Cyprian's Carthage by its barbarian rulers, and the heretical control of the churches there (and in particular those containing the martyr's relics) are linked. Yet the perfidious are not limited to being barbarians, nor vice versa; they remain separate groups doing separate (if equally abominable) things.

The two polemical strands come closest to convergence outside Victor in the Pseudo-Fulgentian sermon *On the True Vine*, which is impossible to date but clearly from the period of Vandal rule in Africa (and possibly its early stages).[111] The text is one of seventy-nine sermons preserved in a turn-of-the-tenth-century manuscript that seems to transmit the structure of an original fifth- or sixth-century collection. The preface to the collection indicates that these sermons were written by a Nicene bishop standing in for a colleague in a different diocese from his own: most likely, the usual Nicene bishop was in exile.[112] *On the True Vine* opens with an arresting metaphor, drawn from Psalm 79, of the church as a vineyard despoiled by cruel cultivators. The psalm text would have seemed particularly apt for a Nicene preacher looking to discuss Vandal conquest and persecution, given its juxtaposition of the *gentes* to the vineyard planted by God: late-antique exegetes like Cassiodorus often read it as an allegory for the fall of Jerusalem to the "gentile" Romans in 70 CE.[113] The preacher complains that the "atria of the churches

---

109. On these sermons, see (with caution) Courcelle (1964), 188–89; Isola (1990), 15, 17–18, 46–49, 55–56; Modéran (2003), 43; Howe (2007), 22, 149.

110. Ps.-Victor, *Hom. Cyp.* (*PL* 58); Modéran (2003), 40, with n. 146 (agnostic on attribution).

111. Ps.-Fulg., *Serm.* 46 (*PL* 65: 912A–913A).

112. On the sermon collection and manuscript transmission, see Grégoire (1980), 89–125; Dossey (2010), 166. The text of the preface (attributed as sermon 1 of a collection of eighty by Grégoire) was recorded in an edition of 1633 without identification of the manuscript (Grégoire [1980], 91–92).

113. See Heydemann (2013), 157–63. I am grateful to her for discussion of this psalm and its interpretation.

have been contaminated," most likely a reference to Homoian use of formerly Nicene churches. As his metaphor unfurls, the preacher describes merciless barbarians cutting off God's vines and sets out a clear contrast between Christ's eschatological protection of the true church and the barbarians' current maltreatment of it: "Behold, Christ our Lord, who 'was given for our sins' [Rom. 4:25]; let us live in his shade among foreign peoples." Like Victor's, his message is clear: individual Christians should not shrink from this suffering, and meanwhile not let their maltreatment dissuade them from staying true to their faith and receiving God's grace.

It is hard to do justice to the doctrinal, exegetical, and political complexities of this sermon and its rich use of the psalm text. Its hostility to the Vandals and their (incipient?) rule of Africa is clear. The barbarian presence in Africa causes the harsh treatment of the true church. Oblique reference is made to heretical use of Nicene churches; the juxtaposition is once more suggestive. Compared to the scriptural exegesis in the rest of the sermon collection, *On the True Vine* is exceptionally explicit in its contemporary frame of reference and detailed in its application of typology to explain those present-day circumstances. Many in the audience would surely have joined the dots. Yet again, though, the barbarians are not called Arians or heretics. They are stereotypical savages, allegorized as the wild boars of the psalm and characterized by a punning tag (which only really works in Latin): "nesciunt putare, sed amputare" (they do not know how to think, only how to cut things off).

The only generic association of Vandals and Arianism in the works of Fulgentius of Ruspe again emphasizes the absence of straightforward polemic against specifically barbarian heretics. In the doctrinal text *To Thrasamund*,[114] Fulgentius praises the king for his scriptural studies, which, Fulgentius states, were rare for a barbarian king and more customary for a Roman. Fulgentius portrays Thrasamund as the conduit through which learning (*studia disciplinae*) might take over the customs of a barbaric people (*iura barbaricae gentis*) "that is accustomed to champion its own ignorance as if by its native character" (*quae sibi uelut uernacula proprietate solet inscitiam uindicare*).[115] If *disciplina* is intended in a Christian sense, implied by the context of the king's biblical study, this is an association of the Vandals with some ignorance of Christian truth, playing on barbaric stereotypes. Whether Arianism is implied is unclear, although the text's emphasis on Nicene doctrine as Christian truth might suggest so. Once more, this is far from the strident statement of the inseparability of barbarism and Arianism found in the *History of the Persecution*. It also has to be set in its specific rhetorical context. The

---

114. See pp. 82–83, 161–63.
115. Fulg., *Ad Tras.* 1.2 (ed. Fraipont: 99). Bianco (2010), 20 n. 16, rightly emends *soles* to *solet*.

statement comes as part of a panegyrical section praising Thrasamund's exceptional qualities as a ruler.[116] Fulgentius may have played up the Vandals' general Christian ignorance on this particular occasion to make the king's piety and learning that much more remarkable, a strategy used by a number of sixth-century Nicene authors writing to recent or possible royal converts.[117]

A number of Nicene authors in Vandal Africa made reference to impious, destructive, bestial, and dim-witted barbarians. These references were meant to shape Nicene Christians' perceptions of the king and military aristocracy who now dominated African society. For readers or listeners who had already internalized an association of barbarians and Arians, such allusions may have acted as a sort of dog whistle, especially since the same dehumanizing characteristics were frequently given to heretics in late-antique Africa. The juxtaposition of barbarians and Arians may have been intended to play upon wider cultural notions of Arianism as a heresy of barbarians. At the same time, the allusiveness of this connection suggests that these Nicene writers did not seek to profit from such cultural ideas (which were available to them from earlier authors, whether or not they were widely shared within their Christian communities). Christians standing in the basilicas of Pseudo-Fulgentius and Pseudo-Victor were not encouraged to feel antipathy toward Vandals because they were Arians, or Homoians because they were barbarians. Instead, these preachers (like Quodvultdeus of Carthage) presented a dual interpretation of contemporary events that did not require such a linkage. Impious barbarians (the Vandal king and his agents) had inflicted persecution on their true Christian community; heretics (of unidentified ethnicity or cultural identity) had benefited from those acts of persecution. The explanations of African ecclesiastical politics that these preachers set out preserve a sense of separation between these two sets of immoral agents even as they bring them into close proximity. The message of these sermons seems simple: Arians had profited from the actions of the barbarians, and both were to be mistrusted and maligned—but not necessarily because they were the same people.

When other Nicene writers of the period construe a relationship between Vandals/barbarians and Christianity, they portray it in sympathetic if patronizing terms, following in the footsteps of earlier writers.[118] Victor of Vita himself hints at such a possibility. As Howe has demonstrated, Victor uses topoi of barbarian behavior only for Vandals who were Arians. Two Nicene Vandal confessors are described

---

116. Fulg., *Ad Tras.* 1.1–2 (ed. Fraipont: 97–99); see also pp. 161–62.
117. Cf. Isola (1994–95), 57–62; see also p. 237.
118. See p. 184 n. 98.

positively, without ethnographic stereotyping.[119] For Victor, it was Arianism that made Vandals (and others) barbarian. His work holds out the possibility that Nicene Vandals were valued members of church and society. Of course, in Victor's case this argument should not be pushed too far. The *History*'s overall impression is still one of an alliance between and fusion of barbaric heretics and heretical barbarians. Nevertheless, Victor's nod to other ways to represent Vandal Christianity is important. Two other Nicene writers exploited these possibilities to a far greater degree.

The author of the *Carthaginian Epitome*, an African continuation of the chronicles of Jerome and Prosper, imaginatively reconstructs barbarian conversion to Arianism.[120] He explains away the barbarians' heresy in a manner that permits them a genuine if naïve piety. In the epitomator's account, the Antichrist (personified as Arians expelled from the churches by Theodosius; the passage alternates between nominatives singular and plural), "not finding a place any longer" in the empire, crosses the frontiers and goes to "the barbarian nations, as if proffering apostolic testimony." The Arians tell the barbarians there, "We had been sent to the Romans, but because they judged themselves unworthy of the word of God, we turned to the *gentes*. For you were worthy to receive the true faith." The barbarians are thus presented with missionaries who claim to be true Christians and tell them that they are God's chosen people, as the epitomator then emphasizes: "And transferring all the things about the calling of the gentiles, of which the holy scriptures are full, to those persons, they occupied the souls of the barbarians." The Arians preach to the barbarians that the "one God, one faith, one baptism" of Ephesians 4:5 belongs to the Arians alone: precisely the type of exclusivist claim that one would expect Christian missionaries to make. Demonically inspired heretics convert the barbarians to Arianism, but the role of the latter is both passive and innocent. They are then co-opted into the Antichrist's cunning plan to divide the Christian people and kill Christian souls by rebaptism. Yet the barbarians continue to play a passive role. The demonic Arians are the real culprits, exploiting barbarian rule to forward the Antichrist's agenda. There is no reason to think that the Christianity of the barbarians is anything other than sincere. They had simply been misled by the Arians.

---

119. Howe (2007), 156-217, 283-318. Howe also notes that a number of Victor's martyrs and confessors have likely non-Roman names (e.g., Armogas, Dagila). Great care must be taken here: as already discussed, attributing ethnicity to names is a risky business (see p. 46, with n. 72, and 174 n. 42). Even if these names were indeed of Vandal origin, that would not necessarily convey the identity ascribed to these individuals by themselves or by others. What can be said is that these names' possibly "Germanic" connotations provided an opportunity for Victor to represent their bearers in ethnographic terms had he wished. That he did not is suggestive.

120. *Epit. Carth.* (ed. Mommsen: 496). On the text see pp. 114-18. The full quotation is at pp. 117-18.

This explanation is reminiscent of Salvian of Marseille's sympathetic account of barbarian Christianity in his *On the Government of God*.[121] Salvian excuses the heresy of the Christian Goths and Vandals: their biblical text had been incorrectly translated and interpreted. They had been led astray by their (Roman) teachers; their error was not their fault. These barbarians saw themselves as orthodox and Catholic; in any case, their superior Christian lifestyle outweighed their misguided faith.[122] Several late-antique Nicene accounts of the conversion of Fritigern's Goths to Christianity in 376 find similarly sympathetic explanations for their heresy.[123] Like those Goths, the epitomator's Arian converts have every right to believe that they have been converted to the true Christian faith; it is their teachers who are to be blamed.

The epitomator may allow for the possibility of genuine barbarian piety, but he still sets it in a context of heresy and persecution. The author of the *Conference of Augustine with Pascentius* makes a bolder statement of the validity of barbarian Christianity.[124] Augustine ends this debate, centered upon ὁμοούσιος, with a long final oration that convinces the judge and stumps his opponent.[125] Pascentius had attacked the Greek Christological term because of its absence from scripture, arguing that doctrinal statements should be made only from the Bible's explicit testimony.[126] Augustine points out that the original biblical texts were written in Hebrew and Greek. If only the original words were permissible, that would have implications for the authority of translations (15.92–104). This played into an argument about ὁμοούσιος made by the real Augustine in the genuine debate from which this imaginary dialogue was constructed: To understand and evaluate the word, it had to be translated into Latin and its meaning explained. That meaning could be found in scripture, even if the word was not.[127]

The Augustine in the dialogue makes this argument in a strikingly novel way, inspired by the presence of barbarian Christians in Africa. The barbarians are given a stake in translation problems:[128] "What if a Greek should object that the

---

121. On Salvian see p. 184 n. 98.

122. Salv., *Gub. Dei* 5.2–3 (ed. Lagarrigue: 314–20); see too 6.2.9, 7.9.38, and, e.g., 5.4 on charity (366, 456, 320–22).

123. In Orosius 7.33.19 (ed. Arnaud-Lindet: 3:92), followed by Isid., *HG* 7–8 (ed. Mommsen: 270–71), Goths ask Valens for Christian teachers; he sends Arians; they know no better. In Soc., *HE* 4.33 (ed. Hansen: 269), Goths semiconsciously choose Arian Christianity out of obedience to Valens. In Soz., *HE* 6.37 (ed. Bidez and Hansen: 294–97), (previously Catholic Christian) Goths adopt Arianism from both obligation to Valens and trust in Ulfila.

124. On this text see pp. 73–75.

125. *Coll. Pasc.* 15 (ed. H. Müller, Weber, and Weidmann: 88–116).

126. Ibid., 4 (78–80); see too 7, 11–14 (80–82, 84–88).

127. Aug., *Ep.* 238.4 (ed. Goldbacher: 4:535–36).

128. See G. Clark (2011), 39; Burton (2012), 115–16, on Augustine and languages.

divulging of words pertaining to the faith should be permitted neither to a Latin nor to a barbarian but only to himself?" (15.92–93). *Amen* and *alleluia* were used everywhere in Hebrew: they could not be translated into Latin or "barbarian" (15.94–96). The word was made flesh and the faith strengthened in Syria and Greece, not in Africa or "the whole of *barbaria*" (15.96–99). Moses, the prophets, the apostles, and the evangelists wrote "not in the Latin or barbarian language" but in Hebrew or Greek (15.99–102). "Barbarian" is used nonjudgmentally throughout, as shorthand for a certain language and a set of Christians who used it for worship.

Later, Augustine returns to this language point, apparently to attack the idea that the Greekness of the word ὁμοούσιος might be the problem.[129] His point again is that words of different languages should be acceptable (15.139–92). His clincher is the use of the barbarian language in Christian worship:[130] "If it is not permitted in the least that the one substance of the Father, Son, and Holy Spirit be manifested by the Greek language, therefore neither also ought God be praised in the barbarian one" (15.192–94). As the faithful used the Greek word ὁμοούσιος for the one substance of the Trinity,

> so the one nature of the one God is asked for mercy by all Latins and barbarians, that the barbarian language might not be in any way foreign to the praises of the one God. For we say in Latin, *Domine, miserere*. Therefore ought this mercy from that one God, Father, Son, and Holy Spirit, be begged only in the Hebrew or Greek language, or at the outside in Latin, and not also in the barbarian language? For if it is permitted, not only to barbarians in their language, but also to Romans, to say *Froia arme*, which is translated *Domine, miserere*, why would it not be permitted in the councils of the fathers in that land of the Greeks, whence the whole faith was set down, to confess ὁμοούσιος in their own language, that is the one substance of Father, Son, and Holy Spirit? (15.194–206)

In Augustine's argument, barbarians become an important part of the universal Christian community, with a language as valid as any other. Moreover, the author notes (without any hint of hostile commentary) that barbarians and Romans join together in church services conducted in the "barbarian" language. Barbarian Christianity is just another form of the true faith, in which Roman Christians too could unproblematically participate—provided it is Nicene.

This may seem only a sensible position for a Nicene cleric to take. There are many examples of barbarians in late antiquity who presented themselves as Nicene Christians, were represented as such, or interacted with Nicene clerics as

---

129. See Amory (1997), 199; Kitchen (2011), on contemporary anti-Greek polemic.
130. See pp. 38–41.

Christians.¹³¹ John Chrysostom set aside a church in Constantinople to provide Nicene services in Gothic for barbarian Christians; his preaching used their presence to make similar points about Christian universality.¹³² However, references to barbarian Christians as Arians, and the strident polemic of Victor in particular, have led to a sense in modern treatments that these individuals always had to be definitively other. What makes this passage so compelling is the very normality of barbarian Christianity within it.¹³³

Of course, this is not a disinterested plea to ensure that the linguistic needs of barbarian Christians continued to be addressed. Coming as part of a polemical anti-Arian text, these passages use barbarian Christians to score points against the Arians.¹³⁴ In effect, Augustine argues that, by Pascentius's logic, the barbarians cannot be proper Christians (nor can Pascentius by his own strict definition).¹³⁵ Thus, the very group whose rulers enforced Homoian Christianity within Africa is used to undermine its coherence. The total divorce of barbarian Christians from any connection with Pascentius, the Arians, or Christian deviance reinforces this point. Instead, their recurring conjunction with the Nicene faithful impresses upon the reader that they should be—indeed, already were—part of the true church, those who were "Catholics in the whole world" (15.152).

The *Conference*'s portrayal of barbarians as normal members of the Christian community should not be read as the author's consistent opinion about the nature of Vandal Christianity. The same goes for the epitomator's innocent barbarian victims of Arian cunning. These were rhetorical devices adapted to fit the particular polemical or narrative context in which they were deployed (in the case of the latter, to connect the Arians of 490s Carthage to those of 380s Milan).¹³⁶ Of course, the same should be said for the hostility with which other Nicene authors portrayed the Christian Vandals and their impiety, ignorance, or heresy. Quodvultdeus and Victor wrote in the aftermath of major anti-Nicene measures undertaken by Vandal rulers—in Quodvultdeus's case, partly after his exile from Africa by Geiseric. These were moments of particular tension when such polemic may have seemed the best response. The sermon on Cyprian's martyr day was likewise preached on an occasion that required clarifying statements of definition and defamation. The anony-

---

131. Bearing in mind that such ascriptions are rarely other than provisional (see pp. 205–6), see individual examples at *PLRE* 2:288–90 (Chlodovechus), 293–94 (Chrotchildis 1 and 2), 400 (Erelieva *quae et* Eusebia), 484 (Fredericus 1), 620–21 (Fl. Jordanes 3), 657 (Lantechildis), 935 (Rechiarius), 1009 (Sigismundus); Schäferdiek (1978), 496–97; Amory (1997), 476–77; Heil (2011), 48–65. On such interactions see p. 184 nn. 95–99.

132. Chauvot (1998), 429–35; G. Clark (2011), 39–40.

133. Cf. Vössing (2008), 201–2.

134. Tiefenbach (1991), 254.

135. See *Coll. Pasc.* 11 (ed. H. Müller, Weber, and Weidmann: 84).

136. See p. 118.

mous preacher had to explain why his Christian opponents possessed the basilicas in which Cyprian's remains were held, which meant simultaneously attacking the political authority that had transferred those churches. It is hard not to wonder how welcome a Vandal would have been in his or Pseudo-Fulgentius's church; their dehumanizing rhetoric of barbarism and bestiality, if repeatedly invoked, might have inculcated in those present a sense of themselves as a "non-Vandal" Christian community. But the contents of the rest of the sermon collection do not suggest that this was a frequent frame of reference. At the same time, the more sympathetic alternatives shown by the authors of the *Epitome* and the *Conference* make it equally likely that such a new arrival would have led a Nicene cleric to a change of tack. Victor of Vita's passage on the Vandal confessors underscores the extent to which extant descriptions were shaped by the needs of their authors in a particular instance. Vandal Christians could pass for non-Vandal Nicenes when it suited the case he wanted to make. Neither outright hostility nor untroubled acceptance should be interpreted as the "real" opinion of Nicene clerics regarding the Vandal Christians of Africa. The attitudes that these clerics expressed would have depended on the particular context in which they operated, the individual or group they had in mind, and the situation to which they had to respond.

It is in this regard that the spectrum of Nicene clerical descriptions of Vandal/ barbarian Christianity is revealing. It shows a variety of approaches that Nicene clerics could have taken in concrete situations. Vandal Christians could be definitively other: barbaric intruders, associated with heresy or persecution. They could also be treated like any other Christians and accepted as part of a Christian community that straddled the age-old boundary of Roman/barbarian. On this point, the sheer absence of explicit references to Vandals or barbarians as Arians—and to Catholics as Romans—is instructive. In Vandal Africa, only Victor fully took up the opportunity that these two negative stereotypes afforded. This is not to say that Nicene writers did not talk about Vandals and Arian heresy. It was just that, when they did, they rarely talked about them as Vandal or barbarian Arians.

CONCLUSION

In his recent book *Rethinking Ethnicity*, Richard Jenkins argues that the importance of ethnicity in a given social context should be judged by its consequences.[137] The consequences of Vandalness or Romanness for Christians in Vandal Africa are not immediately obvious. The extant statements and actions of kings and clerics rarely treat Vandals and Romano-Africans as separate groups. Both sets of authority figures sometimes took ethnicity into account. Ethnic discourse could be a useful tool, especially for Nicene clerics, who turned to ethnography to explain away

137. Jenkins (2008), 49.

the embattled status of their communities in the kingdom. Yet even in instances where ethnicity is involved, invocations of ethnic self-identification or ethnographic stereotyping can rarely be followed through to demonstrably differential treatment of Christians. There are scenarios in which Christianity and an exclusive definition of ethnicity could conceivably have been simultaneously relevant facets of an individual's identity. Being Vandal or Roman may have had implications for particular individuals that are simply invisible. Yet the very inaccessibility of these effects limits the utility of ethnicity as a category of analysis for Christian matters in Vandal Africa. From the perspectives of contemporaries, it does not appear as a decisive factor in shaping the effects that membership in different Christian groups had on social relations. This is not to abandon the categories of Vandal and Roman altogether, nor to suggest that identikit and harmonious congregations of mixed ethnicity and confession populated the Christian landscape of post-imperial Africa. Rather, it is to emphasize the severe limitations on what ethnic categories can explain.

When thinking through how affective ties and social circumstances might impact the integrity of (ideally) exclusive Christian communities, contemporaries latched on to a different social factor. For kings and clerics alike, participation in the kingdom's service aristocracy marked out an individual as deserving of particular attention for their confessional identity. The Hasding dynasty was especially concerned to ensure the orthodoxy of courtiers and bureaucrats. For Nicene clerics, the same efforts to tie political authority and social advancement to Homoian Christianity presented a threat to the integrity of their communities and the orthodoxy of individual Catholic Christians. Their efforts to persuade and censure those led by promises of power and status into compromising or abandoning their faith had an obvious target in aristocrats (and hopeful arrivistes) in the kingdom. Both Vandals and Romano-Africans were potential recipients of this royal coercion and clerical chastisement. Their bracketing together as servants of the Hasding dynasty and prominent members of post-imperial African society is not limited to discussions of Christian exclusivity. This cultural, social, and political intermingling of elite individuals of different ethnicities is similarly attested in contemporary classicizing literature and material evidence. The behaviors and customs of Vandals and Romano-Africans show the marks of common strategies of social distinction. Given the manner in which their doctrinal affiliations were policed, the Christian identities of the ruling elite should also be considered together, as, at least in part, products of the same social logic that provoked these other aspects of their public self-expression. When the contemporary observers most exercised by Christian exclusivity—and thus most likely to want to identify telling differences—took Vandal and Romano-African aristocrats together, it makes sense for us to do so as well.

7

Elite Christianity, Political Service, and Social Prestige

At some point in the mid-fifth century, a man named Arifridos was buried at the west end of the right-hand aisle of a church in Thuburbo Maius (modern-day Henchir Kasbat, Tunisia), and a mosaic inscription was installed to commemorate his interment ("Arifridos in [pace] uixit annos [...] depositus di[e...] idus nouem[b]").[1] The deceased was buried with prestigious grave goods comprising an oval gold fibula and metal shoe buckles. As a result of these accoutrements and his name,[2] Arifridos—alongside a handful of other recipients of furnished burials—has been associated with the newcomers to Africa of the 430s. Of the small number of "Vandals" whose remains have been found in Africa, Arifridos has received particular attention. His tomb has featured prominently in the examinations of Vandal identity discussed in the last chapter because his funerary ensemble isolates the insufficiency of ethnic categories to describe either mortuary practice or elite self-identification.[3] Arifridos's costume is best seen simply as an expression in militarized terms of membership in Vandal Africa's ruling elite. The claim that he (and, naturally, his heirs) sought to make with his burial costume was one of social superiority rather than necessarily, or exclusively, ethnic identity.[4]

---

1. Von Rummel (2007), 337–38.
2. On the problems of names and ethnic self-identification, see p. 174 n. 42.
3. See (best) Von Rummel (2007), 337–42; (2008), 158–64. See also Merrills and Miles (2010), 83–88; Steinacher (2011), 68–71; Steinacher (2016), 273–75. On this insufficiency see pp. 173–75.
4. For recent critical approaches to furnished burial, see Brather (2002); Brather (2008); H. Williams (2005); Halsall (2010), esp. 91–197; Halsall (2011). See also Carroll (2006), esp. 58, 142–48; Cooley (2012), 128–45, on the performance of (inter alia) social status through Roman funerary practice.

This claim was not limited to the rich grave goods with which he was doubtless ostentatiously buried. Arifridos was interred in a prime location inside a prominent church (the former temple of Baal-Tanit), with an epitaph to advertise the locus. This sort of privileged burial was a classic means of expressing status in late Roman Africa.[5] Its prevalence in Vandal Africa both shows a fundamental continuity in the commemoration of the dead and suggests that the creation of distinctions between Vandals and Romans was not at issue here. Arifridos's tomb confounds ethnic interpretation.[6] The commemorative practices of Vandals and Romans may have been more alike than many have countenanced—precisely because being Vandal or Roman does not primarily seem to have been at stake.

If the social implications of Arifridos's burial have rightly been recognized, the fundamentally Christian nature of this means of prestigious display has not received sufficient emphasis. With his privileged burial in the sacred space of a church, Arifridos expressed not only his status but also his piety and importance within a Christian community—and in this context the two went hand in hand.[7] Arifridos was not alone: other members of the secular elite buried in this way include an anonymous woman interred at the entrance to the same church in Thuburbo Maius, the so-called Vandal boy at Theveste (modern-day Tébessa, Algeria; discussed below), and the Suevic woman Ermengon at Hippo Regius (modern-day Annaba, Algeria).[8] These are rare examples of the happy survival of an inscription in situ above a tomb datable by either a recorded regnal year or specific grave goods. Nevertheless, numerous other Vandal-era privileged burials have been identified within the precincts of African churches, through either stratigraphic and phase analysis of tombs or dates recorded in mosaic epitaphs now divorced from their original contexts.[9] It was not only members of the new military aristocracy who expressed their status in this way. In the middle of a chapel at Ammaedara (modern-day Haïdra, Tunisia), funerary epitaphs were set up to commemorate members of the Astii family, urban notables who proudly recorded their service as part of the city's civilian elite.[10] These inscriptions have

---

5. N. Duval (1986); Fevrier (1986); Yasin (2009), esp. 69–100; Cooley (2012), 237–38.

6. See Von Rummel (2007), 270–323; Von Rummel (2008), 160–63, for similar conclusions regarding other furnished burials in Africa; Halsall (2011) for *comparanda*.

7. N. Duval (1986), 27–28; Handley (2003), 44–45; Yasin (2009), 91–94; Cooley (2012), 237.

8. On all of these burials, see Bockmann (2013), 155, 190–92, 220–21; the "Vandal boy," p. 215; Ermengon, Marec (1958), 62–63.

9. See (best) Bockmann (2013), 104–5, 163–66, 168, 210–13, 241; Stevens (1993), 93; Ben Abed-Ben Khader et al. (2004), 101–11, 122–23; Raynal (2005), B.10, at 2:494–95, 408–11; with the review of the last two by Stevens (2007); Bejaoui (2008), 201–2. See also p. 152 n. 41 on bishops' burials.

10. N. Duval and Mallon (1969); N. Duval and Prévot (1975), nos. 413 (dated to 526), 401, 424, with Chastagnol and Duval (1974), 95; Bockmann (2013), 210–13. See too, in the same church, the epitaph of Festa, dated to the fourteenth year of Thrasamund's reign (510): N. Duval and Prévot (1975), no. 419.

excited much interest because of references to three priests of the imperial cult: two former keepers of the imperial flame (*flamen perpetuus*) and one former priest of the province of Africa (*sacerdotalis prouinciae Africae*).[11] Without becoming mired in the fascinatingly unsolvable riddles that these titles pose, it is possible to say that the continued existence and epigraphic display of these offices suggest that, at Ammaedara at the very least, old markers of curial status and civic participation remained significant. Controlling stakes within the "salvation economy" of post-imperial Africa were sought by all sorts of aristocrats, whether they touted traditional roles as priests of the imperial cult or dressed the part of military men.[12] Undoubtedly, many more privileged burials from the Vandal period lie hidden within the vast corpus of undated Christian epitaphs found in late-antique African churches.[13] Burial and commemoration in church were still used as expressly Christian means of prestigious display in Vandal Africa.

Such funerary arrangements often illustrate a moment of social stress, as a family attempted to maintain its status for a new generation.[14] In this sense, they distill a constant elite concern. Aristocrats in the fifth-century Mediterranean increasingly commandeered various Christian practices for their claims to social standing. Such adaptations of preexisting norms and habits were a necessary corollary of the Christianization of the late Roman aristocracy. As Michele Renee Salzman has rightly put it, "To the late Roman aristocrat, religious affiliation was meant to secure and augment status." Members of that elite thus found ways to express their Christianity to make it, like participation in traditional cults had been, a "status-confirming aspect of their social identity."[15]

As a result, it was not necessarily in the interest of elite Christians to present themselves in unambiguous religious terms. Elite sociability often required the seclusion of religious and other differences behind a carefully constructed facade of mutual appreciation, whether to maintain patronage networks and secure favors or simply to keep up appearances. For a number of reasons, elite figures might modulate their statements and activities to avoid clear signals of religious

11. There has been considerable speculation regarding whether these were merely honorific titles or implied continued observances of some form and, if the latter, whether the recipients of those gestures of loyalty were Roman emperors or Vandal kings. The existence of the *sacerdotalis prouinciae Africae* has also been used to suggest that the old council of the province of Africa continued to meet. See esp. Chastagnol and N. Duval (1974); Clover (1982), 12–13; Clover (1989), 60–61; N. Duval (1984); Merrills and Miles (2010), 212–13; Alan Cameron (2011), 171, 795–96; Leone (2013), 87–99.

12. On mosaic inscriptions as participation in "l'économie du salut," see Caillet (1993), 468.

13. Cf. N. Duval (1986), 27. More speculative attributions have also been made, based on stylistic grounds and "Germanic" names: see esp. Ennabli (1982), 146–71; (1991), 31–33, for a list. See in this context the privileged burial of one Hildeguns at Mactar: Prévot (1985), 43–45. On problems with "Vandal names," see p. 174 n. 42.

14. See, e.g., Halsall (2010), 167.

15. Salzman (2002), 1–68, 138–219, quotations at 66, 13; see also Curran (2000), 260–320.

affiliation. This downplaying or suppression of religious difference has been highlighted particularly with respect to exchanges between pagans and Christians,[16] but the same can be said for Christians with different confessional allegiances. Too firm an insistence on adherence to a particular form of Christianity could disrupt the recognition of social status by peers whose religious affiliations were far from uniform. Some of the most successful late fourth- and fifth-century Christian aristocrats were slippery in their precise doctrinal or confessional definition. Christian figures whom contemporaries linked to a particular faction often maintained polite contact on both sides of rancorous Christian disputes.[17] Texts produced by individuals like Paulinus of Nola, though effusive in their piety, rarely articulate clear-cut statements of particular doctrinal positions.[18] Similarly, the iconography of churches dedicated by powerful fifth-century figures frequently bears no trace of a particular confessional affiliation.[19] The sincerity of these individuals' Christianity or the extent of their Christian knowledge should not be questioned. The point is that these aristocrats had (subtly) different priorities from the bishops with whom they exchanged artfully crafted pleasantries.

The same fundamental imperatives have been identified in Vandal Africa, where a diverse ruling elite operated in a shared sphere of social and political competition. Such concerns of social cohesion, combined with the demands of political accommodation, have been seen as a useful context for the poems of the *Latin Anthology*, which constitute the most extensive evidence for the culture of the Vandal court and Carthaginian elite.[20] These works present their Romano-African and Vandal patrons as prestigious individuals united by common praiseworthy activities, possessions, and qualities (and, at a basic level, by their shared literary taste). The poems very rarely mention Christianity. As such, they have been profitably interpreted as an example of the irrelevance of religious differences or of their deliberate cloaking to avoid potential antagonism, whether between members of the elite or between elite figures and their Vandal rulers, in a courtly context where Christian affiliation held potentially perilous political and legal significance. The

---

16. See esp. Sandwell (2007), 114–19, on "the feel for the game"; Alan Cameron (2011), esp. 173–205, 353–98; also the classic P. Brown (1961).

17. See, e.g., the "Arian" general Aspar (who donated to Nicene churches and was petitioned by Theodoret): p. 145 n. 10; Gundobad and Theoderic ("Arian" kings of the Burgundians and Ostrogoths respectively) and various Nicene clerics: Shanzer and Wood (2002), 8–27; Moorhead (1992a), 91–93; Heather (1996), 222–25; Amory (1997), 196–216; Augustine's correspondence with both the (apparently Nicene) general Boniface—some of whose entourage had, to Augustine's mind, been rebaptized by heretics—and potentially "Donatist" landowners: Aug., *Ep.* 220.4 (ed. Goldbacher: 4:433–34); Lancel (2002b), 276.

18. On Paulinus see Trout (1999), 218–19.

19. Mathisen (2009); Ward-Perkins (2010).

20. *AL* (ed. Shackleton-Bailey).

classicizing world of religious neutrality conjured by these poems was a safe space for both elite interaction and competition and for effusive displays of political loyalty.[21]

This is a convincing argument, excepting its corollary: that the disruptive effects of doctrinal controversy precluded similar opportunities for Christian prestigious display and political accommodation. Christianity did not have to be a divisive aspect of social life in Vandal Africa. There were ways in which elite individuals could convincingly express their piety and social distinction to contemporaries, whatever their confessional or ethnic identity. This chapter explores a series of individual texts and incidents to show the possibilities for definitively Christian elite self-expression. It argues that the demands of Christian orthodoxy found concrete expression in the identities of elite figures in Vandal Africa, but only within contexts circumscribed by the influence of the other demands upon their loyalties. The confessional identities evident at certain fixed points in time were not necessarily consistent or monolithic, either as experienced by those individuals or understood by their peers. The existence of rival, mutually exclusive Christian orthodoxies did not prevent definitively Christian elite social interaction, competition, or political loyalty.

DEFINING MOMENTS

The most visible elite Christians of Vandal Africa are Victor of Vita's martyrs and confessors. Just as the *History of the Persecution* has dictated the terms upon which Vandal Africa is understood, so the work's steadfastly Nicene courtiers have been central to discussions of the relationship between Christian identity and political loyalty in the kingdom.[22] During the episodes that Victor describes, these men and women self-identify in a manner that clearly marks them out as Nicene Christians. When pressured to perform an action which they think threatens that Christianity—usually a demand, made by kings, officials, and Homoian clerics, that they receive rebaptism—they choose to prioritize it over their political position, social standing, and even bodily integrity. As Jonathan Conant has stated, "Nicene Christians who refused to change their confession even in the face of strong external pressure clearly defined themselves to a meaningful degree in

---

21. Miles (2005); Merrills and Miles (2010), 219–27.

22. For elite lay martyrs and confessors, see *HP* 1.19–21, 1.43–50, 2.8–11, 3.21–30, 3.33, 3.38, 3.47–51 (ed. Lancel: 105–6, 116–21, 125–26, 184–91, 192, 195, 199–202). Courtois (1954) is classic; see also (best) Shanzer (2004); Howe (2007), 120–356; Fournier (2008), 164–263; Merrills and Miles (2010), 184–92; Merrills (2011); Conant (2012), 166–70, 180–86. See too the four Spanish courtiers executed in 437: Conant (2012), 166–67, with references. This section is limited to Victor of Vita's examples for ease of discussion.

terms of their faith."[23] Of course, part of the reason these courtiers and notables resemble model orthodox Christians is that a Nicene cleric narrates their stories. It is thus tempting to adopt a position of acute skepticism. Certainly, it cannot be assumed that the individuals involved understood their actions exactly as Victor explains them.[24] All the same, Victor's martyr and confessor stories present an unrivaled opportunity to explore potential intersections of elite Christian identity, political loyalty, and the enforcement of religious uniformity in Vandal Africa.

Whatever the precise circumstances of their loss of office and standing, an exclusive definition of orthodox Christianity was evidently important for the individuals in these stories. They decided that being an orthodox Christian was indeed relevant to their activities as members of the kingdom's ruling elite, whether at the Vandal court in Carthage or in other African cities, and incompatible with those other affiliations. In so doing, they acted as clerics in contemporary texts exhort the faithful to do. When their political service could no longer coexist with their Christian faith, they renounced it.[25] Of course, agents of the Vandal government no less meaningfully decided that the martyrs and confessors of the *History of the Persecution* were heretics and thus forbidden from officeholding unless they agreed to receive Homoian baptism. If they refused, this action would confirm their heresiological categorization in the minds of those enforcing the law. External definitions set the parameters for Christian courtiers and notables to define their identities. During such episodes, being Homoousian (in those external terms) was also relevant to and incompatible with political service.

While external definition and the use of coercion were important, they do not make the Nicene Christian identity of these individuals in those contexts any less meaningful. Identity always results from a combination of external social forces and self-definition;[26] moreover, the pressure in this particular situation actually pushed in the opposite direction from that which they took. It should also be remembered that those under duress previously had to have been identifiable as Homoousians. For example, Saturus, Huneric's *procurator domus* when the future king was still merely the heir to the throne, was said to have "frequently denounced the error [*prauitatem*] of the Arians with the freedom of a Catholic [*libertate catholica*]."[27] Similarly, the noblewoman and wife of a royal attendant Dagila, who suffered religious coercion under Huneric, "had already frequently been a confessor in the time of Geiseric."[28] Others may have been similarly outspoken and thus

23. Conant (2012), 194.
24. See esp. the murder of Sebastian: *HP* 1.19–21 (ed. Lancel: 105–6), with the accounts of Berndt (2007), 219–20, and Fournier (2008), 230–31; though cf. Steinacher (2016), 190.
25. See p. 178.
26. See p. 174 n. 44.
27. *HP* 1.48 (ed. Lancel: 119).
28. Ibid., 3.33 (192).

aligned themselves with one contemporary ecclesiastical faction. Those who decided to undergo rebaptism, however willingly, also made their affiliation publicly clear: for some, as true Christians; for others, Arian heretics. At the very least, the Nicene confessors and martyrs of the *History of the Persecution* present a distinctly confessional Christian identity: one irreconcilable with loyalty to Vandal kings.

As is so often the case in early Christian history, the difficulty is deciding how representative a set of martyrs and confessors were among contemporary Christians.[29] Many scholars of Vandal Africa have seen Victor's elite Catholics as the thin end of the wedge. They were the visible manifestation of a silent Catholic majority that opposed Vandal rule.[30] Others have contrasted them to a different majority: the secular-minded Romano-African aristocrats who supported their new masters without religious scruple.[31] Most recently, Conant has neatly characterized elite responses to Hasding Christian policies as a spectrum running from variously motivated Homoian adherents and converts to Nicene martyrs and confessors. Between these poles "doubtless lay an extensive middle ground populated by crypto-Nicenes, by those on whom conversion rested as an uneasy burden, and by Nicene Africans willing to confine themselves to private life in order to avoid the conversionary pressures associated with public office."[32] If there is a problem with his "extensive middle ground," it is that it is still not broad enough. Even in this shrewd analysis, there remains the presumption of a consistent clarity of Christian affiliation and its implications that was not necessarily present outside the defining moments experienced by the likes of Saturus and Dagila.

CHRISTIAN COURTIERS

> To be sure, he [Thrasamund] forced the Christians to change their ancestral doctrine ... but he pretended not to know in the least what sort [of Christian] those who refused were [τοὺς ἀπειθοῦντας, ὁποῖοί ποτε εἶεν, ἥκιστά γε εἰδέναι ποιούμενος].
>
> —PROCOPIUS, *VANDAL WARS*

Procopius's pithy assessment of Thrasamund's pragmatic approach to religious conformity is a signal reminder that Vandal kings, like Roman emperors, had interests countervailing the strict heresiological categorizations that they put into

---

29. A central problematic of study of pre-Constantinian Christianity: see, most recently, Rebillard (2012a), 9–60.
30. See p. 10 n. 47.
31. Miles (2005); Merrills and Miles (2010), 225–27.
32. Conant (2012), 185–86.

law.³³ The need to ensure political stability and the integration of key figures into government ran alongside and was sometimes of greater concern than the establishment of religious uniformity.³⁴ This might partly explain the intermittent promulgation and fluctuating enforcement of anti-Nicene edicts across the reigns of all the Vandal kings.³⁵ At times when religious uniformity was less of a priority at court, the precise ecclesiastical affiliation of a courtier was less likely to become a political or legal issue.

The effects of these alternative priorities and the inconsistent patterns of enforcement they produced were experienced not only en bloc but also in the differential treatment of particular individuals. It is notable that, on a number of occasions in Victor's *History*, Geiseric and Huneric seek to personally persuade a Nicene official to convert, invoking a preexisting relationship to do so.³⁶ This is partly a useful narrative tool, allowing Victor to emphasize the magnitude of the worldly honor that his characters rejected, but it also represents a plausible consideration. Personal relationships and loyalties likely affected royal decisions. A case in point concerns the pious Felix, a Nicene Christian and the estate manager (*procurator domus*) of Geiseric's son Theoderic, who appears in Victor of Vita's *History* arranging for the burial of his ex-colleague Armogas.³⁷ The differential treatment of the two is striking: while Armogas suffered the full application of legislation against Nicene political service (and, in Victor's account, the full armory of Vandal extrajudicial punishment), Felix continued to hold office. It does not seem a coincidence that Felix, as *procurator domus*, was a close ally of his royal lord Theoderic, while Armogas was a mere dependent whose precise role is not supplied. Felix may have had corresponding protection from the recently issued law. Without an alternative social logic of this sort, there hardly seems another explanation for, say, the appointment of the unnamed royal cellarer (*cellarita regis*) mentioned later in Victor's text, given that his wife, Dagila, had professed her Nicene Christianity on multiple occasions.³⁸ On the other hand, the "eminent and noble" Servus, a citizen of Thuburbo Maius targeted under Huneric, may have been more vulnerable because he had previously fallen foul of Geiseric for withholding information.³⁹

---

33. Proc., *BV* 1.8.9–10 (ed. Dewing: 74, 76). Although his information on specific kings requires careful treatment, this portrayal of Thrasamund's policies chimes with the description of *V. Fulg.* 20 (ed. Isola: 202). On Roman emperors see Shaw (2011), 490–505; Hermanowicz (2008), 188–92; Humfress (2008), 132–42.

34. Considerations plausibly adduced to explain inconsistent Roman enforcement: see, e.g., Tomlin (1998), 37–39; Lee (2013), 151–52.

35. See pp. 15–16.

36. *HP* 1.19, 1.47, 3.27 (ed. Lancel: 105, 118, 188).

37. Ibid., 1.43–46 (116–18). See also pp. 213–14.

38. *HP* 3.33 (ed. Lancel: 192); though cf. Merrills (2011), 114.

39. *HP* 3.25 (ed. Lancel: 187); translation from Moorhead (1992b), 73.

The influence possessed by officeholders and other members of the social elite caused them to be singled out in antiheretical edicts;[40] at the same time, it made it more likely that a blind eye would be turned to their offenses.[41]

It is important to note that laws against Nicene Christians at court and elsewhere do not seem to have been repealed even when rulers were conciliatory. Thus, the possibility of prosecution remained beyond their promulgation.[42] Nevertheless, a current desire to ensure uniformity, even as signaled through the issue or reissue of antiheretical laws, was important. It made individuals more likely to see advantages in and disregard the disincentives to the reporting and prosecution of lay heretics.[43] Those potentially liable were often influential individuals whose clout made it less attractive for others to publicly raise their Christian affiliation and try to use the law against them. It was not necessarily wise to do so when the individuals concerned could be patrons, allies, or dangerous enemies. In this context, it is unsurprising that the original denunciations of Nicene Christians in the *History* are sometimes made by Homoian clerics, whose status was more, though by no means fully, independent of court politics.[44]

There were a number of reasons why courtiers and civic notables who publicly self-identified as Nicene Christians might have escaped the implications of heresiological and legal definition. It must also be remembered that individual aristocrats' self-definition was not always clear cut. Victor's martyrs and confessors again provide useful anecdotal corroboration. When push came to shove, these individuals decided that orthodox Christianity was more important than office and standing. Nevertheless, their officeholding suggests that they had been able to serve the Vandal regime before, despite the policies that caused their removal.[45] It may be that some of these individuals had not previously seen their Christianity in such a doctrinally bounded way, since no one had forced them to define themselves as orthodox Christians as opposed to Homoousians or Arians. Their confessional identity crystallized only when they were forced to choose. Others clearly had presented themselves as specifically Nicene Christians before[46] but still had not seen this as incompatible with political service. This should not be surprising. Elite individuals across late antiquity served rulers whose religious affiliations and policies conflicted with their own. In Vandal Africa, even Nicene clerics found

---

40. Merrills (2011), 114.
41. Cf. Kelly (1998), 157–62; Harries (1999), 77–98.
42. See pp. 15–16, 99.
43. On possible advantages see p. 217 n. 105. On reluctance see Lepelley (1979–81), 1:395–402; Harries (1999), 91; Humfress (2007), 254; Hermanowicz (2008), esp. 106–8, 134, 164–68; Shaw (2011), 496–508, 542.
44. *HP* 1.19, 1.48 (ed. Lancel: 105, 119); see also pp. 44–45.
45. Miles (2005), 313.
46. See p. 200.

ways to downplay differences with their rulers when it suited them.[47] Courtiers and officeholders could be Nicene Christians without this necessarily preventing an effective political relationship with Vandal kings.

Courtiers could reconcile their political service with their sense of their Christianity through various means. Which particular route they took may not, practically speaking, have been that important, simply because others may have been ignorant of their specific confession. There were ways in which this affiliation could be made manifest, with varying degrees of volition on the part of an individual. Yet other than the public rite of rebaptism or explicit statements about doctrine or ecclesiastical loyalty, the unambiguous performance of a confessional identity became more difficult. The most obvious means to publicly display Christianity was church attendance.[48] This was the undoing of the courtiers who entered the basilica of the Nicene bishop of Carthage, Eugenius, *in habitu barbaro*.[49] Yet for extended periods Carthage had no Nicene bishop.[50] This leaves the tantalizing question of where these courtiers had worshiped before a doctrinally suitable bishop was appointed; the same goes for Christian aristocrats in other cities where exile or prohibition left a see empty. Victor's *History* provides glimpses of illicit services at which members of the ecclesiastical hierarchy presided.[51] It could also be that these aristocrats in Carthage (and elsewhere) attended churches that had been handed over to Homoian clerics.

Such a pragmatic choice may have been unnecessary. The *History of the Persecution* dramatizes sporadic attempts by Vandal kings and Homoian clerics to ensure adherence to Christian orthodoxy through more or less forcible acts of rebaptism. Vandal legislation embedded in the text also prohibits Nicene public worship. Yet even at times of state-sanctioned coercion, there is no mention of enforced attendance at any Homoian church anywhere.[52] Private observance may well have been a means to escape the implications of public worship. On one occasion, Victor of Vita describes a Nicene aristocratic circle worshiping in private. In an unnamed African town, a noblewoman named Dionysia had her son Maioricus's tomb installed at home after he suffered a martyr's death. She would then pray there; a coterie seems to have formed around her.[53] This Christian group had at its core an aristocratic family whose ecclesiastical affiliation was clearly known; the

---

47. See ch. 5.
48. See Rebillard (2012a), 67–68.
49. *HP* 2.8–11 (ed. Lancel: 125–26); see pp. 181–83.
50. Conant (2012), 164–65.
51. *HP* 1.41–42, 3.29 (ed. Lancel: 115–16, 190).
52. Cf. Maxwell (2006), 133–36; Maxwell (2012), 866; Sandwell (2007), 189–90, on surprisingly low late-antique expectations of churchgoing.
53. *HP* 3.22–24 (ed. Lancel: 185–86); see also the assembly in a private house at Tipasa: 3.29 (190). On private observance in late antiquity, see Bowes (2008).

doctrinal attitudes of other such groups may have been less publicly obvious. In Vandal Africa, Christian identity was both less clear cut and less evident to contemporaries than has often been thought.

Even when individuals made decisions that presented a clear and doctrinally bounded Christian identity to the world, this should not be understood in terms of Victor of Vita's straightforward contrast between pure faith and worldly ties. His martyrs and confessors saw Nicene Christianity as more important than any other aspect of their social identity, but this confessional identity itself meant not just a set of beliefs but also belonging to a group and membership in a social network. This produced a set of social expectations and pressures just as much as officeholding at court. The choices made by individuals were "worldly" even when contrary to their apparent political and status interests and involved factors beyond the profession of a set of orthodox doctrines: the authority of clerics with whom they had dealings, the Christianity of social contacts, or even the ecclesiastical control of certain churches and martyrs' shrines.[54] The full social logic of martyrs' and confessors' actions is not accessible, since they can now be seen only through the eyes of clerics like Victor of Vita. Ironically, it is easier to identify other rationales when clerics talk about errant individuals.

The martyr and confessor stories of the *History of the Persecution* show that elite actors at court, in administration, or generally prominent in the kingdom could be placed in positions where they had to define themselves in bounded confessional terms. There were situations when ecclesiastical affiliation had implications regarding both an individual's continued political service and their liability for punishments. Individuals could also deliberately express this affiliation and decide for themselves its incompatibility with political loyalty. Yet it required a precise set of circumstances for the doctrinal affiliation of a Christian courtier to become not only relevant but also the object of attempts to enforce religious uniformity. This affiliation had to be in some way publicly visible to contemporaries. Another powerful figure at court had to decide that it was in their interests to pursue an accusation of heresy, considering in their calculations the influence upon which the accused could call. Finally, if it came to it, the king had to be willing to sanction—or, at the very least, unwilling to retrospectively censure—any actions taken on his behalf. The safeguarding of religious uniformity may have been a key element of his rule in both ideological and practical terms, but other factors also intruded upon such decisions. As a result, Christian ecclesiastical affiliations could be as clear or as opaque as individual, king, and court made them. Victor's confessors and martyrs turn up at both ends of this spectrum. They were individuals who were decidedly Nicene Christians when forced to make up their minds.

54. On the last see pp. 215–17.

Otherwise, they were simply Christian courtiers, in the eyes of the public, the law, and perhaps even themselves.

POETIC JUSTICE

Dracontius has never been far from the minds of Vandal historians. The unfortunate poet and *uir clarissimus* was imprisoned by Gunthamund (r. 484-96) for a crime he enigmatically describes as "writing about one who, though a lord, was unknown to me" (*ignotumque mihi scribere uel dominum*).[55] Dracontius was traditionally the poster boy for a Catholic Romano-African elite subjugated to barbarian masters and longing for Roman (or, at the very least, more Roman) rule.[56] The blandishments of his apology to Gunthamund for this crime, the *Satisfactio*, were seen as forced praise of a tyrant.[57] More recently, Dracontius has become a more plausibly ambivalent figure: a prominent member of the Carthaginian elite, implicated in Vandal rule by his activities in the city's lawcourts. The precise nature of his offense remains contested. Praise of a foreign ruler has normally been conjectured; more recently, Andy Merrills and Étienne Wolff have each suggested delivery of a panegyric to rulers closer to home: Gunthamund's royal rivals, whether Huneric (his predecessor, who tried to cut him out of the succession) or Hilderic (the Hasding dynast who almost replaced him in those alternative arrangements).[58] As Ian Fielding has noted, it requires a tortuous reading of the Latin text to make this *dominus* "unknown" to Dracontius a Vandal king. At the same time, *scribere* requires neither a formal panegyric nor even praise per se, somewhat lessening the possible ideological impact of his actions.[59] (Of course, downplaying the extent of his crime was one of Dracontius's rhetorical strategies.) The exact nature and significance of Dracontius's communications remain enigmatic, but his actions hardly seem a firm basis on which to portray him as the voice of a generation of disenfranchised Catholic Roman aristocrats. His activities before his incarceration and his requests for the intercession of prominent members of the Romano-African elite during his imprisonment instead suggest a figure bound up in the politics of the Vandal court at Carthage.[60] As to the *Satisfactio*, questions of sincer-

---

55. Drac., *Satis.* 94 (ed. Moussy: 181). For this translation and astute analysis of this difficult phrase, see Fielding (2017), 89-97.
56. Useful references are in Merrills (2004a), 146 n. 8; for this approach, see also Schmidt (1942), 110-11; Bright (1999), 194-96; Wolff (2004), 123; Arweiler (2007), 150. Cf. Conant (2012), 373.
57. Diesner (1966a), 142; Diesner (1966b), 38, 63; cf. Courcelle (1964), 195.
58. Merrills (2004a); Wolff (1998), 381-83. See also Miles (2005), 317; Merrills and Miles (2010), 220.
59. Fielding (2017), 93-94, with n. 21.
60. Miles (2005), 317; Merrills and Miles (2010), 220-21.

ity seem as unhelpful here as in the analysis of any late-antique praise. It was simply an attempt by a courtier to use his oratorical skills to regain favor.

Dracontius is now rightly set within a much more finely textured Vandal court. Nevertheless, he remains a symbol for the incompatibility of Nicene Christianity and political service. Merrills and Richard Miles have suggested that Dracontius was unusual in praising Gunthamund in religious terms in the *Satisfactio* and that the poem's failure may have resulted from this idiosyncratic choice.[61] The *Satisfactio* is said to show a figure deaf to the harmoniously secular tones of praise at the Vandal court: "For a Catholic Romano-African to present such a work to a Vandal king was politically crass. It is hardly surprising that Dracontius was left languishing in his prison cell."[62] The *De laudibus Dei*, the poet's three-book plea for (and exegetical treatment of) divine forgiveness, thus becomes his rhetorical backup strategy: self-representation as a Nicene martyr, seeking forgiveness from God alone. Dracontius's marginalization would then show that neither pious Nicene Christians nor open Christian displays had a place at court.[63]

Whether as exemplar or exception, Dracontius has remained a test case for Christianity's impact on interactions between Romano-African elites and Vandal rulers. It is thus disconcerting to discover the fragility of the widely accepted narrative of his career.[64] It has only three fixed points: the lost text written about or to the *ignotus dominus*; the *Satisfactio*, addressed to Gunthamund; and a lost panegyric to his successor, Thrasamund. A number of scholars assume that the last was a *gratiarum actio* for the poet's release on the new king's accession.[65] There is absolutely no evidence for this.[66] It is based on the assumption that, since a poem of thanksgiving would have been necessary to recognize a ruler's clemency and no such text to Gunthamund is known, Dracontius must have remained in prison until 496 at the least.[67] The *De laudibus Dei* is then slotted in after the *Satisfactio*'s failure as a sequel under Gunthamund showing that the poet had given up hope of release. In fact, although the text was also written in prison and shares the *Satisfactio*'s central theme of forgiveness, its third book's confession of sins does not include Dracontius's panegyrical treachery, focusing instead on apparent legal

---

61. Merrills and Miles (2010), 219–25; see also Miles (2005), 318.
62. Merrills and Miles (2010), 225.
63. Drac., *DLD* (ed. Moussy); Merrills and Miles (2010), 225.
64. Standard reconstructions include Schanz, Hosius, and Krüger (1920), 58–68; *PLRE* 2:379–80 (Dracontius 2); *PCBE I* 329; Moussy (1985), 7–31; Bright (1987), 14–20; Bright (1999); Simons (2005), 1–3.
65. E.g., Moussy (1985), 30; Bright (1999); Miles (2005), 317, 318; Berndt (2007), 153; Hen (2007), 87; Merrills and Miles (2010), 225.
66. See the sixteenth-century description of the text in Bernardino Corio's *Historia di Milano*, in Bright (1999), 200 n. 22.
67. As noted by Wolff (1998), 383 n. 33.

corruption.[68] The frailty of this biography, based on internal evidence from the poems, an argument from silence, and psychological readings of highly rhetorical texts, should be obvious. It is plausible that Gunthamund refused to release Dracontius and likewise that the *De laudibus Dei* represents a further poetic response to the same imprisonment, but this is far from the only way the poems can be put together.[69] It seems better to analyze their contents instead of using them to create an uncertain biography.

When detached from speculative narratives, the *Satisfactio* demonstrates the possibilities for conformity available to a Christian courtier. The poet presents himself as a pious Christian and loyal subject seeking forgiveness from both Gunthamund and God. Gunthamund is provided with exempla of clement rulers from biblical and Roman history, to whom he is implicitly compared. As Lavinia Galli Milić has noted, a number of obvious borrowings cast Dracontius as Ovid and place the king in the role of Augustus: the Vandal ruler is effectively offered an opportunity to better the first Roman emperor.[70] Dracontius's Christian praise of Gunthamund is equally striking. The king is assimilated to God using the classic "divine insinuation" of the panegyrist; the same regal qualities are applied interchangeably, most notably the clemency (*pietas*) that Dracontius expects both to display.[71] Dracontius even compares his crime to that of the *ingrati* who, "since they do not know the Lord, worship vain idols."[72] Christianity and loyalty go hand in hand; disobeying Gunthamund is tantamount to paganism. In constructing his image of Gunthamund as an idealized Christian ruler, Dracontius probably drew on contemporary representations; a number of texts from the period suggest portrayal of Vandal rule as God given.[73] Dracontius's panegyric implies that Christians could praise Vandal kings in Christian terms whatever their confessional allegiance.[74] It is important to note that Christological and Trinitarian doctrine are entirely absent from the *Satisfactio*. Dracontius chose to ignore any doctrinal differences between himself and Gunthamund and instead to play up their common

---

68. On this problem see Wolff (2004), 124–25; restated by various authors in Wolff (2015); cf. Moussy (1985), 26–29.

69. For alternatives see previous note.

70. Galli Milić (2009), 259–60; cf. Wolff (2004), 127.

71. Galli Milić (2009), 252–57, at 253; see now Goldlust (2015); cf. Saylor Rodgers (1986); Kelly (1998), 139–42.

72. Drac., *Satis.* 93–96, quotation at 96 (ed. Moussy: 181); see also Conant (2012), 183.

73. See p. 147.

74. Fielding (2017), 89–127, argues that this praise is ironic or, at the least, that Dracontius's *comparationes* to Augustus and other Roman emperors are sufficiently ambiguous to give readers doubts in case Gunthamund failed to act appropriately. The *Satisfactio* may well have worked at this sophisticated level, but it still suggests that Dracontius's audience at the Carthaginian court had expectations of Christian praise of Vandal rulers; it was such expectations that (in this interpretation) he sought to subtly subvert.

Christianity. In the *Satisfactio*, Dracontius appears as a pious Christian without making any statement that would suggest a specific doctrinal affiliation.

This self-presentation might seem to jar with the Catholic martyr and spiritual cousin to Boethius sometimes described in modern accounts.[75] Yet Dracontius's self-definition as a Christian is much less clear cut than has generally been thought. The quality of his exegesis evinces considerable Christian learning.[76] In a passage of his *De laudibus Dei* that resembles nothing so much as a creedal statement, Dracontius does present himself as Nicene (although the importance of these fifty-odd lines within a three-book, 2,300-line exegetical poem on divine clemency can be overplayed).[77] However, this cannot be used as evidence for his Christian identity at the time of the *Satisfactio*. His beliefs or the Christian faction to which he adhered (the two are not necessarily identical) may have changed in the meantime. Dracontius could also have been Nicene in his Christology at the time of the *Satisfactio* but not thought that this was the defining or even a particularly significant feature of his Christianity. Finally, he may have seen himself as a Nicene Christian but without clearly expressing his allegiance to contemporaries. Given that Nicene clerics could also praise Vandal kings as ideal Christian rulers,[78] it is entirely possible that Dracontius, as a determinedly Nicene Christian, could reconcile himself in this manner without it being necessarily insincere or incongruous. However, the poet did not make his doctrinal standpoint, whatever it was and however important it was to his Christian self-definition, relevant to his praise of Gunthamund. To ascribe a particular religious label to Dracontius is to miss the point of his verses.

The poet brought the flexibility symptomatic of late-antique courtly discourse and of the classicizing Vandal-era poets of the *Latin Anthology* into Christian affairs. He was certainly not the first late-antique court poet to defy religious labeling.[79] Of course, the success or failure of his initiative has an important effect upon the contextualization of this Christian praise. The poem's results are unknown, although it seems more likely a failure than a success. At the same time, that probable result may not have stemmed from the poem's contents. Dracontius's choice of panegyric as the vehicle of his appeal encourages this idea, but other

---

75. See Merrills (2004a), 145–48, on the Boethian parallel.

76. Arweiler (2007).

77. Drac., *DLD* 1.562–564, 2.60–110 (ed. Moussy: 1:181, 199–201), has references to a triune God; 2.100–105 contains a short passage of polemic against unnamed individuals "devoid of reason," which seems to be an anti-Arian attack, though a very roundabout one. Strikingly, both sections lack the heresiological and technical terminology prevalent in contemporary Nicene literature.

78. See pp. 153–54, 158, 161–62, 164.

79. See, e.g., Ausonius: McLynn (1994), 82–83; Pacatus: Alan Cameron (2011), 227–30; Claudian: Alan Cameron (1970) and now Alan Cameron (2011), 207–8. See also Humphries (2010b); Lepelley (2010).

factors were no doubt at play (as is implied by Dracontius's later condemnation and praise of individuals who respectively ignored and aided his quest for release).[80] That Dracontius later addressed a panegyric to Thrasamund suggests that his Christian flattery was not so far off target. For the question of Christian identity at the Vandal court, the royal reception of these verses is perhaps less important than Dracontius's capacity to produce them. The *Satisfactio* shows that an elite actor and learned Christian could portray himself and his relationship to Vandal power in decidedly religious terms without taking an obvious stance in ecclesiastical politics. Being Christian at the Vandal court did not necessarily mean being Nicene or Homoian.

A CHRISTIAN ACHILLES

A sixteenth-century manuscript from Monte Cassino preserves a letter exchange between two late-antique African correspondents: a count, Sigisteus, and a presbyter, Parthemius.[81] This literary conversation most likely took place under Vandal rule, although the attribution cannot be certain.[82] Sigisteus wrote to Parthemius to praise him and requested a reply; Parthemius granted his plea and returned the favor. Little of substance is conveyed, but that was not the point. Letter writing in late antiquity was an important means of elite sociability and literary competition. These two florid prose compositions would not look out of place alongside Symmachus's or Sidonius Apollinaris's more baroque epistolographic exercises—save for the frequently awkward grammar.[83] The letters present Sigisteus as both cultured and militarily active. Parthemius addresses him as "exalted lord" (*domino sublimi*) and describes him as better than the heroes of Greece, as an Achilles, and as a man whom "our warlike Africa" had "borne to the stars." This combination of a quintessentially Roman form of social interaction, a smattering of classical allusions, and an emphasis on military prowess represents a perfect distillation of the culture of elite representation common to individuals of all ethnicities in Vandal Africa.[84]

---

80. See, e.g., Moussy (1985), 29–30.

81. All references to these texts come from Sig., *Ad Parth.* (ed. Bianco), and Parth., *Ad Sig.* (ed. Bianco). See (best) Bianco (1988a); (1988b).

82. On the Vandal date see *PCBE I* 821, 1077; *CPL* 271–72; Hays (2004), 126; Merrills and Miles (2010), 99; Conant (2012), 55. For similar exchanges in late Roman and Byzantine Africa, see, e.g., Aug., *Epp.* 185, 185A, 189, 220, 229–31 (ed. Goldbacher: 4:1–44, 131–37, 431–41, 497–510); Aug., *Ep.* 17* (ed. Divjak: 88); Ferr., *Ep.* 7 (*PL* 67: 928B–950A). Part of the reason that this letter exchange cannot be unequivocally dated is precisely its lack of clear references to barbarians, Arians, or Christian conflict.

83. See Bianco (1988b); Hays (2004), 132. On late-antique epistolography and *amicitia*, see Matthews (1974), 58–64; Matthews (1975), 5–9; Ebbeler (2009); Van Waarden (2010), 30–34, 61–66. On letters between generals and clerics, see Lee (2007), 154–62, esp. 160–62.

84. Merrills and Miles (2010), 99. See also pp. 173–75.

The strongly Christian tone of both letters is thus all the more striking. They present Sigisteus as a Christian who reveres God, the church, and his clerical correspondent (the count rather bombastically describes Parthemius as "an equal of the apostolic see"). Sigisteus looks forward to Parthemius's "salvific speech," presents himself as a sick man requiring healing from a clerical doctor, and begs the presbyter to pray for him. In turn, Parthemius describes a humble Christian whom God had fashioned to enact good works and to understand the difference between good and evil. Parthemius even takes this relationship with God into the military sphere in the letter's closing metrical lines: "Let the almighty arm you from heaven with shield and mail and helmet and let your life be blessed" (*te clipeo loricaque et galea caelitus armet / omnipotens et sit uita beata tibi*).[85]

Pious Christianity is made an important part of Sigisteus's membership in the African elite. Yet there is nothing in these texts that would permit an identification of Sigisteus or Parthemius with the confessional terminology used by either moderns or ancients. They vault doctrinal issues effortlessly, simply presenting Sigisteus not only as socially important and a pious Christian but socially important *because* he is a pious Christian. The formal prose of the letter exchange afforded both Sigisteus and Parthemius a means to assert a specifically Christian status that maximized the potential for contemporaries to recognize it, whatever their ethnic or confessional allegiance.

A RESPONSIBLE LANDLORD

The demands of prestigious display could align nicely with a nonexclusive Christian piety. On occasion, they could also intersect with the requirements of a more rigorous confessional identity. In the first book of his *History*, Victor of Vita narrates the unhappy tale of a group of slaves on the estate of an unnamed Vandal military commander (*millenarius*) in the time of Geiseric.[86] The Vandal married his arms bearer, Martinianus, to the slave who looked after his household, Maxima.[87] On the wedding night, Maxima, dedicated to Christ, persuaded her husband to join her in submission to the heavenly bridegroom, and he then

---

85. Lines clearly influenced by Vergilian epic: see Bianco (1988a), 254–56.
86. *HP* 1.30–35 (ed. Lancel: 110–13). On the *millenarius* as a military commander (of about one thousand men), see Gil Egea (1998), 332–33; Liebeschuetz (2003), 68; Maier (2005), 225–31; Merrills and Miles (2010), 69; Vössing (2014), 91. This office has been much debated. Analogy with the Ostrogothic and Visigothic kingdoms suggests judicial responsibilities (see, e.g., Maier [2005], 228–29; but cf. Merrills and Miles [2010], 69). This putative jurisdiction has been characterized as ethnically defined (e.g., Liebeschuetz [2003], 68), but this hypothesis seems to rely on a view of an ethnically divided African society. In any case, it is not the *millenarius*'s official duties but his status as a landowner that is at stake in this passage.
87. On the legal and literary contexts of this marriage, see Cooper (2016), 240–43.

convinced his three brothers, also slaves on the estate, to do likewise. All went happily into monasteries at Thabraca (modern-day Tabarka, Tunisia). When he found out, the *millenarius* was rather less pleased and brought the slaves back: to be tortured for their disobedience and, just as important, to be rebaptized as Homoian Christians. When Geiseric heard about the situation, he ordered, first, further punishments for the slaves (from which, naturally, they escaped miraculously unharmed) and then their banishment.

The relationship among the *millenarius*, his slaves, and Christianity forms the core of this story and is a revealing example of the intersection of Christian identity and the maintenance of social status. Victor of Vita represents the Vandal as a barbarian persecutor and his actions, particularly his recalling of the slaves from the monastery, as illegitimate. Victor states that they were no longer his slaves but instead those of Christ. The *millenarius*'s actions could alternatively be read as those of a *dominus* reestablishing his authority over his property.[88] The same can be said of the slaves' rebaptism. As Kim Bowes has shown, late Roman *domini* often expected their dependents to join them in worship.[89] Like most aspects of life in aristocratic households, Christian observance was predominantly shaped around the proprietor and his nuclear family. Bishops in late antiquity alternately criticized and exploited the authority that landowners exerted over their dependents in this regard. An instructive comparison can be drawn from Augustine's letters. The bishop of Hippo frequently chastised landlords for not doing more to ensure that their dependents were Catholic, including using force.[90] It was just this responsibility that the Vandal *millenarius* sought to fulfill—only, in Victor's eyes, according to the wrong definition of the true faith.

By acting to control the Christian observance of his dependents in this way, the anonymous *millenarius* made his confessional allegiance clear. The Homoian baptism of these slaves would have required the involvement of Homoian clerics—whether his own clergy from his estate or a bishop or cleric who held a more formal ecclesiastical post in the region.[91] The *millenarius*'s actions also signaled that the Christianity of his household was to be orthodox according to the bounded categories of contemporary ecclesiastical controversy: in modern terms, Homoian and not Nicene. Given that late-antique estates were supposed to reflect the self-image of their aristocratic owners, this must be seen as a statement of his Christian

---

88. Cf. Vössing (2011), 164 n. 74.
89. Bowes (2008), 125–88.
90. Ibid., 168–69; Lancel (2002b), 276; Dossey (2010), 139, 188–89. See also Hermanowicz (2008), 146, 152, for an earlier ban on Donatist landowners rebaptizing their slaves.
91. See *V. Fulg.* 6–7 (ed. Isola: 171–77), for a Homoian presbyter, Felix, located on a *fundus*. Since African estates often gained representatives of the ecclesiastical hierarchy, whether Catholic or Donatist—see Dossey (2010), 125–44, 205–7—Felix's precise remit is unclear.

identity. The anonymous Vandal *millenarius* portrayed himself as a specifically orthodox Christian.

Of course, if the *millenarius* here conformed to and reinforced the norms of contemporary Christian heresiology, this did not necessarily mean that he considered orthodox Christianity the most important aspect of his identity, even in this particular instance. Christian affiliation did not obviate his other concerns as a social actor; in fact, imperatives of status played a significant role. His actions pertained as much to the slaves' disobedience—and thus the preservation of his authority within his household and his status within his community—as to questions of Christian conflict. The two issues intersected in the confessional identity of these five slaves, their divergence from the Christian norms of the *familia*, and the duties of a Christian aristocrat regarding the heterodoxy of his dependents. The demands pressed by his status as an orthodox Christian and as a landowner pushed the *millenarius* in the same direction. The reception of these actions by Victor of Vita illustrates once again the possibilities of interpretation by contemporaries. For Victor, the *millenarius*'s actions were those of a barbarian Arian and oppressive lord. For Homoian Christians or for those less invested in clear doctrinal distinctions, they could have been those of a responsible Christian landowner.

AD SANCTOS

Victor of Vita may have disapproved of the actions taken by the Vandal lord, but he would have agreed that the profession of Catholic Christianity should secure worldly status for an individual. This is nowhere clearer than in the story (cited earlier) of Armogas, a dependent of the king's son Theoderic, who fell foul of a recent law against Nicene Christians serving at royal courts in the latter part of the reign of Geiseric.[92] According to Victor, Armogas was tortured, then condemned to menial agricultural labor. As the degraded aristocrat approached death, he summoned Theoderic's estate manager (*procurator domus*), Felix, and requested a simple burial beneath a carob tree. Felix, "a revered Christian," did not consider this fitting for a "revered confessor" and replied, "I will bury you in one of the basilicas with the triumph and recognition [*gratia*] that you deserve" (1.45, 1.46). Armogas remained insistent and was duly rewarded for his unyielding modesty. At that very spot, a wonderful marble sarcophagus was miraculously uncovered.

This story, as the *History of the Persecution* relates it, suggests that the rewards for orthodox Christianity were not merely heavenly. Armogas was reduced to a far more humble station because he refused to "convert" to what he saw as heresy. At the same time, by this action he acquired social prestige in what Victor saw as a more appropriate form: status within his Christian community. The concluding

---

92. *HP* 1.43–46 (ed. Lancel: 116–18). See also p. 176 n. 58.

miracle neatly essays this paradox of renunciation. Felix wished to give Armogas the funerary pomp and privileged burial requisite not only for a remarkable confessor but also for a Christian aristocrat.[93] Armogas's refusal was vindicated by a discovery that supplied him this moment of prestigious display. Victor's hagiographical account of the death of this erstwhile Vandal official is open to skeptical reading on numerous levels, but it remains plausible that those who maintained a decidedly orthodox Christian identity, particularly in the face of hostile treatment, could secure an honored position within a Christian community. At the very least, the Armogas episode shows that clerics sought to increase the appeal of doctrinal rigidity by singling out individuals in this way and couching Christian prestige in terms of aristocratic values.[94] Clerics had frequently used such rhetoric to help ease what could be an abrupt transition for prominent congregants and correspondents from worldly to spiritual honor.[95]

Armogas's privileged burial also highlights yet again an issue critical for evaluating the scope that aristocrats possessed to represent their status in Christian ways beyond the Vandal court, as well as the consequences of heresiology more broadly. Contemporaries understood the implications of privileged burial—a long-standing social practice—for the status of the deceased. Whether and by whom that claim to status was recognized is another matter. The degree of acceptance accorded to the claims made by and for the Christian dead depended on the extent to which heresiological divisions were imprinted upon local Christian communities. On a practical level, the audience for a burial like that of Arifridos (described at the beginning of this chapter) was limited to those who entered his church in Thuburbo Maius. If that church served an exclusive community of Homoian or Nicene Christians, many simply might not have had the chance to see Arifridos's funeral or epitaph. Christians who did not worship there might still have been aware of the honor accorded to him within the basilica. Yet if they shared the heresiological mind-set encouraged by their clerics, they might have decided that Arifridos's assertion of his status as an elite Christian was invalidated by the doctrinal affiliation of that church. Equally, if the deceased, his heirs, or his fellow congregants thought their church had a local monopoly on Christian orthodoxy, this might have meant that a circumscribed audience was intended. It is here that our ignorance of local circumstances at Thuburbo Maius and elsewhere becomes a serious stumbling block.

This book has repeatedly questioned the extent to which the congregation of even a determinedly orthodox Christian church would—and could—uphold such exclusivity; the reasons do not require another airing here. It is nonetheless

---

93. On privileged burials see pp. 195–97.
94. See pp. 177–80. See also Hon., *Ep. consol. ad Arcad.* (*PL* 50).
95. Curran (2000), 316–17; Salzman (2002), 200–219.

worth elaborating another factor that might have led individuals to continue to worship at a particular church whatever its cleric's ecclesiastical affiliation. Christians might have seen attendance at the church of a martyr, especially on a festival day, as more important to their praxis than the doctrinal affiliation of the cleric who preached there.[96] The funerary arrangements of the "Vandal boy" in the massive, transregional pilgrimage site at Theveste offer a crucial example.[97] In 508, a mosaic epitaph for this five-year-old was set up in the heart of the complex, probably by his parents.[98] The deceased has received his (somewhat misleading) nickname because his portrait depicts him in military clothing of the sort worn by soldiers and government officials (see figure 3). Whoever installed this funerary mosaic wished to emphasize the status of the boy and his family as members of the ruling elite and perhaps to acknowledge a glittering future that would now never come to pass. The boy was buried next to relics generally accepted as those of the local martyr Crispina and her companions (though this must remain a hypothesis). It seems unlikely that pilgrims would have been put off by the particular doctrinal affiliation of the cleric who used the basilica in the first decades of the sixth century. The many travelers who came to gain proximity to the saints' relics would have seen the boy's tomb and recognized the elite Christian status that it implied.[99]

The great pilgrimage church at Theveste may be an extreme case, but it nonetheless isolates something important. In certain circumstances, Christians may have self-identified more strongly as devotees of a holy martyr than as Christologically orthodox Christians. They would have been aided in this regard by the striking continuities in the local material commemoration of martyrial cults within a number of African basilicas. As Ralf Bockmann has noted, these continuities do not have to mean that these buildings remained in the same hands throughout.[100] As in many conflicts, clerics from both factions sought to harness the authority of the same martyrs and holy persons. So, at Carthage, Homoian clerics took over the basilica *maiorum*, where Perpetua, Felicitas, Celerina, and the Scilitian martyrs were buried, and the two extramural basilicas dedicated to

---

96. See Sandwell (2007), 134–37, 189; Sizgorich (2009), 56–65.

97. On the boy see Von Rummel (2007), 190–91; Bockmann (2013), 220–25. On the complex (including hypothesized relics), see Christern (1976); Gui, Duval, and Caillet (1992), 311–16; Sears (2007), 51–52; Yasin (2009), 161–64.

98. Bockmann (2013), 220–21.

99. On burial *ad sanctos*, see Y. Duval (1988), with critical comments by Yasin (2009), 70–71, 212–22. There are forms of martyrial commemoration close to a number of the burials mentioned at p. 196; however, given that the precise locations both of epitaphs and of martyrial inscriptions and depositions are unknown, it is not always certain that proximity was a prime concern.

100. Bockmann (2013), 116–17, 164–66, 254.

FIGURE 3. Epitaph of the "Vandal boy" at Theveste (Tébessa, Algeria). From Bockmann (2013), plate 18, fig. 1, reproduced with kind permission of Reichert Verlag.

Cyprian.[101] They celebrated the Cypriana festival held in the city on his martyr day.[102] Nicene Christians also commemorated all of these figures.[103] Contests for possession of the martyrs are most easily identified in the crowded—and archaeologically and textually well attested—Christian topography of Carthage, but it is plausible that similar competition occurred within other urban centers. When those on either side of religious boundaries shared reverence for particular holy figures, Christian bishops had to work hard to convince their congregations that their opponents' use of such cults was illegitimate.[104] Martyrial cults may have allowed individual Christians to reconcile with their personal convictions what was, to an inevitable degree, a pragmatic choice. Discussions of these problems

101. *HP* 1.9, 1.16 (ed. Lancel: 100–101, 104).
102. Proc., *BV* 1.21.17–25 (ed. Dewing: 180–84); see also p. 93.
103. For an example see p. 186.
104. Fournier (2008), 236–38; Sizgorich (2009), 24–45, 56–65.

frustratingly have to remain largely in the realm of the hypothetical, given their contingency upon unknowable local conditions. At the very least, however, there were ways in which the use and perception of churches could allow for a broader and more receptive audience for the display of prestige by socially prominent congregants, alive or dead.

CONCLUSION

This chapter has argued that Christian members of the African elite were able to serve the Vandal kings and engage in (now traditional) Christian practices of elite competition in spite of doctrinal and ecclesiastical differences. Even avowedly pious Christians did not necessarily relate their Christianity to a particular creed or ecclesiastical faction. Those aristocrats who did had other interests that militated against the unambiguous public expression of that affiliation. They were aided by the limitations to the ability and desire of other major players, kings and clerics included, to seek a clear statement of specific adherence or the enforcement of antiheretical laws. Courtiers and aristocrats operated in a social and political climate conducive to the maintenance of a helpful ambiguity regarding confessional identity. This was not always the case: sporadic bouts of active enforcement, the heresiological rigor of some clerics, or even a rivalry at court or within a civic elite could necessitate a clear moment of definition.[105] Equally, not all Christian aristocrats would have chosen to take up these opportunities, whether because of conviction or the pursuit of alternative strategies of distinction. The Christian prestige accorded to a signally orthodox member of a Christian community—and especially one who had renounced the world for their faith—could be pursued instead of the broader social prestige commensurate with elite status. On the other hand, as in the case of the Vandal *millenarius*, the requirements of orthodoxy and social standing sometimes aligned. The difficulty in such cases was the disruption that a clear statement of doctrinal affiliation could cause for the acceptance of status. It is thus important that worldly and Christian prestige could come together in less problematic combinations. Christian aristocrats like Dracontius, Sigisteus, and the family of the "Vandal boy" found ways to express their piety without limiting their prospective audience. Similarly, the Nicene martyrs and confessors of the *History of the Persecution* were able to serve at the Vandal court or occupy prominent roles in civic politics until their hands were forced. For others, like the *procurator* Felix, that moment may never have arrived. Being Christian was not a problem unless it was made into one.

---

105. On rivalries see Halsall (2007), 323; Merrills and Miles (2010), 192.

Epilogue

Homoian Christianity in the Post-Imperial West

Vandal Africa came to an abrupt end. In 533, the imperial army under Belisarius took Carthage with startling ease. Gelimer's insurgency was soon put down. The ousted Vandal king and his troops were shipped off to the East: pensioned off and enlisted respectively. After a century of rule in Africa, the Hasding regime had collapsed in short order.[1] The speed with which Vandal power folded has sometimes been read as the sign of a failed state, but military defeats could topple even the most successful ancient and early medieval regimes. Vandal rule cannot be judged by its ending.

The kingdom's Homoian Christians disappear almost as suddenly as the Vandal state. After a brief period of continued license, petitions from Africa's Nicene bishops, seconded by the bishop of Rome, forced Justinian's hand. The emperor ordered the properties of Arian and other heretical churches to be transferred to the Nicene establishment and punishments to be reintroduced for Arians (among other religious deviants).[2] There are a few hints of a continuing Homoian presence in Africa. Procopius alludes to Arian soldiers among the occupying Eastern forces and attributes a military revolt to a harsh anti-Arian law.[3] Ferrandus of Carthage, a Nicene cleric and protégé of Fulgentius of Ruspe, advised an incoming imperial count, Reginus, on how to treat heretical soldiers and what to do when sent to a

---

1. Merrills and Miles (2010), 228–55; Conant (2012), 306–16.
2. Iust., *Nov.* 37 (ed. Schöll and Kroll: 244–45); Modéran (1998b), 702–3; Merrills and Miles (2010), 239–41.
3. Proc., *BV* 2.14.12–21 (ed. Dewing: 330–32).

region populated by heretics.[4] The creed he supplied to Reginus is explicitly *contra Arium*, indicating the heretics he had in mind.[5] Otherwise, Africa's Homoian Christians do not resurface. If their presence in Vandal Africa had transpired something like a "bizarre replaying"[6] of the Donatist schism, here was history repeating itself once more. Just as the Donatists disappear from (modern) view in the 430s, so too do the Homoians a century later.

Whatever their post-Vandal fate, these Christians' activities had lasting effects. Already in Byzantine Africa, what had now become the Vandal interregnum was folded into the Nicene master narrative so prevalent in the histories and tractates of the previous century. In another of the ironies that seem characteristic of late-antique African ecclesiastical politics, the imperial saviors of African Nicene Christianity became its new enemies. For hard-liners, the condemnation of Theodoret of Cyrrhus, Theodore of Mopsuestia, and Ibas of Edessa by Justinian and the churchmen who sided with his policy of reconciliation undermined the doctrinal settlement set out at the Council of Chalcedon (451).[7] Nicene polemic was reformulated to malign a new (tyrannical) ruler and his creatures; erstwhile rivals were pressed into service once more. As part of a polemical tome against Mocianus, an opponent in this new controversy over the "Three Chapters," Facundus, the bishop of Hermiane in Byzacena, accuses the *scholasticus* of repeated prevarication: he had apparently sided with the Arians under the Vandals before rejoining the Nicene faith. The Vandal persecution joins a familiar historical litany:

> That is the way to Gehenna, which the Sirmian multitude entered upon in those times according to the will of Constantius at Rimini and Seleucia, which multitude he [Mocianus] himself has followed, who was an Arian under Vandal rule. Then, when the Roman Empire succeeded them, he changed with the times and seemed to be Catholic. Now, since orders prejudicial to Catholic religion have arisen from the palace, he again follows the same [route], because, just as you see, those counselors have prescribed an action; not satisfied with that, he still does not stop grasping to secure something more elevated even if it comes about from the perdition of others.[8]

Justinian and the condemnation of the Three Chapters are bundled up with Constantius II, Sirmium, Rimini and Seleucia, and the Vandal persecution as way stations on the same road to hell (and certainly, at least in the case of Mocianus, one paved with malign intentions). The history and cultural associations of Arianism

---

4. Ferr., *Ep.* 7.5.11–14 (*PL* 67: 939A–942D); see also Cooper (2007), 31–37.
5. Ferr., *Ep.* 7.5.12 (*PL* 67: 939C).
6. Shaw (2011), 804.
7. On Africa and the Three Chapters controversy, see Markus (1966); Markus (1979); Maas (2003b), 42–64; Sotinel (2005), 279–84; Modéran (2007); Conant (2012), 316–30.
8. Fac., *C. Moc.* 64 (ed. Clement and Vander Plaetse: 415).

remained available for African Christians as rhetorical weapons to discredit opponents in Byzantine Africa.

This was to be the enduring legacy of Africa's Homoian Christians. The outpouring of Nicene polemic against them as Arians made a major contribution to the continued framing of correct Christian belief and practice as non-Arian in early medieval Europe. The extensive Trinitarian discussions of African Nicene writers provoked by their Homoian rivals proved eminently useful for Carolingian clerics as they too sought to define what it was to be Christian.[9] The Vandal kingdom has often been portrayed as an outlier among the new polities of the post-imperial West as a result of its ongoing Christian controversy.[10] The ease with which Christian writers in the early medieval West appropriated African anti-Arian texts for their programmatic treatments of the true faith signals that the Christian politics of post-imperial Africa were not as anomalous as they have often been made out.[11] Dialogue and conflict over correct belief and practice patterned Christianity in late antiquity and the early middle ages.

This book has sought to normalize Vandal Africa and its ecclesiastical conflict by setting it against a broader backdrop of late-antique Christianity. The church politics of post-imperial Africa represent an extension of earlier controversies; they also bear comparison with fifth-century Eastern Christological debates. Part 1 argued that, as in those other conflicts, these politics centered on the definition of the true Christian faith and the identity of the church that embraced it. Its Nicene and Homoian participants conducted their disputes on terms all too familiar from the Trinitarian debates of the middle decades of the fourth century. Homoian writers accused their rivals of fomenting a Homoousian heresy through the creation and profession of the Nicene Creed and cited the creed of the universal Councils of Rimini and Seleucia as a definitive statement of faith. Nicene writers defended Nicaea and its definitions and characterized and rebutted the Arianism of their opponents through the arguments and precedents of better-known late fourth- and early fifth-century churchmen. While the writings of both sides seem to pick up where Latin Nicene and Homoian disputants had left off in 380s Milan, the methods they used to contest these fundamental issues of Christian self-definition and ecclesiastical legitimacy evoke earlier disputes in Africa and contemporary Eastern developments. The textual forms and debate tactics employed by both parties come straight from the playbook of veteran controversialists like Augustine of Hippo and

---

9. For the use of Nicene anti-Arian texts from Vandal Africa in Carolingian creedal commentaries, see the helpful catalog of Keefe (2012), nos. 8, 15, 19, 37, 83, 93, 96–97, 102, 121, 124, 126, 131, 137, 148, 166, 184, 194, 199, 241, 301, 311–12. For the use of Vig., *Dial.*, in the *Opus Caroli*, see Bullough (2003), 348–49, 354; Meeder (2005), 147–49.

10. Most recently in Castritius (2010).

11. See Schwank (1961b); (1961a), xv, on Caesarius of Arles's wholesale use of the *C. Var.* for his *Breuiarium*.

Cyril of Alexandria. Above all, the continued importance of legal categorization in shaping the power relations of the African Christian community signals that the old world of acrimonious heresiological disputation lived on. The fact that it was now Homoian clerics who received the benefits of the Constantinian revolution only underlines this point. The process of defining and contesting the true Christian faith that had received its irresistible momentum from the intervention of the late Roman state continued apace in Vandal Africa. The end of empire did not mean new ground rules for ecclesiastical controversy.

Many contemporaries shared this view of overriding continuity. The Nicene and Homoian writers considered in part 1 did not distinguish between the Christian politics of the Vandal present and those of the late Roman past. In contrast to more influential voices (at least to moderns) like Possidius of Calama and Victor of Vita, they did not characterize the conquest as a rupture. Unlike modern patristic scholars, they did not see the events of the 380s as the end of a discrete phase of Trinitarian controversy. Instead, they wrote the events of contemporary ecclesiastical controversy into continuous histories stretching back into the fourth-century past. Of course, writers showed awareness of historical contingency and changing circumstances: for instance, the contrast between the Theodosian settlement and its reversal in post-imperial Africa. Nonetheless, again and again, the Vandal present was interpreted through key moments of the late Roman past. As these writers saw it, their African Church was not post-Roman. Its events and protagonists were made part of unbroken narratives of the church intended to shape the identity of African Christians. Extant Christian polemic writings present contemporary conflict not as something revolutionary but as a new iteration of an ancient battle. These Christian polemicists fought it using the methods of a fifth-century Mediterranean Church that, even as it moved on to new problems, still turned to the archetypal heresy and its history for solutions. Nicene and Homoian writers did not simply look to the authoritative figures of a heroic age of Trinitarian debate now long past. These African churchmen claimed to be their heirs and equals, defending Christian truth from the same heretical threats that had imperiled the church for more than a century, living in the same era of ecclesiastical history. As a result, they were not just arguing once again over the questions of Trinitarian doctrine debated incessantly within the fourth-century church. They were writing a new chapter in "the Arian controversy."

This Christian controversy had consequences far beyond the institutional church. The maintenance of correct Christian faith was an important consideration not only for the bishops of the new polity but also for its kings and ruling elite. Yet, as part 2 sought to demonstrate, the nature of individual identities meant that this shared concern for orthodoxy competed with a host of other considerations. Royal attempts to fulfill Christian ideals of a ruler who ensured the correct belief of his subjects were part of a broader nexus of efforts to secure political legitimacy, stability, and loyalty. Aristocrats had to trade off multiple forms of prestige and allegiance: Christian status, which was partly based upon the correct expression of their faith in God, and the broader social prestige and political loyalty that buttressed their positions as elite actors. The enforcement of religious uniformity or the articulation of a clear confessional identity could align with these alternative sets of interests; at other times, these different elite priorities could be less compatible. Bishops, to establish themselves against competing Christian authority figures, attempted to persuade other social actors to share their definitions of orthodoxy and heresy and to consider those definitions crucial to their behavior and conduct; where possible, these representatives of ecclesiastical institutions sought the implementation of legislation to enforce orthodoxy in practical terms. At the same time, bishops both Nicene and Homoian were embedded within society as elite actors and subject to similar demands as their aristocratic counterparts. Nicene bishops may have seen the Vandal kings as Arian heretics and the treatment they received at their hands as persecution. Yet they also pragmatically engaged with their rulers and sought concessions. Even for Nicene clerics, the expectation that heresiological distinctions would govern social actions could be outweighed by the need to harness the political power of kings who, after all, were unlikely to be suddenly overthrown.

Part 2 explored the different ways that individuals found to ease or even resolve the tensions that these conflicts of interests could produce. Vandal Africa, like its late Roman predecessor and post-imperial counterparts, was a polity deeply influenced by Christianity. Kings, bishops, and aristocrats could stay Christian even as they lessened or evaded the implications of the heresiological mind-set that they themselves encouraged. In the final reckoning, this conclusion may not seem so far from that of much recent scholarship on Vandal Africa, which has played down the role of Christian conflict and stressed a more pragmatic, "secular" basis for the politics of the kingdom. Both accounts are in many ways compatible, but with important differences. The chapters of part 2 attempted to recast this pragmatism as a result of how even decidedly Christian individuals approached their world and thus shaped the social and political possible in Vandal Africa. This part aimed to reincorporate Christianity and the evident consequences of contemporary ecclesiastical controversy into the workings of the polity, to avoid the curious sense of bipolarity that can result from a tidy compartmentalization of the secular and the religious. Vandal Africa may have diverged from the other successor kingdoms—although not the Theodosian empire—in the considerable extent to which its clerics engaged in doctrinal controversy and its kings sought religious uniformity. It nevertheless remained a viable political entity because being Christian was not always synonymous with the adoption of a rigorous and inflexible doctrinal affiliation and heresiological world view. Piety and pragmatism were not mutually exclusive.

By appropriating and adapting recent approaches to orthodoxy, heresy, and identity in late antiquity, this book has sought to reintegrate Vandal Africa into the study of late-antique Christianity. The kingdom, society, and church that have emerged do not conform to the traditional picture of an anomalous outlier. The profound similarities between its Christian politics and those of other late-antique polities suggest that Vandal Africa's supposed exceptionalism needs to be approached on a different footing. On these terms, it is not post-imperial Africa that requires explanation. Rather, the received view of the other successor kingdoms—as polities largely vacant of the consequences of the same Christian differences—seems unusual. It is this traditional image of Homoian Christianity in the post-imperial West that this epilogue revisits.

VANDAL EXCEPTIONALISM

By signaling fruitful comparisons across the western Mediterranean, I do not mean to say that all of the successor kingdoms looked like Vandal Africa. The social and political consequences of the same basic Christian difference that inspired such vibrant debates in Africa had varying parameters across the regions of the post-imperial West. Important contrasts can be drawn; the following pages will explore them at greater length. Rulers were less willing than their Vandal counterparts to pursue Christian uniformity. Tied to this, ecclesiastical disputes were conducted at a lower pitch and frequency, and there was greater leeway for explicit acceptance of Christian difference on the parts of clerics, kings, and elites. In the absence of major efforts to enforce Homoian Christianity as orthodoxy, Christian communities probably matched up more closely to ethnic ones in these kingdoms. For all of these reasons (and others), ecclesiastical politics took a rather different form in fifth- and sixth-century Gaul, Italy, and Spain than in Africa.

This book has deliberately refused to present (yet another) explanation of why Vandal Africa was different. Many plausible suggestions have, of course, been made.[12] The Vandal war band's relatively recent conversion may have made its members particularly zealous in support of their new (Homoian) faith, although this verges on psychological explanation. The greater independence of the Hasding dynasty's establishment in the African provinces, compared to Visigothic or Ostrogothic initiatives, may have resulted in a sense of greater freedom from imperial censure when it came to questions of orthodoxy.[13] It certainly produced a more confrontational approach to land redistribution than in Aquitaine or Italy.[14] The African Catholic Church's experience of prolonged controversy with its

---

12. Cf. Heather (2007a) 142–46, with discussion of various possible motives.
13. As suggested by T. Brown (2007), 419.
14. See p. 173 n. 37.

Donatist rival seems to have made its representatives more prone to mark and challenge perceived Christian difference.[15] Indeed, a number of scholars have put a strident case for the distinctive nature of Christianity in Roman Africa[16]—the "Bible belt" of late antiquity, in Paula Fredriksen's evocative phrase[17]—as part of a broader awareness of the divergent profiles of provincial churches.[18] Variation should only be expected. Rome's western provinces (and the kingdoms that inherited them) followed different late and post-Roman trajectories, with divergences in ecclesiastical institutions, power structures, socioeconomic conditions, and cultural traditions. Any one of these manifold facets of the post-imperial West could be adduced, in a dizzying kaleidoscope of combinations.

As this rehearsal of the differences between Vandal Africa and its transmarine neighbors should suggest, the pursuit of any programmatic or monocausal explanation is inherently problematic. Even the plausible individual features identified above could point in different directions. The lack of imperial recognition for Vandal conquest and settlement might just as easily be seen as a pressing reason for conciliatory moves toward the Nicene Church.[19] Similarly, the concerns of "Catholic" churchmen with Donatism could (in another context) have led historians to expect a more sanguine attitude toward Arianism.[20] As a result, it is much easier to pursue the individual logic of how events proceeded in each kingdom than to explain why these same factors did not lead individual actors to take different courses. Above all, it should be remembered that the differences that require explanation do not support a stark contrast. A fair (if somewhat crude) summary of the current consensus on this issue in studies of the Burgundian, Ostrogothic, and Visigothic kingdoms would be that the presence of powerful Homoian Christians provoked intermittent flash points of conflict amid a more general coexistence. The same could easily be said for Vandal Africa. (At any rate, it is what this book has been arguing.) What generalization of this sort tends to conceal is finer (but nonetheless crucial) differences of degree, like the greater quantity and focus of African Christian polemic or the sharper consequences for Nicene Christians on those occasions when Huneric or Thrasamund mobilized the Hasding dynasty's governmental machinery. In that sense, the social and political implications of Homoian Christianity in the post-imperial West are better understood not in terms of a dichotomy (Africa and the rest) but rather as a spectrum of possible consequences, latent across all of the polities ruled by Homoian kings.

15. See, e.g., Fournier (2012), 248.
16. E.g., Jensen (2013); see also Patout Burns and Jensen (2014).
17. Fredriksen (1991), 155.
18. See Mathisen (1989); Sotinel (2012), 127.
19. As noted by Heather (2007a), 137.
20. A similar argument has been applied to bishops of Rome and their apparent prioritizing of Eastern doctrinal issues over the challenges of Arians in Ostrogothic Italy: e.g., Amory (1997), 197–98.

UNIFORMITY AND ITS ALTERNATIVES

The marked limitation of royal intervention is perhaps the most substantial difference between the ecclesiastical politics of Vandal Africa and those of the other successor kingdoms. Only rarely did kings in the rest of the West use the military dominance and administrative structures at their disposal to seek Christian uniformity in the manner that had become customary in the later Roman Empire. This is not to say that the Hasding dynasty's desire for Christian uniformity was unparalleled. The closest *comparanda* are the concerted efforts of the Visigothic kings Leovigild (r. 568–86) and Reccared (r. 586–601) to unite the Homoian and Nicene churches of their Spanish kingdom in the 580s and 590s, using methods up to and including coercion.[21] In 580 an assembly of Homoian clerics convoked by Leovigild produced and subscribed to a twelve-book treatise in support of a new doctrinal compromise, whereby they stated that the Father and Son were equal but the Holy Spirit lesser and decided that a new baptism should no longer be required of Nicene Christians entering their communities.[22] Nicene bishops seem to have been a particular target of Leovigild's enforcement of this doctrinal settlement. Some converted; vocal episcopal opponents were sent into exile, including Masona of Merida and the future historian John of Biclar.[23] After Leovigild's death, his son Reccared continued his policy of seeking ecclesiastical unity to match hard-won Spanish territorial unification.[24] Yet he took the opposite approach, publicly affirming his support for the Nicene-Constantinopolitan creed of 381 at the Third Council of Toledo, in 589. At the same meeting, the kingdom's Homoian bishops and "the whole of the Gothic *gens*" anathematized the Arian heresy and professed Nicene Christianity.[25] That conciliar unanimity was illusory, at least in the late 580s; the introduction and enforcement of this new religious settlement seem to have been causal factors in several revolts against Reccared's rule, backed by prominent Homoian bishops.[26] Reccared and Leovigild's

---

21. Heather (1996), 280–83; Velazquez (2003), 168–87; Koch (2012), 190–213; Koch (2014); J. Wood (2012), 43–50.

22. Toledo III (589), anathema 16 (ed. Vives: 119); Ioh. Bicl., *Chron.* 57 (ed. Cardelle de Hartmann: 71–72).

23. Ioh. Bicl., *Chron.* 57 (ed. Cardelle de Hartmann: 72); Isid., *HG* 49–50 (ed. Mommsen: 287–88); Isid., *De uir. illust.* 28, 30, 31 (ed. Codoñer Merino: 149–52). On Masona see *VPE* 5.1–13 (ed. Maya Sánchez: 47–98). This doctrinal policy may also have been a factor in the revolt of Leovigild's son Hermenegild, who presented himself as a Nicene Christian, though since issues of Christian affiliation are absent from all Spanish accounts of the revolt, their role is hotly contested: see most recently Koch (2012), 195–99; J. Wood (2012), 45–46, 221–22; Koch (2014), 261–62, with detailed bibliography in n. 17.

24. Heather (1996), 280–83; Velazquez (2003), 169–70; J. Wood (2012), 39–50; Koch (2014), 261–64.

25. Toledo III (589) (ed. Vives: esp. 109–10, 122–23); Ioh. Bicl., *Chron.* 91 (ed. Cardelle de Hartmann: 81–82); Isid., *HG* 52–54 (ed. Mommsen: 288–90). On Toledo III see Velazquez (2003), 168–75; Koch (2012), 331–53.

26. Heather (1996), 282–83; Collins (2004), 67–69; Koch (2012), 204–5; J. Wood (2012), 49.

attempts to secure Christian orthodoxy and uniformity stemmed from the same ideals of late-antique rulership that inspired the likes of Huneric. In the aftermath of the Council of Toledo, John of Biclar was quick to paint Reccared as a new Constantine and a new Marcian (reenacting Nicaea and Chalcedon respectively).[27]

As the policy decisions of Leovigild and Reccared show, Homoian kings outside Africa could represent themselves as ideal Christian rulers and include within that remit ensuring correct religious observance. When kings took on board the implications of this requirement—acknowledgment and reinforcement of the claims of Homoian clerics to orthodoxy—it could lead to conflict with the Nicene bishops of their kingdoms. The actions of the Ostrogothic king Theoderic (r. 493–526) in the final years of his reign are a case in point.[28] Reports of Homoian converts to Nicene Christianity in the East led Theoderic to send an embassy to the eastern emperor Justin I in 525 requiring their return to (his) true faith. This attempt at patronage over the wider Homoian Christian community failed. In response, Theoderic incarcerated John the Nicene bishop of Rome, tasked with that delicate mission; much to the detriment of the king's posthumous reputation, the pope died in prison. Theoderic also produced an edict (probably never implemented) seizing Nicene churches across an unspecific area.[29] The precise fallout is complicated by the exceedingly polemical (and somewhat bizarre) account of the Anonymus Valesianus.[30] In the first half of the narrative, Theoderic receives treatment as an ideal ruler, respectful to the Nicene Church; in the second, which includes the mission and the edict, all of his actions reveal a tyrannical persecutor. Victor of Vita faced a similar problem in discussing Huneric's promising early years and his later "persecutory" actions. The Anonymus Valesianus's abrupt U-turn could be seen as an alternative (and perhaps less elegant) solution to Victor's accusations of barbarian deceit.[31] It remains evident that protection of what he considered the true Christian faith had motivated Theoderic's actions.

The deployment of religious coercion was always possible in the successor kingdoms. A perceived need for Christian uniformity intermittently shaped the formation of royal policies. Crucially, though, such moments came along much less frequently than in Africa. Before Leovigild, there is little evidence for such sustained initiatives or even isolated episodes in Visigothic Spain.[32] As the first half of the Anonymous Valesianus's binary narrative suggests, Theoderic's treatment of

27. Ioh. Bicl., *Chron.* 91 (ed. Cardelle de Hartmann: 81–82).
28. *AV* 81–96 (ed. Rolfe: 558–68), with Barnish (1983) and Noble (1993), 417–23.
29. *AV* 88–95 (ed. Rolfe: 562–68). On Theoderic's posthumous reputation, see p. 233.
30. See (best) Barnish (1983).
31. See pp. 155–56.
32. Writing in the 610s and 620s, Isidore of Seville characterized the respective support of and hostility toward the Nicene Church of two sixth-century Visigothic rulers but provided little to substantiate his point of view: Isid., *HG* 41, 45 (ed. Mommsen: 283–84, 285).

John and putative anti-Nicene edict were marked departures from the stance he had taken up to that point: one marked by elaborate (and self-conscious) self-restraint in ecclesiastical affairs.[33]

Homoian rulers outside Africa did offer patronage of various kinds to fellow members of that church: allocating preexisting church buildings, facilitating the construction of new ones, and welcoming clerics at their courts.[34] Yet this support rarely extended to the employment of coercive force in favor of Homoian Christianity. When Homoian kings acted against Nicene bishops, it was generally as a result of specific issues of political security: most notably, accusations of sedition or treason.[35] Suspicions of allegiance to the imperial court in Constantinople clearly contributed to Theoderic's treatment of Pope John after his failed embassy.[36] Vandal regimes too worried about Nicene clerics as possible agents of collaboration across the new internal political frontiers of the Roman world, and faith and loyalty were similarly bound together in Christian (and specifically royal) discourse in post-imperial Africa.[37] Yet those African regimes seem to have taken a much broader view of the implications. Through lawmaking, the association of orthodoxy and loyalty was made into something resembling a general principle, if one observed intermittently and inefficiently in practice. The late Roman antiheretical legislation helpfully collected in book 16.5 of the *Theodosian Code* (and subversively appropriated by Huneric in February 484) is notably absent from Visigothic, Burgundian, and Ostrogothic codifications of late and post-Roman laws.[38] For much of the period, the political context for Christian confession in Italy, Gaul, and Spain was one of studied legal ambiguity overlaid with carefully balanced royal patronage of both ecclesiastical factions.[39]

---

33. On Theoderic and the Nicene Church, see (best) Moorhead (1992a), 54–60, 92–93, 114–39; Noble (1993); Amory (1997), 195–221.

34. On Homoian churches in Ostrogothic Italy, see Deliyannis (2010), 146–87; in Visigothic and Burgundian Gaul, Heil (2014b), 280–82, 289–91. Mathisen (1997a) has useful references on clerics' presence at court, though unhelpfully portraying them as "court bishops."

35. For examples of exile or maltreatment of Nicene bishops as a result of suspicions of treason, see I. Wood (1994), 46; Heather (1996), 213–14; Mathisen (1997b), 536–37; James (2008), 46–49.

36. See p. 227.

37. See esp. Steinacher (2011), 54–55.

38. On the Visigothic *Breuiarium* and the Burgundian *Liber constitutum*, see Dumézil (2005), 209, 247. The one exception is *NVal* 18 (ed. Mommsen and Meyer: 103–5) = *NVal* 2 in the *Breuiarium*, an anti-Manichaean edict of Valentinian III. On the Ostrogothic *Edictum Theoderici* see Lafferty (2013); on the absence of doctrinal issues in the royal and official letters collected in Cass., *Variae* (though noting its potential to mislead), Bjornlie (2013), 72. On Vandal appropriation of *CTh* 16.5, see p. 16.

39. A conclusion drawn by modern commentators regarding, e.g., Theoderic in Ostrogothic Italy: Moorhead (1992a), 54–60, 138–39; Noble (1993); Heather (1996), 222–23, 245, 257–58; Gundobad in Burgundian Gaul: Shanzer and Wood (2002), 163–207; I. Wood (2012), 144; Alaric II in Visigothic Aquitaine: Heather (1996), 198, 212–15; Mathisen (1997b); Koch (2012), 72–93; Halfond (2012).

Partly as a result of this, ecclesiastical controversy between Nicene and Homoian clerics was of a lesser scale and frequency. There is a step change in the quantity of evidence. In particular, large-scale Homoian efforts to promote their Christianity as orthodoxy are rarely attested in fifth- and sixth-century Gaul, Spain, and Italy. The lack of dedicated anti-Arian tractates from those regions partly explains this paucity of evidence, since the activities and self-presentation of Homoian Christians are generally recorded for posterity by the Nicene heresiologists who condemned them. Yet this serves only to defer the issue, as the dearth of dedicated and sustained anti-Arian polemic outside Africa is itself revealing.[40] References to Arians tend to come as allusive asides in texts about other matters. This is not to say that heresiology is lacking; individuals certainly still felt the need to account for the presence of Christians whose Trinitarian doctrine and claims to authority conflicted with their own.[41] Still, the differential quantity and quality of evidence suggest that this particular issue of correct doctrine and ecclesiastical affiliation was less charged than in post-imperial Africa.

In this regard, the contrast between the policies of the regimes in Toulouse, Lyon, Ravenna, and Toledo and the enactments of the Hasding dynasty in Carthage is undoubtedly crucial. As part 1 explored, Vandal anti-Homoousian legislation and its enforcement were key determinants of the forms that ecclesiastical politics took. The absence of a supportive political and legal context in the rest of the western Mediterranean was similarly formative. It likely dissuaded Homoian clerics from active proselytism of and public disputation with Nicene Christians. More subtly, it also made it less likely that contemporary texts would record those conflicts that did occur. The ambivalent stances adopted by post-imperial regimes did little to encourage churchmen to deliberately document their controversies in a manner conducive to their presentation to secular authority figures (and their reconstruction by modern scholars). At the same time, the infrequency and localization of open conflict may have helped rulers to avoid handing down unhelpfully precise rulings about Christian truth. The relatively isolated instances of ecclesiastical controversy between Nicene and Homoian churchmen often did not escalate to the point that decisive or generalizing royal intervention was sought or required. The political climate for confessional identity and the treatment of Christian difference resulted from a reciprocal and ongoing process of triangulation among clerical, royal, and elite interests. However it came about, the reluctance of post-imperial regimes to enforce religious uniformity lowered the stakes of ecclesiastical controversy.

The more limited efforts of rulers and clerics to inculcate a heresiological mindset provided greater discursive space for the unselfconscious articulation of

---

40. Conant (2012), 174–76.
41. See pp. 237–48.

coexistence and compromise. Christians in Vandal Africa also found ways to turn a blind eye to doctrinal differences,[42] but writers in Italy and Gaul (in particular) seem to have more comfortably bypassed heresiological distinctions, whether by prudent avoidance of religious topics, exploitation of shared aspects of Christian belief and behavior, or nonpolemical description of alternative ecclesiastical affiliation.[43] Most notably, Nicene clerics seem to have interacted more (if not wholly) straightforwardly with Homoian kings than their colleagues in Africa, securing sympathetic arbitration in disputes and recognition of their privileges.[44] Contemporary letters show Nicene bishops turning to the Ostrogothic regime to resolve all manner of conflicts, from disputed papal elections through simoniac priests to property issues.[45] In exceptional circumstances, such polite contact could even take in the problems of doctrinal difference that (potentially) divided these kings and bishops. The most striking case is the relationship between the Nicene bishop Avitus of Vienne (r. c. 494–517) and the Burgundian king Gundobad (r. c. 473–516).[46] The kingdom established by the Gibichung dynasty in the Rhone valley was the site of considerable dialogue between Nicenes and Homoians. As Ian Wood has noted, the Homoian Gundobad seems to have afforded Avitus and his Nicene colleagues substantial license to discuss controversial doctrinal subjects publicly, and sometimes polemically, at his court and within his kingdom.[47] This included surprisingly open and frank discussions of doctrine with the Homoian king.[48]

As might be expected, Avitus's missives to Gundobad intermingled doctrine with extensive flattery. As part of polite interactions, clerics could be unabashed in offering their rulers decidedly Christian panegyrical treatment. In portraying the likes of Gundobad, Theoderic, or the Visigoth Alaric II (r. c. 484–507) as the recipients of divine favor or as the possessors of an exceptional (even "priestly") piety, Nicene bishops furnished those kings with the attributes habitually accorded to Christian emperors as part of the pleasantries of episcopal correspondence.[49] In the

42. See ch. 7.
43. On avoidance see, e.g., Shanzer (2009), 67–69, on Ostrogothic Italy; on shared aspects, e.g., I. Wood (2014), on Avitus and Gundobad's interest in Eastern Christological disputes; on nonpolemical description, Cohen (2014), 200–206; Cohen (2016), 512–15.
44. See the references at n. 49.
45. Cass., *Variae* 1.9, 3.37, 4.44, 8.24, 9.15 (ed. Mommsen: 18, 98, 134, 255, 279–81); *Ep. Theod. uariae* 5 (ed. Mommsen: 390).
46. On Avitus see Shanzer and Wood (2002), with helpful translations and commentaries on individual texts; Heil (2011).
47. E.g., I. Wood (2012), 144.
48. Shanzer and Wood (2002), 163–207.
49. On divine favor attributed to kings in Ostrogothic Italy and Visigothic Gaul, see Heather (1996), 198, 213, 223–25; Heather (2000), 448; Rota (2001), 235–42; in Burgundian Gaul, see, e.g., Avitus, *Ep.* 44 (ed. Peiper: 74). On the piety and Christian learning of Theoderic, see, e.g., *Ep. Theod. uariae* 1 (ed. Mommsen: 389); Ennod., *Ep.* 9.30.7 (ed. Vogel: 319); Ennod., *Pan.* 80 (ed. Rohr: 254), where he is

same vein, kings and their subordinates sought, and Nicene bishops offered, customary prayers for their safety, their salvation, and the stability of their regime.[50] Eugenius and Fulgentius similarly turned their hands to panegyric when it suited their interests.[51] In the other kingdoms, such recourse was both more often desirable and more easily defensible to potentially critical coreligionists.

The manner in which Nicene clerics approached Homoian kings in Ravenna, Lyon, and Toulouse says much for the status of these political centers as sites of religious diversity (as, indeed, the palace in Carthage remained, in spite of efforts to weed out heretical courtiers). Again, the contrast was in the willingness of contemporaries to acknowledge that social reality without resorting to heresiological polemic or invoking ideal strategies of exclusion. When providing a budding courtier (his brother-in-law Agricola) with a portrait of the daily routine of the household of the Visigothic king Theoderic II (r. c. 453–66) at Toulouse, Sidonius Apollinaris (at that time a prominent Gallo-Roman lay aristocrat) described the king's attendance at Homoian matins in the company of his closest confidants. Sidonius not only avoided anti-Arian polemic but also, by the mere inclusion of this part of Theoderic's schedule, suggested that his ambitious correspondent might attend. That Nicene courtiers joined the king is, in any case, implied by Sidonius's presentation of his knowledge of Theoderic's devotions in the form of an eyewitness account.[52] The priorities of contemporaries can be unexpected. Avitus found it worthy of comment when the Nicene deacon and doctor to Theoderic at Ravenna, Helpidius, sent him a letter via Homoian priests. Yet his response finds the bishop of Vienne less annoyed with this choice ("the character of the carriers did not diminish the esteem of the writer") than with another perceived breach of epistolary protocol: Avitus's prior missive to Helpidius had mysteriously gone missing despite its carriage by the latter's *maior domus*.[53] In any case, that a Nicene deacon could entrust correspondence with a Nicene bishop to Homoian

---

"a priest in your mildness" (*mansuetudine sacerdotem*); Ennod., *V. Epiph.* 122–46 (ed. Vogel: 99–102); of Gundobad, see, e.g., Avitus, *C. Eut.* (ed. Peiper: 15); Avitus, *C. Arr.* 30 (ed. Peiper: 12); Avitus, *Epp.* 4, 30 (ed. Peiper: 29, 61–62).

50. On Ostrogothic Italy see Cass., *Variae* 8.8, 10.34, 11.3 (ed. Mommsen: 237, 320, 332–33); Rome (501), 1, 2, 4 = *Praeceptiones regis* (ed. Mommsen: 420, 422, 424); Ennod., *Ep.* 9.30.10 (ed. Vogel: 319). On Visigothic Gaul see Agde (506), prologue, 48 (ed. Munier: 192, 212).

51. See pp. 155–63.

52. Sid., *Ep.* 1.2.4 (ed. Anderson: 1:336–38). On this portrait, see (best) Harries (1994), 13–14, 127–28; Kitchen (2010), 59–60. Mathisen (2014), 186, suggests that Sidonius himself had attended, though this is far from a necessary implication of the passage. It is worth noting that Sidonius suggests that Theoderic merely went through the motions in these devotions; this, of course, usefully dissembled possible anxieties about attendance as a Nicene Christian.

53. Avitus, *Ep.* 38 (ed. Peiper: 67); Moorhead (1992a), 167. On the importance of carriers and the niceties of protocol within letter exchanges, see Conybeare (2000), 20–40.

priests again suggests something of the everyday sociability fostered in the context of royal courts.

All the same, Nicene observers in Gaul, Spain, and Italy remained conscious that the good relations maintained between competing Christian individuals and communities were fragile. A striking indication of this ongoing threat is evident from a response that Avitus gave in 517 to an episcopal correspondent who had asked whether, under the Nicene king Sigismund (r. c. 516–24), Nicene bishops should take over Arian churches in the Burgundian kingdom. Avitus demurred, since "the heretics will not unreasonably object that they have been persecuted."[54] For Avitus, such an action would provide grounds for a future (Arian) Burgundian king—or a neighboring (Arian) ruler—to retaliate against Nicene churches or clerics.[55] The possibility of a policy change to something more closely resembling the Christian nightmare of heretical persecution—or, from a Homoian perspective, the Christian ideal of pious defense of the Catholic faith against heresy—had to be borne in mind. If, as seems likely, the bishop of Vienne was thinking of Theoderic,[56] he was remarkably prescient, given the Ostrogothic king's treatment of the bishop of Rome just eight years later.[57] Awareness of events in neighboring kingdoms—and perceived persecution in Africa should not go without mention here[58]—informed contemporaries' sense of the politically possible.

In political terms, the possibilities of varying degrees of conflict and coexistence were always open. The maintenance of a studiously ambivalent position in ecclesiastical politics required a delicate balancing act for Homoian kings. The pursuit of alternatives to Christian uniformity and exclusivity demanded a similar finesse from clerics within reach of the new centers of power. Everywhere in the West, the presence of (powerful) Homoian Christians created the potential for disharmony. There is no better indication of this latent potential than the attempts of Nicene clerics to shape collective memories of fifth- and sixth-century Arianism. From the laconically brutal notices in the chronicles of Prosper and Hydatius to the overwrought miracle stories in the collections of Gregory of Tours and Gregory the Great, Nicene authors in the fifth and sixth centuries show a noteworthy tendency to commemorate moments when Arian rulers, groups, or clerics violated norms of

---

54. Avitus, *Ep.* 7 (ed. Peiper: 36); translation (with commentary) in Shanzer and Wood (2002), 295–302, at 297.

55. Avitus, *Ep.* 7 (ed. Peiper: 36).

56. Shanzer and Wood (2002), 298 n. 2.

57. See p. 228.

58. See, e.g., Conant (2012), 76–78, on the popularity of the story of the confessors of Tipasa who traveled to Constantinople; Cain (2005), on Gregory of Tours's use of hagiographical material regarding Eugenius of Carthage. For knowledge of Eugenius at Rome, see Gelasius, *CA* 95.63 = *Epistola ad Dardanos* (ed. Günther: 391).

sacred space and Christian communal solidarity.[59] These Homoian kings were often the very same who had been, on other occasions, conciliatory and even sympathetic to the requests of Nicene churchmen. Mutual accommodation may have been the norm, but it remained unstable. The transformation of Theoderic's reputation among Nicene writers from pious (if incidentally heretical) king to tyrannical persecutor—so crudely charted by the Anonymus Valesianus—demonstrates these fine margins.[60] Such anxieties were not new to the post-imperial West: they were part and parcel of late-antique Christian views of heretical rulers in particular and secular authority more broadly. In their (generally cooperative) interactions, kings, clerics, and courtiers operated in the long shadow of earlier and contemporary confrontations. To borrow a line from Thomas Sizgorich: a post-imperial king, just as much as a Christian Roman emperor, was "always already a persecutor."[61]

ETHNICITY AND CHRISTIANITY

The differing political climate for confessional identity in Italy, Gaul, and Spain had further consequences. In the absence of widespread efforts to gain adherents to Homoian Christianity in these kingdoms, it is probable that the vast majority of Homoian Christians in these areas were Ostrogoths, Burgundians, or Visigoths. Such communities may well have persisted in these regions—especially in northern Italy and the Balkans—long after Theodosius I's antiheretical legislation of the 380s, but their presence can only be mooted, not substantiated.[62] Excepting the possible case of a Homoian church in Rome, they cannot be connected to the Homoian communities evident in the late fifth and sixth centuries.[63] In similar terms, there are few attested Nicene Visigoths, Ostrogoths, and Burgundians.[64]

59. Prosper, *Chron.* 1327, 1329, 1339 (ed. Mommsen: 475–77); Hyd., *Chron.* 79 (89), 110 (118), 112 (120), 228 (232), see also 29 (37), 167 (174), 175 (182), 179 (186) (ed. Burgess: 88–90, 94, 118, 80, 106, 108–10); Greg. Tur., *DLH* 2.2–2.4, 2.25, 3 pref., 3.10, 3.31, 5.38 (ed. Krusch and Levison: 39–45, 70–71, 96–97, 106–7, 126–28, 243–45); Greg. Mag., *Dial.* 2.14, 2.31, 3.29–32, 4.31 (ed. De Vogüé: 2:180–82, 222–26, 376–92, 3:104–6).

60. For two analyses of these successive versions of Theoderic, see Robinson (2004); Goltz (2008), 307–541, 587–607.

61. Sizgorich (2009), 102.

62. See p. 13 n. 67.

63. On Sant'Agata dei Goti at Rome, see Mathisen (2009). Even continuity of Homoian usage of this site is somewhat speculative. This church was founded (or redecorated?) by the general Ricimer (fl. 456–72). It is known to have been Homoian in the late sixth century, since Gregory the Great describes it as Arian and recounts its reconsecration at Greg. Mag., *Dial.* 3.30 (ed. De Vogüé: 2:378–84), but it could easily have changed ecclesiastical hands in the meantime. The only (putative) evidence for Ricimer's doctrinal affiliation is the church itself (see *PLRE* 2:945 [Fl. Ricimer II]).

64. On Visigoths see Koch (2014), 265–68; Burgundians, I. Wood (2012), 143–45; Ostrogoths, the prosopography of Amory (1997), 474–78, tables 6–9, with the justified critique by Heather (2007b), 50–52.

The significance of this paucity should not be exaggerated, given that there are few individuals whose ethnic and confessional affiliations are incontrovertibly attested in any case.[65] Nevertheless, it seems a plausible assumption that ethnic and Christian groups mapped onto each other much more closely in Gaul, Italy, and Spain than in Africa. This may have meant that ethnicity was seen as more "salient" in matters of Christian affiliation in the Visigothic, Burgundian, and Ostrogothic kingdoms.

This seems a commonsensical assumption. Yet it is barely reflected in the writings of contemporaries. As a number of recent studies suggest, the idea that Homoian Christianity or Arian heresy was essentially a matter of ethnic identity is as misleading for fifth- and sixth-century Gaul, Italy, and Spain as for Africa.[66] The practical institutional arrangements of Homoian churches in these regions are obscure, but there is nothing to imply that they differed greatly from their Nicene counterparts.[67] Moreover, the association of Catholic Christianity or Arian or Homoousian heresy with membership in a particular ethnic group was just one way to portray the actions and beliefs of contemporaries, and by no means a dominant one. As in Africa, most of the texts that discuss true Christianity and Arian (or Homoousian) heresy do not even mention ethnicity. In surviving Homoian writings, such an association is astonishingly rare.[68] More often that not, such texts present the ecclesiology of a universal Christian community, not one delimited by ethnic origin.[69] The ethnic composition of specific ecclesiastical communities would certainly have had practical implications, which are not discussed; it may even have made an association of ethnicity and confession more of an underlying assumption, giving a different quality to these texts (i.e., ethnicity not mentioned as too obvious even to point out). Distinctly Gothic Christian cultural traditions would have played an important role, in the Ostrogothic kingdom at the

65. See, e.g., Koch (2014), 266.
66. See Berndt and Steinacher (2014a), esp. the essays by Heil, Koch, and Berndt and Steinacher.
67. See p. 41 n. 51.
68. There are only two cases of Homoian clerics in the West explicitly identifying their doctrinal affiliation in ethnic terms: the anathemas of the Spanish Homoian bishops at the Council of Toledo in 589 (see p. 235), and the deeds of sale and liquidation (with a problematic context) carried out in Byzantine Ravenna. In the latter, the clerics involved refer to themselves as representatives of the "church of the law [sc. religion] of the Goths." The texts are *PItal*. 33 = Marini 117 (July 541, after 16 July) (ed. Tjäder: 84–88) and *PItal*. 34 = Marini 119 (sometime in 551) (ed. Tjäder: 98–104); see discussions by Tjäder (1954–1982), 2:79–84, 91–98; Amory (1997), 251–56, 395, with further discussions under the individual items of his prosopography. These documents have formed the basis of numerous accounts of Homoian/Gothic ecclesiology: Wolfram (1988), 14–17, 325; Amory (1997), 236–76; Geary (1999), 122; Dumézil (2005), 324; Hen (2007), 54; Berndt and Steinacher (2014b), 227 (though cf. 223–24); similarly, but with greater implied reserve, Moorhead (1992a), 95 and Heather (1996), 245. Their date and specific legal context suggest that a minimalist reading is more appropriate: see Whelan (forthcoming).
69. For Ostrogothic Italy see p. 240, with n. 97; for Visigothic Spain, p. 235.

least: rich Gothic and bilingual biblical codices and commentaries survive from late fifth- and early sixth-century Italy.[70] Even so, it remains clear that Christian affiliation was far from being a simple instrument of ethnic identity, in and out of Africa.

When they were deployed, ethnic arguments were more malleable than portrayals of dually opposed ethnic and Christian camps suggest. Homoian Christians in the Visigothic kingdom referred to Nicene Christians as "Romans" and their Christianity as "the Roman religion."[71] This phraseology is attested by a number of contemporary observers, including John of Biclar, apparently quoting an edict of King Leovigild from 580 imposing his Homoian bishops' compromise formula, and the canons signed by those same bishops at the Council of Toledo in 589 as they converted to the Nicene faith.[72] Crucial to the interpretation of this terminology is its semantic counterpart. In his edict, Leovigild, in contradistinction to the religion of the Romans, describes his Christianity as "the Catholic faith."[73] The ethnic designation of Nicene heresy as "Roman" seems to be a mirror image of attacks on Arianism as Vandal, Gothic, or barbaric. The restriction of this form of Christianity to one ethnic group is set out in polemical contrast to the universality of the true Catholic Church. This contrast between an ethnically limited heretical sect and an ethnically integrative Catholic community was used to good effect nine years later at Toledo, as the Visigothic king Reccared and the prominent Nicene bishop Leander of Seville each sought to stage the ceremonial conversion of the Goths.[74] Like the devious Arian missionaries cast out to *barbaricum* in the *Carthaginian Epitome*, both Reccared and Leander saw the calling of the gentiles as a particularly suitable theme.[75] As the bishop of Seville put it, "I say heresies are found to dwell either in one corner of the world or in one people [*gens*]: the Catholicity of the church, just as it is extended through the whole world, thus also is constituted by the society of all peoples."[76]

The foregrounding of the Goths in that moment of conversion shows how much had changed in the western Mediterranean between the 480s and the 580s.

---

70. For basic inventories, see Stutz (1984), esp. 56; Burton (2002), 394–95: Hen (2007), 55–56. On Gothic-Latin bilingual texts, see Gryson (1982a), 77–92; Stutz (1984), 57; Heather and Matthews (1991), 146–48, 158–61; Amory (1997), 249–50; Falluomini (2010); Berndt and Steinacher (2014b), 225 n. 33.

71. Cf. Mathisen (2014), 189–90.

72. Ioh. Bicl., *Chron.* 57 (ed. Cardelle de Hartmann: 71–72); Toledo III (589), anathema 16 (ed. Vives: 119). See also Greg. Tur., *GM* 24, 78–79 (ed. Krusch: 52–53, 90–92).

73. Ioh. Bicl., *Chron.* 57 (ed. Cardelle de Hartmann: 71–72).

74. See (best) Stocking (2000), 59–88; Velazquez (2003), 168–75.

75. Toledo III (589) (ed. Vives: 110); Leander, *Hom. in laud. eccl.* (ed. Vives). On the *Epitome* see pp. 114–18.

76. Leander, *Hom. in laud. eccl.* (ed. Vives: 140). On ethnic and Christian affiliation in 580s Spain, see Whelan (forthcoming).

If Huneric had decided to back the Nicene bishops in 484—or Fulgentius had won over Thrasamund in the 510s—it is unlikely that the result would have been portrayed as a "conversion of the Vandals." In the latter part of the sixth century, as Isabel Velazquez has argued for Spain and Helmut Reimitz for Gaul (or, perhaps better, Francia), political communities begin to be framed more explicitly in ethnic terms.[77] This was not a wholesale change from post-imperial Africa: when worrying about their attendance at a Nicene church in (Vandal) courtly attire, Huneric had conceived of his service aristocracy in ethnic terms.[78] Nor had the political "nation" in Spain become synonymous with the Goths (if it ever did). Nonetheless, this was the beginning of a period that saw (to quote Reimitz) "the formation of a specific social imagination of the world as one divided among Christian peoples which we might call a Western ethnicity."[79] The result of this process—alongside the related development of an "ever-stronger profile as the agents and subjects of history" for "*Gothi, Franci* and *Suevi*"[80]—is evident in works like the Nicene bishop Isidore of Seville's *History of the Goths* (written in the 610s and 620s). This *History* does indeed consider Arian heresy in terms of its implications for ethnic identity, in the manner in which modern scholars have tended to view it, because the titular Goths shape the work.[81] The degree to which Homoian or Nicene Christianity contributed to ethnic identity and group formation is in direct proportion to the significance of ethnic affiliations in a given post-imperial society. As time went on, such affiliations gained in social importance, even as Homoian Christians receded from view.[82]

In contrast to their Homoian counterparts, Nicene writers were much more willing to concurrently deploy ethnography and heresiology from the first intrusions of Homoian *externae gentes* in the West. Nevertheless, the specific articulation of such cultural prejudices more often than not forces us to problematize them. Fiery polemic against stereotyped barbaric heretics is widespread, although noticeably dampened by the establishment of stable political entities; it was easier to inveigh against contemporary or past enemies than current elites.[83] As Sam Cohen has recently noted, Italian polemic against Goths as Arians began in earnest only during the Gothic wars, under the influence of Justinianic ethnographic propaganda. Such an absence of ethnographic heresiology (or heresiological eth-

77. Velazquez (2003); Reimitz (2015).
78. See p. 182.
79. Reimitz (2015), 2.
80. Ibid., 75.
81. Isid., *HG* (ed. Mommsen). On Isidore's history and ethnography, see Velazquez (2003), 188–95; J. Wood (2012), esp. 191–231; Reimitz (2014), 48–53.
82. On the increasingly definitive political role of ethnic identification, see Pohl (2013a).
83. On ethnography and heresiology at the turn of the fifth century, see p. 184 nn. 95–99. See also *Chron. Gall. a. CCCCLII* 51, 138 (ed. Mommsen: 652, 662).

nography) is particularly striking in the case of contemporary bishops of Rome, who were not shy of producing explicit polemic against those whom they saw as heretics and schismatics.[84] As in Africa, when Nicene authors in the other western provinces and successor kingdoms discussed ethnicity and confession together, they construed their connection in any number of ways, including through more sympathetic approaches.[85]

Even polemic had many purposes. Like Fulgentius of Ruspe in *To Thrasamund*, Avitus of Vienne used the notion of habitual barbarian Christian ignorance as a means of providing exceptional praise to rulers. The difference was that his addressees, the Merovingian Clovis (r. 481?–511?) and the Burgundian Sigismund, had in fact taken the plunge (literally, in the case of the former) and become Nicene Christians.[86] Avitus's easy invocation of the "customs of a *genus*" as obstructions and Arian heresy as a polluter of "the fearsome spirits of diverse nations" suggests he was tapping into broader cultural impressions.[87] Still, the bishop of Vienne gave voice to those notions precisely to show how his royal subjects had confounded them. Despite his impeccable ethnographic hauteur, Avitus suggested that membership in a barbarian people did not have to mean ignorance, if its king became Nicene. Whether it is Avitus's vision of Merovingian and Burgundian Christian progress or, to take another example, Ennodius of Milan's politic slandering of the (supplanted) Rugi as barbaric heretics and praise of the (contemporary) Theoderic's biblical knowledge and Davidic piety in the *Life of Epiphanius*,[88] passages of conjoined ethnographic and heresiological chauvinism often signpost the social and political interests that might have led to their suppression.

ORTHODOXY, DIALOGUE, AND CONTROVERSY

Part of the reason that ethnic and Christian identities (or barbaric and heretical stereotypes) were rarely straightforwardly elided in these kingdoms was the continued importance of Christian orthodoxy. The implications for the formation of these polities of the specifically Christian issues that divided true Christians from (Arian or Homoousian) heretics may have been limited. These differences

---

84. Cohen (2014), 207–211; Cohen (2016), 512–21.

85. E.g., Isid., *HG* 7–8, 15–17 (ed. Mommsen: 270–71, 273–74) and Toledo III (589) (ed. Vives: 110), both picking up Orosius's account of the conversion of the Goths (7.33.19 [ed. Arnaud-Lindet: 3:92]); see also p. 190 n. 122).

86. Avitus, *Epp.* 8, 46 (ed. Peiper: 40–42, 75–76). On Sigismund see I. Wood (2004). The conversion of Clovis has engendered a massive historiography. For a helpful recent account (with extensive literature), see Heil (2014a); I. Wood (1985) is classic. On Avitus and Clovis, see Shanzer and Wood (2002), 362–69.

87. Avitus, *Epp.* 46, 8 (ed. Peiper: 75, 40).

88. Ennod., *V. Epiph.* 118–19, 122–46 (ed. Vogel: 99–102).

nonetheless retained a considerable valence for churchmen as they sought to establish their authority and that of their ecclesiastical institutions. The presence of contemporary Arians and Homoousians inspired clerics in the kingdoms of the Visigoths, Burgundians, and Ostrogoths to turn to heresiology.

The absence of large-scale efforts at Homoian proselytism does not seem to have neutralized this ecclesiastical concern. Both Homoian texts and Nicene polemic suggest that Homoian clerics portrayed themselves as Catholic Christians and claimed the heritage of late fourth-century Homoian Christianity. As a consequence of this orthodox mind-set, they entered into disputes with Nicene rivals, which often look rather like those of Vandal Africa. What Nicene writers say about their Arian opponents does not distinguish them from the historical Arians whose defeats these writers were continuing to commemorate. Through heresiological typology and genealogy, Nicene controversialists across the post-imperial West tied their opponents back to Arius and his fourth-century followers. As already noted, these disputes were not of the same frequency—and rarely of the same order—as those in Vandal Africa. The evidence for contemporary heresiology and controversy in Gaul, Spain, and Italy is more episodic and, where it does appear, more sparse and allusive than the extended polemics of African Nicene writers. Even so, what does survive suggests that exclusive definitions of orthodoxy continued to matter to churchmen in the post-imperial West.

Different regions provide alternative routes into similar problems of Christian self-definition. Sixth-century manuscripts and palimpsests from Ostrogothic Italy provide precious evidence of the sorts of texts from which Homoian clerics developed their sense of orthodox Christian identity. Despite the copying of aggressive anti-Nicene polemic, there is little evidence for public controversy between Nicenes and Homoians under Theoderic and his successors or, for that matter, of Nicene anti-Arian literature dating from the period (with the exception of the lost two-book *Against Arius* by Gelasius of Rome).[89] In Gaul, on the other hand, there are numerous references to Nicene and Homoian individuals clashing over their competing definitions of orthodoxy. Prominent Nicene churchmen wrote tractates against Arian heresy or included discussions of its history and teachings in works written for other purposes, but no Homoian texts survive. Neither Homoian texts nor anti-Arian polemic are preserved from Spain before the 580s; few texts survive from sixth-century Spain in any case. Yet, as a result of a series of events that most closely parallel the ecclesiastical politics of Vandal Africa, that decade inspired a flowering of Christian literary activity in the Visigothic kingdom that is revealing of (at the least) the reinvention of heresiological traditions and also, perhaps, of continuities obscured by the silence of previous decades.

---

89. *LP* 51.6 (ed. Duchesne: 2:255).

Whatever that kingdom's reputation for tolerance,[90] Homoian clerics in Ostrogothic Italy cared about orthodoxy. An allusive remark from Theoderic, directed toward another set of churchmen—the Nicene synod assembled at Rome in 502 to judge the city's bishop, Symmachus—casts an intriguing sidelight. In exhorting the Nicene bishops to pass sentence, Theoderic told them to ignore the potential repercussions of causing offence to the powerful parties involved in the schism: "For many bishops, both of your religion and of our own, have been thrown out of their churches and properties on account of disputes about God and yet still live."[91] His frame of reference is frustratingly unspecified but explicitly contemporary. Theoderic's statement takes for granted that various characteristics of the Homoian Church in his kingdom were analogous to those of the Nicene. For individual Homoian clerics to lose their property and churches required institutional mechanisms for the disciplining of individuals for their diversion from agreed norms. Above all, Theoderic's exhortation confirms what should be a commonsensical assumption about any set of late-antique churchmen: they were motivated by correct Christian doctrine and sought to preserve it when necessary.

This concern to uphold and instill their true Christian faith is evident from Latin Homoian texts copied out in a series of manuscripts produced in Ostrogothic Italy. The earlier texts provide indirect insights, insofar as they would have informed how the clerics who copied and studied them understood what it was to be Christian. They suggest an institutional culture resembling that of their colleagues in Africa. Indeed, one manuscript (the *Verona Collection*, produced in the late fifth century in northern Italy) contains sermons on martyr festivals, *Against the Pagans*, and *Against the Jews*, written by a Homoian cleric or clerics in Vandal Africa.[92] Alongside a collection of homilies on the Gospels, these sermons were intended to instruct a wide community as part of bilingual services (although whether lay, clerical, or monastic is unclear).[93] In their discussions of classic themes of Christian morality and discipline,[94] these sermons present little that would have surprised contemporary Nicene preachers like Caesarius of Arles or the anonymous users of the Eusebius Gallicanus collection (barring, of course, the subtle

---

90. On "tolerance" and "noninterference" in Ostrogothic Italy (often bracketed with the *ciuilitas* ideology), see Saitta (1986); Saitta (1999), 204–10; Moorhead (1992a), 92; Noble (1993); T. Brown (2007); Arnold (2014), 73–74, with n. 53; Berndt and Steinacher (2014b), 221–22, 227–28.

91. Rome (501), 5 = *Anagnosticum regis* (ed. Mommsen: 425): "nam multi et uestrae et nostrae religionis episcopi propter dei causas et de ecclesiis et de rebus suis iactati sunt et tamen vivunt."

92. See p. 88.

93. A number of the texts received Gothic glosses that summarize their contents or mark out the relevant biblical passage with which they should be read: Gryson (1982a), 77–92.

94. On sin, see, e.g., *De lect. sanct. euan.* 3.2, 18.2, 19 (ed. Gryson: 10, 34, 36); *De solemn.* 2, 3 (ed. Gryson: 51–59); on perfidy and secular thoughts, *De lect. sanct. euan.* 22.4 (ed. Gryson: 41); on imitation of the martyrs, *De solemn.* 8–18, esp. 18.5 (ed. Gryson, 69–92, at 90–91).

subordination of the Trinity in the creedal statement attributed to the "just and righteous"[95]). As in those Gallic Nicene sermon collections, community building, correct doctrine, and the avoidance of sin were key concerns for the anonymous individual(s) who read them.[96] Most strikingly, these Homoian texts—and others copied in Ostrogothic Italy—consistently set out a vision of a universal Homoian Christian community.[97] The wider Homoian connections (Africa, the Balkans, Constantinople) implied by the presence of these texts in Italy are consistent with these expansive visions of Catholicity.[98]

With such visions came considerable heresiology. The *Verona Collection* includes a short but stridently anti-Homoousian text, *Against the Heretics*;[99] one of its African sermons also sets out the ideal social separation of "the faithful" and "the unfaithful."[100] Heresiological polemic is a particularly pronounced feature of the Bobbio fragments,[101] which preserve portions of two early fifth-century texts: one written against the Macedonians and "those who call themselves orthodox," and another produced to instruct the reader on the (Homoian) Christian faith against classic pagan accusations.[102] The former cites in detail a range of fourth-century Nicene authorities.[103] The author calls his coreligionists "the Christians upon whom the false name of 'Arians' has been imposed."[104] He attacks "those who call themselves orthodox, who have invaded our churches and obtain them in the manner of tyrants,"[105] an accusation that seems to situate the text in the polarized aftermath of the enforcement of Theodosius I's anti-Arian legislation.[106] Its copying in Ostrogothic Italy—alongside the importation of sermons from Vandal Africa—suggests something of that charged heresiological atmosphere carried over into post-imperial Italy.

95. *De solemn.* 15.6 (ed. Gryson: 91).

96. On Caesarius see Klingshirn (1994); on Eusebius Gallicanus, Bailey (2010). For further indications of such pastoral concerns, see the Homoian *Exposition of the Gospel of Luke*, extant in a sixth-century MS palimpsested in eighth-century Milan, which discusses (inter alia) almsgiving, the apostles as model Christians, and the fundamental change of life that accompanies baptism: *Exp. euang. sec. Luc.*, frags. 5, 6.10 (ed. Gryson: 213–22, 224), with Gryson (1982b), xxii–xxiii, on the MS.

97. See esp. *C. Iud.* 4, 9 (ed. Gryson: 93–94, 107–9); *Exp. euang. sec. Luc.*, frags. 5.2, 5.12 (ed. Gryson: 214, 218).

98. On Africa see p. 88; the Balkans, McLynn (1996), 482–84; Constantinople, the fragment of a Gothic martyrology edited and translated with discussion by Heather and Matthews (1991), 119–22.

99. *C. haer.* (ed. Gryson).

100. *De lect. sanct. euan.* 18.4 (ed. Gryson: 35).

101. On its preservation (in the leaves of a sixth-century MS palimpsested in a late seventh-century MS of the Acts of Chalcedon), see Gryson (1982b), xxiii–xxiv.

102. *Adu. orth. et Mac.* (ed. Gryson); *Instr. uer. fid.* (ed. Gryson).

103. *Adu. orth. et Mac.*, frags. 1–2, 4 (ed. Gryson: 229–33, 235–36).

104. Ibid., frag. 6 (237).

105. Ibid., frag. 7 (239).

106. On this context see McLynn (1996), 482–84.

There is no way of knowing if Homoian Christians acted upon the central implications of these texts. No texts survive from Ostrogothic Italy that record Homoian clerics entering into disputes with their Nicene contemporaries. By contrast, late fifth- and early sixth-century Gaul saw a number of public debates between Nicenes and Homoians. In a letter of 475, Sidonius Apollinaris, by then the bishop of Clermont, praised his colleague Basilius of Aix for defeating a Gothic Homoian layman named Modaharius in debate using biblical *testimonia*.[107] A century later, Gregory of Tours debated two visiting envoys from Visigothic Spain on Trinitarian doctrine.[108] The lengthy (pseudo-)verbatim transcripts of these altercations that Gregory provides in the *Ten Books of Histories* contain now traditional Nicene arguments, like exegesis of biblical passages that imply Christ's weakness or subordination as pertaining to his human nature. As Edward James has suggested, these extended debate accounts—and three other such set pieces in the *Histories*—strive for a particular self-fashioning.[109] The textual promotion of public victories over Arian opponents apparently still worked to burnish episcopal authority, even if (as far as Gregory's works permit us to see) there were no resident Homoian clerics in 580s Tours.

The Nicene echo chamber of Gregory's Gaul makes a sharp contrast with the ongoing heretical presences evident in the writings of one of his Gallic heroes: the letters and tractates of Avitus of Vienne are peppered with allusions to the activities of Homoian churchmen within the Burgundian kingdom.[110] Avitus's florid letters and tractates are tricky to decode but contain a number of allusions to debates and conversations between himself, his colleagues, and their Homoian counterparts both at the Burgundian court and in various forms of ecclesiastical meeting.[111] One letter even implies the presence of Nicene bishops at an annual Homoian synod in Geneva.[112] As Uta Heil has shown, the topics that Avitus debated with the Homoians were classics of Trinitarian disputation. He drew on the works of Ambrose and Augustine to refute Homoian arguments, which often focused on the status of the Holy Spirit.[113] As part of his parallel doctrinal discussions with Gundobad,[114] Avitus even wrote a (now lost) imaginary dialogue with the Burgundian king as his interlocutor.[115]

---

107. Sid., *Ep.* 7.6.2 (ed. Anderson: 2:314); for commentary see Van Waarden (2010); Mathisen (2014), 174; Heil (2014b), 279.
108. Greg. Tur., *DLH* 5.43, 6.40 (ed. Krusch and Levison: 249–52, 310–13).
109. James (2009), 334–38, esp. 337–38.
110. On Avitus see n. 46. For Gregory on Avitus, see Greg. Tur., *DLH* 2.34 (ed. Krusch and Levison: 81–84).
111. Avitus, *C. Arr.* 14, 30 (ed. Peiper: 6, 12–15); Avitus, *Epp.* 23, 31, 53–54 (ed. Peiper: 55–56, 62, 81–83).
112. Avitus, *Ep.* 31 (ed. Peiper: 62).
113. Heil (2011), 117–250; (2014b), 293–96.
114. See p. 230.
115. Shanzer and Wood (2002), 187–93; I. Wood (2004), 370.

From Avitus's emollient letters, these discussions and those between Nicene and Homoian clerics in the kingdom often sound quite cordial. A keen royal interest in Eastern anti-Chalcedonian views provided common ground.[116] Yet anti-Arian polemic is far from absent. In letters to the king's Nicene son, Sigismund, Avitus punningly dismisses the *sacerdotes* around Gundobad as "rather his seducers, or, to speak more truly still, his sectaries" (*sacerdotibus, immo magis seductoribus et, ut adhuc uerius dicamus, sectatoribus suis*) and takes great pleasure in the apparent discovery of Bonosiac heresy among the Homoian clerics assembled at the aforementioned synod in Geneva.[117] Avitus's debates with Homoians were not simply polite expressions of erudition for a courtly audience. When writing to Sigismund, Avitus expressed his frustration at the private nature of one debate that he felt he had won, and his desire to publicize the result.[118] The implication is that open-ended debate with Arians was worryingly inconclusive even for the most diplomatic of Nicene churchmen. This is not to say that Avitus would always have appeared triumphant if minutes had been published. The bishop of Vienne sometimes appears on the back foot, most notably when he mistakenly accuses his opponents of misquoting scripture when his own memory has failed him.[119] This contrasts with the impression that Avitus gives of the imminent conversion of the theologically learned Homoian king as a result of his agency—that is, if Gundobad had not already converted in secret.[120] Had Homoian accounts of these same debates and discussions survived, they might have told a different story.

In their explicit references to disputes with specific contemporary individuals, Sidonius, Avitus, and Gregory make clear that Homoian Christians did present themselves as orthodox and, partly as a result, that the refutation of Arianism still mattered to Nicene churchmen. Their colleagues in fifth- and sixth-century Gaul made further references to the problems of Arian heresy. On some occasions, these concerns seem to have pertained to the presence of those perceived as Arian in their midst, but no precise context is established. The Gallic Chronicler of 452 bemoaned the return of Arians to the western provinces.[121] In a notice for the year 451, he laments the crisis of the imperial state that had come about partly as a result of the heresy of the Arians, which "having infused the whole world, claimed the name of Catholic." The circumstances provoking the anonymous author to this alarmist view are unknown.[122] The more developed anti-Arian treatises of Faustus

---

116. See esp. Avitus, *C. Eut.* (ed. Peiper), with I. Wood (2014), 8–12.

117. Avitus, *Epp.* 23, 31 (ed. Peiper: 55, 62). On "Bonosiac" heresy, a set of Christological views that Avitus associated with those of Photinus, see Shanzer and Wood (2004), xvii, 107, 165–66.

118. Avitus, *Ep.* 23 (ed. Peiper: 55–56).

119. Avitus, *C. Arr.* 30 (ed. Peiper: 13–14); Shanzer and Wood (2002), 165.

120. I. Wood (2004), 371–72; (2012), 143.

121. *Chron. Gall. a. CCCCLII* 51, 138 (ed. Mommsen: 652, 662).

122. Steinacher (2016), 45–46, suggests that this is a reference to Alaric's Goths.

the bishop of Riez in southern Gaul (r. c. 457–90) are similarly elusive. Faustus responded to the letter of an unnamed episcopal colleague seeking advice on how to respond to Arians who asserted that the Son was lesser (*iunior*), and wrote a treatise called *On the Holy Spirit* that includes dialogue with imagined Arians and Macedonians.[123] Without further information, it is difficult to tell whether these works were inspired by the interventions of real Homoians in mid fifth-century Gaul or to discern what exactly Faustus meant by his intent "to arm and reinforce against Arian depravities."[124] Still, to frame this issue in terms of whether or not the threat of "real" contemporary Arians inspired the writings of Nicene churchmen like Faustus is to miss the point. Christian errors—and those of Arianism more than most—were always on the minds of "Catholic" churchmen, whether or not they were personified in the near vicinity or rival clerics made direct moves to challenge those "Catholics."

Visigothic Spain also saw episodes of controversy between Nicenes and Homoians. These events cluster in the 580s, the period when first Leovigild and then his son Reccared sought ecclesiastical unity.[125] Best attested is the running battle between Masona, the Nicene bishop of Merida, and Sunna, a Homoian bishop appointed to the same city.[126] The events are recorded in a biography of Masona in the *Lives of the Fathers of Merida*, written by an anonymous cleric of the church of Eulalia in the 630s.[127] Their dispute culminated in a public debate in the episcopal palace at Merida. As the hagiographical *Lives* describes them, the proceedings seem much closer to the charged legalistic encounters of Vandal Africa than to the more cordial discussions in Burgundian Gaul. Masona and Sunna discussed Trinitarian doctrine with judges present; in accordance with legal precedent, Sunna, as the accuser, spoke first. At stake was possession of the prestigious basilica of Eulalia: the judges were to decide who was orthodox and hand the church over to that party. Masona triumphed but was soon exiled as a result of a petition from Sunna to Leovigild.[128] As in Vandal Africa, royal commitment to the enforcement of a particular definition of orthodoxy raised the stakes of Christian debate.

The conflict between Masona and Sunna isolates another feature of ecclesiastical controversy that the other successor kingdoms shared with Vandal Africa. Prestigious basilicas and martyrs remained sites of contestation between Nicene and Homoian Christians; indeed, their importance only grew as a result of the

---

123. Faustus, *Ep.* 3 (ed. Engelbrecht: 168–81); Faustus, *De spir. sanct.* (ed. Engelbrecht); see also Mathisen (1999a), 239–40; Heil (2014b), 282–84.

124. Faustus, *Ep.* 3 (ed. Engelbrecht: 173).

125. See pp. 226–27.

126. *VPE* 5.1–13 (ed. Maya Sánchez: 47–98).

127. On the text, see Fear (1997) xxix–xxxiii; I. Wood (1999); Stocking (2000), 89–117; Koch (2012), 273–309.

128. *VPE* 5.5–6 (ed. Maya Sánchez: 56–71).

marked expansion of interest in the cult of saints and the miraculous in the sixth-century West. Nicene ecclesiastical authors rarely mentioned transferred Nicene churches while Homoian clerics and communities possessed them, but the provisions of later Gallic and Spanish councils make clear that such redistributions had taken place.[129] If public controversy is lacking in texts from Ostrogothic Italy, Deborah Deliyannis has nonetheless convincingly suggested that the high-profile building activity of Homoian clerics within the monumental center of Ravenna during the reign of Theoderic would have acted as an equally profound statement of orthodox status.[130] These lavish constructions may have provoked the new phase of Nicene church building from the late 520s, which produced (among others) the basilica of San Vitale.[131] Of course, as the *Lives of the Fathers of Merida* suggests, just as important as church buildings were the holy individuals whose relics they contained. Leovigild's apparent desire to appropriate the authority of Eulalia was matched, a decade earlier, by the Lombard king Alboin's supposed reverence for apostolic sites in Rome.[132] As part of the growing centrality in Christian discourse of the saints and their wonder working, mid-to-late-sixth-century Nicene authors rehearsed the argument that Arians could not perform miracles, unlike their Nicene rivals both living and dead.[133] This argument may already have been elaborated in Vandal Africa, if Gregory of Tours's story of the trial by miracle between Eugenius and Cyrila in a public square in Carthage does indeed derive from an African life.[134]

Such arguments could just as easily show the appropriation of orthodoxy and (Arian) heresy for assertions about the saints as the reverse. When Gregory of Tours and Gregory the Great contrasted the failure of Arian miracles with the success of Nicene holy men, they sought to construct the authority of particular figures as wonder workers and even that of miraculous postmortem agency in general.[135] In a broader sense, the majority of Nicene references to Arians and Arian heresy outside Vandal Africa come in passing. As a result, this polemic is qualitatively different from that found in dedicated anti-Arian tractates. At the

129. For Gaul, see Orléans (511), canon 10 (ed. De Clercq: 7–8); Epaon (517), canon 33 (ed. De Clercq: 33); see also Avitus, *Ep.* 7 (ed. Peiper: 35–39); Greg. Tur., *GC* 47 (ed. Krusch: 326–27). For Spain, see Toledo III (589), canon 9 (ed. Vives: 127); Zaragoza II (592), canons 2–3 (ed. Vives: 154–55).

130. Deliyannis (2010), 143–44, 146–87.

131. Ibid., 199–200.

132. *Ep. Austr.* 8 (ed. Gundlach: 121).

133. Greg. Tur., *DLH* 9.15 (ed. Krusch and Levison: 429–30); Greg. Tur., *GM* 24–25, 39, 78–81 (ed. Krusch: 52–53, 63, 90–93); Greg. Tur., *GC* 13–14, 47 (ed. Krusch: 305–6, 326–27); *Ep. Austr.* 8 (ed. Gundlach: 121–22). For saints' miracles involving Arians, see Greg. Mag., *Dial.* 2.31, 3.29–32, 4.31 (ed. De Vogüé: 2:222–26, 376–92, 3:102–4).

134. Greg. Tur., *DLH* 2.3 (ed. Krusch and Levison: 42–44); see also Cain (2005).

135. See Van Dam (1993), 105–10, on anti-Arianism as part of Gregory of Tours's theology of the miraculous; Dal Santo (2012) on Gregory the Great and debates over the cult of saints.

same time, it is still suggestive of a Nicene instinct to shape orthodoxy and ecclesiastical authority in dialogue with the archetypal heresy. Real Homoian opponents did not have to be on their minds—nor Arians the main target of a text—for Arianism to be useful for Nicene writers. The history of the heresy provided a touchstone for Vincent, a prominent monk at the monastery of Lérins in the 430s and 440s, when he laid out ground rules to help the faithful identify Catholic doctrine as opposed to heresies. In his *Admonition*, Vincent makes the Arian "fraud" of Rimini an illustration of his principle that the Catholic faith always follows tradition.[136] Polemic against Arians may not have been the major point of his work, but this did not stop him from describing in pitiful detail the social and political turmoil that their novel doctrines wrought in the fourth-century empire. In similar terms, as Martin Heinzelmann has argued, Gregory of Tours's *Ten Books of Histories* is not antiheretical or anti-Arian as such.[137] Nevertheless, it does begin with an explicitly anti-Arian creedal formula, and fourth-, fifth-, and sixth-century Arians are among the colorful cast of characters whose activities Gregory narrates to set out, by means of contrast, correct Christian behavior.[138] For Vincent and Gregory, defining true Christianity remained a question of not doing what the Arians (among others) did.

Vincent was just one of many authors to engage closely with the history of the Arian controversy when defining orthodoxy in the fifth and sixth centuries. Just as in Vandal Africa, elsewhere in the West, Homoian and Nicene churchmen alike drew on the resources of this past. The two Homoian texts preserved in the Bobbio fragments contain hostile commentary on long quotations from Athanasius, Ambrose, Hilary of Poitiers, and Phoebadius of Agen, as well as more approving citations from Theognis of Nicaea and two (perhaps less likely) other authorities: Constantine (a unique citation) and Constantius II (writing to a synod, most likely that at Rimini).[139] The death day of Constantius II (misspelled or misstated as "Constantine") also features in a fragment of a (probably Constantinopolitan) Gothic martyrial calendar copied out in the same manuscript. The Homoian community in northern Italy that used the calendar would have celebrated him as a martyr.[140] The crucial middle decades of the fourth century seem to have been similarly foundational for Homoian churchmen in Visigothic Spain. The episcopal converts at the Council of Toledo in 589 pointedly anathematized profession of the

---

136. Vinc. Ler., *Comm.* 4–5 (ed. Demeulenaere: 150–53).

137. Heinzelmann (1998).

138. See esp. Greg. Tur., *DLH* 1 pref., 3 pref. (ed. Krusch and Levison: 3–5, 96–97).

139. *Adu. orth. et Mac.*, frags. 1–6 (ed. Gryson: 229–36). On the citations of Constantine and Constantius, see Meslin (1959).

140. Heather and Matthews (1991), 119–22.

creed of Rimini,[141] and King Reccared renounced all councils "that existed against the holy Nicene synod."[142]

Those anathemas were made in the aftermath of the conversions of Reccared, a group of Homoian bishops, and a number of Gothic aristocrats. As a result they reflect, in the first instance, a Nicene understanding of what Arianism was. The Third Council of Toledo shows a decidedly historical perception of Arianism comparable to the deep dives of African Nicene churchmen into the minutiae of the 320s, 350s, and 380s. Both Reccared and the newly Nicene bishops set out a (now familiar) Chalcedonian narrative of the transmission of orthodoxy through Nicaea, Constantinople, Ephesus, and Chalcedon, with a particular stress on Nicaea.[143] Writing soon afterward, the Nicene bishop and historian John of Biclar not only portrayed Reccared as a new Constantine or Marcian, overseeing a new Nicaea and Chalcedon, but also characterized the work of the council as the final end of a heresy that had persisted for almost three hundred years: "From the twentieth year of the rule of Emperor Constantine, at which time the Arian heresy began, up to the eighth year of Maurice, the emperor of the Romans, which is the fourth year of the reign of Reccared, 280 years passed, in which the Catholic Church struggled against the attack of this heresy. But with the Lord's support it won, because it is built upon a rock."[144] For John, the last Arians of Spain were not new; they were part of a continuous history of heresy that went all the way back to Arius.

Gallic authors similarly understood the Arianism of the late and post-Roman West as the same phenomenon. From reading the Gallic Chronicler of 452—as with the *Carthaginian Epitome*—one would get the impression that the same Arians whom Theodosius had exiled from the empire in the 380s had returned in 406:[145] "From this time, the Arians who had fled far off from the Roman world began to be raised up by the aid of the barbarian nations, with whom they had united themselves."[146] Certainly, the anti-Arian arguments deployed by Faustus of Riez, Avitus of Vienne, and Gregory of Tours hark back to earlier disputes with Homoian Christians. Gallic authors were just as keen as their Spanish counterparts to find in the fourth century the interpretive key for their experience of royal conversion: that of Clovis. Drawing in particular upon Sulpicius Severus's account of the 350s and 360s,[147] Gregory and Venantius Fortunatus present Clovis's victories over neighboring Homoian kings as stemming from the miraculous

---

141. Toledo III (589), anathema 17 (ed. Vives: 119).
142. Ibid. (111–12).
143. Ibid. (111–16, 119–22).
144. Ioh. Bicl., *Chron.* 91 (ed. Cardelle de Hartmann: 82).
145. *Chron. Gall. a. CCCCLII* 22 (ed. Mommsen: 648). On the *Epitome* see pp. 114–18.
146. *Chron. Gall. a. CCCCLII* 51 (ed. Mommsen: 652).
147. Sulp. Sev., *Chron.* 2.38–45 (ed. Halm: 91–99).

agency of two famously anti-Arian saints, Hilary of Poitiers and Martin of Tours. Both writers explicitly state that it was like Hilary was fighting Arianism again; as Fortunatus saw it, Hilary thought the Visigoth Alaric II was another Constantius.[148]

Even in Ostrogothic Italy, where Nicene writers are unnervingly silent on the Arians in their midst, there are telltale signs after Justinian's reconquest. It does not seem a coincidence that the two most important Homoian churches were rededicated to Martin and Eusebius the Martyr (most likely the bishop of Vercelli and ally of Hilary against Constantius) once they had been handed over to Agnellus of Ravenna in the late 560s.[149] Agnellus himself wrote a telling response to a query from another bishop regarding the true faith. He formatted the main body of his letter as a dialogue between himself and Arius, a literary choice of which Quodvultdeus of Carthage and Vigilius of Thapsa would surely have approved.[150] Once more, the sharp historiographical contrast between the debates and controversies of the post-imperial West and those of the later Roman Empire does not seem to capture contemporary views. As Nicene writers told it in 560s Italy, 580s Spain, and Gaul across this whole period, their Arians were directly related to those who had been active in the middle decades of the fourth century.

Vandal Africa did not have a monopoly on Nicene and Homoian dialogue and controversy. Nicene and Homoian clergymen throughout the post-imperial West cared deeply about the maintenance of orthodoxy. In Gaul, Italy, and Spain, just as in Africa, engaged churchmen of both affiliations placed themselves in traditions of Christian teaching and ecclesiastical self-definition that, at least as they perceived them, stretched back into the fourth century. What was different was the extent and frequency under Homoian rulers of the mutual controversy that resulted from these competing definitions. In this regard, it is telling that an outpouring of Nicene historical triumphalism in all three regions followed in the wake of conquest or conversion. Even without a supportive political environment, some clerics sought to profit by engaging in dialogue and polemic against their heretical rivals (whether real or imagined). Controversy between Nicenes and Homoians was more localized than in Africa but nonetheless important for its practitioners. Gregory of Tours's dialogues are a case in point.[151] Clerical authority still depended on the profession of orthodoxy and the refutation of heresy. As a result, individuals continued to set their performance of priestly office in the context of a much longer (and decidedly anti-Arian or anti-Homoousian)

---

148. Greg. Tur., *DLH* 2.37, cf. 3 pref. (ed. Krusch and Levison: 85–86, 96–97), and Ven. Fort., *Lib. uirt. sanct. Hil.* 8.23 (ed. Krusch: 9–10), with Deliyannis (2012). See also Ven. Fort., *V. Hil.* (ed. Krusch).
149. Deliyannis (2010), 144–45; (2012). For a resume of Eusebius's career, see Flower (2013a), 155–56.
150. Agnellus, *Ep. ad. Arm.* (*PL* 68: 381–86). See also Moorhead (1992a), 91; T. Brown (2007), 423.
151. See p. 241.

ecclesiastical history. In that sense, Homoian Christianity and its heresiological shadow, Arianism, would never really go away.

HOMOIANS IN THE POST-IMPERIAL WEST

A sharp distinction between polemic against "real" and "imagined" heretics is not always useful. All heretics were in some sense inventions of the heresiologists who perceived and described them. There is a danger in seeking to separate "real" opponents or controversies from ecclesiastical shadowboxing. It can lead to too easy a dismissal of certain interpretative possibilities (like the potential influence of "real" contemporary Homoians on the thinking of a Vincent or Faustus). More than that, it obscures the common purpose of all attacks on heretics: the definition of correct Christianity and the edification of those who (are supposed to) profess it. Of course, the presence or absence of flesh-and-blood Homoian Christians does make an important difference. Accusations of Arianism in fifth-century Africa meant something rather different from the same charges in eighth- and ninth-century Byzantium or Francia (or, for that matter, in the new heresiological arenas of eleventh- and twelfth-century Europe).[152] In this transition, the disappearance of Homoian Christians from the early-medieval west is self-evidently crucial. Accusations of Arianism were always a rhetorical maneuver; from the seventh century, our possibilities for interpreting the cultural meaning of this specific maneuver narrow.

This was not yet the case in fifth- and sixth-century Gaul, Italy, and Spain. Vandal Africa was no exception in the post-imperial West. Homoian Christianity had a similar range of potential consequences across the Visigothic, Burgundian, and Ostrogothic kingdoms. The presence of Christian authority figures with differing Trinitarian views could lead to dialogue, heresiology, and controversy. Participants in these debates and conflicts drew on polemical resources inherited from earlier Trinitarian debates. At the same time, broader social and political pressures encouraged the pursuit of coexistence and the downplaying or even suppression of difference. The late-antique ideal of religious uniformity framed the actions of kings and bishops alike, but more often than not as a point of reference for much less confrontational forms of interaction.

Much the same can be said for Vandal Africa. What separates the Vandal kingdom from Burgundian Gaul, Ostrogothic Italy, or Visigothic Aquitaine and Spain are crucial differences of degree. These manifest themselves most clearly in those

---

152. On Arianism and iconoclasm in Byzantium, see Gwynn (2007b). For individual accusations of Arianism in Carolingian Francia, see Ganz (1995), 767; Chazelle (2001), 55–56, 65–68, 120, 127–28; Noble (2009), 295. For some eleventh- and twelfth-century accusations, see Pegg (2008), 18–25; Moore (2012), 62, 68–69; Caldwell Ames (2015), 154, 200.

moments when ecclesiastical controversy was made to matter. There is nothing from Gaul, Italy, or Spain that approaches the concerted mobilization by Geiseric, Huneric, and Thrasamund (in particular) of the coercive force at their disposal against Nicene Christians on those (intermittent) occasions when uniformity was pursued. Likewise unparalleled is the less tangible (but no less significant) shift in the balance of power that the Hasding dynasty's anti-Homoousian legislation produced. Above all, the sheer quantity and pointedness of contemporary anti-Arian (and anti-Homoousian) polemical literature marks Vandal Africa out. Numerous contemporary African writers sought to frame what we might call the sociology of post-imperial Africa in terms of the effects of particular ecclesiastical affiliations. As a result, it is relatively straightforward and indeed hard not to frame social and political life in the new kingdom in terms of the impact of heresiological patterns of thought and exclusivist forms of Christian belonging. It seems telling that the same cannot be said for Gaul, Italy, or Spain, where such issues tended to be secondary. They can be read into many texts and episodes, not least since, as has been shown, a number of authors work hard to deliberately bypass or downplay such issues.[153] Nevertheless, compared to African Christian texts, there is a much more obvious gap between such an interpretative framework and that provided by Gallic, Italian, and Spanish authors. While doctrinal differences certainly did not matter to Nicene and Homoian Christians in post-imperial Africa all of the time, Christian authority figures there were more prone than their transmarine counterparts to think that those differences *should* matter all of the time and to seek to make them meaningful.

It is this explicit contemporary theming of (orthodox) Christian identity and ecclesiastical affiliation that, more than anything else, makes Vandal Africa different from its western neighbors. It is indicative of a deep-rooted culture of ecclesiastical controversy. The sophistication of the Christian polemical literature produced in Vandal Africa is symptomatic of distinctive forms of continuity from the later Roman Empire and the perpetuation of particular aspects of late Roman culture—indeed, aspects that have often been taken as definitive of the late-antique period as a whole. All of the first successors to Roman rule in the fifth- and early sixth-century West are best understood, in the first place, as late-antique polities. The ecclesiastical controversy explored in this book demonstrates how that late-antique inheritance framed post-imperial Africa.

---

153. See pp. 231–32.

BIBLIOGRAPHY

SERIES AND REFERENCE WORKS

CCSL	*Corpus Christianorum, series Latina.*
CPL	Dekkers, E. (1995), *Clavis patrum latinorum*, 3rd ed., Turnhout.
CSEL	*Corpus Scriptorum Ecclesiasticorum Latinorum.*
MGH	*Monumenta Germaniae Historica.*
MGH AA	*Monumenta Germaniae Historica, Auctores Antiquissimi.*
PCBE I	Mandouze, A. (1982), *Prosopographie chrétienne du bas-empire*, vol. 1: *Prosopographie de l'Afrique chrétienne (305–533)*, Paris.
PL	*Patrologia Cursus Completus, series Latina*, ed. J.-P. Migne (1844–64), 221 vols., Paris.
PLRE	Jones, A. H. M., J. R. Martindale, and J. Morris, eds. (1971–92), *The Prosopography of the Later Roman Empire*, 4 vols., Cambridge.
PLS	*Patrologiae Cursus Completus, series Latina, Supplementum.*

PRIMARY TEXTS

Acta conc. Aquil.	*Acta concilii Aquileiensis*, ed. M. Zelzer (1982), *CSEL* 82.3, 325–68.
Adu. orth. et Mac.	*Aduersus orthodoxos et Macedonianos*, ed. R. Gryson (1982), *Scripta Arriana latina I*, CCSL 87, Turnhout, 229–47.

Agde (506)	*Concilium Agathense a. 506*, ed. C. Munier (1963), *Concilia Galliae a. 314–a. 506*, CCSL 148, Turnhout, 192–228.
Agnellus, *Ep. ad. Arm.*	Agnellus of Ravenna, *Epistula ad Armenium*, PL 68, 381–86.
AL	*Anthologia Latina*, ed. D. R. Shackleton-Bailey (1982), *Anthologia Latina I, Carmina in codicibus scripta*, Stuttgart.
Alt. Her.	*Altercatio Heracliani cum Germinio episcopo*, ed. C. P. Caspari (1883), *Kirchenhistorische Anecdota: nebst neuen Ausgaben patristischer und kirchlich-mittelalterlicher Schriften*, Oslo, 133–47.
Ambrose, *De fide*	Ambrose of Milan, *De fide*, ed. O. Faller (1962), CSEL 78, Vienna.
Ambrose, *Ep.*	Ambrose of Milan, *Epistulae liber decimus*, ed. M. Zelzer (1982), CSEL 82.3, Vienna, 1–140.
Anon., *H. Vind.* 5a	Anonymous, *Homiliare Vindobonense* 5a, ed. P.-M. Bogaert (1967), PLS 4, Paris, 1911–12.
Anon., *S. Morin*	Anonymous, *Sermones 30 collectionis Morin dictae*, ed. G. Morin (1967), PLS 4, Paris, 741–834.
Ath., *De syn.*	Athanasius of Alexandria, *De synodis*, ed. H.-G. Opitz (1940–41), *Athanasius Werke*, zweiter Band, erster Teil: *Die Apologien, 8.–9. Lieferungen*, Berlin, 231–78.
Ps.-Ath., *De trin.*	Pseudo-Athanasius, *De trinitate libri duodecim*, PL 62, 237–334.
Aug., *C. Iul.*	Augustine of Hippo, *Contra Iulianum opus imperfectum*, ed. M. Zelzer (1974), CSEL 85, Vienna.
Aug., *C. Max.*	Augustine of Hippo, *Contra Maximinum Arianorum episcopum*, ed. P.-M. Hombert (2009), *Scripta Arriana latina II*, CCSL 87A, Turnhout, 489–692.
Aug., *C. serm. Arian.*	Augustine of Hippo, *Contra sermonem Arianorum*, ed. P.-M. Hombert (2009), *Scripta Arriana latina II*, CCSL 87A, Turnhout, 181–256.
Aug., *Coll. cum Max.*	Augustine of Hippo, *Collatio cum Maximino Arianorum episcopo*, ed. P.-M. Hombert (2009), *Scripta Arriana latina II*, CCSL 87A, Turnhout, 383–470.
Aug., *De haer.*	Augustine of Hippo, *De haeresibus*, ed. L. G. Müller (1956), *The De haeresibus of Saint Augustine*, Catholic University of America Patristic Studies 90, Washington DC.
Aug., *Ep.*	Augustine of Hippo, *Epistulae*, ed. A. Goldbacher (1895–1923), 5 vols., CSEL 34.1-2, 44, 57-58, Vienna.

Aug., *Ep.*	Augustine of Hippo, *Epistulae (Divjak)*, ed. J. Divjak (1981), *Epistolae ex duobus codicibus nuper in lucem prolatae*, CSEL 88, Vienna.
Aug., *Gesta cum Emerito*	Augustine of Hippo, *Gesta cum Emerito*, ed. M. Petschenig (1910), *Sancti Aureli Augustini scripta contra Donatistas*, vol. 3, CSEL 53.3, Vienna, 179–96.
Aug., *Psalm.*	Augustine of Hippo, *Psalmus contra partem Donati*, ed. R. Anastasi (1957), Pubblicazioni dell'Istituto universitario di magistero di Catania, Serie litteraria, Testi critici 1, Padua.
Ps.-Aug., *S. spur.*	Pseudo-Augustine, *Sermones spurii*, PL 39, 1735–2354.
Ps.-Aug., *Serm. Cai.* I.7	Pseudo-Augustine, *Sermo Caillau-Saint-Yves* I.7, ed. A. Caillau and B. Saint-Yves (1960), *PLS* 2, Paris, 909–25.
Ps.-Aug., *Serm. Mai* 42	Pseudo-Augustine, *Sermo Mai* 42, ed. A. Mai (1960), *PLS* 2, Paris, 1141–43.
Ps.-Aug., *Solutiones*	Pseudo-Augustine, *Solutiones diversarum quaestionum ab haereticis obiectarum*, ed. B. Schwank (1961), *Florilegia Biblica Africana saec. V*, CCSL 90, Turnhout, 141–223.
Auson., *Ep.* 12	Ausonius, *Epistula* 12, ed. H. G. Evelyn-White (1921), *Ausonius*, vol. 2, Loeb Classical Library 115, Cambridge, MA, 33–41.
AV	*Anonymi Valesiani pars posterior*, ed. J. C. Rolfe (1952), *Ammianus Marcellinus*, vol. 3, Loeb Classical Library 331, Cambridge, MA, 530–68.
Avitus, *C. Arr.*	Avitus of Vienne, *Contra Arrianos*, ed. R. Peiper (1883), *MGH AA* 6.2, Berlin, 1–15.
Avitus, *C. Eut.*	Avitus of Vienne, *Contra Eutychianam haeresim*, ed. R. Peiper (1883), *MGH AA* 6.2, Berlin, 15–29.
Avitus, *Ep.*	Avitus of Vienne, *Epistulae*, ed. R. Peiper (1883), *MGH AA* 6.2, Berlin, 1–103.
Breu. Hipp.	*Breuiarium Hipponense*, ed. C. Munier (1974), *Concilia Africae, a. 345–a. 525*, CCSL 149, Turnhout, 22–53.
C. Fel.	Pseudo-Vigilius of Thapsa, *Contra Felicianum Arianum de unitate Trinitatis liber*, PL 42, 1155–72.
C. haer.	*Contra haereticos*, ed. R. Gryson (1982), *Scripta Arriana latina I*, CCSL 87, Turnhout, 142–45.
C. Iud.	*Contra Iudaeos*, ed. R. Gryson (1982), *Scripta Arriana latina I*, CCSL 87, Turnhout, 93–117.
C. pag.	*Contra paganos*, ed. R. Gryson (1982), *Scripta Arriana latina I*, CCSL 87, Turnhout, 118–40.
C. Var.	Pseudo-Vigilius of Thapsa, *Contra Varimadum*, ed. B. Schwank (1961), *Florilegia Biblica Africana saec. V*, CCSL 90, Turnhout, 1–134.

CA	*Collectio Avellana*, ed. O. Günther (1895–98), *Epistulae imperatorum pontificum aliorum inde ab a. CCCLXVII usque ad a. DLIII datae Avellana quae dicitur collectio*, 2 vols., CSEL 35, Vienna.
Carthage (390)	*Concilium Carthaginense a. 390*, ed. C. Munier (1974), *Concilia Africae, a. 345–a. 525*, CCSL 149, Turnhout, 11–19.
Carthage (419)	*Concilia Carthaginense anni 419 acta diei 25 Maii*, ed. C. Munier (1974), *Concilia Africae, a. 345–a. 525*, CCSL 149, Turnhout, 88–94.
Carthage (525)	*Concilium Carthaginense 5–6. Februarii 525*, ed. C. Munier (1974), *Concilia Africae a. 345–a. 525*, CCSL 149, Turnhout, 254–82.
Cass., *Chron.*	Cassiodorus, *Chronica*, ed. T. Mommsen (1894), *Chronica minora saec. IV. V. VI. VII.*, vol. 2, MGH AA 11, Berlin: 109–61.
Cass., *Variae*	Cassiodorus, *Variae*, ed. T. Mommsen (1894), *Cassiodori senatoris Variae*, MGH AA 12, Berlin, 1–385.
Cer. c. Max.	*Disputatio Cerealis contra Maximinum*, ed. I. Baise (2006), "La *Disputatio Cerealis contra Maximinum* (CPL 813, CE): Tradition manuscrite et édition critique," *Révue Benedictine* 116, 262–86.
Chron. Gall. a. CCCCLII	*Chronica Gallica a. CCCCLII*, ed. T. Mommsen (1892), *Chronica minora saec. IV. V. VI. VII.*, vol. 1, MGH AA 9, Berlin, 646–62.
Coll. Pasc.	*Collatio Augustini cum Pascentio Ariano*, ed. H. Müller, D. Weber, and C. Weidmann (2008), Österreichische Akademie der Wissenschaften, philosophisch-historische Klasse, Sitzungsberichte 779, Veröffentlichungen der Kommission für die Herausgabe des Corpus der Lateinischen Kirchenväter 24, Vienna, 73–121.
Comm. in Iob	*Anonymi in Iob commentarius*, ed. K. B. Steinhauser (2006), CSEL 96, Vienna.
CTh	*Codex Theodosianus*, ed. T. Mommsen and P. M. Meyer (1904), Berlin.
De lect. sanct. euan.	*De lectionibus sanctorum euangeliorum*, ed. R. Gryson (1982), *Scripta Arriana latina I*, CCSL 87, Turnhout, 7–46.
De solemn.	*De solemnitatibus*, ed. R. Gryson (1982), *Scripta Arriana latina I*, CCSL 87, Turnhout, 47–92.
Drac., *DLD*	Dracontius, *De laudibus Dei*, ed. C. Moussy (1985–88), *Dracontius: Œuvres*, vols. 1–2, Paris.
Drac., *Rom.*	Dracontius, *Romulea*, ed. J. Bouquet and É. Wolff (1995–96), *Dracontius: Œuvres*, vols. 3–4, Paris.
Drac., *Satis.*	Dracontius, *Satisfactio*, ed. C. Moussy (1988), *Dracontius, Œuvres*, vol. 2, Paris, 175–91.

Ennod., *Ep.*	Ennodius of Pavia, *Epistulae*, ed. F. Vogel (1885), *Magni Felicis Ennodii opera*, MGH AA 7, Berlin.
Ennod., *Pan.*	Ennodius of Pavia, *Panegyricus regi Theoderico*, ed. C. Rohr (1995), *Der Theoderich-Panegyricus des Ennodius*, MGH Studien und Texte 12, Hannover.
Ennod., *V. Epiph.*	Ennodius of Pavia, *Vita Epiphanii*, ed. F. Vogel (1885), *Magni Felicis Ennodii opera*, MGH AA 7, Berlin, 84–109.
Ep. Austr.	*Epistulae Austrasicae*, ed. W. Gundlach (1892), *Epistolae Merowingici et Karolini aevi*, MGH Epistolae 3, Berlin, 110–53.
Ep. Theod. uariae	*Epistulae Theodericanae uariae*, ed. T. Mommsen (1894), *Cassiodori senatoris Variae*, MGH AA 12, Berlin, 387–92.
Epaon (517)	*Concilium Epaonense 517. Sept 15.*, ed. C. De Clercq (1963), *Concilia Galliae, a. 511–a. 695*, CCSL 148A, Turnhout, 20–37.
Epit. Carth.	*Epitome Carthaginiensis*, ed. T. Mommsen (1892), *Chronica minora saec. IV. V. VI. VII.*, vol. 1, MGH AA 9, Berlin, 493–97.
Exp. euang. sec. Luc.	*Arriani cuiusdam expositionis euangelii secundum Lucam fragmenta rescripta*, ed. R. Gryson (1982), *Scripta Arriana latina I*, CCSL 87, Turnhout, 197–225.
Fac., *C. Moc.*	Facundus of Hermiane, *Contra Mocianum*, ed. J.-M. Clement and R. Vander Plaetse (1974), CCSL 90A, Turnhout, 401–16.
Fastidiosus, *Sermo*	Fastidiosus, *Sermo*, ed. J. Fraipont (1968), *Sancti Fulgentii episcopi Ruspensis opera*, CCSL 91, Turnhout, 280–83.
Faustus, *De spir. sanct.*	Faustus of Riez, *De spiritu sancto*, ed. A. Engelbrecht (1891), CSEL 21, Vienna, 99–157.
Faustus, *Ep.*	Faustus of Riez, *Epistulae*, ed. A. Engelbrecht (1891), CSEL 21, Vienna, 159–220.
Felix II (III), *Ep.*	Felix II (III), *Epistulae*, ed. A. Thiel (1867), *Epistolae Romanorum Pontificum genuinae et quae ad eos scriptae sunt a. S. Hilario usque ad Pelagium II*, Brunsberg, 221–84.
Ferr., *Ep.*	Ferrandus of Carthage, *Epistulae et opuscula*, PL 67, 887–950.
Fil., *Haer.*	Filastrius of Brescia, *Diversarum hereseon liber*, ed. F. Heylen (1957), CCSL 9, Turnhout, 215–324.
Fulg., *ABC.*	Fulgentius of Ruspe, *Psalmus abecedarius*, ed. A. Isola (1983), *Fulgenzio di Ruspe: Salmo contro i vandali ariani*, Corona patrum 9, Turin.
Fulg., *Ad Mon.*	Fulgentius of Ruspe, *Ad Monimum*, ed. J. Fraipont (1968), CCSL 91, Turnhout, 1–64.
Fulg., *Ad Tras.*	Fulgentius of Ruspe, *Ad Trasamundum*, ed. J. Fraipont (1968), CCSL 91, Turnhout, 95–185.

Fulg., *C. Fab.*	Fulgentius of Ruspe, *Contra Fabianum fragmenta*, ed. J. Fraipont (1968), *CCSL* 91A, Turnhout, 761–866.
Fulg., *De fide ad Petrum*	Fulgentius of Ruspe, *De fide ad Petrum*, ed. J. Fraipont (1968), *CCSL* 91A, Turnhout, 709–60.
Fulg., *De rem. pecc.*	Fulgentius of Ruspe, *De remissione peccatorum*, ed. J. Fraipont (1968), *CCSL* 91A, Turnhout, 647–707.
Fulg., *De Trin. ad Fel.*	Fulgentius of Ruspe, *Liber de Trinitate ad Felicem*, ed. J. Fraipont (1968), *CCSL* 91A, Turnhout, 631–46.
Fulg., *De uerit. praed.*	Fulgentius of Ruspe, *De ueritate praedestinationis et gratiae libri III ad Iohannem et Venerium*, ed. J. Fraipont (1968), *CCSL* 91A, Turnhout, 458–548.
Fulg., *Dict. Tras.*	Fulgentius of Ruspe, *Dicta regis Trasamundi et responsiones Fulgentii*, ed. J. Fraipont (1968), *CCSL* 91, Turnhout, 65–94.
Fulg., *Ep.*	Fulgentius of Ruspe, *Epistulae*, ed. J. Fraipont (1968), 2 vols., *CCSL* 91–91A, Turnhout, 187–629.
Fulg., *Serm.*	Fulgentius of Ruspe, *Sermones*, ed. J. Fraipont (1968), *CCSL* 91A, Turnhout, 887–942.
Fulg., *Serm. dub.*	Fulgentius of Ruspe, *Sermones dubii*, ed. J. Fraipont (1968), *CCSL* 91A, Turnhout, 943–59.
Ps.-Fulg., *Serm.*	Pseudo-Fulgentius of Ruspe, *Sermones*, *PL* 65, 855–954.
Ps.-Fulg., *Trin.*	Pseudo-Fulgentius of Ruspe, *Liber de Trinitate*, ed. J. Fraipont (1961), *Florilegia Biblica Africana saec. V*, *CCSL* 90, Turnhout, 239–59.
Genn. and Ps.-Genn., *Uir. inlust.*	Gennadius of Marseille and Pseudo-Gennadius, *De uiris inlustribus*, ed. E. C. Richardson (1896), Texte und Untersuchungen zur Geschichte der altchristlichen Literatur 14.1, Leipzig, 57–97.
Gesta con. Carth.	*Gesta conlationis Carthaginiensis*, ed. S. Lancel (1974), *CCSL* 149A, Turnhout.
Greg. Mag., *Dial.*	Gregory the Great, *Dialogi*, ed. A. De Vogüé (1979–80), *Grégoire le Grand: Dialogues*, 3 vols., Sources chrétiennes 251, 260, 265, Paris.
Greg. Tur., *DLH*	Gregory of Tours, *Libri historiarum X*, ed. B. Krusch and W. Levison (1951), rev. ed., *MGH Scriptores rerum Merovingicarum* 1.1, Hannover.
Greg. Tur., *GC*	Gregory of Tours, *Liber in gloria confessorum*, ed. B. Krusch (1895), *MGH Scriptores rerum Merovingicarum* 1.2, Berlin, 294–370.
Greg. Tur., *GM*	Gregory of Tours, *Liber in gloria martyrum*, ed. B. Krusch (1885), *MGH Scriptores rerum Merovingicarum* 1.2, Berlin, 34–111.
Hier., *Altercatio*	Jerome, *Altercatio Luciferiani et Orthodoxi*, ed. A. Canellis (2000), *CCSL* 79B, Turnhout.

Hil., *Ad Const.*   Hilary of Poitiers, *Liber II ad Constantium*, ed. A. Feder (1916), CSEL 65.4, Vienna, 195–205.
Hil., *Adu. Val.*   Hilary of Poitiers, *Liber aduersus Valentem et Ursacium*, ed. A. Feder (1916), CSEL 65.4, Vienna, 39–187.
Hil., *C. Aux.*   Hilary of Poitiers, *Contra Auxentium*, PL 10, 609–18.
Hil., *In Const.*   Hilary of Poitiers, *Liber in Constantium*, ed. A. Rocher (1987), *Hilaire de Poitiers: Contre Constance*, Sources chrétiennes 334, Paris.
Hon., *Ep. consol. ad Arcad.*   Honoratus of Constantia, *Epistula consolatoria ad Arcadium*, PL 50, 567–70.
HP   Victor of Vita, *Historia persecutionis Africanae provinciae*, ed. S. Lancel (2002), *Histoire de la persécution vandale en Afrique*, Collection des universités de France, série latine 368, Paris, 93–212.
Hyd., *Chron.*   Hydatius, *Chronicon*, ed. R. W. Burgess (1993), *The Chronicle of Hydatius and the Consularia Constantinopolitana: Two Contemporary Accounts of the Final Years of the Roman Empire*, Oxford, 69–172.
Instr. uer. fid.   *Instructio uerae fidei*, ed. R. Gryson (1982), *Scripta Arriana latina I*, CCSL 87, Turnhout, 248–65.
Ioh. Bicl., *Chron.*   John of Biclar, *Chronicon*, ed. C. Cardelle de Hartmann (2001), *Victoris Tunnunensis Chronicon: Cum reliquiis ex Consularibus Caesaraugustanis et Iohannis Biclarensis Chronicon*, CCSL 173A, Turnhout, 59–83.
Iord., *Get.*   Jordanes, *De originis actibusque Getarum*, ed. F. Giunta and A. Grillone (1991), *Iordanis De origine actibusque Getarum*, Fonti per la storia d'Italia pubblicate dall'Istituto storico italiano per il Medio Evo 117, Rome.
Isid., *De uir. illust.*   Isidore of Seville, *De uiris illustribus*, ed. C. Codoñer Merino (1964), *El "De Viris Illustribus" de Isidiro de Sevilla: Estudio y edición critica*, Theses et studia philologica Salamanticensia 12, Salamanca.
Isid., *HG*   Isidore of Seville, *Historia Gothorum*, ed. T. Mommsen (1894), *Chronica minora saec. IV. V. VI. VII.*, vol. 2, MGH AA 11, Berlin, 241–303.
Iust., *Nov.*   Justinian, *Novellae*, ed. R. Schöll and G. Kroll, 6th ed. (1928), Corpus juris civilis 3, Berlin.
Lat. reg. Vand. Alan.   *Laterculus regum Vandalorum et Alanorum*, ed. R. Steinacher (2004), "The So-Called *Laterculus regum Vandalorum et Alanorum*: A Sixth-Century Addition to Prosper Tiro's Chronicle?," in A. H. Merrills, ed., *Vandals, Romans and Berbers: New Perspectives on Late Antique North Africa*, Aldershot, 164–68.

Leander, *Hom. in laud. eccl.*	Leander of Seville, *Homilia in laude ecclesiae*, ed. J. Vives (1963), *Concilios visigóticos e hispano-romanos*, España Cristiana, textos 1, Barcelona, 139–44.
Lib. gen.	*Liber Genealogus*, ed. T. Mommsen (1892), *Chronica minora saec. IV. V. VI. VII.*, vol. 1, MGH AA 9, Berlin, 154–96.
LP	*Liber pontificalis*, ed. L. Duchesne (1886–1957), *Le Liber pontificalis: Texte, introduction et commentaire*, 3 vols., Paris.
Max., *Diss.*	Maximinus, *Dissertatio*, ed. R. Gryson (1982), *Scripta Arriana latina I*, CCSL 87, Turnhout, 147–96.
Min. Fel., *Oct.*	Minucius Felix, *Octavius*, ed. B. Kytzler (1982), *M. Minucii Felicis Octavius*, Leipzig.
Not. prov.	*Notitia provinciarum et civitatum Africae*, ed. S. Lancel (2002), *Histoire de la persécution vandale en Afrique*, Collection des universités de France, série latine 368, Paris, 251–72.
NVal	Valentinian III, *Novellae*, ed. T. Mommsen and P. Meyer (1904), *Theodosiani libri XVI cum constitutionibus Sirmondianis*, Berlin, 69–154.
Opt., *C. Parm.*	Optatus of Milevis, *Contra Parmenianum*, ed. M. Labrousse (1995–96), *Optat de Milève: Traité contre les Donatistes*, 2 vols., Sources chrétiennes 412–13, Paris.
Orléans (511)	*Concilium Aurelianense 511. Iul. 10.*, ed. C. De Clercq (1963), *Concilia Galliae, a. 511–a. 695*, CCSL 148A, Turnhout, 3–19.
Orosius	Orosius, *Historia contra paganos*, ed. M.-P. Arnaud-Lindet (1990–91), *Orose: Histoires (contre les païens)*, 3 vols., Paris.
Parth., *Ad Sig.*	Parthemius, *Rescriptum ad Sigisteum*, ed. M. G. Bianco (1988), "Uno scambio di epistole nell'Africa del VI secolo: Le lettere di Sigesteo e Partenio," *Annali della Facoltà di Lettere e Filosofia* 21, 408–9.
Passio beat. mart.	*Passio beatissimorum martyrum qui apud Carthaginem passi sunt sub impio rege Hunirico die VI non. iul.*, ed. S. Lancel (2002), *Histoire de la persécution vandale en Afrique*, Collection des universités de France, série latine 368, Paris, 213–20.
Philostorgius, *HE*	Philostorgius, *Ecclesiastical History*, ed. J. Bidez (1981), *Philostorgius: Kirchengeschichte: Mit dem Leben des Lucian von Antiochien und den Fragmenten eines arianischen Historiographen*, rev. ed. by F. Winkelmann, Berlin.

PItal. 33 = Marini 117		PItal. 33 = Marini 117, ed. J.-O. Tjäder (1982), *Die nichtliterarischen lateinischen Papyri Italiens aus der Zeit 445-700*, vol. 2, Skrifter utgivna av Svenska institutet i Rom. 40 19.2, Stockholm, 79-89.
PItal. 34 = Marini 119		PItal. 34 = Marini 119, ed. J.-O. Tjäder (1982), *Die nichtliterarischen lateinischen Papyri Italiens aus der Zeit 445-700*, vol. 2, Skrifter utgivna av Svenska institutet i Rom. 40 19.2, Stockholm, 91-104.
Poss., *V. Aug.*		Possidius of Calama, *Vita Augustini*, ed. A. A. R. Bastiaensen (1997), *Vita di Cipriano, Vita di Ambrogio, Vita di Agostino*, Scrittori greci e latini, Vite dei santi 3, Milan, 127-241.
Proc., *BV*		Procopius of Caesarea, *De bello vandalico*, ed. H. B. Dewing (1916), *Procopius*, vol. 2: *History of the Wars, Books III and IV*, Loeb Classical Library 81, Cambridge, MA.
Prosper, *Chron.*		Prosper of Aquitaine, *Chronicon*, ed. T. Mommsen (1892), *Chronica minora saec. IV. V. VI. VII.*, vol. 1, MGH AA 9, Berlin, 341-499.
Quod., *Adu. haer.*		Quodvultdeus of Carthage, *Aduersus quinque haereses*, ed. R. Braun (1976), CCSL 60, Turnhout, 259-301.
Quod., *C. Iud., pag. et Arr.*		Quodvultdeus of Carthage, *Contra Iudaeos, paganos et Arrianos*, ed. R. Braun (1976), CCSL 60, Turnhout, 225-58.
Quod., *De acc. ad grat. I*		Quodvultdeus of Carthage, *De accedentibus ad gratiam I*, ed. R. Braun (1976), CCSL 60, Turnhout, 439-58.
Quod., *De acc. ad grat. II*		Quodvultdeus of Carthage, *De accedentibus ad gratiam II*, ed. R. Braun (1976), CCSL 60, Turnhout, 459-70.
Quod., *De sym. I*		Quodvultdeus of Carthage, *De symbolo I*, ed. R. Braun (1976), CCSL 60, Turnhout, 303-34.
Quod., *De sym. III*		Quodvultdeus of Carthage, *De symbolo III*, ed. R. Braun (1976), CCSL 60, Turnhout, 349-63.
Quod., *De ult. quart. fer.*		Quodvultdeus of Carthage, *De ultima quarta feria*, ed. R. Braun (1976), CCSL 60, Turnhout, 393-406.
Quod., *DTB I*		Quodvultdeus of Carthage, *De tempore barbarico I*, ed. R. Braun (1976), CCSL 60, Turnhout, 421-37.
Quod., *DTB II*		Quodvultdeus of Carthage, *De tempore barbarico II*, ed. R. Braun (1976), CCSL 60, Turnhout, 471-86.
Quod., *Lib. prom.*		Quodvultdeus of Carthage, *Liber promissionum et praedictorum Dei*, ed. R. Braun (1976), CCSL 60, Turnhout, 1-223.
Rome (501)		*Acta synhodi a. DI*, ed. T. Mommsen (1894), *Cassiodori senatoris Variae*, MGH AA 12, Berlin, 393-455.

Ruf., *HE*	Rufinus of Aquileia, *Historia ecclesiastica*, ed. T. Mommsen (1903–8), *Die Kirchengeschichte*, 2 vols., Die griechischen christlichen Schriftsteller der ersten drei Jahrhunderte 9, Eusebius Werke 2, Leipzig.
Ruf., *Lib. Adam. Orig. adu. haer.*	Rufinus of Aquileia, *Libri Adamantii Origenis aduersus haereticos*, ed. V. Buchheit (1966), *Tyranii Rufini librorum Adamantii Origenis aduersus haereticos interpretatio*, Studia et testimonia antiqua 1, Munich.
Salv., *Gub. Dei*	Salvian of Marseille, *De gubernatione Dei*, ed. G. Lagarrigue (1975), *Salvien de Marseille: Œuvres*, vol. 2, Sources chrétiennes 220, Paris.
Serm. Arian.	*Sermo Arianorum*, ed. P.-M. Hombert (2009), *Scripta Arriana latina II*, CCSL 87A, Turnhout, 157–75.
Sid., *Ep.*	Sidonius Apollinaris, *Epistulae*, ed. W. B. Anderson (1936–65), *Sidonius: Poems and Letters*, 2 vols., Loeb Classical Library 296, 420, London.
Sig., *Ad Parth.*	Sigisteus, *Epistola ad Parthemium*, ed. M. G. Bianco (1988), "Uno scambio di epistole nell'Africa del VI secolo: Le lettere di Sigesteo e Partenio," *Annali della Facoltà di Lettere e Filosofia* 21, 407–8.
Soc., *HE*	Socrates of Constantinople, *Historia ecclesiastica*, ed. G. C. Hansen (1995), *Sokrates: Kirchengeschichte*, Die griechischen christlichen Schriftsteller der ersten Jahrhunderte, n. f. 1, Berlin.
Soz., *HE*	Sozomen, *Historia ecclesiastica*, ed. J. Bidez, rev. ed. by G. C. Hansen (1995), *Sozomen: Kirchengeschichte*, Griechischen christlichen Schriftsteller der ersten drei Jahrhunderte, n. f. 4, Berlin.
Sulp. Sev., *Chron.*	Sulpicius Severus, *Chronicorum libri duo*, ed. K. Halm (1866), CSEL 1, Vienna, 1–105.
Test. Pat. Fil. et Spir. Sanct.	*Testimonia de Patre et Filio et Spiritu Sancto*, ed. D. De Bruyne (1961), *Florilegia Biblica Africana saec. V*, CCSL 90, Turnhout, 225–33.
Theod., *Eranistes*	Theodoret of Cyrrhus, *Eranistes*, ed. G. H. Ettlinger (1975), *Theodoret of Cyrus: Eranistes: Critical Text and Prolegomena*, Oxford.
Theodulf, *De Spir. Sanct.*	Theodulf of Orleans, *De Spiritu Sancto*, PL 105, 239–76.
Toledo III (589)	*Toletana synodus tertia*, ed. J. Vives (1963), *Concilios visigóticos e hispano-romanos*, España Cristiana, textos 1, Barcelona, 107–45.
V. Fulg.	*Vita Fulgentii*, ed. A. Isola (2016), CCSL 91F, Paris.
Ven. Fort., *Lib. uirt. sanct. Hil.*	Venantius Fortunatus, *Liber de uirtutibus sancti Hilarii*, ed. B. Krusch (1885), MGH AA 4.2, Berlin, 7–11.

Ven. Fort., *V. Hil.*	Venantius Fortunatus, *Vita Hilarii*, ed. B. Krusch (1885), *MGH AA* 4.2, Berlin, 1–7.
Vict. Tonn., *Chron.*	Victor of Tunnuna, *Chronicon*, ed. C. Cardelle de Hartmann (2001), *CCSL* 173A, Turnhout, 1–55.
Ps.-Victor, *Hom. Cyp.*	Pseudo-Victor of Vita, *Homilia de sancto Cypriano episcopo et martyre*, *PL* 58, 265–68.
Vig., *C. Eut.*	Vigilius of Thapsa, *Contra Eutychetem*, *PL* 62, 95–154.
Vig., *Dial. I*	Vigilius of Thapsa, *Contra Arianos, Sabellianos, Photinianos dialogus*, 1st version = pref. I, 1–2, ed. P.-M. Hombert (forthcoming), *CCSL* 90B, Turnhout, 245, 253–354.
Vig., *Dial. II*	Vigilius of Thapsa, *Contra Arianos, Sabellianos, Photinianos dialogus*, 2nd version = pref. II, 1–3, sententia, ed. P.-M. Hombert (forthcoming), *CCSL* 90B, Turnhout, 246–414.
Vig., *Solutiones*	Vigilius of Thapsa, *Solutiones obiectionum Arrianorum*, ed. P.-M. Hombert (2010), "Les *Solutiones obiectionum arrianorum*: Une œuvre authentique de Vigile de Tapse. Édition intégrale, traduction et commentaire," *Sacris erudiri* 49, 202–41.
Ps.-Vig., *Dial.*	Pseudo-Vigilius of Thapsa, *Contra Arianos dialogus*, *PL* 62, 155–80.
Vinc. Ler., *Comm.*	Vincent of Lérins, *Commonitorium*, ed. R. Demeulenaere (1985), *CCSL* 64, Turnhout, 147–95.
VPE	*Vitas sanctorum patrum Emeritensium*, ed. A. Maya Sánchez (1992), *CCSL* 116, Turnhout.
Zaragoza II (592)	*Concilium Cesaraugustanum*, ed. J. Vives (1963), *Concilios visigóticos e hispano-romanos*, España Cristiana, textos 1, Barcelona, 154–55.

SECONDARY LITERATURE

Adams, J. N. (2003), *Bilingualism and the Latin Language*, Cambridge.

——— (2007), *The Regional Diversification of Latin, 200 BC–AD 600*, Cambridge.

Aiello, V. (2005), "I vandali nell'Africa romana: Problemi e prospettive di ricerca," *Mediterraneo Antico* 8, 547–69.

——— (2006), "Che fine ha fatto l'*élite* burocratica romana nel regno dei Vandali?," in R. Lizzi Testa, ed., *Le trasformazioni delle élites in età tardoantica*, Saggi di storia antica 28, Rome, 15–40.

Albl, M. C. (1999), *"And Scripture Cannot Be Broken": The Form and Function of the Early Christian Testimonia Collections*, Supplements to *Novum Testamentum* 96, Leiden.

Amory, P. (1997), *People and Identity in Ostrogothic Italy, 489–554*, Cambridge Studies in Medieval Life and Thought, 4th ser., 33, Cambridge.

Arnold, J. (2014), *Theoderic and the Roman Imperial Restoration*, Cambridge.

Arweiler, A. (2007), "Interpreting Cultural Change: Semiotics and Exegesis in Dracontius' *De laudibus Dei*," in W. Otten and K. Pollmann, eds., *Poetry and Exegesis in Premodern Latin Christianity: The Encounter between Classical and Christian Strategies of Interpretation*, Supplements to *Vigiliae Christianae* 87, Leiden, 147–72.

Ashbrook Harvey, S., and D. G. Hunter, eds. (2008), *The Oxford Handbook of Early Christian Studies*, Oxford.

Aubineau, M. (1966), "Les 318 serviteurs d'Abraham (Gen. XIV, 14), et le nombre des Pères au Concile de Nicée (325)," *Revue d'Histoire Ecclésiastique* 61, 5–43.

Ayres, L. (2004), *Nicaea and Its Legacy: An Approach to Fourth-Century Trinitarian Theology*, Oxford.

——— (2010), *Augustine and the Trinity*, Oxford.

Bailey, L. K. (2010), *Christianity's Quiet Success: The Eusebius Gallicanus Sermon Collection and the Power of the Church in Late Antique Gaul*, Notre Dame, IN.

Baise, I. (2006), "La *Disputatio Cerealis contra Maximinum* (*CPL* 813, CE): Tradition manuscrite et édition critique," *Revue Bénédictine* 116, 233–86.

Bakhuyzen, W. H. v. d. (1901), *Der Dialog des Adamantius*, Die griechischen christlichen Schriftsteller der ersten drei Jahrhunderte 4, Leipzig.

Baratte, F., and F. Bejaoui (2001), "Églises urbaines, églises rurales dans la Tunisie paléochrétienne: Nouvelles recherches d'architecture et d'urbanisme," *Comptes Rendus de l'Académie des Inscriptions et Belles Lettres* 145, 1447–98.

Bardy, G. (1932–33), "La littérature patristique des 'Quaestiones et responsiones' sur l'écriture sainte," *Revue Biblique* 41: 210–36, 341–69, 515–37; 42: 14–30, 211–29, 328–52.

——— (1957), "Der Dialog (christlich)," *Reallexikon für Antike und Christentum* 3, 945–55.

Barnes, M. R. (1993), "The Arians of Book V, and the Genre of *De trinitate*," *Journal of Theological Studies* 44, 185–95.

——— (2007), '*De trinitate* VI and VII: Augustine and the Limits of Nicene Orthodoxy," *Augustinian Studies* 38, 189–202.

Barnes, M. R., and D. H. Williams, eds. (1993), *Arianism after Arius: Essays on the Development of the Fourth Century Trinitarian Conflicts*, Edinburgh.

Barnes, T. D. (1993), *Athanasius and Constantius: Theology and Politics in the Constantinian Empire*, Cambridge, MA.

Barnish, S. J. B. (1983), "The *Anonymus Valesianus* II as a Source for the Last Years of Theoderic," *Latomus* 42, 572–96.

Barnish, S. J. B., and F. Marazzi, eds. (2007), *The Ostrogoths from the Migration Period to the Sixth Century: An Ethnographic Perspective*, Studies in Historical Archaeoethnology 7, Woodbridge.

Barnwell, P. S. (1992), *Emperors, Prefects and Kings: The Roman West, 395–565*, London.

Barth, F. (1969), *Ethnic Groups and Boundaries: The Social Organization of Culture Difference*, Oslo.

Bauer, W. (1971), *Orthodoxy and Heresy in Earliest Christianity*, R. A. Kraft and G. Krodel, trans., Philadelphia (appeared in 1964 as *Rechtgläubigkeit und Ketzerei im ältesten Christentum*, ed. G. Strecker, 2nd ed., Beiträge zur historischen Theologie 10, Tübingen).

Bejaoui, F. (2008), "Les Vandales en Afrique: Témoignages archéologiques. Les récentes découvertes en Tunisie," in G. M. Berndt and R. Steinacher, eds., *Das Reich der Vandalen und seine (Vor-)Geschichten*, Vienna, 197–212.

Ben Abed-Ben Khader, A., and N. Duval (2000), "Carthage, la capitale du royaume et les villes de Tunisie à l'époque vandale," in G. Ripoll and J. M. Gurt, eds., *Sedes regiae (ann. 400–800)*, Memorias de la Real Academia de Buenas Letras de Barcelona 25, Barcelona, 163–218.
Ben Abed-Ben Khader, A., M. Fixot, M. Bonifay, and S. Roucole (2004), *Sidi Jdidi I: La basilique sud*, Collection de l'École française de Rome 339, Rome.
Berndt, G. M. (2007), *Konflikt und Anpassung: Studien zu Migration und Ethnogenese der Vandalen*, Historische Studien (Matthiesen Verlag) 489, Husum.
―― (2010), "Hidden Tracks: On the Vandal's Paths to an African Kingdom," in F. Curta, ed., *Neglected Barbarians*, Turnhout, 537–69.
Berndt, G. M., and R. Steinacher, eds. (2008a), *Das Reich der Vandalen und seine (Vor-) Geschichten*, Vienna.
―― (2008b), "Minting in Vandal North Africa: Coins of the Vandal Period in the Coin Cabinet of Vienna's Kunsthistorisches Museum," *Early Medieval Europe* 16, 252–98.
――, eds. (2014a), *Arianism: Roman Heresy and Barbarian Creed*, Aldershot.
―― (2014b), "The *ecclesia legis Gothorum* and the Role of 'Arianism' in Ostrogothic Italy," in Berndt and Steinacher, eds., *Arianism: Roman Heresy and Barbarian Creed*, Aldershot, 219–29.
Bianco, M. G. (1988a), "I versi di Partenio presbitero a Sigesteo *comes*," in V. Tandoi, ed., *Disiecti membra poetae: Studi di poesia latina in frammenti, III*, Foggia, 243–57.
―― (1988b), "Uno scambio di epistole nell'Africa del VI secolo: Le lettere di Sigesteo e Partenio," *Annali della Facoltà di Lettere e Filosofia* 21, 399–431.
―― (2010), "Noterella fulgenziana: *Ratio* e *rationabilitas* nel dibattito teologico Fulgenzio-Trasamundo," in A. Piras, ed., *Lingua et ingenium: Studi su Fulgenzio di Ruspe e il suo contesto*, Studi e ricerche di cultura religiosa, nuova serie 7, Cagliari, 17–28.
Bjornlie, M. S. (2013), *Politics and Tradition between Rome, Ravenna and Constantinople: A Study of Cassiodorus and the Variae, 527–554*, Cambridge Studies in Medieval Life and Thought, 4th ser., 89, Cambridge.
Bockmann, R. (2013), *Capital Continuous: A Study of Vandal Carthage and Central North Africa from an Archaeological Perspective*, Spätantike—Frühes Christentum—Byzanz: Kunst im ersten Jahrtausend, Reihe B: Studien und Perspektiven 37, Wiesbaden.
―― (2014), "The Non-archaeology of Arianism—What Comparing Cases in Carthage, Haïdra and Ravenna Can Tell Us about 'Arian' Churches," in G. M. Berndt and R. Steinacher, eds., *Arianism: Roman Heresy and Barbarian Creed*, Aldershot, 201–18.
Bonner, G. (2002), *St Augustine of Hippo: Life and Controversies*, 3rd ed., Norwich.
Bouhot, J.-P. (1981), "Origine et composition des 'scolies ariennes' du manuscrit Paris, B. N., lat. 8907: À propos des travaux de Roger Gryson," *Revue d'histoire des textes* 11, 303–23.
Bourdieu, P. (1984), *Distinction: A Social Critique of the Judgement of Taste*, trans. R. Nice, Cambridge, MA (appeared in 1979 as *La distinction: Critique sociale du jugement*, Paris).
Bourgeois, C. (1980), "Les vandales, le vandalisme et l'Afrique," *Antiquités Africaines* 16, 213–28.
Bowersock, G. W., P. R. L. Brown, and O. Grabar (1999), *Late Antiquity: A Guide to the Postclassical World*, Cambridge, MA.
Bowes, K. D. (2008), *Private Worship, Public Values, and Religious Change in Late Antiquity*, Cambridge.

Boyarin, D. (2004), *Border Lines: The Partition of Judaeo-Christianity*, Philadelphia.
Brather, S. (2002), "Ethnic Identities as Constructions of Archaeology: The Case of the Alamanni," in A. Gillett, ed., *On Barbarian Identity: Critical Approaches to Ethnicity in the Early Middle Ages*, Studies in the Early Middle Ages 4, Turnhout, 149–75.
—— (2004), *Ethnische Interpretationen in der frühgeschichtlichen Archäologie: Geschichte, Grundlagen und Alternativen*, Ergänzungsbände zum Reallexikon der germanischen Altertumskunde 42, Berlin.
—— (2008), "Kleidung, Grab und Identität in Spätantike und Frühmittelalter," in G. M. Berndt and R. Steinacher, eds., *Das Reich der Vandalen und seine (Vor-)Geschichten*, Vienna, 283–93.
Braun, R., ed. (1976), *Opera Quodvultdeo Carthaginiensi episcopo tributa*, CCSL 60, Turnhout.
Brennecke, H. C. (1988), *Studien zur Geschichte der Homöer: Der Osten bis zum Ende der homöischen Reichskirche*, Beiträge zur historischen Theologie 73, Tübingen.
—— (2007), "Auseinandersetzung mit sogenannten 'Arianern,'" in V. H. Drecoll, ed., *Augustin Handbuch*, Tübingen, 208–12.
—— (2008a), "Augustin und der 'Arianismus,'" in T. Fuhrer, ed., *Die christlich-philosophischen Diskurse der Spätantike: Texte, Personen, Institutionen*, Philosophie der Antike 28, Stuttgart, 175–87.
—— (2008b), "Lateinischer oder germanischer 'Arianismus'? Zur Frage einer Definition am Beispiel der religiösen Konflikte im nordafrikanischen Vandalenreich," in H. Müller, D. Weber, and C. Weidmann, eds., *Collatio Augustini cum Pascentio: Einleitung, Text, Übersetzung*, Österreichische Akademie der Wissenschaften, philosophisch-historische Klasse, Sitzungsberichte 779, Veröffentlichungen der Kommission für die Herausgabe des Corpus der Lateinischen Kirchenväter 24, Vienna, 125–44.
—— (2014), "Deconstruction of the So-Called Germanic Arianism," in G. M. Berndt and R. Steinacher, eds., *Arianism: Roman Heresy and Barbarian Creed*, Aldershot, 117–30.
Bright, D. F. (1987), *The Miniature Epic in Vandal Africa*, Norman, OK.
—— (1999), "The Chronology of the Poems of Dracontius," *Classica et Mediaevalia* 50, 193–206.
Brown, P. R. L. (1961), "Aspects of the Christianization of the Roman Aristocracy," *Journal of Roman Studies* 51, 1–11.
—— (1992), *Power and Persuasion in Late Antiquity: Towards a Christian Empire*, Madison, WI.
—— (1995), *Authority and the Sacred: Aspects of the Christianisation of the Roman World*, Cambridge.
—— (2000), *Augustine of Hippo: A Biography*, 2nd ed., London.
—— (2002), *Poverty and Leadership in the Later Roman Empire*, London.
—— (2012), *Through the Eye of a Needle: Wealth, the Fall of Rome, and the Making of Christianity in the West, 350–550 AD*, Princeton, NJ.
—— (2013), *The Rise of Western Christendom: Triumph and Diversity, A.D. 200–1000*, 3rd ed., Chichester.
Brown, T. S. (2007), "The Role of Arianism in Ostrogothic Italy: The Evidence from Ravenna," in S. J. B. Barnish and F. Marazzi, eds., *The Ostrogoths from the Migration Period to the Sixth Century: An Ethnographic Perspective*, Studies in Historical Archaeoethnology 7, Woodbridge, 417–41.

Brubaker, R. (2002), "Ethnicity without Groups," *Archives Européennes de Sociologie* 43, 163–89.
Buchheit, V. (1966), *Tyranii Rufini librorum Adamantii Origenis aduersus haereticos interpretatio*, Studia et testimonia 1, Munich.
Buell, D. K. (2005), *Why This New Race: Ethnic Reasoning in Early Christianity*, New York.
Buenacasa Pérez, C. (2007), "La persécution du donatisme et l'imposition de l'orthodoxie en Afrique du Nord (IVe–Ve siècles): Comment effacer la mémoire des hérétiques?," in S. Benoist and A. Daguet-Gagey, eds., *Mémoire et histoire: Les procédures de condamnation dans l'Antiquité romaine*, Metz, 225–42.
Bullough, D. (2003), "Charlemagne's Court Library Revisited," *Early Medieval Europe* 12, 339–63.
Burgess, R. W. (1993), *The Chronicle of Hydatius and the Consularia Constantinopolitana: Two Contemporary Accounts of the Final Years of the Roman Empire*, Oxford.
Burgess, R. W., and M. Kulikowski (2013), *Mosaics of Time: The Latin Chronicle Traditions from the First Century BC to the Sixth Century AD*, vol. 1: *A Historical Introduction to the Chronicle Genre from Its Origins to the High Middle Ages*, Studies in the Early Middle Ages 33, Turnhout.
Burns, T. S. (1984), *A History of the Ostrogoths*, Bloomington, IN.
Burrus, V. (1995), *The Making of a Heretic: Gender, Authority and the Priscillianist Controversy*, Transformation of the Classical Heritage 24, Berkeley, CA.
Burton, P. (2002), "Assessing Latin-Gothic Interaction," in J. N. Adams, M. Janse, and S. Swain, eds., *Bilingualism in Ancient Society: Language Contact and the Written Text*, Oxford, 393–418.
——— (2012), "Augustine and Language," in M. Vessey, ed., *A Companion to Augustine*, Chichester, 113–24.
Bussières, M.-P., ed. (2013), *La littérature des questions et réponses dans l'antiquité profane et chrétienne: De l'enseignement à l'exégèse*, Turnhout.
Caillet, J.-P. (1993), *L'évergétisme monumental chrétien en Italie et à ses marges: D'après l'épigraphie des pavements de mosaïque (IVe–VIIe s.)*, Collection de l'École française de Rome 175, Rome.
Cain, A. (2005), "Miracles, Martyrs and Arians: Gregory of Tours' Sources for his Account of the Vandal Kingdom," *Vigiliae Christianae* 59, 412–37.
Cain, A., and N. E. Lenski, eds. (2009), *The Power of Religion in Late Antiquity*, Aldershot.
Caldwell Ames, C. (2015), *Medieval Heresies: Christianity, Judaism, and Islam*, Cambridge.
Cameron, Alan (1970), *Claudian: Poetry and Propaganda at the Court of Honorius*, Oxford.
——— (2011), *The Last Pagans of Rome*, Oxford.
Cameron, Av. (1994), "Texts as Weapons: Polemic in the Byzantine Dark Ages," in A. K. Bowman and G. Woolf, eds., *Literacy and Power in the Ancient World*, Cambridge, 198–215.
——— (1999), "Heresiology," in G. W. Bowersock, P. R. L. Brown, and O. Grabar, *Late Antiquity: A Guide to the Postclassical World*, Cambridge, MA, 488–90.
——— (2002), "Apologetics in the Roman Empire—a Genre of Intolerance?," in J.-M. Carrié and R. Lizzi Testa, eds., *'Humana sapit': Études d'antiquité tardive offerts à Lellia Cracco Ruggini*, Bibliothèque de l'Antiquité Tardive 3, Turnhout, 219–27.
——— (2003), "How to Read Heresiology," *Journal of Medieval and Early Modern Studies* 33, 471–92.

―― (2007), "Enforcing Orthodoxy in Byzantium," in K. Cooper and J. Gregory, eds., *Discipline and Diversity*, Studies in Church History 43, Woodbridge, 1–24.

―― (2008), "The Violence of Orthodoxy," in E. Iricinschi and H. M. Zellentin, eds., *Heresy and Identity in Late Antiquity*, Texte und Studien zum antiken Judentum 119, Tübingen, 102–14.

―― (2013), "Can Christians Do Dialogue?," *Studia Patristica* 63, 103–20.

―― (2014), *Dialoguing in Late Antiquity*, Hellenic Studies 65, Cambridge, MA.

Cameron, Av., B. Ward-Perkins, and M. Whitby, eds. (2000), *The Cambridge Ancient History*, vol. 14: *Late Antiquity: Empire and Successors, A.D. 425–600*, Cambridge.

Cardelle de Hartmann, C., ed. (2001), *Victoris Tunnunensis chronicon*, CCSL 173A, Turnhout.

Carroll, M. (2006), *Spirits of the Dead: Roman Funerary Commemoration in Western Europe*, Oxford.

Casiday, A., and F. W. Norris, eds. (2007), *The Cambridge History of Christianity*, vol. 2: *Constantine to c. 600*, Cambridge.

Castritius, H. (2006), "Wandalen," in *Reallexikon der germanischen Altertumskunde* 33, 2nd ed., Berlin, 168–209.

―― (2007), *Die Vandalen: Etappen einer Spurensuche*, Kohlhammer Urban-Taschenbücher 605, Stuttgart.

―― (2010), "Barbaren im Garten 'Eden': Der Sonderweg der Vandalen in Nordafrika," *Historia* 59, 371–80.

Chadwick, H. (2009), *Augustine of Hippo: A Life*, Oxford.

Chalon, M., G. Devallet, P. Force, M. Griffe, J.-M. Lassère, and J.-N. Michaud (1985), "*Memorabile factum*: Une célébration de l'évergétisme des rois vandales dans l'Anthologie latine," *Antiquités Africaines* 21, 207–62.

Chastagnol, A., and N. Duval (1974), "Les survivances du culte impérial dans l'Afrique du Nord à l'époque vandale," in *Mélanges d'histoire ancienne offerts à William Seston*, Publications de la Sorbonne, série études 9, Paris, 87–118.

Chauvot, A. (1998), *Opinions romaines face aux barbares au IVe siècle ap. J.-C.*, Paris.

Chazelle, C. M. (2001), *The Crucified God in the Carolingian Era: Theology and Art of Christ's Passion*, Cambridge.

Christern, J. (1976), *Das frühchristliche Pilgerheiligtum von Tebessa: Architektur und Ornamentik einer spätantiken Bauhütte in Nordafrika*, Wiesbaden.

Chuvin, P. (1990), *A Chronicle of the Last Pagans*, trans. B. A. Archer, Revealing Antiquity 4, Cambridge, MA (appeared in 1990 as *Chronique des derniers païens: La disparition du paganisme dans l'empire romain, du règne de Constantin à celui de Justinien*, Paris).

Clark, E. A. (2004), *History, Theory, Text: Historians and the Linguistic Turn*, Cambridge, MA.

Clark, G. (2011), "Augustine and the Merciful Barbarians," in R. W. Mathisen and D. R. Shanzer, eds., *Romans, Barbarians and the Transformation of the Roman World*, Aldershot, 33–42.

Clover, F. M. (1982), "Carthage and the Vandals," in J. H. Humphrey, ed., *Excavations at Carthage Conducted by the University of Michigan VII*, Ann Arbor, MI, 1–22 (repr. in Clover [1993], *The Late Roman West and the Vandals*, Collected Studies 401, Aldershot, VI).

―― (1986), "Felix Carthago," *Dumbarton Oaks Papers* 40, 1–16 (repr. in Clover [1993], *The Late Roman West and the Vandals*, Collected Studies 401, Aldershot, IX).

―― (1989), "The Symbiosis of Romans and Vandals in Africa," in E. K. Chrysos and A. Schwarcz, eds. (1989), *Das Reich und die Barbaren*, Veröffentlichungen des Instituts für Österreichische Geschichtsforschung 29, Vienna, 57–73 (repr. in Clover [1993], *The Late Roman West and the Vandals*, Collected Studies 401, Aldershot, X).
―― (1993), *The Late Roman West and the Vandals*, Collected Studies 401, Aldershot.
―― (2003), "Timekeeping and Dyarchy in Vandal Africa," *Antiquité Tardive* 11, 45–63.
Cohen, S. (2014), "Heresy, Authority and the Bishops of Rome in the Fifth Century: Leo I (440–461), and Gelasius (492–496)," PhD diss., University of Toronto.
―― (2016), "Religious Diversity," in J. J. Arnold, M. S. Bjornlie, and K. Sessa, eds., *A Companion to Ostrogothic Italy*, Leiden, 503–32.
Collins, R. (2000), "The Western Kingdoms," in Av. Cameron, B. Ward-Perkins, and M. Whitby, eds., *The Cambridge Ancient History*, vol. 14: *Late Antiquity: Empire and Successors, A.D. 425–600*, Cambridge, 112–34.
―― (2004), *Visigothic Spain, 409–711*, Oxford.
―― (2010), *Early Medieval Europe, 300–1000*, 3rd ed., London.
Conant, J. P. (2004), "Literacy and Private Documentation in Vandal North Africa: The Case of the Albertini Tablets," in A. H. Merrills, ed., *Vandals, Romans and Berbers: New Perspectives on Late Antique North Africa*, Aldershot, 199–224.
―― (2010), "Europe and the African Cult of Saints, circa 350–900: An Essay in Mediterranean Communications," *Speculum* 85, 1–46.
―― (2012), *Staying Roman: Conquest and Identity in Africa and the Mediterranean, 439–700*, Cambridge Studies in Medieval Life and Thought, 4th ser., 82, Cambridge.
―― (2013), "Public Administration, Private Individuals and the Written Word in Late Antique North Africa, c. 284–700," in W. C. Brown, M. Costambeys, M. Innes, and A. K. Kosto, eds., *Documentary Culture and the Laity in the Early Middle Ages*, Cambridge, 36–62.
―― (2016), "Donatism in the Fifth and Sixth Centuries," in R. Miles, ed., *The Donatist Controversy in Context*, Translated Texts for Historians, Contexts 2, Liverpool, 345–61.
Conant, J. P., and S. T. Stevens, eds. (2016), *North Africa under Byzantium and Early Islam*, Washington DC.
Conybeare, C. (2000), *Paulinus Noster: Self and Symbols in the Letters of Paulinus of Nola*, Oxford.
―― (2005), "Spaces between Letters: Augustine's Correspondence with Women," in L. Olson and K. Kerby-Fulton, eds., *Voices in Dialogue: Reading Women in the Middle Ages*, Notre Dame, IN, 57–72.
Cooley, A. E. (2012), *The Cambridge Manual of Latin Epigraphy*, Cambridge.
Cooper, K. (2007), *The Fall of the Roman Household*, Cambridge.
―― (2016), "Marriage, Law, and Christian Rhetoric in Vandal Africa," in J. P. Conant and S. T. Stevens, eds., *North Africa under Byzantium and Early Islam*, Washington DC, 237–49.
Cooper, K., and J. Gregory, eds. (2007), *Discipline and Diversity*, Studies in Church History 43, Woodbridge.
Cooper, K. and J. Hillner, eds. (2007), *Religion, Dynasty and Patronage in Early Christian Rome, 300–900*, Cambridge.
Costanza, S. (1980), "Vittore di Vita e la *Historia persecutionis Africanae prouinciae*," *Vetera Christianorum* 17, 229–68.

Courcelle, P. (1964), *Histoire littéraire des grandes invasions germaniques*, 3rd ed., Paris.
Courtois, C. (1954), *Victor de Vita et son œuvre: Étude critique*, Algiers.
——— (1955), *Les Vandales et l'Afrique*, Paris.
Croke, B. (2001), *Count Marcellinus and His Chronicle*, Oxford.
Curran, J. (2000), *Pagan City and Christian Capital: Rome in the Fourth Century*, Oxford.
Curta, F., ed. (2010), *Neglected Barbarians*, Turnhout.
Dagron, G. (1974), *Naissance d'une capitale: Constantinople et ses institutions de 330 à 451*, Bibliothèque byzantine, Études 7, Paris.
Dal Santo, M. (2012), *Debating the Saints' Cult in the Age of Gregory the Great*, Oxford.
De Bruyne, D. (1930), "Un florilège biblique inédit," *Zeitschrift für die Neutestamentliche Wissenschaft* 29, 197–208.
de Ste. Croix, G. E. M. (2006), *Christian Persecution, Martyrdom, and Orthodoxy*, ed. M. Whitby and J. Streeter, Oxford.
Dearn, A. (2016), "Donatist Martyrs, Stories and Attitudes," in R. Miles, ed., *The Donatist Controversy in Context*, Translated Texts for Historians, Contexts 2, Liverpool, 70–100.
Decret, F. (1996), *Le christianisme en Afrique du nord ancienne*, Paris.
Deliyannis, D. M. (2010), *Ravenna in Late Antiquity*, Cambridge.
——— (2012), "Ravenna, Saint Martin and the Battle of Vouillé," in R. W. Mathisen and D. R. Shanzer, eds., *The Battle of Vouillé, 507 C.E.: Where France Began*, Millennium Studies in the Culture and History of the First Millennium C.E. 37, Berlin, 167–80.
Delmaire, R. (1987), "La date de l'ambassade d'Alexander à Carthage et l'élection de l'évêque Eugenius," *Revue des Études Augustiniennes* 33, 85–89.
Diesner, H.-J. (1966a), *Das Vandalenreich: Aufstieg und Untergang*, Leipzig.
——— (1966b), *Fulgentius von Ruspe als Theologe und Kirchenpolitiker*, Arbeiten zur Theologie, 1. Reihe, Heft 26, Aufsätze und Vorträge zur Theologie und Religionswissenschaft 38, Stuttgart.
——— (1968), "Prolegomena zu einer Prosopographie des Vandalenreiches," *Jahrbuch der Österreichischen Byzantinischen Gesellschaft* 17, 1–15.
Dolbeau, F. (2006), "Brouillons et textes inachevés parmi les œuvres d'Augustin," *Sacris Eruditi* 45, 191–221.
Dörrie, H., and H. Dörries (1966), "Erotapokriseis," *Reallexikon für Antike und Christentum* 6, 342–70.
Dossey, L. (2003), "The Last Days of Vandal Africa: An Arian Commentary on Job and Its Historical Context," *Journal of Theological Studies* 54, 60–138.
——— (2010), *Peasant and Empire in Christian North Africa*, Transformation of the Classical Heritage 47, Berkeley, CA.
Doyle, D. E. (2005), "Spread throughout the World: Hints on Augustine's Understanding of Petrine Ministry," *Journal of Early Christian Studies* 13, 233–46.
Drake, H. A. (2000), *Constantine and the Bishops: The Politics of Intolerance*, Baltimore.
Drinkwater, J., and B. Salway, eds. (2007), *Wolf Liebeschuetz Reflected: Essays Presented by Colleagues, Friends and Pupils*, BICS Supplement 91, London.
Dumézil, B. (2005), *Les racines chrétiennes de l'Europe: Conversion et liberté dans les royaumes barbares, V^e–VIIIe siècle*, Paris.

Durst, M. (1998), "Das Glaubensbekenntnis des Auxentius von Mailand: Historischer Hintergrund—Textüberlieferung—Theologie—Edition," *Jahrbuch für Antike und Christentum* 41, 118–68.

Duval, N., ed. (1981), *Recherches archéologiques à Haïdra 2: La basilique I dite de Melléus ou de Saint-Cyprien*, Collection de l'École française de Rome 18, Rome.

——, (1984), "Culte monarchique dans l'Afrique vandale: Culte des rois ou culte des empereurs?," *Revue des Études Augustiniennes* 30, 269–73.

—— (1986), "L'inhumation privilegiée en Tunisie et en Tripolitaine," in Y. Duval and J.-C. Picard, eds. *L'inhumation privilegiée du IVe au VIIIe siècle en Occident*, Paris, 25–42.

Duval, N., and J. Mallon (1969), "Les inscriptions de la 'chapelle vandale' à Haïdra d'après l'abbé Delapard," *Bulletin de la Société des Antiquaires de France*, 99–120.

Duval, N., and F. Prévot (1975), *Recherches archéologiques à Haïdra 1: Les inscriptions chrétiennes*, Collection de l'École française de Rome 18, Rome.

Duval, Y. (1988), *Auprès des saints, corps et âme: L'inhumation 'ad sanctos' dans la chrétienté d'Orient et d'Occident du IIIe au VIIe siècle*, Paris.

Duval, Y., and J.-C. Picard, eds. (1986), *L'inhumation privilegiée du IVe au VIIIe siècle en Occident*, Paris.

Duval, Y.-M. (1969), "La 'manœuvre frauduleuse' de Rimini: À la recherche du *Liber aduersus Vrsacium et Valentem*," in E. R. Labande, ed., *Hilaire et son temps*, Paris, 51–103 (repr. in Duval [1998], *L'extirpation de l'Arianisme en Italie du Nord et en Occident: Rimini (359/60) et Aquilée (381), Hilaire de Poitiers (367/8) et Ambroise de Milan (397)*, Collected Studies 611, Aldershot, II).

—— (1974), "L'influence des écrivains africains du IIIe siècle sur les écrivains chrétiens de l'Italie du Nord dans la seconde moitié du IVe siècle," in S. Tavano, ed., *Aquileia e l'Africa*, Antichità altoadriatiche 5, Aquileia, 191–225.

—— (1998), *L'extirpation de l'Arianisme en Italie du Nord et en Occident: Rimini (359/60) et Aquilée (381), Hilaire de Poitiers (367/8) et Ambroise de Milan (397)*, Collected Studies 611, Aldershot.

Ebbeler, J. (2009), "Tradition, Innovation, and Epistolary Mores," in P. Rousseau, ed., *A Companion to Late Antiquity*, Chichester, 270–84.

—— (2012), *Disciplining Christians: Correction and Community in Augustine's Letters*, Oxford.

Edwards, M. J., M. D. Goodman, and S. R. F. Price, eds., with C. C. Rowland (1999a), *Apologetics in the Roman Empire: Pagans, Jews, and Christians*, Oxford.

Edwards, M. J., M. D. Goodman, S. R. F. Price, and C. C. Rowland (1999b), "Introduction: Apologetics in the Roman World," in Edwards, Goodman, and Price, eds., with Rowland, *Apologetics in the Roman Empire: Pagans, Jews, and Christians*, Oxford, 1–13.

Elm, S., É. Rebillard, and A. Romano, eds. (2000), *Orthodoxie, christianisme, histoire = Orthodoxy, Christianity, History*, Collection de l'École Française de Rome 270, Rome.

Ennabli, L. (1982), *Les inscriptions funéraires chrétiennes de Carthage*, vol. 2: *La basilique de Mcidfa*, Collection de l'École française de Rome 62, Rome.

—— (1991), *Les inscriptions funéraires de Carthage*, vol. 3: *Carthage intra et extra muros*, Collection de l'École française de Rome 151, Rome.

Eno, R. B. (1997), *Fulgentius: Selected Works*, Fathers of the Church 95, Washington DC.

Eshleman, K. (2012), *The Social World of Intellectuals in the Roman Empire: Sophists, Philosophers and Christians*, Cambridge.
Evers, A. W. H. (2010), *Church, Cities and People: A Study of the Plebs in the Church and Cities of Roman Africa in Late Antiquity*, Interdisciplinary Studies in Ancient Culture and Religion 11, Leuven.
Falluomini, C. (2010), "Il codice gotico-latino di Gießen e la Chiesa vandalica," in A. Piras, ed., *Lingua et ingenium: Studi su Fulgenzio di Ruspe e il suo contesto*, Studi e ricerche di cultura religiosa, nuova serie 7, Cagliari, 309–40.
Fear, A. T. (1997), *Lives of the Visigothic Fathers*, Translated Texts for Historians 26, Liverpool.
Feder, A. (1933), "Die Entstehung und Veröffentlichung des gennadischen Schriftstellerkatalogs," *Scholastik* 8, 217–32.
Ferguson, E. (2009), *Baptism in the Early Church: History, Theology, and Liturgy in the First Five Centuries*, Grand Rapids, MI.
Ferguson, T. C. (2005), *The Past Is Prologue: The Revolution of Nicene Historiography*, Supplements to *Vigiliae Christianae* 75, Leiden.
Fevrier, P.-A. (1986), "Tombes privilegiées en Mauretaine et Numidie," in Y. Duval and J.-C. Picard, eds. *L'inhumation privilegiée du IVe au VIIIe siècle en Occident*, Paris, 13–23.
Fialon, S. (2015), "Arianisme 'vandale' et controverse religieuse: Le cas de la *Disputatio Cerealis contra Maximinum*," in É. Wolff, ed., *Littérature, politique et religion en Afrique vandale*, Collection des études Augustiniennes, série antiquité 200, Turnhout, 137–55.
Ficker, G. (1897), *Studien zu Vigilius von Thapsus*, Leipzig.
Fielding, I. (2017), *Transformations of Ovid in Late Antiquity*, Cambridge.
Fischer, A., and I. Wood, eds. (2014), *Western Perspectives on the Mediterranean: Cultural Transfer in Late Antiquity and the Early Middle Ages, 400–800 AD*, London.
Fischer, B. (1942), "Der Bibeltext in den Pseudo-Augustinischen 'Solutiones diversarum quaestionum ab haereticis obiectarum' im Codex Paris B. N. Lat. 12217," *Biblica* 23, 139–64.
Flower, R. A. (2011), "Genealogies of Unbelief: Epiphanius of Salamis and Heresiological Authority," in C. M. Kelly, Flower, and M. S. Williams, eds., *Unclassical Traditions, Volume 2: Perspectives from East and West in Late Antiquity*, Cambridge, 70–87.
——— (2013a), *Emperors and Bishops in Late Roman Invective*, Cambridge.
——— (2013b), "'The Insanity of Heretics Must Be Restrained': Heresiology in the Theodosian Code," in C. M. Kelly, ed., *Theodosius II: Rethinking the Roman Empire in Late Antiquity*, Cambridge, 172–94.
Fournier, É. (2008), "Victor of Vita and the Vandal 'Persecution': Interpreting Exile in Late Antiquity," PhD diss., University of California, Santa Barbara.
——— (2012), "Rebaptism as a Ritual of Cultural Integration in Vandal Africa," in D. Brakke, D. M. Deliyannis, and E. Watts, eds., *Shifting Cultural Frontiers in Late Antiquity*, Aldershot, 243–54.
——— (2013), "Victor of Vita and the Conference of 484: A Pastiche of 411?," *Studia Patristica* 62, 395–408.
——— (2015), "Éléments apologétiques chez Victor de Vita: Exemple d'un genre littéraire en transition," in G. Greatrex and H. Elton, eds., with L. McMahon, *Shifting Genres in Late Antiquity*, Aldershot, 105–17.

Fraipont, J. (1961), "Incerti auctoris liber de trinitate," in *Florilegia Biblica Africana saec. V*, CCSL 90, Turnhout, 235–59.

Francovich Onesti, N. (2002), *I vandali: Lingua e storia*, Lingue e letterature Carroci 14, Rome.

—— (2010), "Le testamonianze linguistiche dei Vandali nel regnum Africae fra cultura latina ed eredità germaniche," in A. Piras, ed., *Lingua et ingenium: Studi su Fulgenzio di Ruspe e il suo contesto*, Studi e ricerche di cultura religiosa, nuova serie 7, Cagliari, 359–84.

Fredriksen, P. (1991), "Apocalypse and Redemption in Early Christianity: From John of Patmos to Augustine of Hippo," *Vigiliae Christianae* 45, 151–83.

Frend, W. H. C. (1952), *The Donatist Church: A Movement of Protest in Roman North Africa*, Oxford.

Gaddis, M. (2005), *There Is No Crime for Those Who Have Christ: Religious Violence in the Christian Roman Empire*, Transformation of the Classical Heritage 39, Berkeley, CA.

—— (2009), "The Political Church: Religion and the State," in P. Rousseau, ed., *A Companion to Late Antiquity*, Chichester, 512–24.

Galli Milić, L. (2009), "Stratégies argumentatives dans la *Satisfactio* de Dracontius," in H. Harich-Schwarzbauer and P. Schierl, eds., *Lateinische Poesie der Spätantike: Internationale Tagung in Castelen bei Augst, 11.–13. Oktober 2007*, Schweizerische Beiträge zur Altertumswissenschaft 36, Basel, 245–66.

Galvao-Sobrinho, C. R. (2013), *Doctrine and Power: Theological Controversy and Christian Leadership in the Later Roman Empire*, Transformation of the Classical Heritage 51, Berkeley, CA.

Ganz, D. (1995), "Theology and the Organisation of Thought," in R. McKitterick, ed., *The New Cambridge Medieval History*, vol. 2: *c. 700–c. 900*, Cambridge, 758–85.

García Mac Gaw, C. (2008), *Le problème du baptême dans le schisme donatiste*, Ausonius Éditions, Scripta Antiqua 21, Pessac.

Gardiner, L. C. A. (2012), "'The Truth Is Bitter': Socrates Scholasticus and the Writing of a History of the Christian Roman Empire," PhD diss., University of Cambridge.

—— (2013), "The Imperial Subject: Theodosius II and Panegyric in Socrates' *Church History*," in C. M. Kelly, ed., *Theodosius II: Rethinking the Roman Empire in Late Antiquity*, Cambridge, 244–68.

Geary, P. J. (1983), "Ethnic Identity as a Situational Construct in the Early Middle Ages," *Mitteilungen der Anthropologischen Gesellschaft in Wien* 113, 15–26.

—— (1999), "Barbarians and Ethnicity," in G. W. Bowersock, P. R. L. Brown, and O. Grabar, *Late Antiquity: A Guide to the Postclassical World*, Cambridge, MA, 107–29.

Gemeinhardt, P. (1999), "Lateinischer Neunizänismus bei Augustin," *Zeitschrift für Kirchengeschichte* 110, 149–69.

George, J. W. (2004), "Vandal Poets in Their Context," in A. H. Merrills, ed., *Vandals, Romans and Berbers: New Perspectives on Late Antique North Africa*, Aldershot, 133–43.

Gil Egea, M. E. (1998), *África en tiempos de los Vándalos: Continuidad y mutaciones de las estructuras sociopolíticas romanas*, Memorias del Seminario de Historia Antigua 7, Alcalá de Henares.

Gillett, A. (2002a), "Introduction: Ethnicity, History, and Methodology," in Gillett, ed., *On Barbarian Identity: Critical Approaches to Ethnicity in the Early Middle Ages*, Studies in the Early Middle Ages 4, Turnhout, 1–18.

———, ed. (2002b), *On Barbarian Identity: Critical Approaches to Ethnicity in the Early Middle Ages*, Studies in the Early Middle Ages 4, Turnhout.

——— (2002c), "Was Ethnic Identity Politicized in the Earliest Medieval Kingdoms?," in Gillett, ed., *On Barbarian Identity: Critical Approaches to Ethnicity in the Early Middle Ages*, Studies in the Early Middle Ages 4, Turnhout, 85–121.

——— (2009), "The Mirror of Jordanes: Concepts of the Barbarian, Then and Now," in P. Rousseau, ed., *A Companion to Late Antiquity*, Chichester, 392–408.

Goetz, H.-W., J. Jarnut, and W. Pohl, eds., with S. Kaschke (2003), *Regna and gentes: The Relationship between Late Antique and Early Medieval Peoples and Kingdoms in the Transformation of the Roman World*, Transformation of the Roman World 13, Leiden.

Goldhill, S., ed. (2008), *The End of Dialogue in Antiquity*, Cambridge.

Goldlust, B. (2015), "La *persona* de Dracontius dans la *Satisfactio*: Quelques réflexions sur la posture discursive du poète," in É. Wolff, ed., *Littérature, politique et religion en Afrique vandale*, Collection des études Augustiniennes, série antiquité 200, Turnhout, 243–57.

Goltz, A. (2008), *Barbar, König, Tyrann: Das Bild Theoderichs des Großen in der Überlieferung des 5. bis 9. Jahrhunderts*, Millennium-Studien 12, Berlin.

González Salinero, R. (2002), *Poder y conflicto religioso en el norte de África: Quodvultdeus de Cartago y los vándalos*, Graeco-Romanae religionis electa collectio 10, Madrid.

Graumann, T. (2002), *Die Kirche der Väter: Vätertheologie und Väterbeweis in den Kirchen des Ostens bis zum Konzil von Ephesus (431)*, Beiträge zur historischen Theologie 118, Tübingen.

——— (2009), "The Conduct of Theology and the 'Fathers' of the Church," in P. Rousseau, ed., *A Companion to Late Antiquity*, Chichester, 539–55.

——— (2012), "Orthodoxy, Authority and the (Re-)construction of the Past in Church Councils," in J. Ulrich, A.-C. Jacobsen, and D. Brakke, eds., *Invention, Rewriting, Usurpation: Discursive Fights over Religious Traditions in Antiquity*, Early Christianity in the Context of Antiquity 11, Frankfurt am Main, 219–37.

Gray, P. T. R. (1989), "'The Select Fathers': Canonizing the Patristic Past," *Studia Patristica* 23, 21–36.

Greatrex, G. (2001), "Justin I and the Arians," *Studia Patristica* 34, 72–81.

Grégoire, R. (1980), *Homéliaires liturgiques médiévaux: analyse de manuscrits*, Biblioteca degli "Studi medievali" 12, Spoleto.

Grillmeier, A. (1987), *Christ in Christian Tradition*, vol. 2: *From the Council of Chalcedon (451) to Gregory the Great (590–604), Part 1: Reception and Contradiction: The Development of the Discussion about Chalcedon from 451 to the Beginning of the Reign of Justinian*, trans. P. Allen and J. Cawle, 2nd ed., Atlanta (appeared in 1979 as *Jesus der Christus im Glauben der Kirche*, Basel).

Gryson, R. (1980), *Scolies ariennes sur le Concile d'Aquilée*, Sources chrétiennes 267, Paris.

——— (1982a), *Le recueil arien de Vérone*, Instrumenta patristica 13, Steenbrugis.

———, ed. (1982b), *Scripta Arriana latina I*, CCSL 87, Turnhout.

Gui, I., N. Duval, and J.-P. Caillet (1992), *Basiliques chrétiennes d'Afrique du nord*, vol. 1: *Inventaire des monuments de l'Algérie*, Collection des études Augustiniennes, série antiquité 129, Paris.

Guidi, P. (2005), *Vigilio di Tapso: Contro gli Ariani*, Testi patristici 184, Rome.

Gwynn, D. M. (2007a), *The Eusebians: The Polemic of Athanasius of Alexandria and the Construction of the "Arian Controversy,"* Oxford.

────── (2007b), "From Iconoclasm to Arianism: The Construction of Christian Tradition in the Iconoclast Controversy," *Greek, Roman and Byzantine Studies* 47, 225–51.

────── (2012a), *Athanasius of Alexandria: Bishop, Theologian, Ascetic, Father*, Oxford.

────── (2012b), "Episcopal Leadership," in S. F. Johnson, ed., *The Oxford Handbook of Late Antiquity*, Oxford, 876–915.

Gwynn, D. M., and S. Bangert, eds. (2010), *Religious Diversity in Late Antiquity*, Late Antique Archaeology 6, Leiden.

Halfond, G. I. (2012), "Vouillé, Orléans (511), and the Origins of the Frankish Conciliar Tradition," in R. W. Mathisen and D. R. Shanzer, eds., *The Battle of Vouillé, 507 C.E.: Where France Began*, Millennium Studies in the Culture and History of the First Millennium C.E. 37, Berlin, 151–65.

Hall, S. G. (2000), "The Organization of the Church," in Av. Cameron, B. Ward-Perkins, and M. Whitby, eds., *The Cambridge Ancient History*, vol. 14: *Late Antiquity: Empire and Successors, A.D. 425–600*, Cambridge, 731–44.

Halsall, G. (2007), *Barbarian Migrations and the Roman West, 376–568*, Cambridge.

────── (2010), *Cemeteries and Society in Merovingian Gaul: Selected Studies in History and Archaeology, 1992–2009*, Brill's Series on the Early Middle Ages 18, Leiden.

────── (2011), "Ethnicity and Early Medieval Cemeteries," *Arqueología y Territorio Medieval* 18, 15–27.

Handley, M. A. (2003), *Death, Society, and Culture: Inscriptions and Epitaphs in Gaul and Spain, AD 300–750*, BAR International Series 1135, Oxford.

────── (2004), "Disputing the End of African Christianity," in A. H. Merrills, ed., *Vandals, Romans and Berbers: New Perspectives on Late Antique North Africa*, Aldershot, 291–310.

────── (2011), *Dying on Foreign Shores: Travel and Mobility in the Late-Antique West*, Journal of Roman Archaeology Supplementary Series 86, Portsmouth, RI.

Hanson, R. P. C. (1988), *The Search for the Christian Doctrine of God: The Arian Controversy, 318–381 AD*, Edinburgh.

Harries, J. (1994), *Sidonius Apollinaris and the Fall of Rome, AD 407–485*, Oxford.

────── (1999), *Law and Empire in Late Antiquity*, Cambridge.

Haubrichs, W. (2012), "*Nescio latine!* Volkssprache und Latein im Konflikt zwischen Arianern und Katholikern im wandalischen Afrika nach der *Historia persecutionis* des Victor von Vita," in S. Patzold, A. Rathmann-Lutz, and V. Scior, eds., *Geschichtsvorstellungen: Bilder, Texte und Begriffe aus dem Mittelalter: Festschrift für Hans-Werner Goetz zum 65. Geburtstag*, Vienna, 13–42.

Hays, G. (2004), "'*Romuleis Libicisque litteris*': Fulgentius and the 'Vandal Renaissance,'" in A. H. Merrills, ed., *Vandals, Romans and Berbers: New Perspectives on Late Antique North Africa*, Aldershot, 101–32.

────── (2010), "Fulgentius of Ruspe and His Medieval Readers," in A. Piras, ed., *Lingua et ingenium: Studi su Fulgenzio di Ruspe e il suo contesto*, Studi e ricerche di cultura religiosa, nuova serie 7, Cagliari, 105–45.

Heather, P. J. (1996), *The Goths*, Oxford.

——— (1999), "The Barbarian in Late Antiquity: Image, Reality, and Transformation," in R. Miles, ed., *Constructing Identities in Late Antiquity*, London, 234–58.

——— (2000), "State, Lordship and Community in the West (c. A.D. 400–600)," in Av. Cameron, B. Ward-Perkins, and M. Whitby, eds., *The Cambridge Ancient History*, vol. 14: *Late Antiquity: Empire and Successors*, A.D. 425–600, Cambridge, 437–68.

——— (2005), *The Fall of the Roman Empire: A New History*, London.

——— (2007a), "Christianity and the Vandals in the Reign of Geiseric," in J. Drinkwater and B. Salway, eds., *Wolf Liebeschuetz Reflected: Essays Presented by Colleagues, Friends and Pupils, BICS Supplement 91*, London, 137–46.

——— (2007b), "Merely an Ideology? Gothic Identity in Ostrogothic Italy," in S. J. B. Barnish and F. Marazzi, eds., *The Ostrogoths from the Migration Period to the Sixth Century: An Ethnographic Perspective*, Studies in Historical Archaeoethnology 7, Woodbridge, 31–79.

——— (2009), *Empires and Barbarians: Migration, Development and the Birth of Europe*, London.

——— (2013), *The Restoration of Rome: Barbarian Popes and Imperial Pretenders*, London.

——— (2015), "Migration," *Networks and Neighbours* 3, 1–21.

Heather, P. J., and J. Matthews (1991), *The Goths in the Fourth Century*, Translated Texts for Historians 11, Liverpool.

Heil, U. (2007), "Augustin-Rezeption im Reich der Vandalen. Die *Altercatio sancti Augustini cum Pascentio Arriano*," *Zeitschrift für Antikes Christentum* 11, 6–29.

——— (2011), *Avitus von Vienne und die homöische Kirche der Burgunder*, Patristische Texte und Studien 66, Berlin.

——— (2014a), "Chlodwig, ein christlicher Herrscher: Ansichten des Bischofs Avitus von Vienne," in M. Meier and S. Patzold, eds., *Chlodwigs Welt: Organisation von Herrschaft um 500*, Roma aeterna 3, Stuttgart, 67–90.

——— (2014b), "The Homoians in Gaul," in G. M. Berndt and R. Steinacher, eds., *Arianism: Roman Heresy and Barbarian Creed*, Aldershot, 271–96.

Heinzelmann, M. (1998), "Heresy in Books I and II of Gregory of Tours' *Historiae*," in A. Callander Murray, ed., *After Rome's Fall: Narrators and Sources of Early Medieval History: Essays Presented to Walter Goffart*, Toronto, 67–82.

Hen, Y. (2007), *Roman Barbarians: The Royal Court and Culture in the Early Medieval West*, Basingstoke.

Hermanowicz, E. T. (2008), *Possidius of Calama: A Study of the North African Episcopate at the Time of Augustine*, Oxford.

Heydemann, G. (2013), "Biblical Israel and the Christian *gentes*: Social Metaphors and the Language of Identity in Cassiodorus' *Expositio psalmorum*," in W. Pohl and Heydemann, eds., *Strategies of Identification: Ethnicity and Religion in Early Medieval Europe*, Cultural Encounters in Late Antiquity and the Middle Ages 13, Turnhout, 143–208.

Hombert, P.-M. (2010), "Les *Solutiones obiectionum arrianorum*: Une œuvre authentique de Vigile de Tapse," *Sacris Erudiri* 49, 151–241.

——— (forthcoming), *Vigilius Thapsensis: Contra Arianos, Sabellianos, Photinianos dialogus*, CCSL 90B, Turnhout.

Howe, T. (2007), *Vandalen, Barbaren und Arianer bei Victor von Vita*, Studien zur alten Geschichte 7, Frankfurt.

Humfress, C. (2007), *Orthodoxy and the Courts in Late Antiquity*, Oxford.
—— (2008), "Citizens and Heretics: Late Roman Lawyers on Christian Heresy," in E. Iricinschi and H. M. Zellentin, eds., *Heresy and Identity in Late Antiquity*, Texte und Studien zum antiken Judentum 119, Tübingen, 128–42.
—— (2011), "Bishops and Law Courts in Late Antiquity: How (Not) to Make Sense of the Legal Evidence," *Journal of Early Christian Studies* 19, 375–400.
—— (2012), "Controversialist: Augustine in Combat," in M. Vessey, ed., *A Companion to Augustine*, Chichester, 323–35.
Humphries, M. (2010a), "Gog Is the Goth: Biblical Barbarians in Ambrose of Milan's *De fide*," in C. M. Kelly, R. A. Flower, and M. S. Williams, eds., *Unclassical Traditions*, vol. 1: *Alternatives to the Classical Past in Late Antiquity, CCJ* Supplementary Volume 34, Cambridge, 44–57.
—— (2010b), "The Sacred and the Secular: The Presence and Absence of Christian Religious Thought in Secular Writing in the Late Antique West," in D. M. Gwynn and S. Bangert, eds., *Religious Diversity in Late Antiquity*, Late Antique Archaeology 6, Leiden, 493–509.
Hunt, E. D. (1989), "Did Constantius II Have Court Bishops?," *Studia Patristica* 19, 86–90.
—— (2007), "Imperial Law or Councils of the Church? Theodosius I and the Imposition of Doctrinal Uniformity," in K. Cooper and J. Gregory, eds., *Discipline and Diversity*, Studies in Church History 43, Woodbridge, 57–68.
Inglebert, H. (1996), *Les Romains chrétiens face à l'histoire de Rome: Histoire, christianisme et romanités en Occident dans l'Antiquité tardive (IIIe-Ve siècles)*, Collection des études Augustiniennes, série antiquité 145, Paris.
—— (2012), "Introduction: Late Antique Conceptions of Late Antiquity," in S. F. Johnson, ed., *The Oxford Handbook of Late Antiquity*, Oxford, 3–28.
Innes, M. (2006), "Land, Freedom and the Making of the Medieval West," *Transactions of the Royal Historical Society* 16, 39–74.
Iricinschi, E. and H. M. Zellentin, eds. (2008a), *Heresy and Identity in Late Antiquity*, Texte und Studien zum antiken Judentum 119, Tübingen.
—— (2008b), "Making Selves and Marking Others: Identity and Late Antique Heresiologies," in Iricinschi and Zellentin, eds., *Heresy and Identity in Late Antiquity*, Texte und Studien zum antiken Judentum 119, Tübingen, 1–27.
Isola, A. (1983), *Fulgenzio di Ruspe: Salmo contro i vandali ariani*, Corona patrum 9, Torino.
—— (1990), *I cristiani dell'Africa vandalica nei sermones del tempo (429–534)*, Edizioni universitarie Jaca 74, Milan.
—— (1994–95), "A proposito dell'*inscitia* dei Vandali secondo Fulg., *ad Tras.* 1, 2, 2," *Romanobarbarica* 13, 57–74.
—— (2016), *Vita Fulgentii*, CCSL 91F, Turnhout.
Jacobs, A. S. (2007), "Dialogical Differences: (De-)Judaizing Jesus' Circumcision," *Journal of Early Christian Studies* 15, 291–335.
James, E. (2008), "Gregory of Tours, the Visigoths and Spain," in S. Barton and P. Linehan, eds., *Cross, Crescent and Conversion: Studies on Medieval Spain and Christendom in Memory of Richard Fletcher*, The Medieval Mediterranean: Peoples, Economies and Cultures, 400–1500, 73, Leiden, 43–64.
—— (2009), "Gregory of Tours and 'Arianism,'" in A. Cain and N. E. Lenski, eds., *The Power of Religion in Late Antiquity*, Aldershot, 327–38.

Jenkins, R. (2008), *Rethinking Ethnicity*, 2nd ed., London.
Jensen, R. M. (2013), "Christianity in Roman Africa," in M. R. Salzman and W. Adler, eds., *The Cambridge History of Religions in the Ancient World*, vol. 2: *From the Hellenstic Age to Late Antiquity*, Cambridge, 264–91.
Johnson, A. P. (2006), *Ethnicity and Argument in Eusebius' "Praeparatio evangelica*," Oxford.
Johnson, S. F., ed. (2012), *The Oxford Handbook of Late Antiquity*, Oxford.
Jones, A. H. M. (1964), *The Later Roman Empire, 284–602: A Social, Economic and Administrative History*, vol. 1, Oxford.
Kahlos, M. (2007), *Debate and Dialogue: Christian and Pagan Cultures c. 360–430*, Aldershot.
Kaster, R. (1988), *Guardians of Language: The Grammarian in Late Antiquity*, Transformation of the Classical Heritage 11, Berkeley, CA.
Keefe, S. (2012), *A Catalogue of Works Pertaining to the Explanation of the Creed in Carolingian Manuscripts*, Instrumenta patristica et mediaevalia 63, Turnhout.
Kelly, C. M. (1998), "Emperors, Government and Bureaucracy," in A. Cameron and P. Garnsey, eds., *The Cambridge Ancient History*, vol. 13: *The Late Empire, AD 337–425*, Cambridge, 138–83.
——— (2004), *Ruling the Later Roman Empire*, Revealing Antiquity 15, Cambridge, MA.
——— (2013a), "Rethinking Theodosius," in Kelly, ed., *Theodosius II: Rethinking the Roman Empire in Late Antiquity*, Cambridge, 3–64.
———, ed. (2013b), *Theodosius II: Rethinking the Roman Empire in Late Antiquity*, Cambridge.
Kelly, C. M., R. A. Flower, and M. S. Williams, eds. (2011), *Unclassical Traditions, Volume 2: Perspectives from East and West in Late Antiquity*, Cambridge.
Kershaw, P. J. E. (2011), *Peaceful Kings: Peace, Power and the Early Medieval Political Imagination*, Oxford.
King, K. L. (2003), *What Is Gnosticism?*, Cambridge, MA.
Kitchen, T. E. (2008), "Contemporary Perceptions of the Roman Empire in the Later Fifth and Sixth Centuries," PhD diss., University of Cambridge.
——— (2010), "Sidonius Apollinaris," in R. Corradini, M. Gillis, R. McKitterick, and I. Van Renswoude, eds., *Ego Trouble: Authors and Their Identities in the Early Middle Ages*, Österreichische Akademie der Wissenschaften, philosophisch-historische Klasse, Denkschriften 385, Forschung zur Geschichte des Mittelalters 15, Vienna, 53–66.
——— (2011), "Italia and Graecia: West versus East in the Rhetoric of Ostrogothic Italy," in C. M. Kelly, R. A. Flower, and M. S. Williams, eds., *Unclassical Traditions, Volume 2: Perspectives from East and West in Late Antiquity*, Cambridge, 116–30.
Klingshirn, W. E. (1994), *Caesarius of Arles: The Making of a Christian Community in Late Antique Gaul*, Cambridge Studies in Medieval Life and Thought, 4th ser., 22, Cambridge.
Koch, M. (2012), *Ethnische Identität im Entstehungsprozess des spanischen Westgotenreiches*, Ergänzungsbände zum Reallexikon der germanischen Altertumskunde 75, Berlin.
——— (2014), "Arianism and Ethnic Identity in Sixth-Century Visigothic Spain," in G. M. Berndt and R. Steinacher, eds., *Arianism: Roman Heresy and Barbarian Creed*, Aldershot, 257–70.
Kulikowski, M. (2007), *Rome's Gothic Wars: From the Third Century to Alaric*, Cambridge.

Kurdock, A. (2007), "*Demetrias ancilla dei:* Anicia Demetrias and the Problem of the Missing Patron," in K. Cooper and J. Hillner, eds., *Religion, Dynasty and Patronage in Early Christian Rome, 300-900*, Cambridge, 190-224.
Lafferty, S. (2013), *Law and Society in the Age of Theoderic the Great: A Study of the Edictum Theoderici*, Cambridge.
Lambert, D. (1999), "The Uses of Decay: History in Salvian's *De gubernatione Dei*," *Augustinian Studies* 30.2, 115-30.
——— (2000), "The Barbarians in Salvian's *De gubernatione dei*," in S. Mitchell and G. Greatrex, eds., *Ethnicity and Culture in Late Antiquity*, London, 103-15.
Lancel, S. (1972-91), *Actes de la Conférence de Carthage en 411*, 4 vols., Sources chrétiennes 194-95, 224, 373, Paris.
——— (1989), "Le sort des évêques et des communautés donatistes après la Conférence de Carthage en 411," in C. Mayer and K. H. Chelius, eds., *Internationales Symposion über den Stand der Augustinus-Forschung*, Cassiacum 39, Res et signa 1, Würzburg, 149-67.
——— (2002a), *Histoire de la persécution vandale en Afrique*, Collection des universités de France, série latine 368, Paris.
——— (2002b), *Saint Augustine*, trans. A. Nevill, London (appeared in 1999 as *Saint Augustin*, Paris).
Le Boulluec, A. (1985), *La notion d'hérésie dans la littérature grecque, IIe-IIIe siècles*, 2 vols., Paris.
Lee, A. D. (2007), *War in Late Antiquity: A Social History*, Oxford.
——— (2013), *From Rome to Byzantium, A.D. 363-565: The Transformation of Ancient Rome*, Edinburgh.
Lenski, N. E. (1995), "The Gothic Civil War and the Date of the Gothic Conversion," *Greek, Roman and Byzantine Studies* 36, 51-87.
Leone, A. (2007), *Changing Townscapes in North Africa from Late Antiquity to the Arab Conquest*, Munera 28, Bari.
——— (2013), *The End of the Pagan City: Religion, Economy, and Urbanism in Late Antique North Africa*, Oxford.
Lepelley, C. (1979-81), *Les cités de l'Afrique romaine au Bas-Empire*, 2 vols., Paris.
——— (1998), "Le patronat épiscopal aux IVe et Ve siècles: Continuités et ruptures avec le patronat classique," in É. Rebillard and C. Sotinel, eds., *L'évêque dans la cite du IVe et Ve siècles: Image et autorité*, Collection de l'École française de Rome 248, Rome, 17-33.
——— (2010), "The Use of Secularised Latin Pagan Culture by Christians," in D. M. Gwynn and S. Bangert, eds., *Religious Diversity in Late Antiquity*, Late Antique Archaeology 6, Leiden, 477-92.
Leppin, H. (2003), *Theodosius der Grosse*, Darmstadt.
Leyser, C. (2007), "'A Wall Protecting the City': Conflict and Authority in the *Life of Fulgentius of Ruspe*," in A. Camplani and G. Filoramo, eds., *Foundations of Power and Conflicts of Authority in Late-Antique Monasticism*, Orientalia Lovaniensia analecta 157, Leuven, 175-92.
Liebeschuetz, J. H. W. G. (1990), *Barbarians and Bishops: Army, Church and State in the Age of Arcadius and Chrysostom*, Oxford.
——— (2001), *The Decline and Fall of the Roman City*, Oxford.

——— (2003), "*Gens* into *regnum*: The Vandals," in H.-W. Goetz, J. Jarnut, and W. Pohl, eds., with S. Kaschke, *Regna and gentes: The Relationship between Late Antique and Early Medieval Peoples and Kingdoms in the Transformation of the Roman World*, Transformation of the Roman World 13, Leiden, 55–83.

——— (2005), *Ambrose of Milan: Political Letters and Speeches*, Translated Texts for Historians 43, Liverpool.

Lienhard, J. T. (1999), "Florilegia," in A. Fitzgerald and J. C. Cavadini, eds., *Augustine through the Ages*, Grand Rapids, MI, 370–71.

Lim, R. (1995), *Public Disputation, Power and Social Order in Late Antiquity*, Transformation of the Classical Heritage 23, Berkeley, CA.

——— (1999), "Christian Triumph and Controversy," in G. W. Bowersock, P. R. L. Brown, and O. Grabar, *Late Antiquity: A Guide to the Postclassical World*, Cambridge, MA, 196–218.

——— (2008), "Christians, Dialogues and Patterns of Sociability in Late Antiquity," in S. Goldhill, ed., *The End of Dialogue in Antiquity*, Cambridge, 151–72.

Lizzi Testa, R. (2009), "The Late Antique Bishop: Image and Reality," in P. Rousseau, ed., *A Companion to Late Antiquity*, Chichester, 525–38.

Löhr, W. A. (2007), "Western Christianities," in A. Casiday and F. W. Norris, eds., *The Cambridge History of Christianity*, vol. 2: *Constantine to c. 600*, Cambridge, 9–51.

Lunn-Rockliffe, S. (2007), *Ambrosiaster's Political Theology*, Oxford.

Lyman, J. R. (1993), "A Topography of Heresy: Mapping the Rhetorical Creation of Arianism," in M. R. Barnes and D. H. Williams, eds., *Arianism after Arius: Essays on the Development of the Fourth Century Trinitarian Conflicts*, Edinburgh, 45–62.

——— (2000), "Ascetics and Bishops: Epiphanius on Orthodoxy," in S. Elm, É. Rebillard, and A. Romano, eds., *Orthodoxie, christianisme, histoire = Orthodoxy, Christianity, History*, Collection de l'École Française de Rome 270, Rome, 149–61.

——— (2007), "Heresiology: The Invention of 'Heresy' and 'Schism,'" in A. Casiday and F. W. Norris, eds., *The Cambridge History of Christianity*, vol. 2: *Constantine to c. 600*, Cambridge, 296–313.

——— (2008), "Arius and Arians," in S. Ashbrook Harvey and D. G. Hunter, eds., *The Oxford Handbook of Early Christian Studies*, Oxford, 237–57.

——— (2009), review of D. M. Gwynn, *The Eusebians: The Polemic of Athanasius of Alexandria and the Construction of the "Arian Controversy*," *Church History* 78, 386–87.

Maas, M. (1992), "Ethnicity, Orthodoxy and Community in Salvian of Marseilles," in J. Drinkwater and H. Elton, eds., *Fifth-Century Gaul: A Crisis of Identity?*, Cambridge, 275–84.

——— (2003a), "'Delivered from Their Ancient Customs': Christianity and the Question of Cultural Change in Early Byzantine Ethnography," in K. Mills and A. Grafton, eds., *Conversion in Late Antiquity and the Early Middle Ages: Seeing and Believing*, Rochester, NY, 152–88.

——— (2003b), *Exegesis and Empire in the Early Byzantine Mediterranean: Junillus Africanus and the Instituta regularia divinae legis*, Studien und Texte zu Antike und Christentum 17, Tübingen.

———, ed. (2005), *The Cambridge Companion to the Age of Justinian*, Cambridge.

——— (2012), "Barbarians: Problems and Approaches," in S. F. Johnson, ed., *The Oxford Handbook of Late Antiquity*, Oxford, 60–91.

Magalhaes de Oliveira, J.C. (2012), *Potestas populi: Participation populaire et action collective dans les villes de l'Afrique romaine tardive (vers 300–430 apr. J.-C.)*, Bibliothèque de l'Antiquité tardive 24, Turnhout.
Maier, G. (2005), *Amtsträger und Herrscher in der Romania Gothica: Vergleichende Untersuchungen zu den Institutionen der ostgermanischen Völkerwanderungsreiche*, Historia Einzelschriften 181, Stuttgart.
Malaspina, E. (1994–95), "L'idrovora di Unirico: Un epigramma (A. L. 387 R.^{2} = 382 Sh. B.), e il suo contesto storico-culturale," *Romanobarbarica* 13, 43–56.
Mandouze, A. (1968), *Saint Augustin: L'aventure de la raison et de la grâce*, Paris.
Mara, M.G. (1986), "Arriani, Arrius," in C. Mayer, ed., *Augustinus-Lexikon I*, Basel, 449–59.
Marec, E. (1958), *Monuments chrétiens d'Hippone: Ville épiscopale de Saint Augustin*, Paris.
Markey, T.L. (1989), "Germanic in the Mediterranean: Lombards, Vandals and Visigoths," in F.M. Clover and R.S. Humphreys, eds., *Tradition and Innovation in Late Antiquity*, Madison, WI, 51–71.
Markschies, C. (1997), "Was ist lateinische 'Neunizänismus'?: Ein Vorschlag für eine Antwort," *Zeitschrift für Antikes Christentum* 1, 73–95.
Markus, R.A. (1966), "Reflections on Religious Dissent in North Africa in the Byzantine Period," *Studies in Church History* 3, 140–49.
——— (1970), *Saeculum: History and Society in the Theology of St Augustine*, Cambridge.
——— (1979), "Country Bishops in Byzantine Africa," *Studies in Church History* 16, 1–15.
——— (1990), *The End of Ancient Christianity*, Cambridge.
——— (1997), *Gregory the Great and His World*, Cambridge.
——— (2003), "Africa and the *orbis terrarum*: The Theological Problem," in P.-Y. Fux, J.-M. Roessli, and O. Wermelinger, eds., *Augustinus Afer: Saint Augustin, africanité et universalité*, Paradosis 45/1, Fribourg, 321–27.
Marrou, H.-I. (1958), *Saint Augustin et la fin de la culture antique*, 4th ed., Paris.
Mathisen, R.W. (1989), *Ecclesiastical Factionalism and Religious Controversy in Fifth-Century Gaul*, Washington DC.
——— (1993), *Roman Aristocrats in Barbarian Gaul: Strategies for Survival in an Age of Transition*, Austin, TX.
——— (1997a), "Barbarian Bishops and the Churches 'in barbaricis gentibus' during Late Antiquity," *Speculum* 72, 664–97.
——— (1997b), "The 'Second Council of Arles' and the Spirit of Compilation and Codification in Late Roman Gaul," *Journal of Early Christian Studies* 5, 511–54.
——— (1999a), *Ruricius of Limoges and Friends: A Collection of Letters from Visigothic Gaul*, Translated Texts for Historians 30, Liverpool.
——— (1999b), "Sigisvult the Patrician, Maximinus the Arian, and Political Strategems in the Western Roman Empire c. 425–40," *Early Medieval Europe* 8, 173–96.
——— (2009), "Ricimer's Church in Rome: How an Arian Barbarian Prospered in a Nicene World," A. Cain and N.E. Lenski, eds., *The Power of Religion in Late Antiquity*, Aldershot, 307–25.
——— (2014), "Barbarian 'Arian' Clergy, Church Organization, and Church Practices," in G.M. Berndt and R. Steinacher, eds., *Arianism: Roman Heresy and Barbarian Creed*, Aldershot, 145–91.

Matthews, J. (1974), "The Letters of Symmachus," in J. W. Binns, ed., *Latin Literature of the Fourth Century*, London, 58–99.
―――― (1975), *Western Aristocracies and Imperial Court, A.D. 364–425*, Oxford.
Maxwell, J. L. (2006), *Christianization and Communication in Late Antiquity: John Chrysostom and His Congregation in Antioch*, Cambridge.
McClure, J. (1979), "Handbooks against Heresy in the West, from the Late Fourth to the Late Sixth Centuries," *Journal of Theological Studies* 30, 186–97.
McLynn, N. B. (1991), "The 'Apology' of Palladius: Nature and Purpose," *Journal of Theological Studies* 42, 52–76.
―――― (1994), *Ambrose of Milan: Church and Court in a Christian Capital*, Transformation of the Classical Heritage 22, Berkeley, CA.
―――― (1996), "From Palladius to Maximinus: Passing the Arian Torch," *Journal of Early Christian Studies* 4, 477–93.
―――― (1999), "Augustine's Roman Empire," *Augustinian Studies* 30, 29–44.
―――― (2005), "'*Genere Hispanus*': Theodosius, Spain and Nicene Orthodoxy," in K. Bowes and M. Kulikowski, eds., *Hispania in Late Antiquity*, The Medieval and Early Modern Iberian World 24, Leiden, 77–120 (repr. in McLynn [2009a], *Christian politics and religious culture in late antiquity*, Collected Studies 928, Aldershot, XII).
―――― (2007), "Little Wolf in the Big City: Ulfila and His Interpreters," in J. Drinkwater and B. Salway, eds., *Wolf Liebeschuetz Reflected: Essays Presented by Colleagues, Friends and Pupils*, BICS Supplement 91, London, 125–35.
―――― (2009a), *Christian Politics and Religious Culture in Late Antiquity*, Collected Studies 928, Aldershot.
―――― (2009b), "Pagans in a Christian Empire," in P. Rousseau, ed., *A Companion to Late Antiquity*, Chichester, 572–87.
―――― (2016), "The Conference of Carthage Reconsidered," in R. Miles, ed., *The Donatist Controversy in Context*, Translated Texts for Historians, Contexts 2, Liverpool, 220–48.
Meeder, S. (2005), "Defining Doctrine in the Carolingian Period: The Contents and Context of Cambridge, Pembroke College, MS 108," *Transactions of the Cambridge Bibliographical Society* 13.2, 133–51.
Merdinger, J. E. (1997), *Rome and the African Church in the Time of Augustine*, New Haven, CT.
Merrills, A. H. (2004a), "The Perils of Panegyric: The Lost Poem of Dracontius and Its Consequences," in Merrills, ed., *Vandals, Romans and Berbers: New Perspectives on Late Antique North Africa*, Aldershot, 145–62.
――――, ed. (2004b), *Vandals, Romans and Berbers: New Perspectives on Late Antique North Africa*, Aldershot.
―――― (2004c), "Vandals, Romans and Berbers: Understanding Late Antique North Africa," in Merrills, ed., *Vandals, Romans and Berbers: New Perspectives on Late Antique North Africa*, Aldershot, 3–28.
―――― (2009), "The Origins of 'Vandalism,'" *International Journal of the Classical Tradition* 16, 155–75.
―――― (2010), "The Secret of My Succession: Dynasty and Crisis in Vandal North Africa," *Early Medieval Europe* 18, 135–59.

——— (2011), "*Totum subuertere uoluerunt*: 'Social Martyrdom' in the *Historia persecutionis* of Victor of Vita," in C. M. Kelly, R. A. Flower, and M. S. Williams, eds., *Unclassical Traditions, Volume 2: Perspectives from East and West in Late Antiquity*, Cambridge, 102–115.
Merrills, A. H., and R. Miles (2010), *The Vandals*, Chichester.
Meslin, M. (1959), "Un témoignage arien sur les empereurs Constantin et Constance II," *Bulletin de la Société des Antiquaires de France*, 73–85.
——— (1967), *Les Ariens d'Occident, 335–430*, Patristica Sorbonensia 8, Paris.
Miles, R., ed. (1999), *Constructing Identities in Late Antiquity*, London.
——— (2005), "The *Anthologia Latina* and the Creation of Secular Space in Vandal North Africa," *Antiquité Tardive* 13, 305–20.
——— (2008), "'Let's (Not) Talk about It': Augustine and the Control of Epistolary Dialogue," in S. Goldhill, ed., *The End of Dialogue in Antiquity*, Cambridge, 135–48.
———, ed. (2016), *The Donatist Controversy in Context*, Translated Texts for Historians, Contexts 2, Liverpool.
Millar, F. (2004), "Repentant Heretics in Fifth-Century Lydia: Identity and Literacy," *Scripta Classica Israelica* 23, 111–30.
——— (2006), *A Greek Roman Empire: Power and Belief under Theodosius II (408–450)*, Sather Classical Lectures 64, Berkeley, CA.
Mitchell, S. (2007), *A History of the Later Roman Empire, AD 284–641: The Transformation of the Ancient World*, Oxford.
Modéran, Y. (1993), "La chronologie de la *Vie de Saint Fulgence de Ruspe* et ses incidences sur l'histoire de l'Afrique vandale," *Mélanges de l'École Française de Rome* 105, 135–88.
——— (1998a), "L'Afrique et la persécution vandale," in L. Pietri, ed., *Histoire du christianisme des origines à nos jours, III: Les Églises d'Orient et d'Occident (432–610)*, Paris, 247–78.
——— (1998b), "Les Églises et la *reconquista* byzantine. A. L'Afrique," in L. Pietri, ed., *Histoire du christianisme des origines à nos jours, III: Les Églises d'Orient et d'Occident (432–610)*, Paris, 699–717.
——— (2002), "L'établissement territorial des Vandales en Afrique," *Antiquité Tardive* 10, 87–122.
——— (2003), "Une guerre de religion: Les deux Églises d'Afrique à l'époque vandale," *Antiquité Tardive* 11, 21–44.
——— (2006), "La *Notitia provinciarum et civitatum Africae* et l'histoire du royaume vandale," *Antiquité Tardive* 14, 165–85.
——— (2007), "L'Afrique reconquise et les trois chapitres," in C. Chazelle and C. Cubitt, eds., *The Crisis of the oikoumene: The Three Chapters and the Failed Quest for Unity in the Sixth-Century Mediterranean*, Studies in the Early Middle Ages 14, Turnhout, 39–82.
——— (2008), "'Le plus délicat des peuples et le plus malheureux': Vandales et Maures en Afrique," in G. M. Berndt and R. Steinacher, eds., *Das Reich der Vandalen und seine (Vor-)Geschichten*, Vienna, 213–25.
——— (2014), *Les Vandales et l'empire romain*, ed. M.-Y. Perrin, Arles.
Moore, R. I. (2012), *The War on Heresy: Faith and Power in Medieval Europe*, London.
Moorhead, J. (1992a), *Theoderic in Italy*, Oxford.
——— (1992b), *Victor of Vita: The History of the Vandal Persecution*, Translated Texts for Historians 10, Liverpool.
——— (2010), "What Names Did the Anti-Nicenes Use for *Catholics* and *Arians*?," *Augustinianum* 50, 423–41.

Moss, C. (2016), "Martyr Veneration in Late Antique North Africa," in R. Miles, ed., *The Donatist Controversy in Context*, Translated Texts for Historians, Contexts 2, Liverpool, 54–69.

Moussy, C. (1985), *Dracontius: Œuvres*, vol. 1: *Louanges de Dieu, livres I–II*, Paris.

Muhlberger, S. (1990), *The Fifth-Century Chroniclers: Prosper, Hydatius and the Gallic Chronicler of 452*, ARCA Classical and Medieval Texts, Papers and Monographs 27, Liverpool.

Mullan, A. (2011), "Latin and Other Languages: Societal and Individual Bilingualism," in J. Clackson, ed., *A Companion to the Latin Language*, Chichester, 527–48.

Müller, C. (2010), "Das Phänomen des 'lateinischen Athanasius,'" in A. Von Stockhausen and H. C. Brennecke, eds., *Von Arius zum Athanasianum: Studien zur Edition der "Athanasius Werke,"* Texte und Untersuchungen zur Geschichte der altchristlichen Literatur, Archiv für die Ausgabe der griechischen christlichen Schriftsteller der ersten Jahrhunderte 164, Berlin, 3–42.

—— (2012), "From Athanasius to 'Athanasius': Usurping a 'Nicene Hero,' or: The Making-Of of the '*Athanasian Creed*,'" in J. Ulrich, A.-C. Jacobsen, and D. Brakke, eds., *Invention, Rewriting, Usurpation: Discursive Fights over Religious Traditions in Antiquity*, Early Christianity in the Context of Antiquity 11, Frankfurt am Main, 19–40.

Müller, H. (2008), "Einleitung," in H. Müller, D. Weber, and C. Weidmann, eds., *Collatio Augustini cum Pascentio: Einleitung, Text, Übersetzung*, Österreichische Akademie der Wissenschaften, philosophisch-historische Klasse, Sitzungsberichte 779, Veröffentlichungen der Kommission für die Herausgabe des Corpus der Lateinischen Kirchenväter 24, Vienna, 24–42.

—— (2012), "Preacher: Augustine and His Congregation," in M. Vessey, ed., *A Companion to Augustine*, Chichester, 297–309.

Müller, H., D. Weber, and C. Weidmann, eds. (2008), *Collatio Augustini cum Pascentio: Einleitung, Text, Übersetzung*, Österreichische Akademie der Wissenschaften, philosophisch-historische Klasse, Sitzungsberichte 779, Veröffentlichungen der Kommission für die Herausgabe des Corpus der Lateinischen Kirchenväter 24, Vienna.

Munier, C. (1974), *Concilia Africae, a. 345–a. 525*, CCSL 149, Turnhout.

Nicolaye, C. (2011), "Episcopal Elections in 5th-century Vandal North Africa," in J. Leemans, P. Van Nuffelen, S. W. J. Keogh, and C. Nicolaye, eds., *Episcopal Elections in Late Antiquity*, Arbeiten zur Kirchengeschichte 119, Boston, 477–98.

Noble, T. F. X. (1993), "Theoderic the Great and the Papacy," in O. Capitani, ed., *Teodorico il Grande e i Goti d'Italia*, vol. 1, Spoleto, 395–423.

—— (2009), *Images, Iconoclasm and the Carolingians*, Philadelphia.

O'Donnell, J. J. (2006), *Augustine: A New Biography*, New York.

Olson, L., and K. Kerby-Fulton, eds. (2005), *Voices in Dialogue: Reading Women in the Middle Ages*, Notre Dame, IN.

Overbeck, M. (1973), *Untersuchungen zum Afrikanischen Senatsadel in der Spätantike*, Frankfurter althistorische Studien 7, Kallmünz.

Papadakis, A. (1991), "*Endemousa synodos*," in A. P. Kazhdan, ed., *The Oxford Dictionary of Byzantium*, Oxford, 697.

Papadoyannakis, Y. (2006), "Instruction by Question and Answer: The Case of Late Antique and Byzantine *erotapokriseis*," in S. F. Johnson, ed., *Greek Literature in Late Antiquity: Dynamism, Didacticism, Classicism*, Aldershot, 91–105.

——— (2008), "Defining Orthodoxy in Pseudo-Justin's 'Quaestiones et responsiones ad orthodoxos,'" in E. Iricinschi and H. M. Zellentin, eds., *Heresy and Identity in Late Antiquity*, Texte und Studien zum antiken Judentum 119, Tübingen, 115–27.

——— (2013), "Didacticism, Exegesis and Polemics in Pseudo-Kaisarios' *erotapokriseis*," in M.-P. Bussières, ed., *La littérature des questions et réponses dans l'antiquité profane et chrétienne: De l'enseignement à l'exégèse*, Turnhout, 271–89.

Parsons, J. K. (1994), "The African Catholic Church under the Vandals, 429–533," PhD diss., King's College, London.

Parvis, S. (2006), *Marcellus of Ancyra and the Lost Years of the Arian Controversy, 325–345*, Oxford.

Patout Burns, J. (1993), "On Rebaptism: Social Organisation in the Third Century Church," *Journal of Early Christian Studies* 1, 367–403.

Patout Burns, J., and R. M. Jensen (2014), *Christianity in Roman Africa: The Development of Its Practices and Beliefs*, Grand Rapids, MI.

Pegg, M. (2008), *A Most Holy War: The Albigensian Crusade and the Battle for Christendom*, Oxford.

Perrin, M.-Y. (2010), "The Limits of the Heresiological Ethos in Late Antiquity," in D. M. Gwynn and S. Bangert, eds., *Religious Diversity in Late Antiquity*, Late Antique Archaeology 6, Leiden, 201–27.

Petri, S. (2003), *Vigilio di Tapso: Contro Eutiche*, Brescia.

Pietri, L., ed. (1998), *Histoire du christianisme des origines à nos jours, III: Les Églises d'Orient et d'Occident (432–610)*, Paris.

Piras, A., ed. (2010), *Lingua et ingenium: Studi su Fulgenzio di Ruspe e il suo contesto*, Studi e ricerche di cultura religiosa, nuova serie 7, Cagliari.

Pohl, W. (1998a), "Introduction: Strategies of Distinction," in Pohl and H. Reimitz, eds., *Strategies of Distinction: The Construction of Ethnic Communities, 300–800*, Transformation of the Roman World 2, Leiden, 1–15.

——— (1998b), "Telling the Difference: Signs of Ethnic Identity," in Pohl and H. Reimitz, eds., *Strategies of Distinction: The Construction of Ethnic Communities, 300–800*, Transformation of the Roman World 2, Leiden, 17–69.

——— (2002), "Ethnicity, Theory, and Tradition: A Response," in A. Gillett, ed., *On Barbarian Identity: Critical Approaches to Ethnicity in the Early Middle Ages*, Studies in the Early Middle Ages 4, Turnhout, 221–39.

——— (2005), "Aux origines d'une Europe ethnique: Transformations d'identités entre Antiquité et Moyen Âge," *Annales: Histoire, Sciences Sociales* 60, 183–208.

——— (2013a), "Christian and Barbarian Identities in the Early Medieval West: Introduction," in Pohl and G. Heydemann, eds., *Post-Roman Transitions: Christian and Barbarian Identities in the Early Medieval West*, Cultural Encounters in Late Antiquity and the Middle Ages 14, Turnhout, 1–46.

——— (2013b), "Strategies of Identification: A Methodological Profile," in Pohl and G. Heydemann, eds., *Strategies of Identification: Ethnicity and Religion in Early Medieval Europe*, Cultural Encounters in Late Antiquity and the Middle Ages 13, Turnhout, 1–64.

——— (2014), "Romanness: A Multiple Identity and Its Changes," *Early Medieval Europe* 22, 406–18.

Pohl, W., C. Gantner, and R. Payne, eds. (2012), *Visions of Community in the Post-Roman World: The West, Byzantium and the Islamic World, 300–1100*, Farnham.
Pohl, W., and G. Heydemann, eds. (2013a), *Post-Roman Transitions: Christian and Barbarian Identities in the Early Medieval West*, Cultural Encounters in Late Antiquity and the Middle Ages 14, Turnhout.
———, eds. (2013b), *Strategies of Identification: Ethnicity and Religion in Early Medieval Europe*, Cultural Encounters in Late Antiquity and the Middle Ages 13, Turnhout.
Pohl, W., and H. Reimitz, eds. (1998), *Strategies of Distinction: The Construction of Ethnic Communities, 300–800*, Transformation of the Roman World 2, Leiden.
Poinssot, L. (1926), "Siméon, évêque de Furnos Majus," *Comptes Rendus de l'Académie des Inscriptions et Belles Lettres* 70, 304–7.
Pottier, B. (2015), "Les donatistes, l'arianisme et le royaume vandale," in É. Wolff, ed., *Littérature, politique et religion en Afrique vandale*, Collection des études Augustiniennes, série antiquité 200, Turnhout, 127–36.
Prévot, F. (1985), *Recherches archéologiques franco-tunisiennes à Mactar*, vol. 5: *Les inscriptions chrétiennes*, Collection de l'École française de Rome 34, Rome.
Price, R. (2012), review of A. M. Schor, *Theodoret's People: Social Networks and Religious Conflict in Late Roman Syria*, *Church History* 81, 662–64.
Price, R., and M. Gaddis (2005), *The Acts of the Council of Chalcedon*, 3 vols., Translated Texts for Historians 45, Liverpool.
Rajak, T. (1999), "Talking at Trypho: Christian Apologetic as Anti-Judaism in Justin's *Dialogue with Trypho the Jew*," in M. J. Edwards, M. D. Goodman, and S. R. F. Price, eds., with C. C. Rowland, *Apologetics in the Roman Empire: Pagans, Jews, and Christians*, Oxford, 59–80.
Ramelli, I. L. E. (2012), "The *Dialogue of Adamantius*: A Document of Origen's Thought? (Part One)," *Studia Patristica* 52, 71–98.
——— (2013), "The *Dialogue of Adamantius*: A Document of Origen's Thought? (Part Two)," *Studia Patristica* 56, 227–73.
Rapp, C. (2000), "The Elite Status of Bishops in Late Antiquity in Ecclesiastical, Spiritual, and Social Contexts," *Arethusa* 33, 379–99.
——— (2005), *Holy Bishops in Late Antiquity: The Nature of Christian Leadership in an Age of Transition*, Transformation of the Classical Heritage 37, Berkeley, CA.
——— (2010), "Old Testament Models for Emperors in Early Byzantium," in P. Magdalino and R. Nelson, eds., *The Old Testament in Byzantium*, Washington DC, 175–97.
Raynal, D. (2005), *Archéologie et histoire de l'Église d'Afrique: Uppenna*, 2 vols., Toulouse.
Rebillard, É. (2012a), *Christians and Their Many Identities in Late Antiquity, North Africa, 200–450 CE*, Ithaca, NY.
——— (2012b), "Religious Sociology: Being Christian in the Time of Augustine," in M. Vessey, ed., *A Companion to Augustine*, Chichester, 40–53.
Reichert, H. (2008), "Die Sprache der Wandalen in Afrika und 'auch Römer dürfen *froia arme* für *domine miserere* sagen,'" in H. Müller, D. Weber, and C. Weidmann, eds., *Collatio Augustini cum Pascentio: Einleitung, Text, Übersetzung*, Österreichische Akademie der Wissenschaften, philosophisch-historische Klasse, Sitzungsberichte 779, Veröffentlichungen der Kommission für die Herausgabe des Corpus der Lateinischen Kirchenväter 24, Vienna, 145–72.

——— (2009), "Sprache und Namen der Wandalen in Afrika," in A. Greule and M. Springer, eds., *Namen des Frühmittelalters als sprachliche Zeugnisse und als Geschichtsquellen*, Ergänzungsbände zum Reallexikon der germanischen Altertumskunde 66, Berlin, 43–120.
Reimitz, H. (2014), "The Historian as Cultural Broker in the Late and Post-Roman West," in A. Fischer and I. Wood, eds., *Western Perspectives on the Mediterranean: Cultural Transfer in Late Antiquity and the Early Middle Ages, 400–800 ad*, London, 41–54.
——— (2015), *History, Frankish Identity and the Framing of Western Ethnicity, 550–850*, Cambridge Studies in Medieval Life and Thought, 4th ser., 101, Cambridge.
Richard, M. (2011), "Dyophysite Florilegia of the 5th and 6th Centuries CE," in Av. Cameron and R. Hoyland, eds., *Doctrine and Debate in the East Christian World, 300–1500*, The Worlds of Eastern Christianity 12, Farnham, 321–45.
Riché, P. (1976), *Education and Culture in the Barbarian West from the Sixth through Eighth Century*, trans. J.J. Contreni, Columbia, SC (appeared in 1962 as *Éducation et culture dans l'Occident barbare, VIe–VIIIe siècles*, 3rd ed., Patristica Sorbonensia 4, Paris).
Robinson, P. (2004), "Dead Boethius: Sixth-Century Accounts of a Future Martyr," *Viator* 35, 1–19.
Rota, S. (2001), "Teoderico il Grande fra *Graecia* e *Ausonia*: La rappresentazione del re ostrogotico nel *Panegyricus* di Ennodio," *Mélanges de l'École Française de Rome: Moyen Age* 113, 203–43.
Rougé, J., and R. Delmaire (2005), *Les lois religieuses des empereurs romains de Constantin à Théodose II (312–438)*, vol. 1: *Code Théodosien, livre XVI*, Sources chrétiennes 497, Paris.
Rousseau, P. (1994), *Basil of Caesarea*, Transformation of the Classical Heritage 20, Berkeley, CA.
———, ed. (2009), *A Companion to Late Antiquity*, Chichester.
Saitta, B. (1986), "*Religionem imperare non possumus*: Motivi e momenti della politica di Teodorico il Grande," *Quaderni Catanesi di studi classici e medievali* 8, 63–88.
——— (1999), "The Ostrogoths in Italy," *POLIS: Revista de ideas y formas políticas de la Antigüedad Clásica* 11, 197–216.
Salzman, M.R. (2002), *The Making of a Christian Aristocracy: Social and Religious Change in the Western Roman Empire*, Cambridge, MA.
Sandwell, I. (2007), *Religious Identity in Late Antiquity: Greeks, Jews and Christians in Antioch*, Cambridge.
Saumagne, C. (1962), "La paix vandale," *Les Cahiers de Tunisie* (= *Mélanges offerts à Ch. Saumagne*) 10, 417–25.
Saylor Rodgers, B. (1986), "Divine Insinuation in the *Panegyrici Latini*," *Historia* 35, 69–104.
Schäferdiek, K. (1978), "Germanenmission," *Reallexikon für Antike und Christentum* 10, 492–548.
——— (2007), "Germanic and Celtic Christianities," in A. Casiday and F.W. Norris, eds., *The Cambridge History of Christianity*, vol. 2: *Constantine to c. 600*, Cambridge, 52–69.
Schanz, M., C. Hosius, and G. Krüger (1920), *Geschichte der römischen Litteratur, IV: Die römische Litteratur von Constantin bis zum Gesetzgebungswerk Justinians, 2. Hälfte: Die Litteratur des 5. und 6. Jahrhunderts*, Munich.
Schmidt, L. (1942), *Geschichte der Wandalen*, 2nd ed., Munich.

Schmidt, P. L. (1977), "Zur Typologie und Literarisierung des frühchristlichen lateinischen Dialogs," in *Christianisme et formes littéraires de l'Antiquité tardive en Occident*, Fondation Hardt pour l'étude de l'Antiquité classique: Entretiens 23, Geneva, 101–90.

Schor, A. M. (2011), *Theodoret's People: Social Networks and Religious Conflict in Late Roman Syria*, Transformation of the Classical Heritage 48, Berkeley, CA.

Schwank, B. (1961a), "Pseudo-Vigilii Thapsensis opus contra Varimadum," in *Florilegia Biblica Africana saec. V, CCSL* 90, Turnhout, 1–134.

——— (1961b), "Zur Neuausgabe von 'Contra Varimadum' nach dem Codex Paris B. N. Lat. 12217 in *Corpus Christianorum Series Latina XC*," *Sacris Erudiri* 12, 112–96.

Schwartz, E., ed. (1934), *Publizistische Sammlungen zum acacianischen Schisma*, Abhandlungen (Bayerische Akademie der Wissenschaften. Philosophisch-Historische Klasse), n. f. 10, Munich.

Sears, G. (2007), *Late Roman African Urbanism: Continuity and Transformation in the City*, BAR International Series 1693, Oxford.

Shanzer, D. R. (2004), "Intentions and Audiences: History, Hagiography, Martyrdom and Confession in Victor of Vita's *Historia persecutionis*," in A. H. Merrills, ed., *Vandals, Romans and Berbers: New Perspectives on Late Antique North Africa*, Aldershot, 271–90.

——— (2009), "*Haec quibus uteris verba*: The Bible and Boethius' Christianity," in A. Cain and N. E. Lenski, eds., *The Power of Religion in Late Antiquity*, Aldershot, 57–78.

Shanzer, D. R., and I. Wood (2002), *Avitus of Vienne: Letters and Selected Prose*, Translated Texts for Historians 38, Liverpool.

Shaw, B. D. (1992), "African Christianity: Disputes, Definitions and 'Donatists,'" in M. R. Greenshields and T. A. Robinson, eds., *Orthodoxy and Heresy in Religious Movements: Discipline and Dissent*, Centre for the Study of North American Religion Series 2, Lampeter, Wales, 5–34 (repr. in Shaw [1995], *Rulers, Nomads and Christians in Roman North Africa*, Collected Studies 497, Aldershot, XI).

——— (1995), *Rulers, Nomads and Christians in Roman North Africa*, Collected Studies 497, Aldershot.

——— (2003), "Judicial Nightmares and Christian Memory," *Journal of Early Christian Studies* 11, 533–63.

——— (2011), *Sacred Violence: African Christians and Sectarian Hatred in the Age of Augustine*, Cambridge.

——— (2015), "Augustine and Men of Imperial Power," *Journal of Late Antiquity* 8, 32–61.

Sieben, H.-J. (2006), "Augustins Auseinandersetzung mit dem Arianismus außerhalb seiner explizit antiarianischen Schriften," *Theologie und Philosophie* 81, 181–212.

Simonetti, M. (1956), *Pseudoathanasii De trinitate libri X–XII*, Bologna.

——— (1978), "Letteratura antimonofisita d'Occidente," *Augustinianum* 18, 487–532.

——— (1986), *La produzione letteraria latina fra romani e barbari (sec. V–VIII)*, Sussidi patristici 3, Rome.

Simons, R. (2005), *Dracontius und der Mythos: Christliche Weltsicht und pagane Kultur in der ausgehenden Spätantike*, Beiträge zur Altertumskunde 186, Leipzig.

Sizgorich, T. (2009), *Violence and Belief in Late Antiquity: Militant Devotion in Christianity and Islam*, Philadelphia.

Slusser, M. (1993), "Traditional Views of Late Arianism," in M. R. Barnes and D. H. Williams, eds., *Arianism after Arius: Essays on the Development of the Fourth Century Trinitarian Conflicts*, Edinburgh, 3–30.
Snee, R. (1998), "Gregory Nazianzen's Anastasia Church: Arianism, the Goths, and Hagiography," *Dumbarton Oaks Papers* 52, 157–86.
Sotinel, C. (1992), "Autorité pontificale et pouvoir impérial sous le règne de Justinien: Le pape Vigile," *Mélanges de l'École française de Rome* 104, 439–63 (repr. in English in Sotinel [2010], *Church and Society in Late Antique Italy and Beyond*, Collected Studies 948, Aldershot, I).
—— (2005), "Emperors and Popes in the Sixth Century: The Western View," in M. Maas, ed., *The Cambridge Companion to the Age of Justinian*, Cambridge, 267–90.
—— (2010), *Church and Society in Late Antique Italy and Beyond*, Collected Studies 948, Aldershot.
—— (2012), "Augustine's Information Circuits," in M. Vessey, ed., *A Companion to Augustine*, Chichester, 125–37.
Spielvogel, J. (2005), "Arianische Vandalen, katholische Römer: Die reichspolitische und kulturelle Dimension des christlichen Glaubenskonflikts im spätantiken Nordafrika," *Klio* 87, 201–22.
Stang, C. M. (2012), *Apophasis and Pseudonymity in Dionysius the Areopagite: "No Longer I,"* Oxford.
Steinacher, R. (2001), "Der *Laterculus regnum Vandalorum et Alanorum*: Eine afrikanische Ergaenzung der Chronik Prosper Tiros aus dem 6. Jahrhundert," MA diss., Institut für Österreichische Geschichtsforschung.
—— (2004), "The So-Called *Laterculus regum Vandalorum et Alanorum*: A Sixth-Century African Addition to Prosper Tiro's Chronicle?," in A. H. Merrills, ed., *Vandals, Romans and Berbers: New Perspectives on Late Antique North Africa*, Aldershot, 163–80.
—— (2008), "Gruppen und Identitäten. Gedanken zur Bezeichnung 'vandalisch,'" in G. M. Berndt and R. Steinacher, eds., *Das Reich der Vandalen und seine (Vor-)Geschichten*, Vienna, 243–60.
—— (2011), "Der vandalische Königshof als Ort der öffentlichen religiösen Auseinandersetzung," in M. Becher and A. Plassmann, eds., *Streit am Hof im frühen Mittelalter*, Super alta perennis, Studien zur Wirkung der klassischen Antike 11, Bonn, 45–73.
—— (2013), "Who Is the Barbarian? Considerations on the Vandal Royal Title," in W. Pohl and G. Heydemann, eds., *Post-Roman Transitions: Christian and Barbarian Identities in the Early Medieval West*, Cultural Encounters in Late Antiquity and the Middle Ages 14, Turnhout, 437–85.
—— (2016), *Die Vandalen: Aufstieg und Fall eines Barbarenreichs*, Stuttgart.
Steinhauser, K. B., ed., with H. Müller and D. Weber (2006), *Anonymi in Iob commentarius*, CSEL 96, Vienna.
Stevens, S. T. (1982), "The Circle of Bishop Fulgentius," *Traditio* 38, 327–41.
—— (1993), *Bir el Knissia at Carthage: A Rediscovered Cemetery Church: Report no. 1*, Journal of Roman Archaeology Supplementary Series 7, Ann Arbor, MI.
—— (2007), "Of Martyrs and Mosaics: Two Early Christian Churches at Sidi Jdidi (Aradi), and Henchir Chigarnia (Uppenna)," *Journal of Roman Archaeology* 20, 689–96.

——— (2012), "North Africa—and the Vandals—Made Manifest," *Journal of Roman Archaeology* 25, 950–53.

Stocking, R. L. (2000), *Bishops, Councils, and Consensus in the Visigothic Kingdom, 589–633*, Ann Arbor, MI.

Stutz, E. (1984), "Codices Gotici," *Reallexikon der germanischen Altertumskunde* 5, 52–60.

Sumruld, W. A. (1994), *Augustine and the Arians: The Bishop of Hippo's Encounters with Ulfilan Arianism*, Selinsgrove, PA.

Swift, E. (2006), "Constructing Roman Identities in Late Antiquity? Material Culture on the Western Frontier," in W. Bowden, A. Gutteridge, and C. Machado, eds., *Social and Political Life in Late Antiquity*, Late Antique Archaeology 3.1, Leiden, 97–111.

Tedesco, P. (2012), "*Sortes Vandalorum*: Forme di insediamento nell'Africa post-Romana," in P. Porena and Y. Rivière, eds., *Expropriations et confiscations dans les royaumes barbares: Une approche régionale*, Collection de l'École française de Rome 470, Rome, 157–224.

Teitler, H. C. (1985), *Notarii and exceptores: An Inquiry into Role and Significance of Shorthand Writers in the Imperial and Ecclesiastical Bureaucracy of the Roman Empire: From the Early Principate to c. 450 A.D.*, Dutch Monographs on Ancient History and Archaeology 1, Amsterdam.

Teske, R. (2004), "Augustine of Hippo and the *quaestiones et responsiones* Literature," in A. Volgers and C. Zamagni, eds., *Erotapokriseis: Early Christian Question-and-Answer Literature in Context*, Contributions to Biblical Exegesis and Theology 37, Leuven, 127–44.

Thompson, E. A. (1966), *The Visigoths in the Time of Ulfila*, Oxford.

——— (1969), *The Goths in Spain*, Oxford.

Tiefenbach, H. (1991), "Das wandalische *Domine miserere*," *Historische Sprachforschung* 104, 251–68.

Tilley, M. A. (1991), "Dilatory Donatists or Procrastinating Catholics: The Trial at the Conference of Carthage," *Church History* 60, 7–19.

——— (1997), *The Bible in Christian North Africa: The Donatist World*, Minneapolis.

Tjäder, J.-O. (1954–82), *Die nichtliterarischen lateinischen Papyri Italiens aus der Zeit 445–700*, 3 vols., Skrifter utgivna av Svenska institutet i Rom. 40 19.1–3, Stockholm.

Tomlin, R. (1998), "Christianity and the Late Roman Army," in S. N. C. Lieu and D. Montserrat, eds., *Constantine: History, Historiography and Legend*, London, 21–51.

Trout, D. E. (1999), *Paulinus of Nola: Life, Letters, and Poems*, Transformation of the Classical Heritage 27, Berkeley, CA.

Ulrich, J. (1997), "Nicaea and the West," *Vigiliae Christianae* 51, 10–24.

Ulrich, J., A.-C. Jacobsen, and D. Brakke, eds. (2012), *Invention, Rewriting, Usurpation: Discursive Fights over Religious Traditions in Antiquity*, Early Christianity in the Context of Antiquity 11, Frankfurt am Main.

Uthemann, K.-H. (1998), "Forms of Communication in the Homilies of Severian of Gabala: A Contribution to the Reception of the Diatribe as a Method of Exposition," in M. B. Cunningham and P. Allen, eds., *Preacher and Audience: Studies in Early Christian and Byzantine Homiletics*, A New History of the Sermon 1, Leiden, 139–77.

Vaggione, R. P. (2000), *Eunomius of Cyzicus and the Nicene Revolution*, Oxford.

Van Dam, R. (1993), *Saints and Their Miracles in Late Antique Gaul*, Princeton, NJ.

Van der Lof, L. J. (1973), "Der fanatische Arianismus der Wandalen," *Zeitschrift für die Neutestamentliche Wissenschaft und die Kunde der Älteren Kirche* 64, 146–51.

Van Nuffelen, P. (2010), "Theology versus Genre? The Universalism of Christian Historiography in Late Antiquity," in P. Liddel and A. Fear, eds., *Historiae mundi: Studies in Universal History*, London, 162–75.

——— (2012), *Orosius and the Rhetoric of History*, Oxford.

Van Rompay, L. (2005), "Society and Community in the Christian East," in M. Maas, ed., *The Cambridge Companion to the Age of Justinian*, Cambridge, 239–66.

Van Slyke, D. (2003), *Quodvultdeus of Carthage: The Apocalyptic Theology of a Roman African in Exile*, Early Christian Studies 5, Strathfield, New South Wales.

Van Waarden, J. A. (2010), *Writing to Survive: A Commentary on Sidonius Apollinaris, Letters, Book 7*, vol. 1: *The Episcopal Letters 1–11*, Late Antique History and Religion 2, Leuven.

Velazquez, I. (2003), "*Pro patriae gentisque Gothorum statu* (4th Council of Toledo, Canon 75, a. 633)," in H.-W. Goetz, J. Jarnut, and W. Pohl, eds., with S. Kaschke, *Regna and gentes: The Relationship between Late Antique and Early Medieval Peoples and Kingdoms in the Transformation of the Roman World*, Transformation of the Roman World 13, Leiden, 161–217.

Vessey, M. (2005), "Response to Catherine Conybeare: Women of Letters?," in L. Olson and K. Kerby-Fulton, eds., *Voices in Dialogue: Reading Women in the Middle Ages*, Notre Dame, IN, 73–96.

———, ed. (2012), *A Companion to Augustine*, Chichester.

Volgers, A. (2004), "Ambrosiaster: Persuasive Powers in Progress," in Volgers and C. Zamagni, eds., *Erotapokriseis: Early Christian Question-and-Answer Literature in Context*, Contributions to Biblical Exegesis and Theology 37, Leuven, 99–125.

Volgers, A., and C. Zamagni, eds. (2004), *Erotapokriseis: Early Christian Question-and-Answer Literature in Context*, Contributions to Biblical Exegesis and Theology 37, Leuven.

Von Rummel, P. (2002), "*Habitus Vandalorum?* Zur Frage nach einer gruppen-spezifischen Kleidung der Vandalen in Nordafrika," *Antiquité Tardive* 10, 131–41.

——— (2007), *Habitus barbarus: Kleidung und Repräsentation spätantiker Eliten im 4. und 5. Jahrhundert*, Ergänzungsbände zum Reallexikon der Germanischen Altertumskunde 55, Berlin.

——— (2008), "Where Have All the Vandals Gone? Migration, Ansiedlung und Identität der Vandalen im Spiegel archäologischer Quellen aus Nordafrika," in G. M. Berndt and R. Steinacher, eds., *Das Reich der Vandalen und seine (Vor-)Geschichten*, Vienna, 151–82.

——— (2011), "Settlement and Taxes: The Vandals in North Africa," in P. C. Diáz and I. M. Viso, eds., *Between Taxation and Rent: Fiscal Problems from Late Antiquity to Early Middle Ages*, Bari, 23–37.

——— (2016), "The Transformation of Ancient Land- and Cityscapes in Early Medieval North Africa," in J. P. Conant and S. T. Stevens, eds., *North Africa under Byzantium and Early Islam*, Washington DC, 105–17.

Voss, B. R. (1970), *Der Dialog in der frühchristlichen Literatur*, Studia et testimonia antiqua 9, Munich.

Vössing, K. (2008), "'Barbaren' und Katholiken: Die Fiktion der Collatio sancti Augustini cum Pascentio Arriano und die Parteien des vandalischen Kirchenkampfes," in H. Müller, D. Weber, and C. Weidmann, eds., *Collatio Augustini cum Pascentio: Einleitung, Text, Übersetzung*, Österreichische Akademie der Wissenschaften, philosophisch-historische Klasse, Sitzungsberichte 779, Veröffentlichungen der Kommission für die Herausgabe des Corpus der Lateinischen Kirchenväter 24, Vienna, 173–206.

―――― (2011), *Victor von Vita: Kirchenkampf und Verfolgung unter den Vandalen in Africa*, Texte zur Forschung 96, Darmstadt.

―――― (2014), *Das Königreich der Vandalen: Geiserichs Herrschaft und das Imperium Romanum*, Darmstadt.

Ward-Perkins, B. (2005), *The Fall of Rome and the End of Civilization*, Oxford.

―――― (2010), "Where Is the Archaeology and Iconography of Germanic Arianism?," in D.M. Gwynn and S. Bangert, eds., *Religious Diversity in Late Antiquity*, Late Antique Archaeology 6, Leiden, 265–89.

Watts, E. (2010), *Riot in Alexandria: Tradition and Group Dynamics in Late Antique Pagan and Christian Communities*, Transformation of the Classical Heritage 46, Berkeley, CA.

―――― (2013), "Theodosius II and His Legacy in Anti-Chalcedonian Communal Memory," in C.M. Kelly, ed., *Theodosius II: Rethinking the Roman Empire in Late Antiquity*, Cambridge, 269–84.

Weber, D. (2008), "Einleitung," in H. Müller, D. Weber, and C. Weidmann, eds., *Collatio Augustini cum Pascentio: Einleitung, Text, Übersetzung*, Österreichische Akademie der Wissenschaften, philosophisch-historische Klasse, Sitzungsberichte 779, Veröffentlichungen der Kommission für die Herausgabe des Corpus der Lateinischen Kirchenväter 24, Vienna, 7–24.

Weidmann, C. (2008), "Einleitung," in H. Müller, D. Weber, and C. Weidmann, eds., *Collatio Augustini cum Pascentio: Einleitung, Text, Übersetzung*, Österreichische Akademie der Wissenschaften, philosophisch-historische Klasse, Sitzungsberichte 779, Veröffentlichungen der Kommission für die Herausgabe des Corpus der Lateinischen Kirchenväter 24, Vienna, 42–64.

Weiskotten, H. (1919), "Sancti Augustini vita scripta a Possidio episcopo," PhD diss., Princeton University.

Wessel, S. (2004), *Cyril of Alexandria and the Nestorian Controversy: The Making of a Saint and a Heretic*, Oxford.

―――― (2012), "Theological Argumentation: The Case of Forgery," in S.F. Johnson, ed., *The Oxford Handbook of Late Antiquity*, Oxford, 916–34.

Westra, L.H. (1997), "Enigma Variations in Latin Patristics: Fourteen Anonymous Sermons *de symbolo* and the Original Form of the Apostles' Creed," *Studia Patristica* 29, 414–20.

―――― (2002), *The Apostles' Creed: Origin, History and Some Early Commentaries*, Instrumenta patristica et mediaevalia 43, Turnhout.

Whelan, R.E. (2014a), "African Controversy: The Inheritance of the Donatist Schism in Vandal Africa," *Journal of Ecclesiastical History* 65, 504–21.

―――― (2014b), "Arianism in Africa," in G.M. Berndt and R. Steinacher, eds., *Arianism: Roman Heresy and Barbarian Creed*, Aldershot, 239–55.

―――― (2017), "Surrogate Fathers: Imaginary Dialogue and Patristic Culture in Late Antiquity," *Early Medieval Europe* 25, 19–37.

―――― (forthcoming), "Ethnicity, Christianity, and Groups: Homoian Christians in Ostrogothic Italy and Visigothic Spain."

Wickham, C. (2005), *Framing the Early Middle Ages: Europe and the Mediterranean 400–800*, Oxford.

Wiles, M. (1993), "Attitudes to Arius in the Arian Controversy," in M. R. Barnes and D. H. Williams, eds., *Arianism after Arius: Essays on the Development of the Fourth Century Trinitarian Conflicts*, Edinburgh, 31–43.

——— (1996), *Archetypal Heresy: Arianism through the Centuries*, Oxford.

Williams, D. H. (1995), *Ambrose of Milan and the End of the Arian-Nicene Conflicts*, Oxford.

Williams, H. (2005), "Review Article: Rethinking Early Medieval Mortuary Archaeology," *Early Medieval Europe* 13, 195–217.

Williams, M. S. (2008), *Authorised Lives in Early Christian Biography: Between Eusebius and Augustine*, Cambridge.

——— (2011), "'Beloved Lord and Honourable Brother': The Negotiation of Status in Augustine, *Letter 23*," in C. M. Kelly, R. A. Flower, and M. S. Williams, eds., *Unclassical Traditions, Volume 2: Perspectives from East and West in Late Antiquity*, Cambridge, 88–101.

——— (2017), *The Politics of Heresy in Ambrose of Milan: Community and Consensus in Late Antique Christianity*, Cambridge.

Williams, R. D. (2001), *Arius: Heresy and Tradition*, 2nd ed., London.

Wolff, É. (1998), "Dracontius revisité: Retour sur quelques problèmes de sa vie et de son œuvre," in B. Bureau and C. Nicolas, eds., *Moussyllanea: Mélanges de linguistique et de littérature anciennes offerts à Claude Moussy*, Bibliothèque d'études classiques 15, Louvain, 379–86.

——— (2004), "*Poeta inclusus*: Le cas de Dracontius," in C. Bertrand-Dagenbach, A. Chauvot, J.-M. Salamito, and D. Vaillancourt, eds., *Carcer II: Prison et privation de liberté dans l'empire romain et l'Occident mediéval*, Paris, 123–28.

———, ed. (2015), *Littérature, politique et religion en Afrique vandale*, Collection des études Augustiniennes, série antiquité 200, Turnhout.

Wolfram, H. (1988), *History of the Goths*, trans. T. J. Dunlap, Berkeley, CA (appeared in 1980 as *Geschichte der Goten: Von der Anfängen bis zur Mitte des sechsten Jahrhunderts: Entwurf einer historischen Ethnographie*, 2nd ed., Munich).

Wood, I. (1985), "Gregory of Tours and Clovis," *Revue belge de philologie et d'histoire* 63, 249–72.

——— (1994), *The Merovingian Kingdoms, 450–751*, London.

——— (1999), "Social Relations in the Visigothic Kingdom from the Fifth to the Seventh Century: The Example of Mérida," in P. J. Heather, ed., *The Visigoths from the Migration Period to the Seventh Century: An Ethnographic Perspective*, Woodbridge, 191–223.

——— (2004), "The Latin Culture of Gundobad and Sigismund," in D. Hägermann, W. Haubrichs, and J. Jarnut, eds., *Akkulturation: Probleme einer germanisch-romanischen Kultursynthese in Spätantike und frühem Mittelalter*, Ergänzungsbände zum Reallexikon der germanischen Altertumskunde 41, Berlin, 367–80.

——— (2012), "Arians, Catholics, and Vouillé," in R. W. Mathisen and D. R. Shanzer, eds., *The Battle of Vouillé, 507 C.E.: Where France Began*, Millennium Studies in the Culture and History of the First Millennium C.E. 37, Berlin, 139–65.

——— (2014), "The Burgundians and Byzantium," in A. Fischer and Wood, eds., *Western Perspectives on the Mediterranean: Cultural Transfer in Late Antiquity and the Early Middle Ages, 400–800 ad*, London, 1–15.

Wood, J. P. (2012), *The Politics of Identity in Visigothic Spain: Religion and Power in the Histories of Isidore of Seville*, Brill's Series on the Early Middle Ages 21, Leiden.

Wood, P.J. (2010), *'We Have No King but Christ': Christian Political Thought in Greater Syria on the Eve of the Arab Conquest (c. 400–585)*, Oxford.

—— (2011), "Being Roman in Procopius' *Vandal Wars*," Byzantion 81, 424–47.

Yasin, A.M. (2009), *Saints and Church Spaces in the Late Antique Mediterranean: Architecture, Cult, and Community*, Cambridge.

Zeiller, J. (1918), *Les origines chrétiennes dans les provinces danubiennes de l'empire romain*, Paris.

INDEX

Adamantius (dialogue character), 78, 103. See also Origen
Africa Proconsularis: diminution of Nicene episcopate of, 38; Nicene episcopal appointments permitted in, 148; restriction of anti-Nicene measures to, 15, 36, 98, 181. See also *sortes Vandalorum*
Against Varimadus, 55–60, 221n11
Agnellus (Nicene bishop of Ravenna), 247
Alaric II (Visigothic king), 228n39, 230; as new Constantius II, 247
Alboin (Lombard king), 244
Alypius (bishop of Thagaste), 74n99
Ambrose (bishop of Milan): in Bobbio fragments, 245; in *Carthaginian Epitome*, 117–18; conflicts with Arians, 117–18, 130; *De Fide*, 112, 162; ethnography and heresiology, 184n96; influence on Avitus, 241; pseudonymous text, 47n74; in Vigilius' *Dialogue*, 70, 71n83, 86
Ammaedara (Haïdra), 29–32, 30*fig.*, 31*fig.*, 36, 196–97
Anonymus Valesianus (historian), 227, 233
Anthologia Latina, 198–99
Anti-Chalcedonians, 121, 136, 144, 242
Antichrist, 117–18, 189
Apostles' Creed, 91
Aradi (Sidi Jdidi), 152n41
Arianism: accusations of in Vandal Africa, 109–37; accusations of in later periods, 248–49; in later Roman Empire, 10–14; in post-imperial West, 237–48; reception of Arian controversy, 69–77, 110–18, 121–30; relationship with ethnic identity, 18–20, 38–46, 175–80, 183–93, 233–37. See also Homoian Christians
Arifridos (privileged burial), 195–96, 214
Arius (presbyter of Alexandria), 10–11; in Agnellus, 247; in anti-Arian polemic, 74, 112–13; in *Carthaginian Epitome*, 116–18; character in Vigilius' *Dialogue*, 69–71, 72, 79, 80, 101–3, 112, 122–25; in Ferrandus, 220; in Fulgentius, 112–13; in John of Biclar, 246; portrayed as Homoian, 90–91, 114, 123; in Quodvultdeus, 113
Armogas (Nicene Romano-African aristocrat), 202, 213–14
Aspar (East Roman general), 145n10, 198n17
Astii (Romano-African family), 196–97
Athanasius (bishop of Alexandria), 50; character in Vigilius' *Dialogue*, 69–71, 72, 78, 80, 101–3, 123–25, 178–79; citation in Bobbio fragments, 245; pseudonymous texts, 51, 71n83, 78; reception in Latin West, 124–25
Augustine (bishop of Hippo Regius): ABC psalm, 49, 134; character in *Book on the Trinity against Felicianus*, 77; character in *Conference*, 40–41, 73–75, 102–3, 178, 190–92; cited by unnamed heretic, 122n70; correspondence with Quodvultdeus, 47; dealings with Arians, 13–14, 73–77; dealings with elites, 106, 198n17,

Augustine *(continued)*
210n82, 212; debates, 80, 82–83, 84, 103; debate with Maximinus, 76–77, 125–26; debate with Pascentius, 73–75, 190; episcopal roles, 153n44; on *homoousios*, 190; influence on Cerealis' *Debate*, 76–77, 125–26; *On heresies*, 47, 106; pseudonymous sermons, 64n53, 88; pseudonymous tractates, 47, 51, 52–3, 59, 73–75; on rebaptism, 106; religious exclusivity, 169–70; role model for Fulgentius, 160; and Roman Africa 1–3; use by Avitus, 241
Augustus (Roman emperor), 208
Aurelius (bishop of Carthage), 135
Auxentius (bishop of Durostorum), 74, 92, 113; putative author of *Commentary on Job*, 88n15
Auxentius (bishop of Milan), 74, 92, 113, 130
Avitus (Nicene bishop of Vienne), 230, 231–32, 237, 241–42, 246

barbarians, 6–7; in African sermons, 65n53; and Arianism, 183–93; conversion of, 13, 117–18; and Homoian Christianity, 13, 18–19, 40–41, 165–69, 235–37; in Victor of Vita, 9, 172–75, 182, 211–13. *See also* identities
Barth, Fredrik, 63
Basilius (Nicene bishop of Aix), 241
Belisarius (East Roman general), 219
Berndt, Guido, 7
Bockmann, Ralf, 215
Boethius (Italo-Roman aristocrat), 209
Boniface (count of Africa), 106, 198n17
Boniface (Nicene bishop of Carthage), 48*table*, 49, 134–37, 163
Boniface (Nicene bishop of Gatiana), 48*table*, 51, 153–54
Bonosiacs (heresy), 242
Book of the Catholic Faith: presentation at Conference of Carthage (484), 39, 51; relationship with other texts, 61, 72, 89, 161; transmission by Victor Vita, 14n70
Bourdieu, Pierre, 174–75
Bowes, Kim, 212
Breviarium (Visigothic law code), 228n38
Brown, Peter, 118
burials, privileged, 29–32, 152n41, 195–97, 213–17
Byzacena (province): autonomy of primate of, 49; exile of Nicene bishops of, 16, 38

Caecilian (bishop of Carthage), 11, 136
Caesarius (bishop of Arles), 221n11
Cain, Andrew, 48–49
Cameron, Averil, 57–58, 81

Carthage: Byzantine reconquest of, 219; churches dedicated to Cyprian, 93, 186, 215–16; continued prosperity, 6–8; Homoian churches in, 36; Homoian clerics in, 36, 45; location of real Augustine-Pascentius debate, 73; martyrial churches, 215–16; Nicene bishops of, 47–49, 204; Nicene clerics in, 45; setting of Cerealis' *Debate*, 76; site of religious violence, 18, 181–82, 204; Vandal court at, 6, 8, 143–44, 181–82, 231
Carthaginian Epitome (*Epitome Carthaginiensis*), 114–18, 133–34, 189–90, 193, 235
Cassiodorus (Italian senator): as exegete, 186; religious neutrality, 228n38
Castinus (Roman general), 7, 12
Cerealis (Nicene bishop of Castellum Ripense), 48*table*, 75–77, 126, 154–55
churches (buildings): built or refurbished under Vandals, 8; competition over, 32–33, 214–17, 243–44, 247; Homoian, 33, 35–38, 186, 244; and martyr cults, 93, 186, 214–17; modern inability to discern confession of, 32, 214–15
ciuitas, 239n90
Clovis (Frankish king), 237, 246–47
Cohen, Sam, 236
Commentary on Job (*Commentarius in Iob*), 87–88, 95, 104–5, 107, 177
Conant, Jonathan, 149, 172, 173, 199–200, 201
Conference of Augustine with Pascentius (*Collatio Augustini cum Pascentio*), 73–75, 80, 101–3, 190–93; on "barbarian" language, 40–41, 190–93; legalism of, 79
Conference of Carthage (411), 16, 40, 97, 131, 136
Conference of Carthage (484), 9, 16, 156; association with *Register*, 35–36; *Book of Catholic Faith* read at, 51, 61, 72, 161; debate over *homoousios*, 102; dubious association of Cerealis' *Debate* with, 75–76; Eugenius' role in convocation, 157–59; Huneric's edicts regarding, 87, 90, 97–98; intervention of Cyrila at, 38–40; possible presence of Vigilius, 72–73; spoofed by Vigilius, 126–27
Constantia (Roman empress), 124
Constantine (Roman emperor): cited in Bobbio fragments, 245; conversion of, 116; in *Carthaginian Epitome*, 117; model for Reccared, 227, 246; in Rufinus' *Ecclesiastical History*, 117; in Vigilius' *Dialogue*, 124
Constantius II: in *Carthaginian Epitome*, 116–17; as character in Vigilius' *Dialogue*, 70, 124, 126–27; cited in Bobbio fragments, 245; in Gothic martyrology, 245; model for Alaric II,

247; and Rimini and Seleucia (359), 12, 129, 179, 220
Council of Aquileia (381), 70
Council of Carthage (525), 49, 51, 71, 134–37, 153
Council of Chalcedon (451), 56, 136, 220, 246
Council of Constantinople (381), 226
Council of Nicaea (325), 10, 12; at Carthage (525), 135; in *Carthaginian Epitome*, 116; compared to Rimini and Seleucia, 91–92, 129; creed of, 13, 40, 90–91, 101, 135; at Toledo III (589), 246; in Vigilius' *Dialogue*, 69, 122
Council of Sirmium (357): the "Blasphemy" creed of, 113
Council of Toledo III (589), 226, 234n68, 235, 245–46
Councils of Rimini and Seleucia (359), 12, 221; anathematized at Toledo III (589), 245–46; Arian "fraud" of, 113, 129–30, 245; attendance, 61–62; in *Carthaginian Epitome*, 117; citation by Huneric, 12, 61–62, 128–30; compared to Nicaea, 61–62, 91–92; creed, 95; in Facundus, 220; in Vigilius' *Dialogue*, 124
Courtois, Christian, 5, 15
Cyprian: churches at Carthage, 93, 186, 215–16; *Homily* about, 186; Homoian citations of, 88, 92–93; martyr's day, 186; on rebaptism, 106; relics at Ammaedara, 29; in *Verona Collection*, 88
Cypriana (martyr festival), 93, 216

Dagila (Nicene Romano-African aristocrat), 200, 202
Debate of Cerealis against Maximinus, 75–77, 80, 125–26, 154–55
debates, 14, 55–84; imagined, in post-imperial West, 243, 245, 247; imagined, in Vandal Africa, 66, 69–84, 101–3, 121–27, 178–79; public, in post-imperial West, 230, 241–43; public, in Vandal Africa, 38–40, 71–72, 156–57, 160–63, 170
Deliyannis, Deborah, 244
Deogratias (Nicene bishop of Carthage), 48, 48table
Dialogue against the Arians, Sabellians and Photinians: characterization of Probus, 78, 178–9; construction of Arius, 90, 123; debates about *homoousios* in, 101–2; details and versions of, 69–73; draws on debate culture, 80–81; heresiology of, 112, 122–25; second edition, 124–25, 126–27; spoofing of Conference of Carthage (484), 126–27; used by *Opus Caroli*, 221n9; use of Rufinus in, 78, 122, 124–25. *See also* Vigilius of Thapsa

dialogues. *See* debates
Diocletian (Roman emperor), 116
Dionysia (Nicene Romano-African aristocrat), 204
Donatist schism: campaigning in, 63–64, 97, 136–37; and Conference of Carthage (411), 40, 136; end of, 35–37; heresiology of, 11, 65–66, 104, 111; and historiography of Roman Africa, 2–3, 4; rebaptism in, 37, 106–8, 111, 133–34, 212n90; reverence of Cyprian in, 93; suspicion of secular power in, 20, 131–32, 144; universality as theme in, 132–33; Vandal-era controversy as replaying of, 16, 61–62, 97–98, 130–34, 219–20
Donatus (bishop of Carthage), 11, 116
Dossey, Leslie, 66
Dracontius (poet), 173, 206–10
Duval, Yves-Marie, 92

Ebbeler, Jennifer, 66
Edict of 20 May 483, 87; cites Geiseric's measures as precedent, 98–99; cited in Vigilius' *Dialogue*, 126–27; discusses Nicene petitions, 157; on *homoousios*, 90. *See also* Huneric
Edict of 24 Feb 484, 9, 87, 97–98; absence of ethnography in, 19; categorizes Homoousians, 91; citation of earlier laws, 16, 97–98, 132, 228; cited in Vigilius' *Dialogue*, 126–27; Conference of Carthage (484) in, 90, 91, 157–58; definition of orthodoxy in, 12, 89, 91, 128–30; justifications of, 61–62, 128–30, 132; responded to by Pseudo-Fulgentius, 61–62; ruler ideal of, 147–48, 151, 158n77; transfer of property in, 147; treats whole kingdom, 36. *See also* Huneric
Edictum Theoderici, 228n38
education, 6, 66, 173
embassies: from Constantinople, 40, 149–50, 156, 157n69
Ennodius (Nicene bishop of Pavia), 237
Epiphanius (bishop of Cyprus), 125
Ermengon (Suevic aristocrat), 196
erotapokriseis, 55–59
Eugenius (Nicene bishop of Carthage), 48–50, 48table, 156–59; appointment of, 156; at Conference of Carthage (484), 38; death of, 75; debates with Homoians, 82; defies prohibition on courtiers in his church, 182, 204; discussed by Gelasius of Rome, 232n58; miraculous activities, 156, 244; panegyrical petition, 158, 231; recalled from exile, 99
Eulalia, church of at Merida, 243, 244

Eunomius (bishop of Cyzicus), 74, 113, 123
Eusebius (bishop of Vercelli), 247
Eutropius (invented judge character), 78
Eutyches (archimandrite at Constantinople), 71n83

Fabianus (learned Homoian Christian), 43*table*, 66, 83, 87, 91, 106
Facundus (bishop of Hermiane), 220–21
Faustus (Nicene bishop of Riez), 242–43, 246, 248
Felicianus (Homoian dialogue character), 77
Felix (correspondent of Fulgentius), 133, 134, 169
Felix (Nicene monk), 45
Ferrandus (Nicene deacon), 48*table*, 219–20
Fielding, Ian, 206
Filastrius (bishop of Brescia), 114
flamen perpetuus, 197
Flower, Richard, 119
Fournier, Éric, 16
Fredriksen, Paula, 225
Fritigern (Gothic leader), 190
Fulgentius (Nicene bishop of Ruspe), 48*table*, 49–50, 53, 160–63; *ABC*, 33–34, 49, 107, 113, 134; anti-Donatist arguments, 134; beaten by Homoian presbyter, 45; debates with Homoians, 65–67, 82–83, 91; debates with Thrasamund, 82–83, 89, 105, 160–63, 187–88, 236, 237; ethnography, 187–88; heresiology, 65–66, 95, 112–13, 133, 169; Homoian opponents, 43*table*; on Homoian charity, 45; on Homoian churches, 33–35; letters, 64, 67, 89, 110, 169; mentor to Ferrandus, 219; panegyrical prose, 161–63, 231; preservation of Homoian texts, 87; pseudonymous texts, 59, 61–62, 88; on rebaptism, 107, 134; *To Thrasamund*, 82–3, 161–63, 187–88, 237
Fundus Gabardilla (estate), 36, 45
Furnos Maius (Aïn Fourna), 152n41

Gaddis, Michael, 20
Galli Milić, Lavinia, 208
Gallic Chronicle of 452, 115, 116n45, 242, 246
Geiseric (Vandal king), 7–8; anti-Nicene measures, 15–16, 98–99, 181, 249; converts to Homoioan Christianity, 12n55; divine support for, 147; expels Quodvultdeus, 47; failed Nicene embassy to, 152; knows not to make martyrs, 145; patronage of Homoian Church, 44; as persecutor, 9, 15–16, 145, 211–12; pressures officials to convert, 202; punishes fugitive Nicene slaves, 211–12; receives *Against Arians*, 51; transfers churches to Homoians, 33

Gelasius (Nicene bishop of Rome), 232n58, 238
Gelimer (Vandal king), 219
Geneva: Homoian synod at, 241
Gennadius of Marseille: *On Illustrious Men*, 47, 49–51, 75
Gog (biblical people), 185
Gothic (language), 13, 39, 192, 234–35, 239n193. *See also* Vandalic (language)
Gratian (Roman emperor), 130
Gray, Patrick, 121
Gregory (Nicene bishop of Tours): African material, 48–49, 156, 232n58; anti-Arian passages, 245; on Clovis, 246–47; debates with Visigothic envoys, 241, 246–47; on Eugenius, 48–49, 156; miracles in, 156, 232–33, 244
Gregory the Great (Nicene bishop of Rome), 232–33, 233n63, 244
Gryson, Roger, 88
Gundobad (Burgundian king): discussions with Avitus, 230, 241–42; good relations with Nicenes, 198n17, 228n39, 230, 231n49;
Gunthamund (Vandal king): anti-Nicene policies, 15; concessions to Nicenes, 99, 159; imprisonment of Dracontius, 206–8, 209

Habetdeum (Nicene bishop of Thamalluma), 48*table*, 143–45, 154, 156–57
Heil, Uta, 241
Heinzelmann, Martin, 245
Helpidius (Nicene deacon and doctor), 231–32
heresiology. *See* polemic
Hermenegild (Visigothic royal), 226n23
Heydemann, Gerda, 186n113
Hilary (bishop of Poitiers): as anti-Arian saint, 247; citation in Bobbio fragments, 245
Hildeguns (privileged burial), 197n13
Hilderic (Vandal king): abortive accession, 159, 206; accession of, 15, 16, 163–64; grant of tolerance to Nicenes, 49, 99, 135, 163–64; relationship with Constantinople, 149n31, 163
Hippo Regius (Annaba), 73–74, 73n94, 196
History of the Persecution of the African Province. *See* Victor of Vita
Home synod, 45
Homily on the Bishop and Martyr Saint Cyprian, 186, 192–93
Homoian Christians, 12–14, 56; in Balkans, 11, 13, 240; in Constantinople, 13, 240; in Eastern Empire, 13, 40, 227, 240; in Gaul, 11, 230, 231–34, 237, 241–43, 244–45, 246–47; in Italy, 13, 231–35, 236–37, 238–40, 244–45, 247; in late Roman Africa, 13–14, 113; in Milan,

117–18, 130, 192, 221; not ethnic church, 38–41, 233–37; not state church, 41–46; in Spain, 11, 226–27, 233–36, 241, 243–44, 245–46; in Vandal Africa, 12–13, 18–20, 35–46, 85–108, 128–30, 189–94. *See also* Arianism

Homoian doctrine, 12–14, 56–57, 95, 112, 123

Homoian priests, African: Antonius (bishop of Thamalluma), 43*table*, 143; Cyrila (patriarch in Carthage), 38–40, 42, 43*table*, 244; claims to be Catholic, 89; elite audience, 177; Fastidiosus (deacon), 43*table*, 65–67, 87; Felix (presbyter), 36, 43*table*, 45, 160, 212n91; heresiology, 95, 104; Jucundus (patriarch in Carthage), 42, 43*table*, 176n55; Marivadus (deacon), 43*table*, 55–57, 67, 70, 125; Victorinus, (bishop of Ammaedara), 29–32, 30*fig.*, 31*fig.*, 34, 43*table*

Homoousians: as accusation in *Conference*, 74–75; as heresiological label, 14, 90–91, 94–108; as legal terminology, 61–62, 96–99, 102–3, 132. *See also* Nicene Christianity

homoousios (ὁμοούσιος): in *Conference*, 74–75, 190–91; as heretical, 12, 14, 61–62, 91–92, 94–97, 101–2; as pagan, 105; in Vigilius' *Dialogue*, 69

Honoratus (Nicene bishop of Cirta), 48*table*

Honorius (Roman emperor): edict of 30 Jan 412, 16, 35, 37, 98, 132

Howe, Tankred, 184, 188–89, 189n119

Humfress, Caroline, 94, 103, 175n50

Huneric (Vandal king): anti-Nicene measures, 9, 15–16, 150, 181–83, 249; attempts to change succession, 158–59, 206; calls Conference of Carthage (484), 9, 16, 38, 72, 157–58; cites Geiseric's measures as precedent, 181; cites Rimini and Seleucia (359) 12; concessions to Nicenes, 16, 40, 148–49, 155–56; confrontation with Habetdeum, 143–45; divine support for, 147–48; interactions with Eugenius, 155–59; patronage of Homoian Church, 44; as persecutor, 9, 15, 150, 181–83; pressures officials to convert, 202; relationship with Marivadus, 125; seeks licence for Homoians in East, 40; torture of Nicenes, 150, 176n55, 181–83. *See also* Edict of 20 May 483; Edict of 24 Feb 484

Hydatius (bishop of Chaves), 115–16, 232–33

identities, 18–21, 139–41, 165–75; confessional, 10–12, 62–63, 65–68, 86–94, 119–21, 165–217; ethnic, 18–21, 38–41, 165–94, 195–97, 233–37; and *habitus*, 174–75; polemically ascribed, 62–65, 94–108, 174, 183–93; porous boundaries of, 62–63, 68, 169–75, 201–17; "salience" of, 167; situational, 19–20, 167; use of history to construct, 8–10, 114–21, 134–37, 165–69, 180–81, 245

Isidore (bishop of Seville): on conversion of Goths, 190n123; ethnography, 236; false attribution of *Carthaginian Epitome* to, 114; *On Illustrious Men*, 76; on religious policies of Visigothic kings, 227n32;

Italian Homoian texts: Bobbio fragments: 240, 245; *Against the Heretics*, 240; *Against the Jews*, 239; *Against the Pagans*, 239; *Exposition of the Gospel of Luke*, 240n96; Verona Collection (*Collectio Veronensis*), 43*table*, 88, 93, 239–40

James, Edward, 241
Jerome, 72, 103, 114–16, 122n71
Job (put-upon prophet), 88, 177
John (Nicene bishop of Rome), 227–28
John Chrysostom (bishop of Constantinople), 169–70, 192
John of Biclar (historian), 226, 227, 235, 246
Jordanes (East Roman historian), 147
Judas (reluctant deicide), 110
Julian (Roman emperor), 117
Justin (second-century apologist), 79
Justin I (East Roman emperor): receives embassy from Theoderic, 227; relationship with Hilderic, 149n31
Justinian (East Roman emperor): ethnography of regime, 236–37; petitioned by primate of Byzacena, 49; reconquest, 2, 219, 236–37, 247; relationship with Hilderic, 149n31; Three Chapters, 220

King, Karen, 57

Latin Anthology, 198–99
Laurentius (invented judge character), 74–75, 102, 178
laws: absence of anti-heretical in post-imperial West, 228–29; against heretics in Roman Empire, 16–17, 63–64, 228, 240; contestation of, 61–62, 100–103, 126–27, 129–32; continuity of legal system, 7; few surviving from Vandal Africa, 151, 155, 172–73; regarding courtiers and administrators, 175–76, 199–206; regarding Homoousians, 15–17, 40, 87, 96–100, 147–49, 170, 181; spoofed by Vigilius of Thapsa, 126–27

Leander (Nicene bishop of Seville), 235
Leovigild (Visigothic king), 226–27, 235, 243, 244
lex Gothorum, 234n68
Liber constitutum (Burgundian law code), 228n38
Life of Augustine, 1–3, 9, 73, 126, 185
Life of Epiphanius, 237
Life of Fulgentius: authorship, 160; on Fulgentius' career, 49–50, 160–61, 163–64; on Hilderic's accession, 163–64; on Homoian bishops, 42–44, 45; on Thrasamund's policies, 177
Lim, Richard, 81
List of the Kings of the Vandals and Alans, 99, 115, 159
Lives of the Fathers of Merida, 243, 244
Lucian (bishop of Antioch), 88
Lucifer (bishop of Cagliari), 13
Luxorius (poet), 173
Lyman, Rebecca, 56, 104

Mactar (Maktar), 197n13
Magog (biblical people), 185
Maier, Gideon, 42
Maioricus (Nicene Romano-African aristocrat), 204
Marcian (Roman emperor): as model for Reccared, 227, 246
Marrou, Henri-Irène, 1
Martin (bishop of Tours): as anti-Arian saint, 247
Martinianus (slave and arms bearer), 211–12
martyrs (African), 215
Masona (Nicene bishop of Merida), 226, 243
Mathisen, Ralph, 41–42, 166–67
Maxima (slave), 211–12
Maximinus (Homoian bishop): debate with Augustine, 76–77, 126; character in Cerealis' *Debate*, 75–77, 113, 126, 154–55; citation of Cyprian, 88, 93; *scolia* of, 86, 88
Maxwell, Jaclyn, 169
Melleus (Nicene bishop of Ammaedara), 29–32, 30*fig.*, 31*fig.*
Merrills, Andy, 100, 152, 175, 206, 207
Miaphysites, 121, 136, 144, 242
Milan: conflicts between Nicenes and Homoians in, 117–18, 130, 221
Miles, Richard, 66, 100, 175, 207
millenarius, 211–13, 211n86, 217
Minucius Felix (apologist), 103
Mocianus (*scholasticus*), 220
Modaharius (Gothic layman), 241

Modéran, Yves, 15, 20, 38, 45, 181
Mommsen, Theodor, 99, 115
monasterium Bagauliense, 153

Nestorius (bishop of Constantinople), 72, 125
Nicene bishops: appeals overseas, 149–50; at Conference of Carthage (484), 38–40, 90–91, 97; careers of, 45–53, 152–53; ethnography of, 183–93; exile of, 38, 147, 156, 158–59, 160–64, 186, 204; numbers, 35–38; petition Vandal court, 154–63
Nicene Christianity: as confessional identity, 169–71, 175–83, 199–211; development in later Roman Empire, 10–13; on Trinity, 56–57, 101–3, 112–14, 121–24, 241
Nicene Christians: coercion of, 8–10, 14–18, 147–48, 199–206, 226–28; service to Vandal rulers, 175–83, 199–210, 213–14

On the True Vine (sermon), 186–87
Origen (third-century exegete), 78n117, 87–88, 125
Orosius (historian), 190n123, 237n85

pagans: coexistence with Christians in late antiquity, 169–70, 198; as heresiological accusation, 104–7, 110, 112; polemic against, 208, 240
Palladius (bishop of Ratiaria), 86, 92, 113, 125
Parsons, Jonathan, 134
Parthemius (African cleric), 210–11
Pascentius (Homoian *comes*): invented character in *Conference*, 73–75, 79, 92, 178, 190–92; real person, 73–75, 92, 113
Perrin, Michel-Yves, 63
Petilian (Donatist bishop), 131
Phoebadius (Nicene bishop of Agen): cited in Bobbio fragments, 245
Photinus (bishop of Sirmium): accusation of Photinian heresy, 122n70; as character in Vigilius' *Dialogue*, 69–70, 112, 122
poetry: Christian, 6, 206–11; classicizing, 6, 8, 146, 173, 198–99
polemic, Christian: audiences of, 58–61, 65–68, 188, 192–93; against court bishops, 42–44, 242; both ethnographic and heresiological, 184–88, 236–37; in dialogue format, 69–84, 101–3, 242–43; guilt by association, 104–8, 111–18, 121–28, 130–34, 246–47; heresiological labeling, 10–11, 14, 94–99, 112–14; heresiological tropes, 63–65, 109–11, 183–84; against

Homoian churches, 32–34; against Homoian kings outside Africa, 229, 232–33; against Homoousians, 94–99, 104–8, 239–40; relative absence outside Africa, 229; role in definition of orthodoxy, 55–63; role in group formation, 62–63, 165–66, 169–71; against Vandal kings, 8–10, 143–44, 148, 155–56; various genres of, 63–65

Pontius Pilate (infamous handwasher), 110

Possidius (bishop of Calama): on Augustine's debate with Maximinus, 126; on Augustine's debate with Pascentius, 73; on Vandal conquest, 1–3, 8, 185, 222;

Probus (invented judge character), 69; evokes philosopher from Nicaea, 122; potential model for elites, 178–79; presents final judgement, 103; symbolic name, 78

Procopius of Caesarea (East Roman historian), 93, 147, 177, 201, 219

procurators, 160, 200, 202, 213

Prosper of Aquitaine (Gallo-Roman historian), 52, 114–16, 117, 232–33

Pseudo-Athanasius, 123, 124

Pseudo-Augustine, 47; *Book on the Unity of the Trinity against Felicianus*, 77; Quodvultdeus' works preserved as, 51–53; *Solutions to the Diverse Questions Objected by the Heretics*, 59. See also *Conference of Augustine with Pascentius*

Pseudo-Fulgentius: *Book on the Trinity*, 59, 61–62, 91–92, 129–32; sermons, 186, 188, 193

Pseudo-Gennadius, 156–57

Quodvultdeus (Nicene bishop of Carthage): anti-Donatist arguments, 107, 133; authorship question, 52–53; *Book on the Promises and Predictions of God*, 52, 185; career and texts, 47–48, 48*table*, 51–53; dialogues in sermons, 83–84; ethnography, 185, 192; heresiology, 113, 133, 185–86; on Homoian charity, 45; on Homoian churches, 32–34; on rebaptism, 107, 133; on Vandals as impious, 185; sermon collection, 51–53, 64, 67, 185

Rajak, Tessa, 79

Ravenna, churches of: 234n68, 244, 247; Eusebius the Martyr, 247; Martin, 247; San Vitale, 244

rebaptism: 105–6; Cyprian and, 93; Donatists and, 37, 106–7, 133–34; Homoians and, 37, 105–7, 117–18, 143–44, 170, 199–200, 211–12; Nicene polemic against, 133–34, 204

Rebillard, Éric, 169

Reccared (Visigothic king), 226–27, 235, 243, 246

reconquest, Byzantine, 2, 219–21, 236–37, 247

Reginus (East Roman ambassador), 157n69

Reginus (East Roman *dux*), 219–20

Register of the Provinces and Cities of Africa, 35–38, 71, 75

Reimitz, Helmut, 236

Ricimer (Roman general), 233n63

Romano-African elites: acceptance of Vandal rule, 7–8; blurring with Vandals, 171–75; Christian identities, 175–83, 195–211, 213–17; continuity of lifestyles, 5–6; seen as secular, 19–20, 139–40

Rome: apostolic sites at, 244; bishops of, 236–37

Royal officials: anonymous cellarer, 202; anonymous *procurator*, 160; Felix (*procurator domus*), 202, 213–14; *maior domus*, 157; Obadus (*praepositus regni*), 158; Saturus (*procurator domus*), 200; Vitarit (notary), 158

Rufinus of Aquileia: account of Nicaea, 122; narrative of 330s, 114; translation of Adamantius dialogue, 78; use by *Carthaginian Epitome*, 116–17; use by Vigilius, 78, 122, 124

Rugi, 237

Sabellius (third-century priest): as character in Vigilius' *Dialogue*, 69–70, 112, 122

sacerdotalis prouinciae Africae, 197

Sack of Rome (455), 48

Salvian (Gallo-Roman writer), 85–86, 190

Salzman, Michele Renee, 197

Sandwell, Bella, 169

Sant'Agata dei Goti (church in Rome), 233n63

Sardinia: exile of Nicene bishops to, 16, 147

Sebastian (Roman general), 200n24

Servus (Nicene Romano-African aristocrat), 202

Shanzer, Danuta, 45

Shaw, Brent, 3, 81

Sidonius Apollinaris (Nicene bishop of Clermont), 210, 231, 241, 242

Sigismund (Burgundian king), 232, 237, 242

Sigisteus (African general), 210–11

Silvester (Nicene Romano-African aristocrat), 160

Sizgorich, Thomas, 119, 122, 233

Socrates (ecclesiastical historian), 190n123

sortes Vandalorum, 7, 172–73, 224; anti-Nicene prohibitions in, 36, 98, 181

Sozomen (ecclesiastical historian), 190n123
Stephania (Fulgentius' correspondent), 66
substance (οὐσία), 12–13, 56, 95–96, 101–2, 112, 123
Sulpicius Severus (Gallo-Roman ecclesiastical historian), 246
Sunna (Homoian bishop of Merida), 243
synodos endemousa, 45

Temple of Memory, Carthage, 159
testimonia collections, 59–62
Testimonies on the Father and the Son and the Holy Spirit, 59
Thabraca (Tabarka), 212
Thamalluma (Telmin): location of Homoian bishop, 36; location of Nicene exile, 143–44
Theoderic (Geiseric's son), 176n55, 202
Theoderic (Ostrogothic king): divine support of, 230n49; on Homoians, 239; in *Life of Epiphanius*, 237; as persecutor, 227, 233; possible reference in Avitus, 232; relationship with Nicenes, 198n17, 227–28, 228n39
Theoderic II (Visigothic king), 231
Theodoret (bishop of Cyrrhus), 50, 72, 198n17, 220
Theodosian Code, 228
Theodosius I (Roman emperor), 13; anti-Arian measures, 117–18, 233, 240, 246; in *Carthaginian Epitome*, 116–18, 189
Theodulf (bishop of Orléans), 71n83
Theognis (bishop of Nicaea), 245
Theveste (Tébessa), 196, 215, 216
Thrasamund (Vandal king): anti-Nicene measures, 15–16, 99, 160, 225, 249; cites *Book of the Catholic Faith*, 89–90; concessions to Nicenes, 148–49; death of, 163–64; debates in reign of, 72; discussions with Fulgentius, 82–83, 148–49, 160–63; excerpts from in Fulgentius, 87; heresiology of, 105, 122n71; patronage of Homoian courtiers, 177, 201–2; receives panegyric from Dracontius, 207, 210; receives praise from Fulgentius, 187–88
Three Chapters controversy, 220
Thuburbo Maius (Henchir Kasbat), 195, 202, 214
Tipasa (Tipaza): famous confessors of, 232n58; Homoian bishop of, 36, 43*table*; private Nicene worship at, 204n53

Ulfila (Homoian bishop), 13, 39, 190n123
Unnamed Vandal king (dialogue character), 75, 126, 154–55
Uppenna (Henchir Chigarnia), 152n41

Valens (Roman emperor), 117, 190n123
Valentinian II (Roman emperor), 117
Valentinian III (Roman emperor), 114
"Vandal boy," privileged burial at Theveste, 196, 215, 216*fig*.
Vandalic (language), 38–41, 46, 174, 190–91. *See also* Gothic (language)
Vandals: as elites, 7–8, 139–41, 171–75, 211–13; Christian identities of, 18–19, 85–86, 175–83; Christian worship of, 40–41, 46, 190–92; conquest of Africa, 1–3; ethnic identity of, 165–69, 171–75, 195–97; Hasding, 7; in Gaul, 7, 85–86; lifestyles of, 7–8, 173–75, 195–97; modern stereotypes of, 1–3, 6, 10; polemically described as barbarians, 9, 183–93; as service aristocracy, 180–83; Siling, 7; as war band, 7, 172–73
Varimadus. *See* Marivadus
Velazquez, Isabel, 236
Venantius Fortunatus (poet), 246–47
Victor (Nicene bishop of Cartenna), 48*table*, 50–51, 156
Victor (Nicene monk), 65–66, 89
Victor of Tunnuna (historian), 49
Victor of Vita (historian), 9–10, 48, 48*table*, 222; on bishops of Carthage, 47–49; on Conference of Carthage (484), 38–39; on embassy from Zeno, 150; ethnography in, 18–20, 165, 168–69, 175–76, 183–85, 188–89, 192–93; on Habetdeum, 143–45; heresiology of, 10–14; on Homoian bishops, 42–44; on Huneric, 9, 15–16, 155–56, 181–83, 202, 227; on illicit Nicene services, 204; on Marivadus, 125; martyr stories in, 178, 199–206; miracles in, 156; on Nicene courtiers, 181–83, 199–206; persecution as theme in, 14–18, 119, 139–40, 143–45, 152; possible authorship of *Homily on the Bishop and Martyr Saint Cyprian*, 186; on privileged burial, 213–14; on rebaptism, 133, 204; relationship with Eugenius, 48; on the Vandal *millenarius*, 211–13; Vandal laws in, 87, 98–99
Vigilius (Nicene bishop of Rome), 71n83
Vigilius (Nicene bishop of Thapsa): *Against Eutyches*, 71n83; *Book on the Trinity against Felicianus* attributed to, 77n111;

career, 48*table*, 51, 71n83; response to Palladius of Ratiaria, 86; *Solutions to the Objections of the Arians (Solutiones obiectionum Arrianorum)*, 59. See also *Dialogue against the Arians, Sabellians and Photinians*
Vincent (monk at Lérins), 245, 248

Von Rummel, Philipp, 182–83
Vössing, Konrad, 42

Wolff, Étienne, 206
Wood, Ian, 230

Zeno (East Roman emperor), 40, 150

www.ingramcontent.com/pod-product-compliance
Lightning Source LLC
Chambersburg PA
CBHW030523230426
43665CB00010B/741